Five Comedies

THE DA PONTE ITALIAN LIBRARY SERIES

Five Comedies

CARLO GOLDONI

Edited by Gianluca Rizzo and Michael Hackett
with Brittany Asaro
Introduction by Michael Hackett
with an essay by Cesare De Michelis

UNIVERSITY OF TORONTO PRESS
Toronto Buffalo London

Toronto Buffalo London
www.utppublishing.com

ISBN 978-1-4426-5028-2

The Lorenzo Da Ponte Italian Library

Library and Archives Canada Cataloguing in Publication

Goldoni, Carlo, 1707–1793
[Plays. English. Selections]
Five comedies / Carlo Goldoni ; edited by Gianluca Rizzo and Michael Hackett ; with Brittany Asaro ; introduction by Michael Hackett ; with an essay by Cesare De Michelis.

(The Da Ponte Italian library series)
Includes bibliographical references.
Contents: The new house – The coffee house – Off to the country – Adventures in the country – Back from the country.
ISBN 978-1-4426-5028-2 (bound)

1. Goldoni, Carlo, 1707–1793–Translations into English. I. De Michelis, Cesare, writer of added commentary II. Hackett, Michael, 1950–, editor, writer of introduction III. Asaro, Brittany, 1984–, editor IV. Rizzo, Gianluca, 1979–, editor V. Goldoni, Carlo, 1707–1793. Smanie per la villeggiatura. VI. Goldoni, Carlo, 1707–1793. Avventure della villeggiatura. VII. Goldoni, Carlo, 1707–1793 . Ritorno dalla villeggiatura. VIII. Goldoni, Carlo, 1707–1793. Bottega del caffè. IX. Goldoni, Carlo, 1707–1793. Casa nova. X. Title. XI. Series: Lorenzo da Ponte Italian library

PQ4695.E5 2016 852'6 C2015-906942-4

This book has been published under the aegis and with the financial assistance of Fondazione Cassamarca, Treviso; Ministero degli Affari Esteri, Direzione Generale per la Promozione e la Cooperazione Culturale; Ministero dei Beni Culturali, Direzione Generale per i Beni Librari e gli Istituti Culturali, Servizio per la Promozione del Libro e della Lettura.

University of Toronto Press acknowledges the financial assistance to its publishing program of the Canada Council for the Arts and the Ontario Arts Council, an agency of the Government of Ontario.

Contents

Foreword

Carlo Goldoni was born in Venice, in 1707. He demonstrated a strong interest in theatre from a very early age. However, he studied to become a lawyer, and eventually obtained his diploma from the University of Padua. Even as a young attorney, his heart was still in the theatre, and he would sometimes appear on stage, acting in various comedies. In 1736 he met Nicoletta Conio – the daughter of a notary – whom he married soon after, and with whom he spent the rest of his life.

When the Medebach Company asked him to become its poet and writer, Goldoni abandoned all other cares and dedicated himself to theatre full time. The open-mindedness of the actors allowed him to begin implementing his reform of the stage. Over the following years, Goldoni presented many of his comedies at the Teatro San Angelo, and then at the Teatro San Luca, where he perfected his reform.

In 1761, he moved to Paris, where he had been called to head the Comédie Italienne. Here he wrote several comedies in Italian and French, as well as a few improvised plays (*a soggetto*). He knew Voltaire, and became friends with Diderot. He received a pension from the crown in recognition of his works, but after the onset of the Revolution, the Convention revoked it. On 7 February 1793, Marie-Joseph Chénier succeeded in having it restored, but it was too late: Goldoni had died the day before, on 6 February 1793.

We mentioned the reform of theatre as one of Goldoni's most important achievements. Before him, the Italian stage was dominated by the commedia dell'arte: actors followed a general plot (*soggetto*) and improvised their parts, employing all sorts of antics and buffoonery. The protagonists of these *commedie a soggetto* were stock characters that often became fixed as masks. Some of the most famous are: Pantalone (Pantaloon), the old, rich, and foolish merchant; Brighella, the rogue and trickster; Arlecchino (Harlequin), the famished servant who came to the city from the countryside; Balanzone, the pedantic doctor from Bologna; and many others, such as the young lovers (Florindo and Rosaura), the clever maid (Colombina), and so on.

The plots are often very complicated, filled with twists and turns and serendipitous reunions of long-lost relatives, and they usually end with a big wedding scene. The enormous popularity of this form of entertainment throughout Europe was due entirely to the art of the actors, whose improvisations lent spontaneity, vigour, and charm to the performances.

Goldoni's reform consists of replacing the *soggetto* with what he called "comedy of character." He would write out all the parts and ask the actors to memorize them and repeat them exactly as they were written. In addition, the engine of the dramatic events was not a complex series of accidents and extraordinary coincidences, as was the rule with commedia dell'arte; rather, each play followed the everyday vicissitudes of easily recognizable characters, taken from the real life of Venice's canals and alleyways.

Goldoni's works have been traditionally praised for their contribution to the advancement of Italian literature. His reform of theatre is often seen as a symptom of a larger trend, a move away from the abstract and formulaic ways of the past to embrace the new era, with its focus on the outside, the objective and observable world of nature. Such a statement could be easily proven by opening any of the many excellent histories of Italian literature available to the general public, but to give an idea of how deeply rooted such an opinion is, we will look at the manual that most influenced the literary critics of the nineteenth and twentieth centuries, Francesco De Sanctis's *Storia della letteratura italiana.*[1] In introducing Goldoni, De Sanctis writes:

> His reform at bottom was the revival of the word, the restoration of literature to the place that belonged to it and with the honors that were due to it; in fact, to put it shortly, it was the New Literature. (De Sanctis, 870)

By "New Literature" De Sanctis means that move away from the past mentioned above. What is notable in this passage is the emphasis on the "word," and its "revival." Up to that point, dramas and comedies

[1] Francesco De Sanctis, *History of Italian Literature, Vol. 2,* translated by Joan Redfern (New York: Barnes and Noble, 1968).

had been written in a pedantic, literary language that bore no resemblance to the idioms spoken by ordinary citizens in their ordinary lives. In fact, Italian did not yet exist as a spoken language at this point in the history of the peninsula: only with the advent of radio, cinema, and television would a common spoken language emerge. At this stage, all cities and regions had different dialects that received a variable influence from the written language, depending on the occasion of the utterance and the degree of erudition of the speaker. Goldoni managed to create a linguistic variety that was not only understood throughout the country, as it was rooted in the traditional language of literature, but at the same time was nimble enough to mimic the spoken conversation of everyday life.

And this brings us to another common critical prejudice towards Goldoni's work: its supposed lack of artifice, its immediate adherence to nature, to reality itself. In part, Goldoni himself is to blame for this gross simplification. In his *Memoirs* he writes: "Speaking for myself, never have I been able to risk a good comedy and perhaps turn it into a bad one for the sake of a prejudice" (quoted in De Sanctis, 870); and the "prejudice" he refers to in this case is the Aristotelian unities of time and place, which pedantic critics prescribed to all playwrights. And the good comedy he had in mind was one that closely resembled the real world. Elsewhere in the *Memoirs* he writes: "In the construction of my pieces I have striven, above all, not to disfigure Nature" (quoted in De Sanctis, 870). So it is easy to understand why critics would emphasize this aspect of his poetics, sometimes exaggerating it. Even De Sanctis seems to believe him, and in fact here is what he says in his *Storia della letteratura italiana*:

> By temperament more a spectator than an actor, while others acted Goldoni observed them, and fixed them in his comedies. It seemed to him that Nature properly observed gave richer results than any combination of fancy, however extraordinary. Art to him was Nature, was the drawing from life. Goldoni may be called the Galileo of the new literature, the telescope here being the true and quick perception of the soul, guided by good sense. Where Galileo banished from science the occult, the hypothetical, the conjectural, the supernatural, Goldoni's aim was to banish from art the fantastic, the declamatory, the rhetorical. (De Sanctis, 869)

The comparison with Galileo might seem a bit of an exaggeration to the contemporary reader, and yet there was something revolutionary in Goldoni's rejection of classical tradition. And the keen observation of his surroundings that he displays in his texts is not completely unlike the spirit of Galileo's scientific revolution. Later on in his discussion of Goldoni's merits, De Sanctis expands further on this idea of immediacy, and adherence to nature:

> The thing in Goldoni that remains eternal, that can never vanish, is that inner world of comedy, gathered from the actual life of that day, and perfectly developed in the situations and the dialogue. His comic world is centered on character – not character conceived as an aggregate of abstract qualities, but true and living character with all its attendant circumstances. ... The characters, as for instance the backbiter, the liar, the miser, the flatterer, the *cavalier servente,* step forth from that mediocre atmosphere alive, vivid, original, and new; and they take their form of life from it. They all have a touch of the gross and the sudden – this, in fact, is the source of the comedy. Their feelings, being natural and undisciplined, spring forth suddenly and directly, uncouthly, just as they are in Nature, not weakened by a sense of decorum; and the result is the purest comedy. (De Sanctis, 871)

In order to emphasize the difference between Goldoni's comedies and those of his predecessors, De Sanctis accentuates this idea of immediacy, of unmediated expression of feelings, characters, and life. He seems to imply that there is no real artifice involved. And this, he argues, is the greatest contribution Goldoni makes to the history of Italian literature. Naturally, as we all know, there is no representation without artifice, without an arbitrary reconstruction of the thing that is represented. The tools that Goldoni uses for his representation, however, are not only literary in nature; they are mostly theatrical. While the former have been amply studied over the centuries, the latter have received very little critical attention ... until now.

The present edition of five of Goldoni's most felicitous comedies aims at correcting these age-old prejudices: the remarkable essay by Michael Hackett – himself an accomplished theatre director, whose productions range from classical Roman theatre to opera and contemporary Polish theatre – presents these masterpieces from the perspective of a practitioner of the dramatic arts. The objective of his analysis is to explain and make the public appreciate all the theatrical subtleties Goldoni infused into his plays. What literary criticism had traditionally considered spontaneous and immediate, Hackett shows to be the result of a painstaking labour that employs all the art, the study, and the artifice Goldoni was able to muster.

Furthermore, he places – possibly for the first time – the few but significant productions of Goldoni's plays staged over the past few decades within the framework of American theatre.

L.B. and M.C.

Credits

The New House is based on the translation by Frederick Davies titled *The Superior Residence*, first published in *Four Comedies by Goldoni* (Harmondsworth: Penguin, 1968).

The Coffee House, translated by Jeremy Parzen, was first published in *The Coffee House* (New York: Marsilio, 1998).

The Holiday Trilogy, translated by Anthony Oldcorn, was first published in *The Holiday Trilogy* (New York: Marsilio, 1992).

Every attempt has been made to identify copyright holders and credit sources for the plays. The publisher would appreciate receiving information as to any inaccuracies or omissions in the credits for subsequent editions.

Chronology

1707 Carlo Goldoni is born in Venice, on 25 February.

1718 The Goldoni family settles in Perugia, where Carlo's father has obtained a medical practice.

1719 Goldoni enters the Jesuit college at Perugia.

1720 The Goldoni family leaves Perugia for Chioggia, passing through Rimini. Carlo is left in Rimini to study philosophy at the Dominican college.

1721 Goldoni flees from Rimini with Florindo de' Maccheroni and his theatrical troupe.

1722 Apprenticed to his uncle, Indric, a lawyer, in Venice.

1723 Enters the Ghislieri College at Pavia, where he studies law.

1725 Expelled from Ghislieri College for writing *Il colosso* (a satire on the women of Pavia). Returns to Chioggia.

1726 Sent to Modena to study law.

1728–9 Appointed clerk in the Criminal Chancellery of Chioggia, and later in that of Feltre. Starts writing his first intermezzos.

1731 Goldoni's father dies at Bagnacavallo. Later that year, Goldoni obtains the Doctorate of Laws from Padua and settles in Venice.

1733 Flees from Venice to escape a difficult love affair. Travels to Milan, Brescia, and Verona.

1734 In Verona he is engaged as playwright by Giuseppe Imer of the Teatro San Samuele of Venice. There he begins his career as a professional dramatist with the tragicomedy *Belisarius.*

1736 In Genoa with the Imer company. Meets and marries Nicoletta Connio.

1737 Appointed director of the Teatro di San Giovanni Grisostomo in Venice.

1741 Appointed honorary consul of Genoa in Venice.

1743 Performance of *La donna di garbo* (*The Lady of Fashion*), his first entirely written comedy. Leaves Venice to escape creditors.

1746 Begins law practice in Pisa.

1745 Writes *Il servitore di due padroni* (*The Servant of Two Masters*) for Antonio Sacchi, an actor of the commedia dell'arte.

1747 In Leghorn, meets Girolamo Medebach, impresario of the Teatro San Angelo of Venice, and signs a provisional agreement with him.

1749 Leaves Pisa for Venice. His first season with Medebach at the Teatro San Angelo opens with *La vedova scaltra* (*The Clever Widow*).

1749 Signs a four-year contract with Medebach.

1750 Announces his intention to write sixteen comedies for the following season at the Teatro San Angelo. The season opens with *Il teatro comico* (*The Comic Theatre*) and includes *La bottega del caffè* (*The Coffee House*).

1752 Signs a three-year contract with the Teatro San Luca in Venice.

1753 Performance of *La locandiera* (*The Mistress of the Inn*) at the Teatro San Angelo.

1754 Falls ill with pneumonia while travelling to Modena. Goes to Milan upon his recovery. Second season at the Teatro San Luca begins.

1755 Contract for the Pitteri Edition of his dramatic works. Third season at the Teatro San Luca.

1756 Makes new contract with the Teatro San Luca. Fourth season opens with *II campiello* (*The Little Town Square*). Literary squabbles start in Venice between Goldoni and his rivals.

1758 Receives invitation from Teatro Tordinona of Rome to write plays and oversee their production.

1759 Leaves Rome. First negotiations with members of the Théâtre Italien of Paris.

1760 Performance of *I rusteghi* (*The Rustics*) and *La casa nova* (*The New House*).

1761 Writes the *Holiday Trilogy* for the Teatro San Luca and accepts a two-year contract with the Comédie Italienne.

1762 Leaves Venice definitively, a decision highly influenced by bitter conflicts between Goldoni and rival playwrights Pietro Chiari and Carlo Gozzi. After *Sior Todero brontolon* (*Grumpy Mr. Todero*) and *Le baruffe chiozzotte* (*Brawling in Chioggia*), bids farewell to the Venetian public with the performance of the autobiographical *Una delle ultime sere de carnovale* (*One of the Last Evenings of Carnival*). Arrives in Paris and assumes his post at the Comédie Italienne.

1763 *Il ventaglio* (*The Fan*), written as a "scenario" for the theatre, is performed in Paris.

1765 Leaves the Comédie Italienne, which is in deep crisis, and settles in Versailles. Appointed to teach Italian to Adelaide, daughter of Louis XV.

1769 Obtains a small annual pension from the French court and returns to Paris.

1771 Premiere of *Le bourru bienfaisant* (*The Beneficent Bear*) in Paris, performed for the marriage of Marie Antoinette and Louis XVI. It is Goldoni's last success.

1775 Back in Versailles, he teaches Italian to Clotilde and Elisabette, sisters of Louis XVI.

1776 Performance of Goldoni's last comedy, *L'avare fasteux* (*The Spendthrift Miser*).

1780 Retires from court and settles definitively in Paris.

1784 Starts writing his memoirs.

1787 Publishes his memoirs.

1788 The printer Antonio Zatta of Venice begins the publication of Goldoni's complete works.

1792 All royal pensions are suppressed by the new Legislative Assembly.

1793 Poverty-stricken and ill, Goldoni dies in Paris at the age of eighty-six. (One day later, the Convention Nationale, unaware of his death, passes a decree to restore him his pension.)

Introduction: The Theatrical Machine of Carlo Goldoni

This introduction is written for all who are dedicated to the theatre ensemble.

The Performance Tradition in the United States

It is impossible to say that there has been a consistent or continuing performance tradition of Carlo Goldoni's plays in the United States. Shakespeare, Molière, and Chekhov are performed so often that it is necessary to speak – not of one – but of many performance "traditions." And unlike Ibsen, Pirandello, and Ionesco, who were represented by intense periods of performance in this country, there has been no particular decade in American theatre history when Goldoni has been regularly performed. Were it not for occasional productions in regional theatres, colleges, and universities, Goldoni's plays would be almost unknown to the theatre public in the United States.[1]

In general, a student educated in theatre history possesses a few "received" impressions or facts about Goldoni – that he was responsible for reforming Italian theatre in the eighteenth century; that he coaxed the comic actors to remove their commedia dell'arte masks; that he created the transition from an improvised scenario to a fully scripted text; that he imitated colloquial speech and presented daily life on the stage; that he was involved in a serious theatrical feud with Carlo Gozzi, who challenged Goldoni's innovations.

What is perhaps less known is that Goldoni was extraordinarily prolific, having created more than two hundred works; that he, in fact, did provide scenarios for commedia dell'arte; that he wrote both in his native Venetian dialect and in the more literary Tuscan language; that he wrote in various genres – domestic and social comedy, elegant comedy of manners, farce, tragedy, and tragicomedy; that he provided texts for intermezzi and libretti for opera seria and opera buffa.

Beyond this, if there is an "idea" of Goldoni, it comes from some collective memory of the 1960 and 1984 American tours of *Arlecchino (The Servant of Two Masters),* performed by the Piccolo Teatro di Milano under the direction of Giorgio Strehler. (A third American tour of *Arlecchino,* adapted from Strehler's original production by Ferruccio Soleri, took place in 2005.) It is impossible to calculate the exact impact or influence that these performances may have had, but they were very successful in displaying the full range and power of Goldoni's theatrical invention.

In the 1980s and early 1990s, a few of the most important companies in the American theatre turned to Goldoni plays – the Guthrie Theatre's *Summer Vacation Madness,* based on the *Holiday Trilogy* and directed by Garland Wright, 1982–3; *Truffles in the Soup,* adapted from *The Servant of Two Masters* and directed by Dan Sullivan for the Seattle Repertory Theater, 1989; Theatre de la Jeune Lune's *Il campiello,* directed by Vincent Gracieux, 1989–90; *Summer Vacation Madness,* another adaptation of *The Holiday Trilogy,* with three abridged plays called *Summer, Vacation,* and *Madness,* directed respectively by Lillian Garrett, Brian Kulick, and David Esbjornson for the Mark Taper Forum at the John Anson Ford Theater in 1990; and *The Servant of Two Masters* at the American Repertory Theatre, directed by Andre Belgrader, 1991–2. Although this cannot be called a "blizzard" of Goldoni activity, it can be viewed as part of a nexus of eighteenth-century theatre production that includes the 1984 Strehler tour and performances of the works of Pierre Marivaux and Carlo Gozzi. These productions occurred throughout the 1980s and 1990s, and interest in eighteenth-century plays still continues. The director and translator Stephen Wadsworth has been most closely associated with the Marivaux revival. Director Andrei Serban and designer-director Julie Taymor have created enormous enthusiasm for Gozzi.

The Goldoni/Gozzi Dichotomy

Ironically, it is the commentary surrounding the production of Gozzi's plays that is responsible for certain misperceptions (or misapprehensions) concerning Goldoni. Robert Brustein, founding director of Harvard's American Repertory Theater, was the motivating force behind the extraordinarily successful *King Stag,* directed by Serban and with costumes and puppets designed by Taymor.[2]

In his review of *King Stag* for the *New York Times,* Mel Gussow identifies Goldoni as "advocating a more realistic psychological approach to the theater," in contrast to Gozzi, whom he considers "an early Italian precursor of our contemporary fabulist theater."[3] The idea of Goldoni as "realist" and Gozzi as "fabulist" is not unwarranted, but it sets up a binary formula for the critical evaluation of these two playwrights that, in Goldoni's case at least, addresses neither the nuances of his dispute with Gozzi nor the complexities of his prodigious career.

In an excellent article written to commemorate the 200th anniversary of Goldoni's death, John Rockwell briefly discusses two seminal post-World War II Italian productions of Goldoni that "reshaped opinion about the playwright":

> Luchino Visconti's staging in 1952 of "La Locandiera" (The Landlady), starring Marcello Mastroianni, reasserted the playwright's credentials as a realist. Mr. Strehler's "Arlecchino" [1947] stressed the fantastical, even Gozzian side to Goldoni's art, investing it with flair and a theatricality that are still very much evident.[4]

Rockwell correctly understands the remarkable combination of the realistic and the fantastic in Goldoni's work, but what he perceives as "fantastical" he attributes to Goldoni's "Gozzian side." In the same article, Rockwell quotes from a conversation with Brustein, who insists on asserting this Goldoni/Gozzi dichotomy:

> What was exciting about Strehler's Goldoni was that he theatricalized him … He did for Goldoni what Gozzi actually did himself.

According to Brustein, whatever is truly theatrical about Goldoni can be attributed to Gozzi and to Strehler's ability to elicit "Gozzian" elements. Brustein's distrust of and even antipathy to Goldoni is clearly expressed in an interview that he conducted with Julie Taymor before her 1990 Broadway premiere of *The Green Bird*:

> It seems very brave of you to do Gozzi on Broadway. One might almost think that Carlo Goldoni, his great rival, would be the more appropriate dramatist since he is linear, realistic, domestic – the kind of thing Broadway normally seems to be interested in. How do you think the fantastical "Green Bird" will go down with Broadway audiences?[5]

The interview promotes an impression of Gozzi's "pure theatricality" in contrast to Goldoni's "impure" dramaturgy. "Linear, realistic, and domestic" are not meant to be flattering adjectives. Brustein casts the Goldoni/Gozzi debate in extremely simplistic terms, with Gozzi as a free-spirited visionary promoting a liberated theatre of improvisation and Goldoni as an establishment literalist who writes to please a pedestrian audience.

In a review of the Serban production of Gozzi's *Serpent Woman,* Mel Gussow analyses Serban's attraction to Gozzi:

> As an archrival of Carlo Goldoni, Gozzi wanted to liberate commedia dell'arte into a world of extravagant theater. His fairy tales explored the mythic connections among divinities, animals and humans ... Gozzi's plays are partly scenarios, open for exploration and allowing for departure. As such, they offer a banquet of possibilities to a director like Mr. Serban who has kinetic, comedic and visual impulses.[6]

Gussow names Serban, Taymor, and Martha Clarke as proponents of a "new fabulism." Others who could be added to this list include Robert Wilson, JoAnne Akalaitis, Ping Chong, and Lee Breuer. These artists are of a generation schooled on Artaud. Their work is a theatre of images and sound – often surreal, hallucinatory, and shaped by their belief in the director as "auteur." In Serban's case, Gozzi is interesting precisely because his plays are "open for exploration" and allow for "departure." Serban, by partaking in Gozzi's "banquet of possibilities," becomes a co-creator in a theatre event called "*Serpent Woman.*"

For Strehler, who possessed prodigious "kinetic, comic and visual impulses," Goldoni's life and plays provided constant inspiration throughout the great director's extraordinary career. His production of *The Servant of Two Masters* was remarkable for its sense of joy, charm, wit, lightness, buoyancy, precision, and speed. Strehler's company performed with an unparalleled virtuosity that seemed to embody the Renaissance ideals of grace and *sprezzatura.* Such elegance of style would have been impossible to accomplish without a strict discipline and adherence to form.

The most compelling difference between Gozzi and Goldoni is not some perceived opposition between fantasy and realism but the actual split between an open dramatic structure and a predetermined one. For Goldoni, dramatic form is fixed – his plays are carefully planned; there is a balance of the component parts; no one element is allowed to dominate; the characters, who would have been interpreted by highly individual actors with special personalities and talents, must nevertheless defer to the demands of the dramatic form; improvisation is banished; the form dominates and becomes transcendent.

In such a theatre, the director is less an auteur who approaches the form from the outside with the intention of completing it and more like a conductor who works from within to release its energies. Although a director of Goldoni has abundant room to shape interpretation, influence characterization, and control rhythm and dynamics, even a director as individual as Strehler must submit to the playwright's form. The antipathy that Brustein, the great spokesman for a "theatre of revolt,"[7] has for Goldoni can be understood in this context. A dramaturgy that demands "submission" seems dangerously close to the politics of the establishment theatre that the "new fabulism" seeks to reject.

Although it is possible to read of a three-hour reduction of *The Holiday Trilogy* performed in New York by the Piccolo Teatro di Milano (2009), a *Trouble in Chiozza* produced by the Classical Theatre Lab in West Hollywood (2013), and a handful of productions of Goldoni plays in small theatres throughout the country, for the twenty-first century in the United States, Goldoni seems to have become almost exclusively a playwright of one play – *The Servant of Two Masters.*

Oregon Shakespeare Theater (2009) and Yale Repertory Theater (2010), with a tour by the Yale to the Guthrie Theater (2012), produced the play just before the Royal National Theatre transfer to Broadway of *One Man, Two Guvnors,* loosely adapted from *The Servant of Two Masters* by Richard Bean. Presumably, the extraordinary success of the London and New York productions has encouraged artistic directors and heads of theatres to schedule the original Goldoni play.[8]

The *Buffa* Finale

Goldoni's dramatic structures are very similar to musical forms that play out over the entire course of the performance. It is this inherent "musicality" that is one of the principal attributes of Goldoni's theatre. Very little has been written in English about the interconnections between Goldoni's opera libretti and his theatre texts. What has been written focuses primarily on discussions of theme and plot rather than on dramatic structure.[9] That Goldoni is considered to have made a major contribution to the development of Italian comic opera and that the invention of the *buffa* finale as practised by Mozart and Rossini is specifically attributed to him relates directly to the structural composition of his plays. The most significant characteristic of the *buffa* finale was its ability to integrate the individual actions (and voices) of each separate character into one great "*tutti*" incorporating the entire ensemble.

At the conclusion of *The New House,* eight major characters, representing the three households of the play, assemble on stage. With extraordinary economy, in the space of less than two and a half pages, the various elements of the plot are resolved; characters who have been in opposition find agreement; the households are united; and a ritual of betrothal takes place. The adept interweaving of plot and character leading inevitably to resolution is one of the key aspects of Goldoni's comic dramaturgy.[10]

Of the eight characters on stage at the end of *The New House,* seven are allowed to speak – some as motivators of the dramatic resolution and others as followers who accept and comment on the ending of the play. These characters assemble on the stage as a gathering force – Cristofolo, alone, speaks in a brief aside to the audience; Cecilia enters and delivers an extended "solo" in the presence of Cristofolo, who then accompanies her in a brief "duet"; they are, in turn, joined by Anzoletto in a short "trio"; immediately afterwards, Checca enters followed by Meneghina, Rosina, Lorenzino, and Lucietta. It is important to imagine the dramatic impact of this *tutti* finale, as characters gather on stage – first there is one – then there are two – three – four – then eight characters assembled on stage (p. 72).

So what specifically do a Goldoni comic ending and a *buffa* finale have in common? There is a complex and virtuosic weaving of characters into one large ensemble. The dramatic and musical momentum towards resolution conveys a sense of inevitability. The endings are, for the most part, "happy" and "harmonic." The dramatic and musical structures are shaped by a conscious geometry of composition. Goldoni inherits a model for the theatre that is at least as old as the Renaissance. The stage becomes the locus for the playing out of life in a great theatrical machine.[11]

At the very end of the play, with eight characters assembled on stage, the actress playing Cecilia "turns and addresses the audience" and speaks on behalf of the entire acting ensemble:

> Let us leave praise and blame to those who are qualified to give it, to those who have a right to give it – to all who, through us, may feel their hearts full of kindness, gentleness, and love. (pp. 72)

In a very short space of time, Goldoni expands the world of the play beyond the characters to the ensemble and from the ensemble to the audience. By inviting them to participate in an experience of "kindness, gentleness, and love," Goldoni reflects an idea of performance that finds its antecedents in Neoplatonism. With its interweaving of philosophical, political, and aesthetic principles, Neoplatonism dominated the major Italian courts of the late Renaissance and early Baroque period and, by extension, most of the courts of Europe.

Love is the motivating force of the Neoplatonic universe – it is the impetus for the Demiurge or Godhead to form celestial bodies from Divine Essence. Because the movements of the planets created by the Demiurge were seen as a "Divine Dance," and the frequencies that the movements elicited were understood to be the "Harmony of the Spheres," participation in dance and music was considered to be an embodiment of the cosmos. So strong is the power of the theatre in the Neoplatonic model as a place to "act out" cosmic patterns that not only the performers but also the spectators experience a communion with Divine Essence – with Divine Love. In performing a dramatic action that leads towards resolution, agreement, and union, and that concludes in a wedding, the ensemble of *The New House* participates in an act of cosmic balancing and realignment.

By Goldoni's time, the locus of cosmic activity has been domesticated. The progress towards harmony is enacted in the commercial theatres of mercantile Venice rather than the Olympic academies of the nobles. Subjects are daily life rather than the exploits of gods, heroes, and mythological creatures. But the *buffa* finale is more than a vestigial remnant of an ancient belief system – it is the Enlightenment's refiguring of late Renaissance/early Baroque theatrical cosmology.

Dramatic Structure

It can be said that the entire dramatic action of Goldoni's plays builds up to the climax of the *tutti* finale. An examination of the full dramatic structure of *The Coffee House* reveals a carefully plotted progression of scenes expanding and contracting in crescendo-decrescendo arcs that accelerate towards the conclusion. Within this structure, the characters become engaged in a subtle and constantly shifting series of relationships.

As an example, the scenes of the first act of *The Coffee House* can be divided into four parts. The scene of the private meeting between Eugenio and Ridolfo and Eugenio's subsequent soliloquy come just after the middle of the act:[12]

1.

Ridolfo/Trappola/Boys
Ridolfo/Pandolfo
Ridolfo/Don Marzio
Ridolfo/Don Marzio/Trappola

2.

Don Marzio/Trappola
Don Marzio/Ridolfo
Don Marzio/Eugenio/Ridolfo
Don Marzio/Eugenio/Pandolfo/Ridolfo
Don Marzio/Eugenio/Ridolfo
Don Marzio/Eugenio/Ridolfo/Boy

3.

Eugenio/Ridolfo
[Eugenio]
Eugenio/Lisaura
Eugenio/Lisaura/Leandro
Eugenio/Placida
Eugenio/Placida/Don Marzio
Eugenio/Don Marzio

4.

Vittoria/Don Marzio
Vittoria/Don Marzio/Trappola
Vittoria/Trappola
Vittoria/Eugenio

In *part one,* each of the first three scenes is a duologue in which Ridolfo interacts in succession with Trappola, Pandolfo, and Don Marzio. These scenes are followed by a brief trio with Ridolfo, Don Marzio, and Trappola. In *part two,* three more dialogues follow. This time Don Marzio is the common factor as he meets in succession with Trappola, Ridolfo, and Eugenio. The first half of this act culminates in a series of scenes with Eugenio and Don Marzio. They meet together first with Pandolfo and Ridolfo followed by the addition of the Boy.

A major scene between Eugenio and Ridolfo follows at the beginning of *part three.* Eugenio is then left on stage alone. Eugenio's solo speech both concludes the first half of the act and introduces the second. The women then make their initial appearance in a sequence of short scenes of relatively equal length. First to appear are Lisaura and Placida. Eugenio's participation is common to their scenes. Following, in *part four* are scenes in which Vittoria is introduced. Her presence binds the scenes together and propels the act towards its exciting conclusion as she confronts her husband, Eugenio.

Examining the dramatic structure in this way reveals a key element that is essential to the staging of the play. There should be a significant contrast between the first half that is inhabited by men and boys and the second half in which the three women are introduced. The small groupings of characters that make up these two halves are like "dances" – first between the men, then between the women and men. Here, structure conveys meaning. In the first half, the audience witnesses the daily life of trade, banking, commerce, and public gambling that excludes women yet drastically affects their lives. The first half also sets up the crises of the dual prodigals, Eugenio and Leandro, in the context of this male world. In the second half, Vittoria and Placida attempt to mitigate the actions of their husbands and claim independence within the dramatic action.

By the second act, the groupings grow progressively from three to four to six to eight characters on stage (with a complement of an undesignated number of waiters):

II.

Ridolfo/Trappola
Ridolfo/Eugenio
Eugenio/Leandro
Don Marzio/Ridolfo
Eugenio/Boy
Eugenio/Pandolfo
Eugenio/Pandolfo/Ridolfo
Ridolfo/Don Marzio
Ridolfo/Don Marzio/Lisaura
Don Marzio/Lisaura/Placida
Don Marzio/Placida

Don Marzio/Ridolfo
Don Marzio/Ridolfo/Eugenio
Don Marzio/Ridolfo/Eugenio/Leandro
Don Marzio/Ridolfo/Leandro/Pandolfo/Eugenio
Don Marzio/Leandro
Don Marzio/Eugenio/Leandro
Don Marzio/Eugenio/Leandro/Lisaura/Waiters
Don Marzio/Eugenio/Leandro/Lisaura/Ridolfo/Waiters
Don Marzio/Eugenio/Leandro/Lisaura/Ridolfo/Trappola/Waiters
Don Marzio/Eugenio/Leandro/Lisaura/Ridolfo/Vittoria
Don Marzio/Eugenio/Leandro/Lisaura/Ridolfo/Vittoria/Waiters
Don Marzio/Eugenio/Leandro/Lisaura/Ridolfo/Placida/Vittoria/Waiters
Eugenio/Ridolfo/Vittoria
Ridolfo/Vittoria
Vittoria/Ridolfo

In terms of characters and dramatic action, the large ensemble scenes at the end of the second act are the most physical of the play as a riot of action breaks out on stage. The various characters get up from the table "in confusion"; Trappola jumps out the window with a plate of food; "Eugenio, with weapon in hand, defends Placida against Leandro, who's following her" (p. 128). These loud, boisterous, chaotic scenes are followed by four small intimate scenes of three, two, and two. Vittoria and Ridolfo confront a chastened Eugenio. His reform, in anticipation of the third act finale, begins here in a moment of silence as a musical antithesis to the chaos that has just ensued.

The third act alternates in groupings of three and two until the gathering of the entire cast in scenes of six, eight, and ten:

III.
Lisaura/Leandro
Lisaura/Leandro/Don Marzio
Don Marzio/Placida
[Placida]
Placida/Ridolfo/Eugenio
Placida/Ridolfo/Eugenio/Boy
Ridolfo/Eugenio
Ridolfo/Trappola/Boys
Trappola/Don Marzio
Trappola/Ridolfo/Don Marzio/Boys

Trappola/Don Marzio/Pandolfo/Boys
Trappola/Don Marzio/Sergeant/Policemen
Don Marzio/Trappola
Don Marzio/Pandolfo/Trappola/Sergeant/Sergeant's men
Don Marzio
Don Marzio/Ridolfo/Leandro
Don Marzio/Ridolfo
Don Marzio/Ridolfo/Boy
Don Marzio/Ridolfo/Vittoria/Eugenio
Don Marzio/Leandro/Placida
Don Marzio/Lisaura
Don Marzio/Lisaura/Placida
Don Marzio/Lisaura/Placida/Eugenio/Vittoria/Ridolfo
Don Marzio/Lisaura/Placida/Eugenio/Vittoria/Ridolfo/Leandro
Don Marzio/Lisaura/Placida/Eugenio/Vittoria/Ridolfo/Leandro/Trappola
Don Marzio/Lisaura/Placida/Eugenio/Vittoria/Leandro/Trappola/Boy
Don Marzio/Lisaura/Placida/Eugenio/Vittoria/Leandro/Trappola/Waiter
[Don Marzio]

In the last four pages of the *Coffee House* (act 3, scenes 20–26, pp. 144–7), eight characters accumulate in various doors and windows to comment on a ninth character, the scandal-mongering Don Marzio, who stands in the middle of the street. The characters appear in rapid succession with short dialogues interspersed between entrances. A climax is reached. With equal rapidity the characters recede behind their doors and windows until Don Marzio, ostracized and in disgrace, addresses his bleak coda to the audience, as he stands alone on stage:

Don Marzio on stage—"Lisaura at the window"—short dialogue—"Placida at the window of the inn"—short dialogue—"Eugenio at a window of the gambling house"—short dialogue—"followed by Ridolfo, opening another"—short dialogue—"followed by Vittoria, opening another"—short dialogue—"Enter Leandro at the door of the inn"—short dialogue—"Enter Trappola"—short dialogue—Ridolfo "leaves the window"—"Enter Barber's boy"—exit line—boy "enters his shop"—"Enter waiter from the inn"—exit line—waiter "enters the inn"—exit line—Leandro "enters the inn"—exit line—Placida "leaves the window"—exit line—Lisaura "leaves the window"—exit line—Vittoria "leaves the window"—exit line—Eugenio "leaves the window"—exit line—Trappola "enters the shop"—Don Marzio on stage alone.

The sequence below indicates the number of characters on stage after each entrance and exit:

1—2—3—4—5—6—7—8—7—8—7—8—7—6—5—4—3—2—1

Because each entrance and exit from the door or window is performed singularly, by only one character at a time, the strict formality of the dramatic structure, in which Don Marzio is left in isolation, is emphasized. The alternating sequences, 7—8—7—8—7—8, represent the entrances and exits of the servants—Trappola, the barber's boy, and the waiter – whose brisk "foot-traffic" across the stage, while avoiding the friendless Don Marzio, adds staccato punctuation to the climax of the scene. While the conclusion of *The New House* integrates all characters assembled on stage, the *buffa* finale in *The Coffee House* becomes the mechanism that spits out the "indigestible" Don Marzio and designates him "harmonically incompatible" with the ensemble.

The Physical Actor

The actors who execute such demanding physical requirements must possess extraordinary stamina and virtuosity. According to Guy Callan, in an article comparing Goldoni and Marivaux, Goldoni's actors brought to the stage a body memory of their original masked roles.[13] The physical bravura needed to play Arlecchino, Brighella, or Colombina was reflected in Goldoni's stage action even when the masks had been removed. The actors also embodied what Callan has called a *jeu physique* – a kinesic style of performance that arrived both from folkloric and social dance.[14] The eighteenth-century actor took command of the stage with a full awareness of his or her connection to the other actors. The arrangements of actors in duets, in trios, and in quartets are like dance changes that embody constant shifts in relationships, power, and psychological states. The actor also understood that he or she did not inhabit the stage in isolation but, according to Callan, as part of a communal dance at once both civic and primal.

In his notes on *The Holiday Trilogy*, Strehler observed that "typical of Goldoni's writing for the stage" was "a comedy of movement and rhythm."[15] One of the most striking aspects of Strehler's *Arlecchino* was the commanding physical display of its ensemble. The actors seemed to embody a common instrument that could execute startling changes in tempo and dynamics – rapid accelerations and decelerations in the dramatic action, carefully orchestrated crescendos and decrescendos, extreme juxtapositions of quietly elegant moments and riotous physical comedy.

Franco Fido, also commenting on *The Trilogy*, has observed that Goldoni's characters "have their roles to play in the ensemble, like the instruments of a well-rehearsed orchestra or the strings of a well-tempered clavier."[16] Fido stresses the integration of the individual actor into the communal performance body. But "well-tempered" becomes an operant word here. Goldoni balanced the extremes inherent in the older improvisational style. His accomplishment can best be understood by examining his contribution to eighteenth-century Italian theatre language.

Goldoni's Language

With its clash of dialects, commedia dell'arte was an exhilarating but frequently incomprehensible mix of vocabularies and linguistic structures. Brighella spoke in Bergamask; Arlecchino in Bergamask and gibberish; Pulcinella in Neapolitan; Pantalone in Venetian; the Doctor in Bolognese and bowdlerized Latin; the Captain in Neapolitan or Spanish; and the Lovers in Tuscan.

As Goldoni's idea of the theatre developed, he moved away from the radically disparate dialects of the commedia dell'arte towards a unified theatre language by writing entirely in Venetian or in Tuscan.[17] The move towards a commonly understood language was a democratic one and is typical of Goldoni's Enlightenment perspective. Gozzi understood the revolutionary nature of Goldoni's new theatre and the characters that it portrayed. By attempting to preserve the commedia dell'arte tradition with its strictly defined class and linguistic structures, Gozzi was also trying to assure his ancient prerogatives as a nobleman. With Goldoni, the old class system implicit in commedia dell'arte is diminished as the dramatic focus shifts towards an urban and urbane perspective consistent with the emergence of the middle class.

This does not mean that Goldoni dispenses with varieties of speech. There are accents and regional colours, distinctions between city and country language, juxtapositions of colloquial and literary expression, differentiations between workers and employers, contrasts between servants and masters.[18] But the thrust of Goldoni's extraordinary achievement remains in his creation of a common theatrical language that allows a diversity of characters to communicate with and comprehend one another.

When performing in English, a sensitive director can do much to reclaim the original effect of Goldoni's language by casting actors with arresting voices and with the ability to project distinct personality through speech. The various combinations of characters, alternating from scene to scene, create a complex interweaving of voices, vocal timbres, and vocal colours, both male and female. For this reason, quality of voice and vocal display are elements that are as important to the actor as physical dexterity. One should imagine that Goldoni's lines were originally spoken by actors whose voices would have been as distinctive and as pliable as their bodies. With this in mind, the director must actively embrace the challenges of Goldoni's language and arrive at a method for activating it in rehearsal.

A Fugue of Words

As significant to Goldoni's dramaturgy as his employment of the *buffa* finale is his fugue-like development of words, phrases, and language sequences. These "word fugues" occur especially at moments when Goldoni concentrates the dramatic action, connects various characters and plot fragments, and progresses towards a resolution or climax. A particularly vivid example can be found in act 3, scene 5, of *Off to the Country*. Learning that Guglielmo has been invited to accompany Fulgenzio and his daughter, Giacinta, to the country, Leonardo becomes exasperated to the point of apoplexy. At the end of a ten-line soliloquy, in a string of three synonyms, he introduces a self-deprecating theme on "the jackass, the madman, the booby." Here Goldoni also initiates a series of tightly organized repetitions beginning with "Fulgenzio." The numbers within the parentheses indicate how many times a word is spoken within a repetitive sequence up to that point in the text:

> LEONARDO ... It must be **Fulgenzio(1)** then. But what reason would **Fulgenzio(2)** have for betraying me? I don't understand anything. It's me who's **the jackass(1), the madman(1), the booby.** (p. 204)

In the following fifteen lines of the Oldcorn translation, "jackass" and its variant "ass"[19] are repeated eleven times; "Fulgenzio/Signor

Fulgenzio" four times; "madman" two times. There are also repetitions of three similar word phrases grouped around the words "drink," "come over/come to" and "make no allowance." These are emphasized below:

CECCO *(enters with the water)*
LEONARDO *(aside, not noticing Cecco)* **Madman! (2) Jackass! (2)**
CECCO Hey, what do you mean **"jackass"? (3)**
LEONARD Yes, that's right. **Jackass! (4) Jackass! (5)** *(takes the water)*
CECCO Sir, I'm not a **jackass. (6)**
LEONARDO No! I am! I'm **the jackass! (7)** *(he drinks)*
CECCO *(aside)* He's right, **a jackass (8) drinks water, and I drink wine.**
LEONARDO Go to **Signor Fulgenzio's (3)** right away. See if he's in. Ask him if **he would be so good as to come over, or should I come to his place.**
CECOO To **Signor Fulgenzio's? (4)** Across the street?
LEONARDO Of course, you **ass (1/9).**[20] Where else?
CECCO Are you talking to me this time?
LEONARDO Yes, you.
CECCO *(aside)* **Ass (2/10)** ... **Jackass (11)** ... There's not a whole lot of difference. *(exit Cecco)*
LEONARDO **I'll make no allowance for his age. I'll make no allowance for anyone.** (p. 204)

With Paolo's re-entry a new section of the "fugue" begins that is organized around the repeated phrase "Leave me alone":

(enter Paolo) Cheer up, sir, don't worry. Everything's going to be ready.
LEONARDO **Leave me alone. (1)**
PAOLO I beg your pardon, sir, I've *done* **my duty (1)**, and more than **my duty. (2)**
LEONARDO **Leave me alone (2)**, I tell you.
PAOLO Has something new come up?
LEONARDO Yes, it certainly has!
PAOLO **The horses are ordered.**
LEONARDO **Cancel the order.**
PAOLO Again?
LEONARDO Oh! Curse my bad luck!
PAOLO What on earth has come over him?
LEONARDO For God's sake, **leave me alone. (3)**
PAOLO *(aside)* Oh, poor me! Things are getting worse by the minute. (p. 205)

In the midst of this second section, Goldoni makes reference to a plot point that has been previously introduced in act 1, scene 1 – the preparation of the horses. The phrases, "The horses are ordered" and "Cancel the order" (emphasized above) contain a repetition of the word "ordered/ order." And the dramatic action is itself a repetition as Paolo is sent once more to cancel the horses that he has twice previously requested. Like the Vaudeville balancing trick of spinning plates, Goldoni must keep all of his plot points current and alive.

In what follows, yet another plot point from act 1, scene 1, is emphasized – Vittoria's "mariage" – the fashionable dress that she has had made for the country. The fourth repetition of the phrase "Leave me alone" completes section two above, while the introduction of the phrase "Go away" emphatically underscores the beginning of section three. This third section is an example of Goldoni's fugal technique at its most complex, as words are repeated and varied, new phrases are introduced as counterpoint, and phrases are split and joined with other phrases.

Enter *Vittoria, carrying a folded dress.*

VITTORIA Brother, would you like to see my "mariage"?
LEONARDO **Go away. (1)**
VITTORIA Is that a way to treat people?
PAOLO *(softly to Vittoria)* **Leave him alone. (4)**
VITTORIA **What the devil's the matter? (1)**
LEONARDO **Yes, the devil's the matter. (2) Go away. (2)**
VITTORIA My, you are certainly in a gay mood for **going (1) to the country! (1)**
LEONARDO **Forget about the country (2), forget about our vacation, forget about everything!**
VITTORIA You don't want to **go to the country? (3)**
LEONARDO No, **I'm not going. (2) And you're not going (3) either.**
VITTORIA Have you taken leave of your senses?
PAOLO *(aside to Vittoria)* Don't upset him any more, for heaven's sake!
VITTORIA *(to Paolo)* Don't you come butting in too!
Enter Cecco.
CECCO *(to Leonardo)* **Signor Fulgenzio (5)** isn't home.
LEONARDO **Where the devil (3)** has **he gone? (3)**
CECCO They told me **he'd gone (4)** to Signor Filippo's.
LEONARDO *(to Paolo)* **My hat and my sword! (1)**

PAOLO Sir?
LEONARDO *(louder, to Paolo)* **My hat and my sword! (2)**
PAOLO Right away, sir. *(he goes to get Leonardo's hat and sword)*
VITTORIA *(to Leonardo)* **What on earth ...? (1)**
LEONARDO **My hat and my sword. (3)**
PAOLO Here you are, sir. *(he gives him his hat and sword)*
VITTORIA *(to Leonardo)* **What on earth's (2)** gotten into you?
LEONARDO **You'll know (1)** soon enough. *(exit Leonardo)*
VITTORIA *(to Paolo)* **What's the matter (1)** with him?
PAOLO I've no idea. I'll follow him at a safe distance. *(exit Paolo)*
VITTORIA *(to Cecco)* Do **you know (2) what's going on? (2/1)**
CECCO **I know (3)** he called me a **jackass. (12)** That's all **I know. (4)** (p. 206)

The phrases "Go away" and "My hat and my sword" are repeated three times each. Variations of the word "go" are used in four different ways in the phrases "Go away," "going to the country," "Where the devil has he gone?" and, "what's going on?" with the effect that the sentences break down and their discrete meanings intersect. Repetitions built around the phrases "going to the country" and "forget about the country" merge. Similarly, repetitions of phrases based on "What the devil's the matter?" intersect with "Go away" and "gone." There are three references to the devil, two to earth, and one to heaven, so that the audience experiences a Dantean word schema swirling humorously in their collective ear. As a final and definitive conclusion to the sequence, there is a final repetition of "jackass."

There are times when Goldoni's words and word clusters are repeated so often that they crowd out other possible vocabulary in a dramatic sequence. The world of barter, counting, and lending is vividly embodied in act 1, scene 8, of *The Coffee House* as the errant Eugenio attempts to borrow money to pay his gambling debts. The audience hears repeated word clusters built around "pay," "sequins," "a sequin a week," and corollary words such as "security," "sale," "sell," "interest," "usury," and "exchange":

EUGENIO Come, come, Pandolfo. Find me the thirty sequins.
PANDOLFO I have a friend who can give you the money, but against security and with interest.
EUGENIO Don't talk to me about security, or we won't get anywhere. I have that cloth at the Rialto, as you know. I'll put it up for sale, and when I sell it, I'll pay.
DON MARZIO *(aside)* "I'll pay." He said, "I'll pay." He lost on his word.

PANDOLFO Very well. How much interest do you want to pay?
EUGENIO You decide how much you believe is appropriate.
PANDOLFO Listen, it'll take at least a sequin a week.
EUGENIO A sequin of usury a week?
RIDOLFO *(with the coffee, to Eugenio)* Here's your coffee.
EUGENIO *(to Ridolfo)* Go away.
RIDOLFO And now a secondary exchange.
EUGENIO *(to Pandolfo)* A sequin a week?
PANDOLFO For thirty sequins, it seems fair to me.
RIDOLFO *(to Eugenio)* Do you want it, or don't you?
EUGENIO *(to Ridolfo)* Go away before I throw it in your face.
RIDOLFO *(aside)* Poor devil! He's drunk with gambling. *(takes the coffee into the back)*(p. 89)

In its most condensed form, the language becomes a manifestation of a blunt naturalism that seems to anticipate the harsh world of David Mamet. While at the same time, as in Pinter, the increasing minimalism moves the language towards poetic abstraction.

Goldoni employs a different approach in act 1, scene 2, of *The New House.* Rather than condensing the language and turning it in on itself as a micro-structure, he uses the repetitions of words and word phrases to integrate long sequences of dialogue. A frazzled Anzoletto confronts his building contractor:

ANZOLETTO You could find some more workmen and get things done quicker.
SGUALDO You let me have some money first.
ANZOLETTO Money! It's always money! That's all I've heard since he's been here. Can't the man forget about it just for one moment? He never stops! It's all he can think of! Money! Money! Money!
SGUALDO No money – no more workmen.
ANZOLETTO Suppose – just suppose – I haven't got any money!
SGUALDO Then I suppose you'd see me and my men walking straight out of here.(p. 11)

The eight repetitions of the word "money" set in motion a recurring motif of "work and payment" that creates a unified macro-structure. Variations on "You let me have the money first" ("No money – no more workmen."/"All right – where's the money?"/"Well, I'll think of the men if you'll start thinking of the money!"/"And tomorrow we'll talk about money") (pp. 11–14) give added meaning to what has already occurred in a previous dialogue with Sgualdo and the maid, Lucietta, as they discuss Anzoletto's waning fortunes (p. 8). The over-arching language structure also sets in motion what will follow (as Anzoletto's household unravels). Within this large macro-structure, Goldoni interweaves smaller micro-sequences of repeated words and phrases.

To the reader contemplating a staging of a Goldoni play, this discussion of word repetitions and the inherent musical structure of his language may seem daunting. How is a company of contemporary actors to accomplish the musical requirements that the plays demand? Certainly, such an awareness of dramatic structure and the skills required to embody it are not generally taught. Yet there is a continuing tradition of comic playing, preserved in film and in television recordings by such great popular artists as the Marx Brothers, Burns and Allen, Monty Python, and the "Not Ready for Primetime Players" of *Saturday Night Live*, that exemplifies the essential elements necessary for the performance of complex comic language. By a sort of theatrical osmosis, succeeding generations of admiring viewers have absorbed from these artists crucial lessons in performing with a consciousness of musical structure.

In "L.A. at Last!," one of the most brilliant episodes of *I Love Lucy*,[21] Lucille Ball, Desi Arnaz, Vivian Vance, and William Frawley exhibit a virtuosic ability to perform dialogue as a unified ensemble. They play together like a venerable string quartet that interacts at the deepest level of communication. The opening scene expository dialogue, which seems commonplace on the printed page, is brought to life by adept attention to rhythm, dynamics, and tonal nuance. The second scene with Ball, Vance, Frawley, and guest star William Holden is a masterpiece of virtuosic performance based on word repetitions integrated with masterly physical comedy. In performance, Ball is said to have known the full script (not only her lines but also those of the entire cast) so that she could calibrate small improvisational moments within the strictly controlled dramatic structure. With their consciousness of musical structure, the *I Love Lucy* cast embody a performance sensibility that has its antecedents in the Goldoni tradition.

In the *Seinfeld* episode "The Dog,"[22] the names of two films that the protagonist Jerry and his friends want to see – *Prognosis Negative* and *Ponce de Leon* – are not only repeated within scenes but throughout the entire half-hour comedy. Unlike *I Love Lucy*, which was filmed in real time before a live audience, *Seinfeld* was recorded in smaller fragments that jump nervously from location to location. It is all the more significant, then, even when the comic structure is no longer inherently "of the theatre" but reflects contemporary television practices, that Julia Louis Dreyfus, Michael Richards, Jason Alexander, and Jerry Seinfeld emphasize the musicality of the repetitions that are enhanced by recurring musical motifs in the soundtrack. The repetitions become a kind of structural "glue" that holds the comic structure together.

The Eighteenth-Century Illustrations

In his note to the reader that precedes *Adventures in the Country*, Goldoni discusses his special method for creating "unity of action" in plays such as the *Coffee House* and *The Holiday Trilogy* that contain multiple characters and plots:

> Unity of action is an indispensable precept, to be observed in dramatic compositions in which the plot chiefly concerns a single character. But when the collective title encompasses a number of persons, unity is itself found in the multiplicity of the actions ... All of the characters act towards the same end, and all of their different actions serve to advance the plot. (p. 226)

The "same end" mirrors Goldoni's opera *buffa* finale – both integrate "different actions" into one great and overriding conclusion. This explains the curious and, at first glance, apparently idiosyncratic depiction of some of these ensemble endings represented in the engravings that accompanied the eighteenth-century editions of Goldoni's plays.[23] A representative example is the illustration for the act 3 final scene of *Off to the Country* (the first play of *The Holiday Trilogy*) (p. 155). Eight characters stand tightly together, shoulder to shoulder, from left to right in a compact rectangular box representing an intimate proscenium. These characters occupy the entire horizontal frame of the box and two-thirds of its vertical space. The most unusual feature of this illustration is that all eight characters are depicted at almost exactly the same height. The image seems strange. Although its compositional elements are repeated over and over in other illustrations, the strangeness never quite dissipates.

It is reasonable to assume that the original illustrations may depict actual or intended stage action. The illustration for act 1, scene 1, captures the opening moments of the play when Leonardo instructs his valet, Paolo, to pack for their vacation. The act 2 illustration is from scene 4. Ferdinando, who plans to join Leonardo and Vittoria on their holiday, enters in his travelling outfit. He is startled to learn that their trip has just been cancelled.

Although the illustrations for acts 1 and 2 attempt to capture stage action in movement, the third-act illustration depicts the "metaphysics" of the finale in which the individual characters become part of a greater ensemble. What is important here is that they are perceived as one body – organically linked shoulder to shoulder – one height in geometric relationship to the horizontal and vertical space. It is not only the gathering of the ensemble that is depicted but also the audience perception of "wholeness" and completion that is represented.

The illustration for the conclusion of the third act of *The Coffee House* (identified as Scene 26, p. 77) offers an almost identical arrangement despite Goldoni's explicit stage directions that place the final action in the doors and windows as discussed above. It is hard to know whether this illustration represents an actual staging or an imagined one. The fact that the conventions of depicting the final ensemble prevail over the intended staging is an indication of how powerful this image of the collective is.

A similar staging configuration can be seen, 123 years later, in a 1911 French film by Georges Mendel. A group of six uncredited actors mime the sextet ("Chi mi frena in tal momento?") from *Lucia di Lammermoor* to a 1908 Victor recording that includes Enrico Caruso as Edgardo.[24] The viewer experiences the same tight horizontal grouping of the ensemble positioned similarly in the vertical space within the film frame. From the tragic Romantic perspective of Donizetti's 1835 opera – if, indeed, the film preserves the vestiges of an earlier performance tradition – the strictly contained ensemble becomes a prison that embodies the repressive world that Lucia and Edgardo inhabit. Each character, in articulating his or her solo line by a distinct movement or physical gesture, seems to struggle to break out of the confines of the ensemble.

In Herbert Graf's 1956 RAI telecast of Verdi's *Falstaff* (conducted by Tulio Serafin with Giuseppe Taddei, Anna Moffo, Fedora Barbieri, Rosanna Carteri, and Luigi Alva), the staging of the final ensemble quadruples the linear arrangement.[25] On a reproduction of an Elizabethan stage, eight principal characters inhabit the foreground and are doubled by at least as many company members in a second row behind. Directly above, on a balcony, four chorus members in front are doubled by a second line. The television cameras cut to smaller groupings within the whole, but they return frequently to the group composition that is remarkably similar in effect to the eighteenth-century illustrations.

The Individual within the Social Collective

For Goldoni, the integration of the individual into a clearly defined social group is a positive act, and the group itself becomes the means for a psychological and social transformation. Comedy, as Goldoni understands it, is a social activity. "If I don't have company," declares an exasperated Filippo in a direct address to the audience, "I might as well be dead" (p. 234). Unable to find his place within a larger group of characters on stage, Filippo turns in frustration to the audience itself in search of an empathetic community.

In Goldoni's comedic universe, the individual must learn to moderate extremes in behaviour, personal vices, and eccentricities that throw that character out of balance with the Enlightenment ideals of order and moderation. The individual character must also suppress desires, ambitions, and passions – no matter how compelling or legitimate – that endanger the well-being of the community.

The gathering of the major characters on the stage, as the plays move irresistibly towards resolution, represents the communities of families, extended families, households including servants, multiple households interrelated by marriage, friends, neighbours, neighbourhoods, urban districts, the city, and the Republic of Venice. While Goldoni presents the inevitable triumph of these corporate bodies with great confidence, he is not afraid to show the psychological and emotional price that the individual characters must pay to be absorbed into the collective.

A "surrender of self" is required to achieve what Callan has called "solidarity with the cosmos."[26] How this surrender is interpreted and, for a contemporary audience, negotiated, is one of the major challenges in staging Goldoni. Surrender means different things in different contexts and in different plays. In *The New House*, Cecilia and Anzoletto willingly submit to the warm embrace of familial obligations and family ties that are enforced with gentle and mildly ironic humour.

In *The Coffee House,* two versions of surrender are offered. By Ridolfo's good counsel, Eugenio is led to a deepening perception of his responsibilities as citizen and husband. His reconciliation with Vittoria is tentatively optimistic and offers the expectation of a lasting reform. In contrast, Flaminio's reunion with Placida is the result of force and shame. There seems to be little chance of a harmonious or successful outcome. For Giacinta, in *Back from the Country*, surrender to marriage with Leonardo is a bitter pill out of which will come, perhaps, a sober wisdom but also regret and a lingering sense of defeat. Guglielmo's petulant and grudging acceptance of Vittoria warns of a loveless and despairing marriage to follow.

The Goldoni Paradox

That Goldoni insists on the supremacy of the collective over the individual leads to a "problem" in interpreting his plays for a contemporary audience. From the vantage point of the eighteenth-century Enlightenment, succumbing to passion was considered a dangerous caprice of the aristocracy. At the time, Goldoni's insistence on the values of the Venetian merchant class, including his focus on the collective, was revolutionary and an expression of a democratic impulse. From a contemporary perspective that has absorbed the tenets of nineteenth-century Romanticism, a sublimation of self or personal expression to that very same collective can seem dictatorial and oppressive.

Another problem in interpreting Goldoni is the paradox of his view of the characters of the women that he creates. In her excellent book on the comedies of Goldoni, *Playing with Gender*, Maggie Günsberg describes the complex interweaving of "money, sex and power" in her chapter on "Masculinity and Materialism" in eighteenth-century Venice.[27] According to Günsberg, daily life was dominated by a prevailing homosocial culture in which men bonded with men to promote mutual interests in commerce, banking, and trade. These bonds also created close psychological and emotional ties. When women attempted to penetrate these male alliances, they were excluded and often punished

> as the inevitable disrupters of homosociality, that patriarchal idyll of all-male harmony and all-male control, and, by extension of patriarchy itself.[28]

Goldoni expects the women that he creates, as he does his male characters, to submit to the fixed structure of the *buffa* finale and to the dominant social order of the Venetian patriarchy. Surrender is especially difficult and painful for daughters and wives who must embrace arranged marriages against their will or instincts. At the same time, Goldoni often gives these characters astonishing things to say – sentiments that apparently subvert the fixity of the male-dominated world. As Giacinta accepts Leonardo with resignation, she speaks candidly to him: "To go from being a free woman to being married is not something a woman can do without violence ..." (p. 347–8). In the last moments of the *buffa* finale, with its expectations of harmonic resolution, Giacinta's comments cut through like a knife to the heart of the audience – with the effect of unsettling the balance of the ending.

Joseph Farrell, in his superb introduction to *Carlo Goldoni and the Eighteenth-Century Theatre,* has noted that the playwright has "the merit of having created some of the strongest, most imaginative, most independently-minded women on the European stage."[29] Yet there is a "dilemma" in Goldoni's writing that Farrell elucidates in his discussion of Mirandolina, the leading character in *La locandiera* and one of the playwright's greatest creations:

> the dilemma could be summed up by pointing out that the creator of Mirandolina is also the author of the preface of the play in which she appears. Inside the drama, Mirandolina is the image of the free spirit who is beholden to no man, the woman who manages her own establishment and who chooses which of the various suitors who pursue her she will have. Her choice is of a man of her own caste, but also someone of lesser attainments and less force of will; someone, in other words, who will permit her the continued possession of her freedom. Nevertheless, in his introductory words, Goldoni condemns his character. The reading of the play preferred by the writer would make it an eighteenth-century *Taming of the Shrew.*[30]

How is it possible that Goldoni the author of the preface is in such direct opposition to Goldoni the writer of the play?

The key to understanding this contradiction can be found in Goldoni's reformation of the character of Pantalone. One of the great masks of the commedia dell'arte, Pantalone is the personification of all that has become warped and corrupt as a result of an unrelenting insistence on male prerogatives. Venice, in fact, can be called the city of Pantalone, and he, most often depicted as a Venetian merchant, is its comic avatar. He is part of a direct continuum of "tyrannical fathers" found in European domestic comedy, from Greek New Comedy, to Attellan Farce in southern Italy, to the plays of Plautus and Terence, to commedia dell'arte, in which the foibles of a despotic patriarch are subverted by wives, sons, nephews, daughters, nieces, servants, and slaves. Pantalone's vanities, his greed, and his unwarranted self-confidence in his potency and sexual prowess have traditionally made him the successful target of those he attempts to suppress.

Farrell identifies Goldoni's reformation of the commedia dell'arte and of the comic mask convention as a radical re-imagining of the character of Pantalone.[31] By balancing the extremes in Pantalone's behaviour, Goldoni brought the character into alignment with Enlightenment values of equanimity and self-control. For Goldoni, the citizen of Venice should aspire to be an "accomplished man" who offers, according to Farrell, "an ideal of honourable conduct as much as the 'gentleman' in England or the 'caballero' in Spain, so that he may be viewed as an updated equivalent of Castiglione's *cortegiano.*"[32] In his *Memoirs,* Goldoni develops his definition of what it means to be "a true Venetian cortesan":

> He is generous without profusion; gay without rashness; fond of women without involving himself; he is prepared to bear part in every thing for the good of society; he prefers tranquillity, but will not allow himself to be duped; he is affable to all, a warm friend or zealous protector.[33]

From an eighteenth-century perspective, the "accomplished man" moderates extreme behaviour and embraces balance. In this context, to be "fond of women" can mean to be affectionate, loving, tender[34] – not attributes associated with the pre-reform Pantalone. But simultaneously, Goldoni's Venetian gentleman must be fond "without involving himself," that is, without being caught up with, or drawn in by, or preoccupied by women. From a post-Romantic perspective, this sentiment seems unduly restricted, dispassionate, and crabbed.

As a gentleman of Venice, Goldoni associates the closed form of his plays and their fixed structure with the social order created by the male-dominated Venetian merchant class. But as an artist and as a man of the theatre, he subverts the fixity of the very system that he extols. This is the great paradox of his plays, but also their great strength. Günsberg successfully articulates the nature of this paradox and discusses its effect on the plays themselves:

> His Enlightenment context means that on one level his plays foreground reason, morality, certainty and the fixed values and identities of dominant power positions. On another level, however, the performative nature of the theatrical medium itself, together with the carnivalesque mobility of the Venetian context, work both to destabilize fixity and to focus attention to the body-as-surface. The theatre audience is presented with surfaces, with

> vestiges of femininity, masculinity and class visually encoded in costumes and deportment, as well as signified verbally. Dramatic tension is set up between the shifting, illusory properties of surfaces that can be styled and manipulated, and the "reality" of what lies beneath.[35]

Although Günsberg's remarks introduce her analysis of "identity, disguise and fashion"[36] in Goldoni's plays, they can be applied, in general terms, to an examination of his entire dramaturgical method. For Günsberg, there is a surface reality that represents the fixed world of the Venetian merchant class. Underlying this fixed world is a deeper "reality" that is released by "the performative nature of the theatrical medium." Goldoni consciously creates dramatic tension by his juxtaposition of the surface and the deeper reality beneath it.

That the stage offers the possibility of an alternative universe is not an idea unique to Goldoni. The metaphysical aspects of theatre are famously explored in Shakespeare's *The Tempest,* Calderon's *Life Is a Dream,* and *The Illusion* by Corneille. These plays, however, display the Neoplatonic ethos of the royal courts that they epitomize. What is new in Goldoni is the perception that an alternative world of the stage can be more real for the middle class than what the surface presents. Even more radical is the correlative idea that the nature of the medium of theatre itself, what Günsberg identifies as "theatrical" and "carnivalesque," is a truer form of expression than the surface reality of eighteenth-century Venetian life.

The Memoirs

In his *Memoirs,* written in French when he was eighty years old, Goldoni identifies his first encounter with the theatre at the age of four when his father and "three or four" of his father's friends entertained the young boy with a puppet show. A defining moment, however, is when an adolescent Goldoni, playing truant from his strict Thomistic school, "sees women on the stage" for the "first time":

> Rimini is in the legation of Ravenna; women are admitted on the theatre, and we do not see there, as at Rome, men without beards or even the signs of them.
>
> The first day or two, I went very modestly into the pit; but seeing young people like myself on the boards, I endeavoured also to get there, and

> succeeded without difficulty. I bestowed a side-glance on the ladies, who looked boldly at me. By-and-by I grew more familiar, and from one subject of conversation to another, and from question to question, they learned that I was a Venetian. They were all country-people of my own, and I received compliments and caresses without number from them.[37]

This is the birth of Goldoni's alternative universe – a world in which women are played by women rather than by beardless men. His theatre awakening is linked to sexual discovery. The women look at him boldly, but he encounters them first with "a side-glance" and then he grows "more familiar." The adolescent Goldoni must look beyond the surface portrayal of femininity, by both women and men, to discover the deeper reality of the women themselves. In the theatre he also recognizes himself and "young people" like himself. And he finds that his identity as a "Venetian," confirmed by "compliments and caresses," is symbiotically joined with his attraction to the theatre troupe. He becomes simultaneously a citizen of Venice and of the theatre, and this dual citizenship transcends geographic boundaries – his place of residence, like that of the itinerant actors, becomes a state of mind.

Once Goldoni steps "on the boards" and passes from surface to depth, he is able to gain access to the culture, language, and conventions peculiar to the theatre. Most of all he is able to enjoy the power of "theatricalization." One of the most interesting aspects of the *Memoirs* is the way Goldoni is seen to play out his life in a series of theatricalizations or performative actions that he himself constructs. As an early and seminal event in the autobiographical narrative, the report of the encounter with the actors allows the octogenarian Goldoni to provide, in hindsight, a *raison d'être* for his entire life.

At the invitation of the theatre troupe, the adolescent Goldoni flees his Dominican school and sets out with the actors on a barge to Chiozza where his mother is living. Unsure of how she will react, Goldoni asks the theatre manager to accompany him to his mother's house:

> he very readily consented and announced himself on his arrival. I remained in the antechamber. "Madam," said he to my mother, "I come from Rimini; I have news from your son."—"How does my son?"—"Very well, madam."—"Is he content with his situation?"—"Not remarkably so, madam; he suffers a great deal."—"From what?"—"From being so far from his tender mother."—"Poor child! I wish I had him beside me." (All this was heard by me, and my heart beat within me.) "Madam," continued the manager,

> "I offered to bring him with me."—"Why then did you not?"—"Would you have been pleased?"—"Undoubtedly."—"But his studies?"—"His studies! Could he not return? Besides, masters are everywhere to be had."—"Then you would willingly see him?"—"With the greatest joy."—"Here he is then, madam."
>
> On this, he opened the door, and I made my entrance: I threw myself at my mother's feet, who cordially embraced me; neither of us could speak for our tears. The actor, accustomed to scenes of this nature, after passing some agreeable compliments, took leave of my mother, and departed …[38]

The young Goldoni, as an initiate in the art of the theatre, relies on the manager of the troupe to demonstrate how one should construct performative actions that will have a desired effect. This particular sequence could be entitled "The Return of the Prodigal Son," but rather than the sombre narrative found in the Gospel of St Luke, Goldoni theatricalizes himself in a light-hearted tale of youthful exuberance and adolescent folly.

The observers of these theatricalizations become participants in them – some willingly, as in the case of the theatre manager, and some unwittingly as, at first, in the case of his mother. The theatre manager performs the role of the "Theatre Manager" in a dialogue with Goldoni's unsuspecting mother. The purpose of the dialogue is to lead Signora Goldoni through her son's emotional journey – that he is not content, that he misses her, that he wants to come home. The dialogue is also constructed to elicit her own feelings – that she longs for him, that she wishes that he were with her, that his school is not so important that he cannot leave. The theatre manager's conversation is precisely calculated to produce such a desired response, and it causes the mother to articulate ideas presumably in contradiction to Goldoni's father. This has all been achieved while Goldoni remains a silent and unannounced witness in the antechamber. At the climax of the dialogue, the manager opens the door on his line, "Here he is then, madam." Goldoni makes his "entrance" and, falling at his mother's feet, joins with her in a tearful embrace.

The theatre manager, "accustomed to scenes of this nature," makes his compliments and departs. On a first reading, Goldoni seems to suggest that the theatre manager, as an actor, is familiar with outpourings of emotion and, perhaps, with the scene itself as similar to a play. But there is also a deeper meaning. What has transpired so far has been a public act, and Signora Goldoni has not been the only member of the young Goldoni's intended audience. There are the citizens on the streets of

Chiozza who direct Goldoni to his mother's house; there are the household servants who must be aware of his presence in the antechamber; and there is the company of actors who will, certainly, learn from their manager of Goldoni's successful enterprise.

When the manager withdraws, the first scene of Goldoni's "play" as a performative act is over and the role assigned to the manager, as both teacher and performer, is finished. What follows is a moment of intimacy between mother and son:

> I remained with her, and frankly owned the folly I had committed; she scolded me one moment, and caressed me the next, and we quite pleased each other.[39]

Goldoni's discussion with his mother is private and beyond the bounds of the readers of the *Memoirs*. This scene is also removed from the "public" that has witnessed his display of the returning prodigal. There is the implication here that the "frank" Goldoni, in these private moments with his mother, presents himself with less premeditation and with more willingness to reveal an "unconstructed" self.

At this point, Goldoni's aunt arrives, and a new act begins. "On her entrance" there is "a repetition of the same surprise and the same caresses." This is the third time in the story that Goldoni is "discovered" with delight. The first is at his point of departure on the barge trip with the actors, when he "sallied out of his hiding place, at which every one began to laugh."[40] The second and third are with his mother and aunt. All three discoveries – with the actors, his mother, and his aunt – end in laughter and caresses and serve as test cases for the ultimate meeting with his father. They also confirm the efficacy of his self-created role as charming prankster, and they are attempts to mitigate what he anticipates will be his father's perception of him as a delinquent truant:

> In six days my father arrived – I trembled all over: my mother concealed me in her dressing-closet, and took the rest on herself. My father ascended the steps; my mother ran to meet him; my aunt did the same, and the usual embraces took place. My father appeared chagrined and thoughtful, and he had not his usual gayety. They supposed him fatigued.
>
> On entering the room, my father's first words were, "Where is my son?" My mother answered with perfect sincerity, "Our youngest son is boarded out." "No, no," replied my father in a rage, "I want the eldest, and he must

be here. In concealing him from me, you are doing very wrong; he must be corrected for his misconduct." My mother was quite at a loss what to do or say: she uttered vaguely, "but—how?"—My father interrupted her, stamping his feet: "Yes, I have been informed of everything by M. Battaglini, who wrote to me in Modena, and I found the letter in passing through it." My mother entreated of him, with an afflicted air, to hear me before condemning me.[41]

Signora Goldoni takes a conscious role as participant and collaborator in this subsequent act of her son's "prodigal play." She conceals her son in her own dressing closet. By fleeing the Dominicans and returning to his mother, Goldoni throws off the role that has been determined for him by his father. The dressing closet is a place of safety where he can return to his "pre-formulated" and "pre-theatricalized" self before he was made to embrace the strict scholastic regimen of his all-male school.

Goldoni's mother takes "the rest on herself" and, with the help of her sister-in-law, she attempts to deflect her husband's anger. The two women seem to fail, but the reader will later come to understand that Signora Goldoni's efforts have prepared her husband to hear their son before "condemning" him:

My father, still in a rage, asked again where I was? I could contain myself no longer, I opened the glass door, but I durst not advance. "Go out," said my father to his wife and sister, "leave me alone with this profligate." When they were gone, I came forward trembling; "Ah, father!"—"How, sir! How do you happen to be here?"—"Father—you have been told."—"Yes, I have been told that, in spite of remonstrances and good advice, and in opposition to everyone, you have the insolence to quit Rimini abruptly."[42]

The scene presents a collision between two strong individuals who have each assigned the other a role as a supporting character in his own play. From Goldoni's perspective, his youthful and exuberant self is pitted against his stern, blustering father:

"What should I have done at Rimini, father?—it was lost time for me."—"How, lost time! Is the study of philosophy lost time?"—"Ah! the *scholastic Philosophy*, the *syllogisms*, the *euthymemas*, the *sophisms*, the *negos propos* and *concedos*; Do you remember them, father?" (He could not avoid displaying a slight movement of the lips which indicated his desire to laugh; I was shrewd enough to perceive it, and I took courage.)[43]

From the moment the father enters the Goldoni household, he is presented by his son's narrative in stereotypical terms. His "chagrin," his "stamping his feet," his "rage," his pointed language are conventional attributes of a non-empathetic patriarch. Signor Goldoni plays his role with enthusiasm, but there are fissures in his performance. His son detects "a slight movement of the lips" that indicates "his desire to laugh." Goldoni's observation of his father is conveyed in a parenthetical insertion that has the same effect as a theatrical aside. The smile itself is also a kind of aside, and it can be viewed as an ironic commentary on the playing out of the conventional scene between father and son. By means of these asides, the conventional form is broken and a new mode of expression becomes possible. Goldoni is "shrewd enough to perceive it" and takes "courage":

> "Ah, father!" I added, "teach me the philosophy of man, sound moral philosophy, and experimental natural philosophy."[44]

The young Goldoni speaks like an apprentice philosopher who attempts to activate Enlightenment sensibilities in his father. Because the context is domestic and the overall effect is one of gentle wit and charm, it is easy to overlook how radical the young Goldoni's propositions are. He has gone into his mother's closet as an adolescent who is expected by the role he has been assigned to be pliant and obedient to his father, but he re-emerges with an adult identity that is born out of republican impulses. "The philosophy of man, sound moral philosophy, and experimental natural philosophy" are subjects antithetical to what he has learned in the Dominican school. Goldoni appeals to his father to break the mould that convention has assigned him and to reinvent his role as patriarch.

Signor Goldoni responds by seeming to shift the conversation: "Come, come; how did you arrive here?" By this one line, something occurs that is typical in Goldoni – a "Goldonian moment." A transition takes place in an instant that connotes a significant psychological shift in the father and signals a deeper communication between him and his son. The young Goldoni has been clever enough to elicit this response and the conversation that follows:

> "Come, come; how did you arrive here?" "By sea."—"With whom?"—"With a company of players."—"Players!"—"They are very respectable people, father."—"What is the name of the manager?"—"He is Florindo on the stage, and they

> call him Florindo de' Macaroni."—"O, I know him; he is a worthy man: he acted Don Giovanni in the *Festino di Pietra*; he thought proper to eat the macaroni belonging to Harlequin, and that is the way he came by that surname."—"I assure you, father, that this company"—"Where is the company gone to?"—"It is here."—"Here?"—"Yes, father."—"Do they act here?"—"Yes, father."—"I shall go see them."—"And I also, father?" "You! rascal! What is the name of the principal actress?"—"Clarice."—"O, Clarice!—excellent, ugly, but very clever."—"Father,"—"I must go to thank them."—"And I, father?"—"Wretch."—"I beg your pardon."—"Well, well, for this time."—[45]

In Goldoni's moment of intimacy with his mother, the reader is excluded from what is private and "frank," but here the reader is invited to witness the reconciliation between father and son. There remains a performative aspect to their relationship that requires an audience. Signor Goldoni's discussion of the stage is meant to be wise and playful – he bonds with his son by discussing the merits of Florindo and the attractions of Clarice. But this dialogue masks a deeper reality that the father, as patriarch, cannot directly acknowledge. His son's performative actions have prevailed over his own. The young Goldoni's theatricalization of the "return of the prodigal" has triumphed, and his father must accept the role that his son has assigned him as the "Benign Father" in the prodigal performance.

Signor Goldoni also accepts cheerfully his son's perception of the itinerant band of actors as "respectable people." Goldoni begs for a reconciliation with his father, not in spite of his embrace of theatre but because of it. The actors are respectable in Goldoni's mind precisely because of their ability to play, joke, laugh, and rally in the face of affliction. This is an essential idea in Goldoni's *Memoirs* – that the theatre offers a model for living one's life more completely and that actors, in perfecting this model, participate in a noble undertaking.

Goldoni's constructed memory of his seminal meeting with the acting troupe is a compendium of narrative elements that, in their theatrical form, become signature components of his dramatic style: (1) As previously discussed, there is a juxtaposition of surface reality with a deeper reality beneath. In addition, (2) characters play out their lives in a series of theatricalizations or performative actions. (3) Typical of the plays is a "Goldonian moment," occurring in an instant, that connotes a significant psychological shift or transition. (4) Characters address the audience in parenthetical comments or asides. And (5) space is defined simultaneously by both its naturalistic and symbolic properties.

The Theatricalization of Self

In theatre scholarship, it has sometimes been noted that, in the same way that the language of psychoanalysis has permeated contemporary consciousness in the United States, the culture of theatre defined Europe in the eighteenth century. The citizens of Venice understood that they were "on stage" acting out a series of both private and public rituals of daily life. The tradition of Carnival and the practice of masquerade intensified audience awareness of theatrical behaviour and the conventions of performance. The theatre also provided a forum where the performative aspects of social ritual could be explored and examined. Goldoni's characters, as products of this environment, frequently present themselves in a series of performative actions or theatricalizations. By playing out a series of performative actions, a character must, by necessity, either merge with or supersede another character's theatricalization of self. The character whose play prevails becomes the dominant force that propels the dramatic action.

In *The New House*, the audience watches Cecilia construct and perform a new role as reformed spendthrift, help Cristofolo transform from irascible curmudgeon to benign uncle, and rehabilitate the person and fortunes of her husband, Anzoletto. Impending financial ruin and social disgrace force Cecilia to confront her imagined life as a grand lady of Venice:

> Oh, what a fool I've been! What an idiot! I could have married into the best families in the town. I could have been covered with gold from head to foot. And here I am burdened with a man who wants to drag me down into the mud! (p. 61)

Without a dowry, Cecilia has entered marriage with expectations that cannot be met. Her new husband's finances are unable to support her in the necessary conditions of her assumed role as a lady of wealth. The extravagant apartment, luxurious clothes, and her sycophantic admirers are props in an unsustainable act. In the last ten minutes of the play, she rejects each – admirers, clothes, and apartment – for a more sober role. She must construct not only her own rehabilitation but her husband's as well:

> CECILIA ... So you're not going to ask your uncle to help you?
> ANZOLETTO Ask him? Not likely! Even if I'd the courage, I know what would happen. He'd only fly into a rage and call me all the names he can think of.
> CECILIA Perhaps I could speak to him?
> ANZOLETTO That wouldn't do any good.

CECILIA Why wouldn't it?
ANZOLETTO Because he can bear the sight of you – even less than he can of me.
CECILIA Oh, I'd be able to calm him down. (p. 65)

Anzoletto is trapped in old modes of behaviour in his relationship with his uncle, but Cecilia's emerging sense of her powers will lead her to succeed in reinventing herself by a new set of performative actions. Learning that Anzoletto's uncle, Cristofolo, is visiting in Signora Checca's apartment above, Cecilia presses her husband to take action immediately:

CECILIA Quick! Come with me!
ANZOLETTO Where?
CECILIA Come with me, I tell you!
ANZOLETTO I don't want to go up there.
CECILIA Come along, you big baby. And you'll see what sort of a wife you've married. (p. 66)

Cecilia's exit line is both an invitation and a rallying cry as she marshals her powers for the performance that she must give upstairs, and she goads Anzoletto, her "big baby," who must prepare his own role as "the chastened prodigal." Cecilia enlists the aid of Checca to intercede with Cristofolo. Signora Checca is a quintessentially Goldonian character – wise, witty, and urbane – who has the interests of the household and her extended family at heart. She is the "resourceful wife" who is able to direct plot elements and bring the play to a satisfactory resolution. Like the theatre manager in the *Memoirs,* she both witnesses Cecilia's play and performs an active role in it. Not only does she arrange the betrothal of her cousin, Lorenzino, to Anzoletto's sister, Meneghina, but she engineers a meeting between Cecilia and the very recalcitrant Cristofolo.

Cecilia and Cristofolo have been locked into two seemingly irreconcilable theatricalizations of self as fashionable spendthrift lady and a middle-class abstemious merchant. For her transformation to be successful, Cecilia must gain Cristofolo's consent to be both audience and participant in her penitent play. At first, he refuses to sit near her:

CECILIA Would you do me the honour of allowing me to pay you my respects.
CRISTOFOLO Y' servant, Signora.
CECILIA Would you do me the great honour of allowing me to seat myself by you?

> CRISTOFOLO Ay, sit if you wish. *(jumps to his feet and moves away)*
> CECILIA Why do you move away?
> CRISTOFOLO Because you don't like the smell of the bacon from my shop.
> CECILIA Dear sir, please do not make me drain my cup of misery to the dregs. Be kind enough to sit here. (p. 69)

Cristofolo's unwillingness to sit indicates his refusal to witness or participate in her performance. Cecilia must arrest Cristofolo's attention and force him to listen. She appeals to him as a "gentleman" and to "subdue his resentment and listen to her." In this way, she shapes, not only her own character, but his as well:

> when a lady humiliates herself, pleads, and begs for forgiveness, any gentleman would subdue his resentment and listen to her. I ask nothing from you – I deserve nothing – only that you listen to me. (p. 69)

What Cecilia asks is that Cristofolo attend her ritual of confession. In the sequence that follows, Cecilia "performs" a long conciliatory speech (one of the longest in this volume of five plays) that is the theatrical mechanism by which she carefully and systematically guides herself, Cristofolo, and the audience through a series of steps towards her transformation:

> And it's true I have spoken badly about you. I have spoken very badly about you. But try to put yourself in my position. I was brought up to a certain way of life, to wear these foolish clothes, to behave in a way completely opposed to all your principles. And if my father wore the sort of clothes that you do, I would even have spoken badly of my own father. And now I am reaping the reward of the ignorant way in which I was brought up. (p. 70)

Cecilia's clothes are a manifestation of her role-playing and self-theatricalization. In her speech, they become a symbol of her transformation – Cecilia enters a metaphorical dressing closet and comes out wearing "new clothes." She puts her past behind her and is prepared to lead a new life. The performative aspect of Cecilia's long speech does not negate its sincerity or capacity to be true. It is simultaneously the process that allows her new identity to be realized and a demonstration of her ability to play her new role successfully. In an aside to the audience, Cristofolo indicates that he has been completely won over by Cecilia's performance and that he is now prepared to hear Anzoletto as well:

> "She could twist anybody round her little finger! Where is he, then, this good-for-nothing husband of yours?" (p. 71)

All that is left is the apartment itself. To complete her metamorphosis, Cecilia must reject the place that has served as the "stage" for her to play out her former role:

> CRISTOFOLO I will pay the rent you owe on this new apartment you've taken. But you will give notice that you're giving it up. It's not the sort of place for you.
> CECILIA Dear Uncle, give us just one little room in your house.
> CRISTOFOLO There isn't one.
> CECILIA Dear Uncle, please. Just while we find somewhere else to go.
> CRISTOFOLO Well, for no longer then, you cunning little minx. While you're in my house you'll both behave yourselves. And mark well, I'll have none of those friends of yours in my house either.
> CECILIA Believe me, I'm so disgusted with those people there's no danger of that. (p. 71)

Cecilia's transformation is now complete – together with Anzoletto, she rejects apartment, clothes, and friends for their new role as niece and nephew of the abstemious grocer.

There is a similar scene in *Back from the Country* that ends with very different results. Fulgenzio, in an advocate's role similar to that of Checca and the theatre manager of the *Memoirs*, attempts to act on behalf of a financially distressed Leonardo by appealing to Leonardo's uncle:

> FULGENZIO My friend, I must talk to you about your nephew Leonardo.
> BERNARDINO Oh, his lordship Leonardo! And what's his lordship up to these days? How is his lordship?
> FULGENZIO To tell you the truth, he hasn't been showing much judgment.
> BERNARDINO Not been showing much judgment? I'd say he has a sight more judgment than we do. We work our fingers to the bone to earn a livelihood, and he enjoys, squanders, parties, and leads the gay life; and you say he doesn't have judgment? (p. 315)

The sarcastic responses are intended to deflect Fulgenzio from his altruistic purpose. Bernardino will not engage in the conversation nor will he accept Fulgenzio's advocacy role:

FULGENZIO … I must tell you that Signor Leonardo has an excellent opportunity to get married.
BERNARDINO I'm happy for him, I'm delighted for him.
FULGENZIO With a dowry of eight thousand crowns.
BERNARDINO I'm happy for him, I'm delighted for him.
FULGENZIO But unless he can put his house in order, he won't get the daughter, and he won't get the dowry.
BERNARDINO What? A man like him? All he has to do is stamp his foot and the money comes up out of every crack! (p. 316)

Leonardo's stability, both economically and emotionally, depends on his uncle's financial assistance, but Bernardino refuses to participate in Leonardo's prodigal play. What follows is humorous, brutal, and poignant. As Leonardo attempts to deliver a set speech of contrition, his uncle cuts him off repeatedly:

LEONARDO *(hat in hand)* Oh, Uncle …
BERNARDINO Put your hat back on.
LEONARDO I regret that my misconduct …
BERNARDINO Put your hat on your head.
LEONARDO Has brought me to this pass.
BERNARDINO Allow me. *(puts Leonardo's hat on for him)*
LEONARDO And unless you help me …
BERNARDINO *(to Fulgenzio)* What's the time?
FULGENZIO *(to Bernardino)* Listen to him, if you will.
LEONARDO Oh, my beloved Uncle … *(takes off his hat)*
BERNARDO Your most humble servant. *(takes off his nightcap)*
LEONARDO Don't turn your back on me.
BERNARDINO *(nightcap in hand)* Oh, I wouldn't dream of doing something as rude as that for the world.
LEONARDO *(hat in hand)* My only mistake was my over-extravagant stay in the country.
BERNARDINO If you'll allow me. *(puts his nightcap back on)* Did you have many guests this year? Did you have a nice time? (p. 318)

Literally with "hat in hand," Leonardo attempts to perform his own version of the play of the repentant prodigal, but his uncle will not permit his gesture of humility or allow its implications. Like an actor stumbling on his own lines, Leonardo is unable to gain the necessary momentum to play out the scene that he intends to perform. Bernardino, as a gentleman of Venice, should at least listen to his nephew's appeal in a spirit of impartiality. By removing his own nightcap, he undermines Leonardo's performative gesture of subservience and refuses to participate in his nephew's theatricalization of self. In fact, Bernardino draws his nephew into his own intractable performance as an unreformed Pantalone and physically manipulates his nephew to achieve a desired result. In Anzoletto's case, despite his inability to save himself, Cecilia's performance of repentance is so virtuosic that she is able to accomplish their dual rehabilitation, but Leonardo's theatricalization of self as contrite penitent fails to accomplish its goal.

These examples from *The New House* and *Back from the Country* have been chosen for their obvious parallels to the *Memoirs* narrative. Prodigality was a major theme in eighteenth-century literature because, in squandering physical, economic, and spiritual resources, the male heir threatened to undermine the stability of the entire household and extended family.[46] What becomes interesting in interpreting the *Memoirs* and these two dramatic sequences is the way that Goldoni is able to construct such individual variations drawn from the same thematic material. This is a key to understanding Goldoni's dramaturgy. He employs fragments of dramatic action – derived from ancient character types, commedia scenarios, and Venetian theatre conventions – to create recurring plot motifs. As with music of the same period, these motifs are developed in a series of variations whose freshness and originality depend on the skill of the playwright and the talents of the performer.

The Goldonian Moment

In the *Memoirs,* Signor Goldoni indicates by an oblique smile, rather than a line of dialogue, that a psychological shift has taken place in his relationship to his errant son. Similarly, there are points in Goldoni's plays when a character transformation seems to occur in the text that is not recorded in the dialogue itself. In *The Coffee House* there is such a "Goldonian moment" designated by the playwright in the stage directions. At the climax of act 2, Ridolfo challenges Eugenio, who has threatened Vittoria with a sword:

> RIDOLFO ... This poor innocent woman may not have anyone to defend her, but I'll defend her to the death. How dare you threaten her, after the way you've treated her? How dare you?
> *(to Vittoria)* Signora, come with me and fear nothing.

VITTORIA No, dear Ridolfo. If my husband wants me dead, let him have his satisfaction. So, then, kill me, you dog, assassin, traitor. Kill me, you scoundrel. You have neither honour, heart, nor conscience.

EUGENIO *(mortified, puts the sword back into its sheath without a word)* (p. 129)

The stage direction alerts the actor playing Eugenio that his "mortification" is real, but Ridolfo and Vittoria, who only see the external signs of Eugenio's change of heart, have opposing reactions to what is occurring:

RIDOLFO *(to Eugenio)* Ah, Signor Eugenio, I see that you are sorry, and I beg your pardon if I spoke too harshly. My lord, you know that I love you, and you know what I've done for you. Even this outburst of mine was the effect of love. I pity this poor woman. How can it be that her tears do not touch your heart?

EUGENIO *(dries his eyes and doesn't speak)*

RIDOLFO *(quietly to Vittoria)* Look, Signora Vittoria, look at Signor Eugenio. He's crying. He's calmed down. He will repent and mend his ways. Rest assured that he loves you.

VITTORIA Crocodile tears. How many times has he promised me that he would mend his ways? How many times has he fooled me with his tears? I won't believe him any more. He's a traitor. I won't believe him any more.

EUGENIO *(trembles, visibly moved and shaken; he throws his hat on the ground like a desperate man, and without a word he enters the back room of the coffee house)* (p. 129)

Again, the stage directions help the actor playing Eugenio to understand that his physical gestures are meant to convey true emotions: he "trembles" and is "visibly moved and shaken," and his tears are meant to be real. Vittoria, who is estranged from Eugenio and does not know his feelings, questions the "meaning" of his gestures.

VITTORIA *(to Ridolfo)* What's the meaning of this silence?

RIDOLFO He's confused.

VITTORIA How can he have changed in one minute?

RIDOLFO I believe he has … (p. 129)

Convinced by Ridolfo's ensuing arguments, Vittoria goes to console Eugenio. Nevertheless, she has asked an essential question. How can his transformation take place "in one minute"? For the scene to make sense, the audience must accept that a real change in Eugenio's character has occurred and that his transformation will have long-term effects. In this example from *The Coffee House,* Goldoni is careful to record the nature of the transformation in his stage directions, because the psychological distance that the actor playing Eugenio must travel is vast – from the extreme anger that provokes him to attack his wife to a silent place of deep mortification and tears.

In *The New House* there is no such stage direction, yet an important Goldonian moment takes place when Anzoletto and Cristofolo finally meet after the double intervention of Checca and Cecilia:

> CECILIA Come in, husband. Providence is being kind to us.
> CRISTOFOLO *(aside)* So he's here as well! This place is Liberty Hall.
> ANZOLETTO I hardly dare face you, Uncle.
> CRISTOFOLO Get to the point. Make out a list of your debts. A transfer of your assets. A resolution to alter your ways. And I'll do what my heart tells me to – and which you don't deserve, you worthless young good-for-nothing.
> ANZOLETTO I promise, I swear, I will always do as you wish. (p. 71)

Anzoletto, like Eugenio, seems to experience his own form of mortification that is salved by Cristofolo's curmudgeonly good humour. Between Anzoletto's brief line, "I hardly dare face you, Uncle" and Cristofolo's response, a transformation takes place in the "heart" of the old man that allows him to come to the aid of his nephew. Whatever happens, the audience must feel that what transpires in these dual transformations of Anzoletto and Cristofolo is satisfactory from a psychological viewpoint. If the actors playing these roles rush through or gloss over these sequences, then the scenes can seem shallow or unmotivated; but if the actors are sensitive to detail and nuance, they have the capacity to reveal the plays as deeply humorous and profoundly compelling experiences.

Goldoni's characters were performed by actors well known to him. He wrote to their special strengths and talents, and he emphasized personality traits that inform the roles but are not necessarily written into the text. In addition, the actors reflected the commedia dell'arte tradition in their portrayal of character types even when they had removed their masks. In *The Coffee House,* Ridolfo (for the Venetian-language version) was originally performed by Giuseppe Marliani in the mask of Brighella. Antonio Collalto, who played the first Eugenio, was also a Pantalone for the same company of Girolamo Medebach.[47] These actors would have brought to their roles layers and textures of meaning, not readily discernible in the text alone, that helped define motivations and relationships. It is very intriguing to think of the Medebach Company's Pantalone in the character of Eugenio. As Eugenio, he incorporates both the attributes of the son of the household and, as an actor who also interprets Pantalone, those attributes of his dead father whom Brighella/Ridolfo has served. By attending the son, Brighella/Ridolfo continues to serve the memory of his deceased master embodied in the actor of Pantalone/Eugenio.

Asides

An actor performing these plays must develop a meta-theatrical awareness, because the world of eighteenth-century Venice portrayed by Goldoni was consciously performative and the characters in that world are frequently cognizant that they are playing roles in both a personal and a societal drama. Goldoni actors need to be both subjective and objective simultaneously. They need to commit themselves to the creation of a surface naturalism that they, as actors and characters, comment on by calling attention to their own participation within the play. Asides have often been thought to represent a sort of primitive or quaint dramaturgy when, in fact, they are one of the most complex elements of Goldoni's plays. In writing of his production of *The Holiday Trilogy*, Strehler discussed his reasons for cutting the asides, along with "repetitions, over-explicit affirmations, [and] the frequent monologues."[48] In his own mind he had not significantly altered the plays, but left them "exactly as they are … somewhat abridged, cut down to proportions manageable on the contemporary stage. Nothing more." Strehler emphasized the Chekovian elements, the "moods and 'atmospheres'" that he found in *The Trilogy*[49] – perhaps in response to critics who considered Goldoni to lack depth or seriousness. He concentrated on the complex character relationships and on closely observed psychological details. But Strehler's approach, no matter how successful as theatre, created a serious distortion of *The Holiday Trilogy* as originally conceived by Goldoni. Anthony Oldcorn, the translator of the *Trilogy* in this volume, has written eloquently concerning the damage done to the plays by Strehler's adaptation:

> The cuts he alludes to amount to nothing less than a radical modernization of the play … he eliminates the 18th-century actor's built in awareness of

> the audience's presence, and of himself or herself as a performer, indeed as *double* performer, playing one role in front of the other actors, and at the same time revealing the falseness and hypocrisy of that role to the lookers on.[50]

Given the contemporary interest in the construction of identity, gender, and social behaviour, it would be a drastic mistake to omit the asides. They have the capacity to call attention to the theatrical game played by each character, and they subvert the fixed surface that the characters intend to present.

In act 1, scene 10, of *Adventures in the Country*, the second play of *The Holiday Trilogy*, there are six asides in the first eight lines of dialogue. Ferdinando and Vittoria have asides to one another; Costanza and Ferdinando each have asides to the audience. The social ritual of paying "respects" and receiving "honour" is undercut by a fierce competition between the women that Ferdinando intentionally exacerbates:

(Enter Vittoria)

VITTORIA Your servant, Signora Costanza. Forgive me if I'm tardy in paying my respects.

COSTANZA What on earth do you mean? It's an honour whenever you come. I consider it a favour. Please sit down. *(they sit down)*

FERDINANDO *(softly to Vittoria, as he sits down)* What do you say, eh? What's that outfit she's wearing?

VITTORIA *(aside to Ferdinando)* All in the worst possible taste! She doesn't even know how to dress.

COSTANZA *(aside)* Oh, blast her! She's wearing a "mariage," the very latest fashion. *(the two women study each other surreptitiously, without speaking)*

FERDINANDO *(aside)* They've been struck dumb, they're not speaking. *(addressing Vittoria and Costanza)* So, ladies, what do you think of the weather?

VITTORIA Oh, not too bad, considering the season.

COSTANZA *(aside)* Now I know why she came to see me, to show off her new dress. But I'm not going to give her the satisfaction, I'm not going to make any comment (p. 240)

The characters must act two "plays" simultaneously. The surface performance encompasses the pleasantries of the weather and the social season, but at a deeper level the growing animus between Vittoria and Costanza is played out by means of the asides. The situation is reminiscent of Molière's *The Misanthrope* where an increasingly agitated Alceste attempts unsuccessfully to suppress his contempt for Oronte's poetry. As in Molière's play, the humour in this scene comes from the characters' attempts to maintain a polite surface despite the ill-mannered impulses that threaten to erupt – impulses that the asides reveal to the audience. As the scene continues, Ferdinando goads Costanza to reveal her true feelings about Vittoria's dress and, by extension, about Vittoria herself:

FERDINANDO But, Signora, that's a dress you can wear on any occasion.
COSTANZA *(aside)* Curse him! What a chatterbox!
FERDINANDO What do you say, Signora Costanza? Isn't it a magnificent dress, and what taste!
COSTANZA Sir, all you seem to be able to do is to interrupt people when they're talking. *(to Vittoria)* What time do you plan to go to Signora Giacinta's?
VITTORIA *(aside)* I can see this dress is driving her crazy. *(to Costanza)* Let me see, Signora, I still have a couple of people to call on, and then I'll go to Signora Giacinta's. If it's still early, we'll have a game of cards. (p. 240)

In the comparatively short time it takes to perform the entire scene, the three characters address each other, themselves, or the audience in twelve separate asides.

The complexity of a scene is potentially increased if the character is aware of other characters' asides even when those asides are spoken privately or to the audience. In act 2, scene 9, of *The New House*, the four actors must decide what they know of one another in relation to the asides:

CECILIA ... I mean to say – if one can't even go to the theatre without one's husband – well! What can one do!
CHECCA Oh, I do not mind. If my husband cannot come with me, I had just as soon stay at home.
CECILIA *(aside)* What a fool!
MENEGHINA *(aside to Rosina)* Did you ever hear such cant and humbug?
ROSINA *(aside to Meneghina)* Yes, I do see what you mean now.
MENEGHINA *(aside to Rosina)* Yet my brother doesn't seem to notice such things.
ROSINA *(aside to Meneghina)* If her husband puts up with it, good luck to her.
CECILIA And at home here, what do you do? Play games?

CHECCA Occasionally we amuse ourselves.
CECILIA What do you play?
CHECCA Cards. Snap and beggar-my-neighbour.
CECILIA But how boring. We play bridge of course ... (p. 45)

Cecilia addresses the audience, but does Checca hear her? As a response to hearing her, are Checca's answers to Cecilia intentionally naive? Is Cecilia aware that Meneghina and Rosina are engaged in a conversation? Does she know that the conversation is about her? Is Checca aware that Meneghina and her Rosina are in conversation? Is she a silent participant in their asides? As the scene progresses, Cecilia seems to become increasingly tactless. Is this a conscious response to the heightened tensions that the asides provoke?

A preliminary examination of the five plays in this volume offers a variety of possible asides:

1. To oneself (unheard by the rest of the characters).
2. To someone else on stage (unheard by the rest of the characters).
3. To the audience (unheard by the rest of the characters).
4. To oneself (overheard by another character or characters).
5. To someone else on stage (overheard by another character or characters).
6. To the audience (overheard by another character or characters).
7. To oneself (overheard by another character or characters but not understood by that character or characters).
8. To someone else on stage (overheard by another character or characters, but not understood by that character or characters).
9. To the audience (overheard by another character or characters, but not understood by that character or characters).

There is also the possibility that actors are interpreting certain asides as "beyond" character – offering meta-theatrical commentaries on the act of performance (both of the characters acting out their constructed selves and of the actors participating in the theatrical event).

It is intriguing to conjecture the style in which asides would be performed. Should they be articulated as naturalistically as possible? Should they be spoken "sotto voce" and as muttered utterances? Or are they expressionist eruptions that burst out of the sides of the characters' mouths like the captions of a cartoon with the head moving in one direction and the body in another? Is it possible that one production can contain different styles, even radically different styles, for performing the asides? Directors and actors need to formulate new acting methods to accommodate the complexity of this stage convention.

Space

Goldoni is often thought of as a proto-"naturalist." This is most true in his imitation of colloquial Italian speech and his depiction of character types that he observed in daily Venetian life. He attributed his quest for verisimilitude to his consultation of two metaphorical books: "The Book of the World" and "The Book of the Theater":

> The first [The Book of the World] shows me the many different types of character that people possess, it depicts them in a most natural way, ... it exhibits the signs, the power, the consequences of all human passions; it produces curious events; it informs me of the latest fashions; it instructs me on the vices and defects which are most common to our time and our nation ... As I leaf through the second one, the Book of the Theater, it teaches me which colors one should use on the Stage to represent characters, passions and events: those found in the Book of the World; how they should be shaded in order to bring them into relief; and which hues make them appear pleasurable to the delicate eyes of the spectator. (Goldoni, *Opere I*, 769–70)[51]

Goldoni populated his stage with merchants, gondoliers, soldiers, grocers, an Armenian fruit seller, fishermen, denizens of the coffee house, gamesters, male and female maskers, actors, maids, valets, kitchen servants, lords, ladies, gentlemen, and stable boys. These characters are often brought "into relief" by compelling psychological details and nuanced dramatic action. As a result, it is possible for a director and his or her design team to stage Goldoni with acute attention to realistic elements in costumes, décor, and props. The texts will sustain this choice.

The original illustration for act 2, scene 10, of *Adventures in the Country* (p. 225) shows Filippo's reception room transformed into a gaming area for the card party sequence. In its seeming attention to detail and in the rich impression it gives of holiday pastimes, the visual information suggests the meticulous stagings of Luchino Visconti. But with a closer examination, the illustration – with only two doors, two paintings, three tables, eight chairs, two candles, and some cards – also possesses the minimalist austerity of a Robert Wilson production.

This, then, is yet another paradox of Goldoni's theatre. He anticipates certain aspects of naturalism, but he is not a naturalist in the nineteenth-century sense. He is defined as much by the past, by the theatrical traditions he builds on, as by the future he helps to create. It is, perhaps, fair to observe that while detail in Goldoni is often naturalistic, the greater mise en scène is as often metaphorical. In the notes for his translation of *Off to the Country*, Anthony Oldcorn discusses the significance of the particular games played by the different characters in the gaming room (see note 12 on p. 220). The specific features of each game – bezique, tresette, and ombre – have both pragmatic implications for staging, if a director wishes to emphasize them, as well as symbolic meanings related to the humour and psychological aspect of each character. In this way, the card scene is at once "real" in its depiction of eighteenth-century life and also symbolic – a place where social intercourse is practised as a game with different stakes and intensities depending on what each participant brings to the table. Costanza addresses the nature of the game that takes place in the card room:

> Oh, yes, I know from experience. I know you have to put people together who do not dislike being together ... And it would be all very well, if they were straightforward about it. The trouble is that half of the time, you're supposed to guess. You have to be so careful, remembering who's friends and who's enemies. Trying to balance the tables according to skill. Choosing the game everybody likes best. Sorting out the ones who leave early and those who stay late, sometimes putting the wife in one room and the husband in another. (p. 253)

In the illustration, the three tables of candlelit card players, sitting in close but isolated proximity, are a poetic manifestation of the inherent competition and potential alienation built into the social groupings. For Goldoni, mise en scène – specifically, the way in which theatrical space is defined – is a nexus of the real, the symbolic, the psychological, and the affective. Each play offers propositions for the meaning and employment of space – specifically, the way that "place" functions in the dramatic action.

The Coffee House is played out in an open piazza. The activities of the various houses burst forth onto the commonly shared playing space. In the scenes that ensue, the audience learns of the private dramas that take place behind the closed facades. At other times, doors and windows are thrown open to reveal what is transpiring inside or to allow actors within to comment on the action outside. As a theatrical space, the piazza is both "real," in that it functions similarly to its actual architectural counterpart, and symbolic, as the locus where interior and exterior meet. Within the piazza, the coffee house is an "eye in the storm" – a place of reflection, observation, negotiation, bartering, and deal making – where the characters can discuss their private concerns before re-entering the public space that the piazza encompasses. The coffee house is both exterior and interior, public and private, within and without.

Instead of being fixed in one public playing space, the dramatic action of *The New House* alternates between two locations – the unfinished apartment of Anzoletto and the upstairs apartment of Signora Checca. The entire first act is performed amidst the chaos of workmen and movers who are in a rush to complete the extravagant new apartment. As in *The Coffee House* the location works on two levels as both a real and a symbolic place of action. The two different illustrations that exist of this first act show a room "under construction" with a man on a ladder holding fabric to be mounted to the wall, another man sawing, and a third man crouching over glue and paint pots. In the larger illustration there is also a worker sanding a door. The room is in flux – neither fixed nor stable. Within this shifting environment "the three workmen enter carrying the parts of a four-poster bed" (p. 19). Later in the scene the men disassemble the same bed. The frequently shifting space is a manifestation of the precariousness of Anzoletto's recent marriage to Cecilia. The assembly and dismantling of the marriage bed is especially significant.

As a contrast, the second act is almost entirely played out in Signora Checca's apartment on the floor above. Checca's environment offers an atmosphere of domestic calm and order in which crises can be dealt with and dispatched. It is fitting, then, that the dramatic action of the third act moves away from the spatial and psychological uncertainty of Anzoletto's space and is resolved in the balanced environment of Signora Checca and her sister.

Of the five plays in this volume, *The Holiday Trilogy* offers the most complex juxtapositions and contrasts in location. There are scenes in receiving rooms and drawing rooms, dressing rooms, a gaming room, the wood, and an open-air cafe. In the receiving rooms, the arrivals and departures of a variety of characters allow groups to form, disband, and reconstitute themselves. The gathering of "company" in these receiving rooms intensifies the commonplace experience of daily existence and accelerates movement towards change. This is especially true in the second play, *Adventures in the Country,* where the urgency to sign the marriage contract between Giacinta and Leonardo is played out in these communal family places.

A number of scenes in *Off to the Country,* including the opening, occur in Leonardo's private dressing room where his manservant, Paolo, packs his master's luggage. As the complications of the plot unfold, Paolo unpacks and repacks. Once again the theatrical location can be interpreted on both a real and a symbolic level. The packing and unpacking, as necessary functions of leaving and staying, are rooted in the requirements of the dramatic action. But the activity of packing also creates a sense of displacement and disorientation and is an extension of Leonardo's psychological state.

In the illustration for the first scene of act 1 in *Adventures in the Country* (p. 224), a garden appears tantalizingly through the open doors of Filippo's reception room. Beyond the garden, the wood beckons. In the third act, two couples find their way to the wood. For the maid Brigida and the valet Paolo, the wood is a place of freedom where they can dream of a life unfettered by the restraints of the masters they serve. For Giacinta and her insistent lover, Guglielmo, the wood, unlike the gaming room, is a place of love and courtship where attractions and passions can be openly expressed.

The open-air cafe, also in act 3 of *Adventures in the Country,* is the most complex symbolic "place" in *The Trilogy.* In his Preface to *Off to the Country,* Goldoni writes of the "pastime of the country holiday" as a "mania":

> The innocent pastime of the country holiday has lately become a passion, a mania, a disorder … ambition has invaded the forests: people going to the country take with them the pomp and tumult of the City, and they have poisoned the pleasures of the shepherds and countrymen … (p. 156)

The cafe, as an outdoor place in the country, should engender freedom, pleasure, and social harmony, but the "coffee house and one or two houses" (p. 272) are impositions of "the City" forced on the natural setting. Something as simple as ordering drinks becomes a complicated and dysfunctional activity for the combined parties of Filippo and Leonardo. As the waiters mix up nine separate orders, the company breaks up into increasingly tired and irritable subgroups. Filippo never even gets his "water with lime juice" (p. 274). The community becomes fragmented, and the false gaiety of the country holiday is exposed.

Dress and the Act of Dressing

Before the conclusion of this introduction, there is a last element that needs to be discussed – dress and the act of dressing. Directors, actors, and designers contemplating a Goldoni production with either historical or contemporary costume should study closely the paintings of Pietro Longhi, Francesco Guardi, and Gianbattista and Lorenzo Tiepolo. In their work, these artists created a detailed and evocative world that is at once both naturalistic and symbolic. In *The Holiday Trilogy*, Vittoria's modish dress, her "mariage," has a defining role for her character. As a fashion statement it seems imposed, a bit too forced, not fully integrated with her personality. Aptly named, her dress is also symbolic of her ill-fated desire to marry Guglielmo.

In Goldoni's Venice, clothes were a powerful means of defining class, rank, gender, occupation, and nationality. Because of its intimate nature in relation to the wearer, clothing had the capacity to fix surface reality to an extent far greater than other social mechanisms. At the same time, the meaning of clothing could be easily subverted or manipulated. In *Back from the Country*, there is an audacity to the way Rosina parades her newly minted boy-husband, Tognino, in his father's clothes. The original illustration shows a goofy adolescent dwarfed by clothing that is many sizes too large for him (p. 288). Yet by wearing the clothing, Tognino defiantly signals to the other characters that he is a man, a husband, and an heir to his father's medical practice. The resulting disjunction that occurs between the reality and the manipulated appearance has an expressionist or surreal power that a director can choose to mitigate or emphasize. Other disjunctions present in *The Holiday Trilogy* include the contrast between Bernardino's old-fashioned dress and his nephew's fashionable town clothes or Sabina's habit of wearing youthful clothes that accentuate rather than disguise her "elderly" presence.

The capacity of dress and of the act of dressing both to fix surface reality and to subvert it is intensified by the phenomenon of masquerade. By the use of masks that covered the face and obscured identity, the citizens of Venice were able to pass through the strict social demarcations of class, rank, marriage, and gender into a transgressive world of disguise. In *The Coffee House*, an atmosphere of disguise permeates the mood of the play. Vittoria's mask helps her to negotiate the exchanges of the piazza as she attempts to liberate her husband, Eugenio, from the gambling house; disguised as a wayfarer, Placida desperately searches among the denizens of Venice for her dissipated husband, Leandro, who is himself in disguise as a nobleman. Even Ridolfo, Trappola, and Eugenio are in a type of meta-theatrical disguise, as the actors who play them unmasked are Brighella, Arlecchino, and Pantalone in their masked form.

The Acting Ensemble

Part of the problem in understanding Goldoni's dramaturgy and the major reason that he is infrequently performed in the United States is that the expectations for the contemporary actor are so different from those of the eighteenth century. In fact, these expectations are antithetical to the ensemble and the idea of the collective. The dominant techniques taught in drama schools today are related to Romantic and post-Romantic conventions of the "sentimental" actor. With their emphasis on self-expression, personal feeling, and individual psychology, these methods trump older theatrical disciplines in which ensemble is emphasized. Nevertheless, embedded in the teaching of the academy and in traditional conservatory training are theatre techniques – including commedia dell'arte, mime, stage combat, ballet, period dance, vaudeville, circus, voice, singing, poetic recitation, and the various systems of Meyerhold, Grotowski, Suzuki, and Bogart – that can serve as the basis for a Goldonian performance method.

Goldoni's plays require the cultivation of group skills that are closely associated with instrumental and choral performance as well as athletic teams – group concentration and communication; choral breathing; an awareness of the kinetic relationship of a performer's body in space in relationship to other bodies; the connection of emotion to movement and of emotion to voice; and a perception of the musical and poetic structure of a performance text.

Even in the world of music, where the expectation of ensemble is a given, it can be difficult to reconcile tensions between individual impulse and group assent. In an analysis of Leonard Bernstein's ability to accomplish ensemble playing at a particularly high level, Alex Ross of *The New Yorker* has written that musicians must be cajoled into creating a particular kind of unison: not a robotic sameness of execution but a deeper unanimity in which spontaneous activities on the part of each player viscerally realize the conductor's vision.[52]

For Ross, participation in the ensemble has metaphysical implications. One can only be truly free as an individual performer by embracing a "deeper unanimity." Speaking in more colloquial terms, Yo Yo Ma, one of the world's premier instrumental soloists, has expressed a similar perspective:

> I'm always an ensemble player. For me, the cello plays more or less one line at a time. For me, what ensemble playing is, is democracy. You know what the big picture is, you know the Constitution, then you exercise your rights as a citizen. Everyone in an ensemble should know what the score is and then you play the right note at the right moment. Sometimes you're in the background, sometimes you're in the foreground. You always need to know what is your exact role from minute to minute, and if you know that, then you'll always do the right thing. That's the same job for a soloist – not to say, "Let's hear me louder than everyone else all the time." You should have that capacity if the need arises, but should always know what your role is so you can always interact.[53]

Ma employs a language of "good citizenship" in relationship to a performing democracy. Even a virtuoso of his calibre or, he implies, especially a virtuoso of his calibre, needs to be cognizant "from minute to minute" of his "exact role" in the ensemble.

Goldoni's plays challenge contemporary directors and actors to set high goals for nothing less than the cultivation of a virtuosic performance community. This is the aspect of Goldoni that was, perhaps, the most attractive to Strehler – the necessity of building and training a company to play as an ensemble. Profoundly influenced by Brechtian ideas of the theatre commune, Strehler idealized the theatre collective and ennobled it. To play Goldoni, directors and actors must aspire to his grace, speed, musicality, physical and vocal virtuosity, and meta-theatrical dexterity. This is a great challenge, but also a great gift for anyone who loves the theatre.

NOTES

1 Some evidence of Goldoni can be found in America as early as 1805 when an English-language version of *The Servant of Two Masters* by Robert Jephson (*The Hotel or The Servant with Two Masters*) was performed in New York. But Goldoni was not acknowledged as the original playwright. Jephson's play was based on *The Hotel or The Double Valet* by Thomas Vaughan, published in 1776 and performed at Drury Lane, again without credit given to Goldoni.

The legendary Italian actress Eleanora Duse performed with great success as Mirandolina in *La locandiera* during her 1893 American tour. Thirty-three years later in 1926, her American disciple Eva Le Gallienne, who wrote a biography of Duse, also performed Mirandolina.

Theatre scholars and members of the literary public have been served for more than one hundred years by Hobart C. Chatfield-Taylor's *Goldoni: A Biography,* the first study of the playwright in English, published in 1913 (New York: Duffield & Company).

No doubt there are other examples of Goldoni in America, but the totality of impact on the American theatre has been meagre.

2 First performed in 1984, this production has had three revivals and has given impetus to many Gozzi projects throughout the country. These include ART's own *Serpent Woman* in 1988, also directed by Serban; the 1996 *Green Bird,* directed by Taymor for the La Jolla Playhouse and its subsequent Broadway run in 2000; and *The Love of Three Oranges,* directed by Nona Cionabu in 2004 for the La Jolla Playhouse.

3 Mel Gussow, "Theater: *King Stag,*" *New York Times,* 19 December 1984. Accessed on the *New York Times* website (www.nytimes.com), 11 August 2008.

4 John Rockwell, "Italy Finds Goldoni as Timely as Ever," *New York Times,* 10 July 1993. Accessed on the *New York Times* website (www.nytimes.com), 11 August 2008.

5 Robert Brustein and Julie Taymor, "Recapturing the Fantasy in Our Lives," *New York Times,* 16 April 2000. Accessed on the *New York Times* website (www.nytimes.com), 1 March 2007.

6 Mel Gussow, "Review/Theater; Fabulist *Serpant Woman,*" *New York Times,* 30 December 1988. Accessed on the *New York Times* website (www.nytimes.com), 1 March 2007.

7 Robert Brustein, *The Theatre of Revolt: An Approach to Modern Drama* (Boston: Little, Brown and Company, 1964).

8 Since the London premiere in 2011 of *One Man, Two Guvnors* there have been a significant number of stagings of *The Servant of Two Masters,* including productions at the Seattle Repertory Theatre (2012); the Washington Shakespeare Theatre Company (2012); the Utah Shakespeare Festival (2013); and the American Shakespeare Center (2013); and at smaller regional theatres within the same period of time. An equally significant number of college and university productions have occurred at such schools as Emerson College (2012); Notre Dame (2012); Virginia Tech (2012); Smith College (2013); University of Athens Georgia; SUNY, Ulster (2013); and Simpson College (2014).

9 See Ted Emery, *Goldoni as Librettist: Theatrical Reform and the "drammi giocosi per musica"* (New York: Peter Lang Publishing, Inc., 1991).

10 Eight characters appear in the final one and a half pages of *Off to the Country* (p. 212–13); in *Adventures in the Country* there are twelve characters and a number of servants in the last four pages (p. 280–3); there are nine characters in the final page and a half (p. 348–50) of *Back from the Country*.

11 "All the world's a stage," says Jaques in his famous speech from Shakespeare's *As You Like It*:

And all the men and women merely players;
They have their exits and their entrances,
And one man in his time plays many parts,
His acts being seven ages.

The stage becomes a place where life, in all its "ages" is enacted (and, in fact, Shakespeare draws from images of commedia dell'arte); but also it is the mechanism that resolves this process from birth to death. In Calderon de la Barca's play *The Great Theater of the World,* God is the Author of the World Play and draws all the characters, even the recalcitrant ones, into a cosmic resolution at the end of his Comedy of Life. Similarly, the individual characters of *The New House* are incorporated into a social body and become part of a greater community.

12 Because Eugenio's speech is delivered in soliloquy, without other characters on the stage, this dramatic moment is being identified separately for the purposes of this structural analysis, and is identified in square brackets.

13 Guy Callan, "Marivaux's *La Fausse Suivante* and Goldoni's *La Bottega del caffè* as Physical Theatre," in *Carlo Goldoni and Eighteenth-Century Theatre,* edited by Joseph Farrell (Lewiston, NY: Edwin Mellen Press, 1997), 37–54; quotation at 39–40.

14 Ibid., 41.

15 Giorgio Strehler, "Goldoni's *Holiday Trilogy*" (from *Per un teatro umano* [Milan: Feltrinelli, 1974], 236–9), in *The Holiday Trilogy,* translated by Anthony Oldcorn (New York: Marsilio Publishers, 1992), 290–5; quotation at 291.

16 Franco Fido, "Introduction," in *The Holiday Trilogy,* translated by Anthony Oldcorn (New York: Marsilio Publishers, 1992), ix–xxxv; quotation at xx.

17 As an example, *The New House* is notable, especially in the first act, for the difference between the volatile and animated speech of the workers and the more evenly phrased articulations of the owners. Admittedly, the elegance of the owners' language masks a desperation caused by growing insolvency and a disintegrating marriage.

18 For this discussion of the evolution of Goldoni's language, I am indebted in part to an informative conversation with Gianluca Rizzo, a co-editor of this book.

19 Goldoni, in the corresponding Italian original, makes a distinction between "*asino*" (ass) and "*bestia*" (beast, animal). The English translation consistently uses "ass" for *asino* and "jackass" for *bestia.* As a result, jackass/ass word clusters are compounded in the English.

20 In the original Italian:

LEONARDO ... Sarà dunque stato **Fulgenzio**; ma per qual ragione mi ha da tradire **Fulgenzio**? Non so niente, son io **la bestia, il pazzo, l'ignorante ...**
CECCO (*viene coll'acqua*).
LEONARDO Sì, **pazzo**, **bestia.** (*Da sé, non vedendo Cecco.*)
CECCO Ma! perché **bestia**?
LEONARDO Sì, **bestia**, **bestia.** (*Prendendo l'acqua.*)
CECCO Signore, io non sono una bestia.
LEONARDO Io, io sono **una bestia**, io. (*Beve l'acqua.*)
CECCO (Infatti **le bestie bevono l'acqua, ed io bevo il vino.)**
LEONARDO Va subito dal **Signor Fulgenzio**. Guarda s'è in casa. Digli che **favorisca venir da me, o che io andrò da lui.**
CECCO Dal **Signor Fulgenzio**, qui dirimpetto?
LEONARDO Sì, **asino**, da chi dunque?
CECCO Ha detto a me?
LEONARDO A te.
CECCO (**Asino**, **bestia**, mi pare che sia tutt'uno). (*Parte.*)
SCENA SESTA
Leonardo, poi Paolo.
LEONARDO **Non porterò rispetto alla sua vecchiaia, non porterò rispetto a nessuno.**
PAOLO Animo, animo, Signore, stia allegro, che tutto sarà preparato.
LEONARDO **Lasciatemi stare.**
PAOLO Perdoni, io ho fatto il **debito mio**, e più del **debito mio.**
LEONARDO **Lasciatemi stare**, vi dico.
PAOLO Vi è qualche novità?
LEONARDO Sì, pur troppo.
PAOLO **I cavalli sono ordinati.**
LEONARDO **Levate l'ordine.**
PAOLO Un'altra volta?
LEONARDO Oh! maledetta la mia disgrazia!
PAOLO Ma che cosa gli è accaduto mai?

LEONARDO Per carità, **lasciatemi stare**.
PAOLO (Oh! povero me! andiamo sempre di male in peggio).
SCENA SETTIMA
Vittoria con un vestito piegato, e detti.
VITTORIA Fratello, volete vedere il mio *mariage*?
LEONARDO **Andate via.**
VITTORIA Che maniera è questa?
PAOLO (**Lo lasci stare**). (*Piano a Vittoria.*)
VITTORIA **Che diavolo avete**?
LEONARDO **Sì, ho il diavolo**; **andate via.**
VITTORIA E con questa bella allegria si ha da **andare in campagna**?
LEONARDO **Non vi è più campagna; non vi è più villeggiatura, non vi è più niente.**
VITTORIA Non volete andare in **campagna**?
LEONARDO No, **non ci vado io**, e **non ci anderete nemmeno voi**.
VITTORIA Siete diventato pazzo?
PAOLO (Non lo inquieti di più, per amor del Cielo). (*A Vittoria.*)
VITTORIA Eh! non mi seccate anche voi. (*A Paolo.*)
SCENA OTTAVA
Cecco e detti.
CECCO **Il Signor Fulgenzio** non c'è. (*A Leonardo.*)
LEONARDO **Dove il diavolo** se l'**ha portato**?
CECCO Mi hanno detto, che **è andato** dal Signor Filippo.
LEONARDO **Il cappello e la spada**. (*A Paolo.*)
PAOLO Signore ...
LEONARDO **Il cappello e la spada**. (*A Paolo, più forte.*)
PAOLO Subito. (*Va a prendere il cappello e la spada.*)
VITTORIA Ma **si può sapere**? (*A Leonardo.*)
LEONARDO **Il cappello e la spada.**
PAOLO Eccola servita. (*Gli dà il cappello e la spada.*)
VITTORIA **Si può sapere**, che cosa avete? (*A Leonardo.*)
LEONARDO **Lo saprete** poi. (*Parte.*)
VITTORIA Ma **che cosa ha?** (*A Paolo.*)
PAOLO Non so niente. Gli vo' andar dietro alla lontana. (*Parte.*)
VITTORIA **Sai tu, che cos'abbia?** (*A Cecco.*)
CECCO Io **so** che m'ha detto **asino**; non **so** altro. (*Parte.*)

21 (Season 4, Episode 16: originally broadcast 7 February 1955); directed by William Archer; written by Bob Carroll, Jr, Madelyn Pugh, and Jess Oppenheimer.

22 (Season 3, Episode 4: originally broadcast 9 October 1991) directed by Tom Cherones; written by Larry David and Jerry Seinfeld; performed by: Julia Louis Dreyfus, Michael Richards, Jason Alexander, and Jerry Seinfeld.

23 The great majority of the engravings are by Antonio Baratti (only a few are by Giuliano Giampiccoli and just one by Giuseppe Daniotto, better known for one of Goldoni's few surviving portraits). The engravings were based on the drawings of Pietro Antonio Novelli. These illustrations are found in two eighteenth-century publications of Goldoni's work. First, there are the octavo volumes that Goldoni decided to publish (at his own expense) after the overwhelming success of his *Baruffe*. These are called the Pasquali edition. The complete publishing project was intended to encompass thirty volumes published over eight years. The first part included comedies, tragedies, and *tragicommedie*; the second was to collect the musical dramas (*drammi musicali*) and the *oratori*; the third was devoted to poetry. However, Goldoni's departure for Paris, the complications posed by his new commitments in France, coupled with the subscribers' waning interest in the least "palatable" of Goldoni's complete works (the *oratori* and the poems) caused the Pasquali edition to be abandoned at volume seventeen, in 1777. The publication of the complete edition of *Opere teatrali del Signor Avvocato Carlo Goldoni veneziano, con rami allusivi* began the following year, thanks to the efforts of Antonio Zatta. Goldoni did not live to see the last of its forty-five volumes, published in 1795 (Gianluca Rizzo).

24 A segment shown in *The Art of Singing: Golden Voices of the Century*, directed by Donald Sturrock for the BBC/IMG Artists/Idéale Audience, 1998; NVC Arts, DVD (116 minutes), release date: 3 September 2002.

25 Video Artists International, DVD (118 minutes), release date: 1 November 2005.

26 Callan, "Marivaux's *La Fausse Suivante* and Goldoni's *La Bottega del caffè* as Physical Theatre"; quotation at 42.

27 Maggie Günsberg, *Playing with Gender: The Comedies of Goldoni* (Leeds: Northern University Press, 2001), 159–81.s

28 Ibid., 164.

29 Farrell, "Introduction," in *Carlo Goldoni and the Eighteenth-Century Theatre*, 7.

30 Ibid., 8.

31 Ibid., 4.

32 Ibid., 4–5.

33 Carlo Goldoni, *Memoirs*, translated by John Black (London: Printed for Henry Colburn, 1814), I: 273.

34 The *Oxford English Dictionary*. In the original French version the phrase is "il aime les femmes sans se compromettre" (he loves women without

compromising himself). See *Memorie di Carlo Goldoni* (Florence: G. Barbera, 1907), I: 231.

35 Günsberg, *Playing with Gender*, 125.

36 For a detailed discussion of a "reality" underlying a fixed surface see ibid., chapter 5, "Surface Mobilities: Identities, Disguise, Fashion," 125–58.

37 Goldoni, *Memoirs*, I: 20–1.

38 Ibid., 25.

39 Ibid.

40 Ibid., 22.

41 Ibid., 30.

42 Ibid., 30–1.

43 Ibid., 31.

44 Ibid.

45 Ibid., 31–2.

46 See Günsberg, *Playing with Gender*, 175–81, for an extended discussion of prodigal masculinity in mercantile Venice.

47 Callan, "Marivaux's *La Fausse Suivante* and Goldoni's *La Bottega del caffè* as Physical Theatre"; quotation at 46.

48 Strehler, "Goldoni's Holiday Trilogy" (1954) in the Appendix for *The Holiday Trilogy*, translated by Anthony Oldcorn, 294.

49 Ibid., 292.

50 Anthony Oldcorn, "Translator's Postscript," in *The Holiday Trilogy*, translated by Anthony Oldcorn (New York: Marsilio Publishers, 1992), 295.

51 Carlo Goldoni, *Opere I*, 769–70. (Text translated by Gianluca Rizzo and Michael Hackett; quoted in Philip L. Sohn, "Pietro Longhi and Carlo Goldoni: Relations between Painting and Theater," in *Zeitschrift für Kunstgeschichte*, 45 Bd., H. 3 [1982]: 256–73; quotation at 259–60.)

52 Alex Ross, "The Legend of Lenny: New York Celebrates Bernstein the Composer," *The New Yorker*, 15 December 2008, 82ff.

53 Yo-Yo Ma, quotation read by Alan Chapman, on a live broadcast for KUSC, Los Angeles, Monday, 13 October 2008 at 10:10 a.m. (before a recorded performance by Ma of the Lalo Cello Concerto).

Five Comedies

The New House

BASED ON A TRANSLATION BY FREDERICK DAVIES[1]

Prose comedy in three acts
Performed for the first time in Venice at the Teatro San Luca on 11 December 1760

Figure 1 *The New House* (La casa nova)

Figure 2 *The New House* (La casa nova), act 1, scene 1

Figure 3 *The New House* (La casa nova), act 2, scene 9

Figure 4 *The New House* (La casa nova), act 3, scene 10

The Author to the Reader

If I hadn't written anything except this single comedy, I think that it would have sufficed to give me the reputation that I now have after writing so many. Reading it and re-reading it, it seems that there is nothing in it that I can critique. If I could flatter myself in considering my works as worthy of being imitated, I would like to offer it to other playwrights as a model.

The plot is presented in such a way that it is easily followed, the action has been stripped of unnecessary ornament, the commentary is true, and the topic is of current interest, and the moral is reasonable, and not pedantic. The characters are all taken from real life, and the dialogue could not be more natural. The tale is believable in all of its parts, and even though there may seem to be two main plot lines, the action is, in fact, singular – for there is one character, Cristofolo, who brings about its resolution.

Do not be shocked, dear Reader, if I praise my Comedy. I am not comparing it to those of other Authors, but to those that I have written, and I think it is admissible that I prefer it to many others, and to place it among my most cherished. The public has justified this opinion of mine, for when the Comedy was performed, it was praised in equal measure not only in Venice but everywhere.

Dramatis Personae

ANZOLETTO	*a Venetian*
CECILIA	*Anzoletto's wife*
MENEGHINA	*Anzoletto's sister*
CHECCA	*a Venetian lady, married*
ROSINA	*Checca's young sister, unmarried*
LORENZINO	*a Venetian, cousin to Checca and Rosina and in love with Meneghina*
CRISTOFOLO	*uncle of Anzoletto and Meneghina*
COUNT	*a friend of Cecilia: an Italian but a stranger to Venice*
FABRIZIO	*a friend of Anzoletto: an Italian but a stranger to Venice*
LUCIETTA	*Meneghina's maidservant*
SGUALDO	*a Venetian building contractor*
WORKMEN	*(three)*
TONI	*servant to Checca and Rosina*
PROSDOCIMO	*a bailiff*

The action of the play takes place in Venice, in the first-floor apartment of Anzoletto and in the second floor apartment of Checca.

ACT ONE

Scene 1

The reception room in the new residence of Signor Anzoletto. Sgualdo, the contractor in charge of the alterations being made to the apartment, enters, followed by three workmen.

SGUALDO Let's try and finish this room off, anyway. It's supposed to be the reception room. Signor Anzoletto's having the furniture brought over from his old house today. So we'd better see what we can do. Onofrio, you finish off those so-called decorations over there, will you? And Prospero, you'd better get the locks on the doors. Lauro, straighten out that door-post first for him, will you? And try not to take all day about it. *(the three men start working, when Lucietta storms in)*

LUCIETTA *(to Sgualdo)* Now just you look here! What are you starting your banging and knocking in here for? Haven't you finished yet? Anybody else could have built a house in the time you've taken to mess up this apartment!

SGUALDO Easy on, Lucietta! There's no need to take on like this. What's the idea?

LUCIETTA What's the idea! I'll tell you what's the idea! The idea is my master's new wife has decided she's moving in here today. So how the devil d'you think I can get the place swept and tidied up when you and your workmen start kicking up more dust and dirt?

SGUALDO It's not our fault, m'dear. It's that master of yours. He doesn't know what he wants. Changes his mind every day. Some friend of his tells him one thing needs altering; somebody else tells him the opposite. Today we must do this; tomorrow we must do that. First of all, three of the bedrooms had to have fireplaces. Then somebody tells him that's not healthy. So we had to bung 'em up. Then somebody else tells him that's all a lot of nonsense. So then it's, "Open up this chimney again!" "No, not that one, this one!" Next it's: "Turn the room next to the kitchen into a dining-room." Then that's altered because of the smoke from the kitchen. Next, the entrance hall must have a partition across it because it's too long. Then the partition has to come down again because it makes the hall too dark. One change after another! One expense after another! But when I ask him for some money – oh, that's quite a different matter! Then he begins wishing the place to the devil – and a certain lady who forced him into renting it!

LUCIETTA You needn't think you can tell me anything I don't know! As if I didn't know it's that new wife of his behind it all. Oh, she doesn't half think herself somebody, that one! Do you know, no sooner had she married him than the master's old house wasn't good enough for her! It hadn't got a water-gate; the entrance hall was too small; it hadn't got three rooms leading into one another; all the decorations weren't modern enough. So now the master's having to pay one of the highest rents in Venice for this new apartment.

SGUALDO Ah, well – I suppose the money will come out of the dowry she brought him.

LUCIETTA Don't make me laugh! D'you know how much dowry she brought him? Nothing! Apart from a bit of old junk and all her lah-di-dah airs and graces. Mind you, my master's no fool by any means. But he will go doing things on the spur of the moment. And then he doesn't like facing up to the consequences. As for that wife of his – well, she's the last person he should have married. Oh, sure, she comes from quite a good family. That's the trouble. The way she's been brought up she should have married somebody with three or four thousand ducats a year.[2] And, of course, my master did start throwing his money about after his father died. And now, poor man, he's not only got his young sister to find a dowry for, but he's got this wife hung like a stone around his neck. Yes, if you ask me, he's certainly got good reason to swear every time you ask him for money. And I'll tell you something else – but don't go repeating it – I wouldn't like it thought I go telling everybody what happens in this house: the master still owes a year's rent on the old house. And that's not all. He hasn't paid the six months' rent due in advance on this apartment yet. The rent collector is calling every day, and the master's told us to say he's not at home. I don't know how it's all going to end. What's more, I've got seven months' wages owing to me. So – now you see how things are!

SGUALDO Well, I'll be damned! If he hasn't been stringing me along as well! D'you know, I've actually been paying these men their wages out of my own pocket! Well, one thing's certain, he won't put me off again with his fine words! Gentleman he may be – but he'll pay me my money or I'll know the reason why!

LUCIETTA Don't you go and let on I've been saying anything. I'm not the gossiping sort – but this wretched apartment has got me so fed up, I might as well be dead. I've never been so absolutely and completely bored in all my life.

SGUALDO Huh! That's one thing your master takes good care I'm not! Anyway, what's wrong with this apartment? He may not be able to afford it, but that doesn't mean to say it's not what they call a very [beautiful] house.

LUCIETTA Oh, yes, it's [beautiful] all right – so [beautiful] you never even see a dog passing here. At our old house I used to get no end of fun just having a look out of the window now and then. And the servants from the other houses round about used to call and we'd have a talk and a bit of a laugh. But as for this lot round here – you've no idea what a stuck-up lot they are. Not one of them's even passed the time of day with me yet. Not even when I've been out on the balcony. Only this morning that little slut of a maid over the street looked straight at me, and then slammed her window in my face!

SGUALDO Oh, I shouldn't worry over that sort of thing. You'll make friends round here in time, you'll see.

LUCIETTA Not the kind I used to have at the old house.

SGUALDO Aha! It's the men servants round by your old house you're missing, I bet.

LUCIETTA Maybe – and maybe not.

SGUALDO Don't they allow your gentlemen friends to call on you?

LUCIETTA Certainly, but I'm not the sort of girl that invites her young men into the house. Sometimes, perhaps, but only briefly, when I go to get wine, we exchange a few words, and that's it. I don't want to seem like one of those, you know.

SGUALDO Of course, I understand.

LUCIETTA Anyway, it's not so much myself that I'm sorry for in that respect. It's my young mistress I'm sorry for.

SGUALDO Why? Isn't the Signorina Meneghina happy about this ["beautiful residence"] either?

LUCIETTA Well, you won't tell a soul, I know, so I'll let you into a secret. Her young man lives exactly opposite our old house. So, of course, back there she used to be able to see him quite often. But now we've moved here, it's been impossible for them to arrange a meeting.

SGUALDO But won't her brother let her marry the young man?

LUCIETTA And what d'you think Signor Anzoletto's got to give her in the way of a dowry?

SGUALDO The old story again, eh?

LUCIETTA Poor girl, I don't know what's to become of her, unless her uncle decides to help her.

SGUALDO Old Cristofolo, you mean? Aye, he's certainly rich enough to help her – if he wanted to.

LUCIETTA Yes, the trouble is the old man's fallen out with his nephew for getting married like this. So, what with her brother and her uncle at daggers drawn, the poor girl can't expect help from either of them.

SGUALDO Sh! This sounds like Signor Anzoletto now!

LUCIETTA You be sure you don't say anything – about what I've been telling you.

SGUALDO Well, I like that, I must say.

LUCIETTA Because don't think I'm not still annoyed I've not been able to clean this room up yet.

SGUALDO Mind I don't get annoyed – I haven't been able to get on with my work – listening to you and your chitter-chatter.

LUCIETTA *(starting to sweep the floor)* Work! That's what you call it, is it?

Scene 2

Enter *Anzoletto.*

ANZOLETTO Oh, dear, oh, dear, isn't this room finished yet? Now what's holding things up? Nothing has gone wrong, I hope?

SGUALDO Everything'll be ready by tomorrow.

ANZOLETTO Tomorrow! Tomorrow! That's all I've been hearing for the last three weeks. Everything will be ready tomorrow!

SGUALDO Look, at least a dozen times you've told me to alter something. And then, as soon as I've done it, you've wanted it altered all over again. You listen to every Tom, Dick, and Harry who thinks he knows how an apartment should be furnished. Well, if you go on trying to follow all the idiotic advice your friends give you, I may as well tell you here and now, this place won't be finished this time next year – never mind tomorrow!

ANZOLETTO Yes, of course, you're quite right, my dear chap. Absolutely right. This time I'll not alter my mind. There – I've said so – and I'll stick to it. Now, you will hurry things, won't you, there's a good chap. My wife has decided to move in today from the old house. I suppose we'll just have to sleep in here for tonight.

SGUALDO Oh, the bedroom's ... all ready.

ANZOLETTO Oh, now really, that's too bad of you! What on earth will people think? To have the bedroom all ready but not the reception room!

SGUALDO Let them think what they like. I can't do any more than I am doing.

ANZOLETTO You could find some more workmen and get things done quicker.

SGUALDO You let me have some money first.

ANZOLETTO Money! It's always money! That's all I've heard since he's been here. Can't the man forget about it just for one moment? He never stops! It's all he can think of! Money! Money! Money!

SGUALDO No money – no more workmen.

ANZOLETTO Suppose – just suppose – I haven't got any money!

SGUALDO Then I suppose you'd see me and my men walking straight out of here.

ANZOLETTO You'll have your money tomorrow.

SGUALDO But I need to pay my men. They all live from hand to mouth.

ANZOLETTO Oh, all right, very well – I'll find some by tomorrow. So please do not mention it again. Let it be understood that I do not wish to discuss the matter any further. Just do what you are told – and remember that you are dealing with a gentleman and a man of honour.

SGUALDO Yes, Signore. Until tomorrow, then.

ANZOLETTO But take care you don't cause me too much expense.

SGUALDO Oh, naturally, Signore. You there, Toni. Go at once to my house and tell the three men there to leave what they're doing and to come here. [*(aside, to himself)*] And if he doesn't pay me tomorrow, I'll find ways of making him.

ANZOLETTO Lucietta!

LUCIETTA Yes, illustrious?

ANZOLETTO Go to the kitchen and give the cook some help if he needs it.

LUCIETTA You're dining here today, then?

ANZOLETTO Yes, with my wife and a few friends.

[LUCIETTA *(aside to herself)* Wonderful!

ANZOLETTO Tell my sister that her sister-in-law and other people are coming, so she can make herself presentable as well.]

LUCIETTA But I don't think she's had all her dresses brought from the old house yet.

ANZOLETTO Tell her I'll have the rest of her things brought over here right away.

LUCIETTA That's not the only thing. All the table linen is still at the old house as well.

ANZOLETTO Very well, very well! I'll have it all brought here.

LUCIETTA How many guests have I to prepare for?

ANZOLETTO Oh, just have the table laid for ten.

LUCIETTA Ten! Oh, yes, of course, Signore. I'll see that it's done, Signore. *(exit Lucietta)*

Scene 3

Anzoletto, Sgualdo, and men that come and go.

SGUALDO *(aside, [to himself])* There's no money for me, but plenty for this dinner of his. Well, we'll see what happens tomorrow.

ANZOLETTO You know, I'm not quite sure whether I like these decorations after all.

SGUALDO Well, I told you what I think of them. But you would listen to that artist friend of yours. They're costing you a tidy packet, and they don't suit the room at all.

ANZOLETTO Yes, I think you're right. You had better take them down again.

SGUALDO Take them down! What the hell d'you think we're going to put in place of them? This room certainly won't be finished this evening if we start messing about with them again.

ANZOLETTO Oh, well, I suppose we'd better leave them – for the time being.

SGUALDO Of course, what you should have had is a large mirror here and plenty of gold braiding round the other walls.

ANZOLETTO You're right, my dear fellow! Absolutely right! So let's get hold of some gold braiding and get it done right away, shall we?

SGUALDO What d'you mean – right away? A job like that would take days!

ANZOLETTO Oh, surely not. Not with these extra men you've sent for?

SGUALDO What about the beading? I'd need at least a hundred feet of gold beading at five soldi[3] a foot.

ANZOLETTO Well, get it.

SGUALDO All right – where's the money?

ANZOLETTO Are you starting that all over again? I've told you I'll settle any accounts tomorrow.
SGUALDO Then it'll have to wait till tomorrow. I haven't that much money either to pay out today.
ANZOLETTO Oh, all right, it's getting late anyway. I suppose we'd better leave things as they are for today.
SGUALDO *(aside, as he goes back to his work)* He's a proper case, this chap!

Scene 4

Enter *Fabrizio.*

FABRIZIO May one enter?
ANZOLETTO Come in! Please do come in, Signor Fabrizio!
FABRIZIO My dear friend, haven't they finished the place for you yet?
ANZOLETTO We are just trying to hasten them a little, my dear fellow. Well, what do you say? Does it please you?
FABRIZIO To tell you the truth – I do not like it at all.
ANZOLETTO You don't? But why ever not?
FABRIZIO Oh, really, my dear fellow! Well, I mean to say, in the first place, you've made the most frightful blunder, you know, in putting the bedrooms on the north side. It's this room facing the south which should be a bedroom. You'll simply die, my dear chap, if you sleep facing the north![4]
ANZOLETTO Oh, good heavens! Did you hear that, Signor Sgualdo?
SGUALDO Now what is it?
ANZOLETTO [*(to Sgualdo)*] D'you want me to catch my death of cold? How would you like to sleep facing the north?
SGUALDO You should have thought of that before.
ANZOLETTO Well, thank heaven we've thought of it now while there's still time to remedy it.
SGUALDO What d'you mean – remedy it?
FABRIZIO Now surely it's not all that difficult to carry a bed from one room to another?
SGUALDO What about these decorations?
FABRIZIO My good man. If one has the men and the money one can do anything.
ANZOLETTO *(to Sgualdo)* Yes, of course, anything can be remedied when you've got the men and the money.

SGUALDO *(becoming angry)* Well, I'll think of the men if you'll start thinking of the money!

ANZOLETTO What way is that to speak? To hear you, anybody might think I refused you your money. Have you ever been short of money?

SGUALDO *(aside)* Now I could show him up in front of his fine friend.

ANZOLETTO Did you hear? That's the way they speak to you nowadays. I've already given him well over a thousand ducats. And I've only just told him that tomorrow I intend settling any accounts that are still outstanding. Dear Signor Fabrizio, would you happen to have ten or twelve ducats to lend me? I would return them tomorrow.

FABRIZIO No, I'm sorry. If I had them I would give them to you gladly. *(aside)* I wouldn't lend him ten liras.

ANZOLETTO *(to Sgualdo)* Well, and what will it cost to move a bed from one room to another?

FABRIZIO Come, sirrah, this is but a puddle in a storm. Do not forget that you are dealing with a gentleman and a man of honour.

SGUALDO *(aside)* Damn me for getting involved with these people. Come along, lads, we've got another removal job on. We've to take one of the beds to bits and put it up again in here.
(to Anzoletto) And there'll be no going back on this!

ANZOLETTO You have my word for that.

SGUALDO *(aside)* And tomorrow we'll talk about money. *(exit Sgualdo)*

Scene 5

Anzoletto and Fabrizio.

FABRIZIO My dear Anzoletto, you have my sympathy. What boors these people are!

ANZOLETTO I sometimes think they will drive me mad. I do nothing but pay out money – and yet never seem to see anything for it.

FABRIZIO By the way, as I passed your kitchen I thought I saw your cook working there?

ANZOLETTO Yes, I am dining here this evening.

FABRIZIO With your wife?

ANZOLETTO With my wife.

FABRIZIO And – er – a few close relatives, I expect?

ANZOLETTO Er – yes – and one or two friends.

FABRIZIO Am I, alas, not numbered among your friends, then?

ANZOLETTO On the contrary, my dear fellow, pray join us, if you wish.

FABRIZIO The pleasure will be mine. I find your wife's company vastly entertaining. She has a charm and a wit, if I may say so, unusual in one so young and so beautiful. Her wit especially pleases me. It is so natural. So sparkling. So unrestrained.

ANZOLETTO And sometimes so damned irritating!

FABRIZIO You complain of her wit?

ANZOLETTO Shall we talk of something else? I am most grateful to you for your suggestion about the rooms facing the north.

FABRIZIO My dear fellow, I take great concern over your health. What's more – your dear wife might have suffered, as well.

ANZOLETTO My dear wife's so damned difficult to please, I am nigh past caring.

FABRIZIO [*(looking towards the background)*] But – pray who is this lady?

ANZOLETTO Lady? Oh, that's my sister. I thought you knew her?

FABRIZIO Not the little Signorina Meneghina? But what a fine young lady she's become!

ANZOLETTO Too fine – for my liking.

FABRIZIO You'd better arrange for her to marry.

ANZOLETTO My dear chap, let's not speak of these sad things, they break my heart.

Scene 6

Enter *Meneghina.*

MENEGHINA [*(from inside)*] May I come in?

ANZOLETTO Of course you can come in. If you want to.

FABRIZIO I am the Signorina Meneghina's most humble and devoted servant!

MENEGHINA My respects to you, sir. *(to Anzoletto, ironically)* Thank you, Brother, for the quite magnificent room you've given me.

ANZOLETTO Now what's the matter? Isn't the room to your liking?

MENEGHINA I never thought that at my age I should find myself buried alive.

ANZOLETTO Buried alive? What the devil are you talking about?

MENEGHINA It was most considerate of you to hide me away in a room looking out on to an enclosed courtyard where you'd never see a dog passing.

FABRIZIO Signorina Meneghina is right.

ANZOLETTO Well, where d'you want me to put you?

MENEGHINA You can hide me under the stairs, under the roof, anywhere you like. But I'm not staying in that room!

ANZOLETTO My dear sister, the apartment is not all that big, you know.

MENEGHINA Not all that big! You can stand there and say that, when there are four rooms on this side alone!

ANZOLETTO Oh, now, be reasonable, my dear girl. These rooms are naturally for me and my wife.

MENEGHINA Of course! Everything's for the new wife! For her, there's a whole apartment! For her, there are four rooms all connected to each other! But for me, there's one tiny closet!

ANZOLETTO What are you talking about? What tiny closet? It's a fine room! Big! Bright! Airy! With two windows! What on earth are you complaining about?

MENEGHINA Yes, and if I look out of the two windows what do I see? Cats – rats – lizards – and a rubbish heap that turns my stomach!

FABRIZIO *(to Meneghina)* Ah! And what you would like to see – is a certain young man? Am I right?

MENEGHINA You, sir, would oblige me by minding your own business!

ANZOLETTO If that's all that's troubling you, you can come in here and look out of the window as long as you like.

MENEGHINA If there's one place I'll never come – it's in here.

ANZOLETTO There you are, then! How do you expect my wife to get to know you and to like you, if you behave so unsociably and ungraciously?

MENEGHINA Well, she needn't put on her airs and graces for me, either. They don't take me in. I know quite well she doesn't want anything to do with me. And I can manage quite well without seeing anything of her.

ANZOLETTO And you've the damned impertinence to tell me so!

MENEGHINA I speak frankly, Brother. I don't go saying behind your back what I wouldn't say to your face.

FABRIZIO Ah! What a fine virtue is sincerity!

ANZOLETTO But what has my wife done to you? What have you got against her?

MENEGHINA D'you think I enjoy having a sister-in-law rummaging the house? I was the mistress of the house as long as our poor mother lived, and I have been ever since. But now her excellency the Signora Cecilia is coming, she'll want to give the orders to the servants.

She'll be the mistress here. I suppose I'll even have to ask her when I want a new pair of shoes.

FABRIZIO May I say that I have found the Signora Cecilia to possess great tact and discretion. Moreover, a younger lady should, undoubtedly, defer to the wishes of a married lady.

MENEGHINA Can't you be quiet? [*(aside)* He makes me so angry I'd kill him.]

ANZOLETTO So! I should not have married my wife – just because you don't want a sister-in-law in the house!

MENEGHINA You should have arranged my marriage, first!

FABRIZIO Yes, your sister's right to a certain extent, my dear fellow.

MENEGHINA Whether I'm right or not, what's that to do with you?

ANZOLETTO If a suitable marriage could have been arranged for you, I would most certainly have arranged it.

MENEGHINA If? If? There's no "if" about it! You had the opportunity and did nothing!

ANZOLETTO What opportunity? D'you mean Lorenzino?

MENEGHINA Yes! Lorenzino! And you said "No"!

ANZOLETTO Yes – and I said "No" because – because that young man's not good enough for you!

MENEGHINA Not good enough for *me*? For *you*, you mean! Who d'you want me to marry, then? A count? A lord? And what wonderful dowry will you be giving me? What her excellency your wife brought you? A lot of fine talk and hot air?

ANZOLETTO The point is I'm able to do what I want! I'm the master of the house. Nobody tells me what I've to do!

MENEGHINA And no sister-in-law is going to tell me what to do, either!

ANZOLETTO Just what d'you think you can do about it?

MENEGHINA Just this. I can go and live with our Uncle Cristofolo.

ANZOLETTO I warn you – if you so much as go anywhere near that old fool – then I've finished with you! D'you hear?

FABRIZIO Excuse me, old fellow, but don't you think that's going a bit too far, what?

MENEGHINA Will you keep out of this! My brother knows what he's talking about! Our uncle's a man of good sense – and can't stand the sight of his nephew here throwing his money away!

ANZOLETTO If you don't hold your tongue, it'll be the worse for you!

FABRIZIO You know, I think if you gave your sister a room with a good view, she'd be happy and forget about all these other matters.

MENEGHINA *(to Fabrizio)* Are you trying to be funny?

FABRIZIO I speak, dear lady, for your own good. I, at least, am trying to show some interest in your welfare.

MENEGHINA I can do without your interest, sir. I am well able to look after myself. I do not intend to remain in that room. And *that* – is *final*! *(exit Meneghina)*

Scene 7

Fabrizio and Anzoletto.

FABRIZIO Your sister is most certainly a young lady with a mind of her own.

ANZOLETTO Obstinate, you mean. As obstinate as the devil.

FABRIZIO Still, your wife will no doubt calm her down and make her see reason.

ANZOLETTO My dear chap, my wife can be more obstinate still.

FABRIZIO Great! Then why did you marry her?

ANZOLETTO I don't even know. Because I gave my word.

FABRIZIO Lucky you, with two such women in your house! Then you'll have to send your sister away.

ANZOLETTO Perhaps you can tell me how!

FABRIZIO How much dowry are you able to give her?

ANZOLETTO At the moment – not a thing.

FABRIZIO But supposing your uncle was prepared to help her?

ANZOLETTO Do not speak to me of my uncle! After the way he has treated me, I wouldn't ask him for a crust of bread if I were starving.

FABRIZIO Shouldn't you make some allowances? He is an old man, after all.

ANZOLETTO My wife would never allow it. He's offended her, as well.

FABRIZIO Well, I suppose it's your own affair, but I think it's a little – inadvisable to allow your wife to come between you and a rich uncle!

ANZOLETTO Look, old chap, I must go to the old house to arrange for the rest of the things to be brought here. Do me a favour and keep an eye on these workmen while I'm away. See that they bestir themselves, there's a good fellow.

FABRIZIO Certainly, my dear Anzoletto, I will do that most willingly.

ANZOLETTO If my wife arrives and sees things unfinished, I won't hear the end of it.

FABRIZIO From what I see, she's been your wife for just fifteen days, and you're already under her thumb.

ANZOLETTO Actually you cannot say I am under her thumb, I am not stupid enough to let her; on the contrary, we get along very well, and we agree on everything: but we are both stubborn. Once, before we got married, when we were still courting each other, for a slight misunderstanding we went two months without talking. Neither of us wanted to be the first to speak, so finally I had to. To avoid this sort of situation I try to dodge any possible scuffle, and I do all I can to make her happy; sometimes I do even more than I can. Enough said, what will be will be. *(aside)* I hope in one of two things: either my uncle will die, or I'll win the lottery. *(exit Anzoletto)*

Scene 8

Fabrizio, followed by Sgualdo.

FABRIZIO There goes a man who has been trying his best to ruin himself for some time. Now he seems to have succeeded – by getting married. Hey, you there!

SGUALDO You called?

FABRIZIO Signor Anzoletto has had to go to the old house. He asked me to tell you to see that everything is finished by this evening. But you are a man of judgment, and you don't need to be instructed on what to do, nor do you need to be prodded. Do your duty and I'll see you at dinner. *(exit Fabrizio)*

Scene 9

Sgualdo, followed by men, followed by Lucietta.

SGUALDO Yes, Signore! You're the sort of friend who never misses an invitation to dinner if he can help it. He could have spared me this sermon. I have to be patient. Come on, lads. Hurry up with that bed. *(the three workmen enter carrying the parts of a four-poster bed)*

LUCIETTA Now what's happening? Don't say you're starting all over again?

SGUALDO Come to poke your nose in again, have you?

LUCIETTA Uh … I almost said what you deserved to hear. *(covering her mouth)*

SGUALDO A good word is never wasted on you.

LUCIETTA He's not really going to let his sister have this room, is he?

SGUALDO If you must know, he's going to have this as his own bedroom.

LUCIETTA Now what's made him do that?

SGUALDO That Signor Fabrizio. Him that was trying to cadge an invitation to dinner. He told your master some nonsense about north and south.

LUCIETTA North and south? Now who can that be? Run off my feet I am! What with answering the door, helping the cook in the kitchen, and trying to tidy up after you lot! I suppose I'd better see who it is. *(exit)*

SGUALDO Always complaining! Like all these servants. They're never happy unless they're moaning about something. If they are old, they are not good for anything any more; if they're young, all they think of is love. It's no use for me to say let's hire them when they're middle-aged, for they go from young to old in a matter of minutes.

LUCIETTA Do you know who it is?

SGUALDO No, you tell me.

LUCIETTA It's the new wife!

SGUALDO Fancy that, now.

LUCIETTA Really, you should have seen the way she came in! You'd have died laughing! All those airs and graces!

SGUALDO Is she by herself?

LUCIETTA By herself! Not likely! She's got one of her lah-di-dah gentlemen friends with her. Some count from Milan.[5]

SGUALDO So soon?

LUCIETTA She doesn't waste any time.

SGUALDO Well, hadn't you better go and tell the Signorina Meneghina?

LUCIETTA Oh, she's locked herself up in her room.

SGUALDO You'll be the one to welcome her, then.

LUCIETTA Not me, you'll see. Since I don't know how she will react, I won't get involved.

[SGUALDO You've never spoken to her?

LUCIETTA No, not me.]

SGUALDO D'you mean to say – she's your master's wife – and you've not spoken to her yet?

LUCIETTA They've only been married a fortnight, and he's been living at her place while I've been trying to clean up here after you.

SGUALDO Quiet. She is coming.

LUCIETTA I'll go to receive her, just out of courtesy. *(she walks towards the door)*

SGUALDO Come on, now, hurry yourselves.

Scene 10

Enter *Cecilia and Ottavio.*

LUCIETTA Your servant, Signora.
CECILIA Ah, yes, who did you say you were?
LUCIETTA Chambermaid, Signora.
CECILIA Has Signor Anzoletto engaged you for me?
LUCIETTA No, Signora, I have been here quite a time.
CECILIA Is there a maid for his sister?
LUCIETTA Yes, Signora.
CECILIA How many maids are there?
LUCIETTA Only me, Signora.
CECILIA And you call yourself a chambermaid?
LUCIETTA What did you want me to say? The maid? You see, Illustrissima, I have a reputation to protect; I honour this house.
CECILIA I see. Well, I shall be bringing my own maid, of course. Which room is this?
LUCIETTA It was to be the reception room, but now it's going to be your bedroom, Signora.
CECILIA Now whose silly idea was that? *(to Sgualdo)* Yours?
SGUALDO Mine? Certainly not!
CECILIA A large room like this should be the reception room. Don't you agree, Count?
OTTAVIO Oh, indubitably, my dear lady.
LUCIETTA *(aside)* He is one to know for sure. These gentlemen are as fickle as the wind.
CECILIA What on earth put it into Signor Anzoletto's head to make such an alteration?
LUCIETTA It's so he won't have to sleep in a room facing the north.
CECILIA Facing the north? Somebody must have put the idea in his head. Was it this blockhead here?
SGUALDO *(getting angry)* I did not suggest any such thing! And what's more – I am not a blockhead!
CECILIA Don't raise your voice to me, my man!
OTTAVIO [*(to Sgualdo)*] Yes, a little more respect, please!
LUCIETTA *(aside)* Lucky us! We have a pompous mistress and a vainglorious captain.
CECILIA [*(to Sgualdo)*] And put this bed back where you got it from.
OTTAVIO This room is to be the reception room.

[SGUALDO As you wish, Signora. *(aside)* Great job, Signor Anzoletto. *(exit Sgualdo)*]

CECILIA *(to Lucietta)* A chair, if you please.

LUCIETTA Yes, Signora. *(she brings a chair to Cecilia, who sits)*

CECILIA And must the Count remain standing? My girl, I shall not take kindly to it, if you have to be told such things.

LUCIETTA I've always given satisfaction before.

CECILIA And a good servant does not answer her mistress back.

[LUCIETTA *(aside)* I'd rather be a hundred miles away.] *(angrily fetches another chair and plonks it beside Cecilia)*

CECILIA Pray, will you be seated, Count. They are not very comfortable, these chairs, are they?

OTTAVIO One does not use such chairs, dear lady.

CECILIA I thought not. I shall have some little armchairs made. *(to Lucietta)* What is it? Did I offend you, too? Such a delicate lot you are! I don't think I can be any kinder than this. I will teach you, don't worry. It really looks like there has never been order in this house. *(to the Count)* What do you think, Signor Count? Am I right?

OTTAVIO Very much so, you couldn't have said it better.

CECILIA That's how I am: whatever I say, whatever I do, I want people to tell me whether I am right or wrong.

LUCIETTA *(aside, ironically)* Be sure the captain will always tell you the truth.

CECILIA Tell me, you have a name, have you not?

LUCIETTA Lucietta. At your service.

CECILIA Well, Lucietta, can you tell me how my sister-in-law is doing?

LUCIETTA She is quite well, Signora.

CECILIA Tell her I asked after her when you see her, will you?

LUCIETTA Yes, Signora.

CECILIA Has she visited here yet?

LUCIETTA Er – yes, Signora.

CECILIA Oh? When did she come?

LUCIETTA This morning, Signora.

CECILIA She has returned to the old house?

LUCIETTA No, Signora.

CECILIA What? Then where is she now?

LUCIETTA She's here in her room.

CECILIA She is here! And does not condescend to come to welcome me! Well? Have you been struck dumb?

LUCIETTA What d'you want me to say?

CECILIA Count, please tell me – is that the way one's sister-in-law should treat one?

OTTAVIO Not in our circles, dear lady.

CECILIA *(to Lucietta)* There, you see! The Count, who is used to going about in society, says she is not behaving well.

[LUCIETTA *(aside)* He encourages her, too!]

CECILIA Go and inform my sister-in-law that if it is not too much trouble to her, I shall come and greet her in her room.

LUCIETTA Yes, Signora. *(aside)* From now on, this house will be the most entertaining place in the world. Hopefully they won't drag me into it. If I can have my back pay, so help me God, I'll be gone in a second. *(exit Lucietta)*

Scene 11

Cecilia and Ottavio.

CECILIA Signor Anzoletto tricked me. If I had known this sister of his would be living with us, being who I am, I wouldn't have agreed to marry him.

OTTAVIO You didn't know he had a sister?

CECILIA I knew it, but he led me to believe she would have moved in with his uncle.

OTTAVIO Maybe she'll move in with him after all.

CECILIA I'm afraid she won't, because he and the uncle are not speaking any more.

OTTAVIO It was foolish of Signor Anzoletto to have quarrelled with his uncle. Signor Cristofolo is not only very rich, he is also a gentleman.

CECILIA I am sorry to say, Count, that I consider him to be nothing of the sort! In my opinion he is a bad-tempered, ill-mannered old blackguard! Do you know, he did everything to stop his nephew marrying me? Actually complained that I didn't bring his nephew a big enough dowry! And he with all his money! I'm quite astonished that you should call him a gentleman!

OTTAVIO My dear lady! I did not know anything of all this! I withdraw what I said completely. The man's a complete boor.

CECILIA He's a blackguard! A lout!

OTTAVIO Whatever you say, dear lady.

CECILIA But I ask you! Should a lady be scorned in such a way by – by such a person?

OTTAVIO Ah, such a lady as yourself deserves to be treated like a queen! Would that I had but had the honour of knowing you before you became engaged to Signor Anzoletto!

CECILIA Ah, my dear Count, that was fate.

OTTAVIO Signor Anzoletto gives you no cause to complain?

CECILIA No, only his uncle. But my husband loves me, and he has the means to support me. So we have no need of his uncle. We are well rid of him. I shall be completely happy when we are rid of my sister-in-law.

OTTAVIO But his uncle could help him a great deal.

CECILIA He can keep his help, we don't need it. My husband has the means to support me. I only want him to rid this house of his sister, and then I'll be content.

OTTAVIO *(aside)* But I know the poor gentleman is in need of money.

Scene 12

Enter *Lucietta.*

LUCIETTA Signorina Meneghina greets the Signora and says she prefers to come here to welcome you, since her room is not a reception room.

CECILIA Were those her exact words?

LUCIETTA I've told you what she said.

CECILIA You see, Count, what she's implying?

OTTAVIO Well, no, to tell the truth. Not exactly.

CECILIA This impertinent young woman is as good as telling me that her room is not as fine as mine.

OTTAVIO Ah, yes, I see what you mean, dear lady.

CECILIA How arrogant of her!

OTTAVIO Well, one can't deny there is some pretension in her words.

LUCIETTA *(aside)* Oh, I want to tell the master to beware of this Signor Count. He's a shameless adulator.

CECILIA What is all that noise?

LUCIETTA Oh, it's only the people in the apartment up above, Signora.[6]

CECILIA But I shan't be able to put up with that sort of thing! Who are these people upstairs?

LUCIETTA They're two ladies, Signora. Sisters. Signora Checca – that's the married one – asked me to let her know when you arrived so that they might pay their respects to you. Oh, they're real ladies – Signora.

CECILIA Has she been to see my sister-in-law?

LUCIETTA Illustrissima, she hasn't. She is one who knows how things work. You'll see! She wouldn't have seen the girl without first seeing the wife.

CECILIA In that case, when you see them you may say that I shall be pleased to receive them. That is the correct procedure, is it not, Count?

OTTAVIO Perfectly, dear lady.

LUCIETTA Wouldn't it be better if I said you hoped –

CECILIA Simply do as you're told. I do not need lessons from scullery maids.

LUCIETTA Who's a scullery maid?

CECILIA That will be all! Get back to your work.

OTTAVIO What can one expect, dear lady? Complete lack of breeding, you know.

LUCIETTA Well, I certainly wouldn't come to you to learn good manners!

CECILIA That's enough! The sooner you go the better! You may consider yourself dismissed.

LUCIETTA Don't worry, I'm going!

Scene 13

Enter *Meneghina.*

MENEGHINA Is something the matter? Stay where you are, Lucietta.

LUCIETTA She says I'm dismissed! But I've told her I was going anyway.

MENEGHINA So, my dear sister-in-law, you've started causing trouble already?

CECILIA That is no way to greet me!

OTTAVIO *(aside)* My God! She is a beautiful girl!

MENEGHINA What has Lucietta done?

CECILIA She was insolent to this gentleman.

OTTAVIO Don't mind me, my dear. Such trifles are beneath me. For heaven's sake, I wouldn't want to be the cause of any trouble. I am your servant. *(to Cecilia)* The most humble servant of the young lady. *(to Meneghina)* Lucietta is a good girl. *(aside)* I would like to be friends with all of them.

MENEGHINA I assume you have your own maid? Lucietta has been with me over a year and I am quite satisfied with her.

CECILIA Oh, keep her, then. But see she doesn't cross my path.
LUCIETTA You needn't worry about that!
MENEGHINA That's enough, Lucietta. Please go to your room.
LUCIETTA *(aside)* Who the hell came into this house? A basilisk? *(exit Lucietta)*

Scene 14

Cecilia, Meneghina, and Ottavio.

MENEGHINA Please forgive me if I didn't come earlier to perform my duty, but I wasn't dressed.
CECILIA Oh, but you didn't need to dress up just for me.
OTTAVIO Signorina Meneghina is beautiful in all kinds of clothes.
CECILIA *(ironically)* Well said, Signor Count.
OTTAVIO It would be truly impossible to find another pair of such beautiful and virtuous sisters-in-law.
MENEGHINA *(aside)* Among his many virtues, one can count that of envy.
CECILIA Would you like to sit down, Signora Sister-in-law?
MENEGHINA Actually, I am not tired.
CECILIA Do as you please, this is your house.
MENEGHINA Oh, no, you see, my room is my house.
CECILIA But the whole house is yours, too.
MENEGHINA Oh, thank you!
OTTAVIO What a beautiful exchange of niceties, courtesies, and affections!
MENEGHINA And how heartfelt they are!
CECILIA And now, Sister-in-law, perhaps you will tell me – where is my husband?
MENEGHINA I have no idea. You see, I never know when he comes and when he goes. Nobody tells me anything.
CECILIA Really? He doesn't talk to you about his affairs?
MENEGHINA Oh, never. He told me he was going to marry only three days before.
CECILIA Would you have preferred to know it in advance?
MENEGHINA Wouldn't you?
OTTAVIO It's always good to have company in the house.
MENEGHINA Well, as far as I am concerned, I am always in my room and I don't bother anybody. After my mother died I have been accustomed to do so.

OTTAVIO Here is an idea: Signora Cecilia will act as your mother.
CECILIA Me as her mother? How can a newlywed of fifteen days be a mother to anyone?
OTTAVIO I'm just saying, since you are married and she is not.
MENEGHINA What did you think he meant?
CECILIA Well – for somebody who never goes into society you have an extremely fashionable hairstyle.
MENEGHINA My maid attends to my hair.
CECILIA That girl Lucietta?
MENEGHINA Yes. Lucietta.
CECILIA But I had no idea she was so gifted. She must do mine as well.
MENEGHINA Oh, I am sure your maid can do better than this.
CECILIA Not really, to be truthful, she does it better than mine. She'll do my hair, too.
MENEGHINA Dear Signora Sister-in-law, please excuse me. Lucietta is a poor girl, but she has never been mistreated. Do me this courtesy. Don't burden her with this additional duty.
CECILIA How dare you speak to me like that! That girl is paid by my husband and I shall certainly make use of her if I want to!
OTTAVIO Ladies, please! One does not become angry over a maid.
CECILIA You won't offend your sister-in-law over the services of a maid, will you?
MENEGHINA Do you want me to send her away? I will send her away.
CECILIA Don't throw a tantrum. You shouldn't be difficult with me.
OTTAVIO Please, for heaven's sake. Let us accommodate her.
MENEGHINA No, I think she came into this house with the intention of ordering me around.
CECILIA I am surprised that you would say such absurdities.
OTTAVIO *(aside)* Poor me. *(aloud)* My dear ladies …
MENEGHINA Not even my mother treated me this way.
OTTAVIO *(to Meneghina)* Please indulge her.
CECILIA What do you mean indulge her? I don't need anybody to indulge me.

Scene 15

Anzoletto, Meneghina, Cecilia, and Ottavio.

ANZOLETTO *(aside)* Oh, poor me!
MENEGHINA Oh, Brother, please tell –

CECILIA Just listen to this, Husband! –

ANZOLETTO My dear Count, a word with you, I beg you.

OTTAVIO *(nearing)* Your servant, Signore.

MENEGHINA Will you please tell me, Brother –

ANZOLETTO Be quiet now, leave me alone.

CECILIA Why don't you listen to me –

ANZOLETTO Dear Wife, be patient. I will be with you in a moment.

OTTAVIO *(quietly to Anzoletto)* What's the matter, dear fellow? You seem quite upset? Is it perhaps because of what the two sisters-in-law were saying?

ANZOLETTO *(aside)* What words! There are facts, and painful facts at that. My dear Signor Count, neither my wife nor my sister is to know about this! I can rely on you?

OTTAVIO *(aside)* Of course, my dear Anzoletto. Please tell me, your secret is safe with me. I'll do whatever I can.

ANZOLETTO *(aside)* I have just been to my old house to collect some things. The landlord refuses to let me take them because I still owe him some rent.

OTTAVIO *(aside)* Oh, I say, that's a bad business!

ANZOLETTO *(aside)* I know that! The point is, can you help me? All I need is somebody to vouch for me.

OTTAVIO *(aside)* Ah, now, one must consider such a situation from every point of view. I'll tell you what I think you –

ANZOLETTO *(aside)* But it's urgent! There's no time to lose! All the table linen's still there, and I'm entertaining people to dinner here this evening.

OTTAVIO *(aside)* I don't know. I will do what I can. It is a difficult situation. *(aloud)* Signore, your most humble servant.

CECILIA You are leaving, Count?

OTTAVIO Alas, dear lady, I have some business to attend to.

CECILIA But you will be dining with us?

OTTAVIO Yes, of course – er – that is, I hope so.

ANZOLETTO *(aside)* You are going to help me?

OTTAVIO *(aside)* I'll see. I'll do what I can.

ANZOLETTO *(aside, while leaving)* In the end, he doesn't want to do anything. I will need to look for help somewhere else.

ANZOLETTO *(aside, accompanying him towards the door)* But you must! I'm depending on you! I'll come with you!

MENEGHINA Are you going out again already?

ANZOLETTO Yes, yes! I shan't be long!

CECILIA But Husband!
ANZOLETTO I said I'll be back soon! *(exit Anzoletto)*
CECILIA There! Because of you my husband's started being rude to me ...
MENEGHINA His rudeness was meant for me. He saw something was wrong, and that Count of yours has told him it's my fault.
CECILIA What d'you mean – that Count of mine?
MENEGHINA Oh, I'm sure I don't care whose Count he is.
CECILIA And I'm sure I don't either. It's my husband I'm concerned about!

Scene 16

Enter *Lucietta.*

LUCIETTA Those two ladies from the apartment upstairs would like to see you.
MENEGHINA Who? Me?
LUCIETTA Well, no – both of you, I expect.
CECILIA Oh, no, they don't! Tell them to make up their minds who they think is mistress here. *(exit Cecilia)*
MENEGHINA Yes! Either her – or me! *(exit Meneghina)*
LUCIETTA Well, if that's the way it is – I'll receive them myself! *(exit Lucietta)*

ACT TWO

Scene I

A room in the Signora Checca's apartment. Checca and Rosina.

CHECCA Well, what d'you make of that? Did you ever know such insolence! They ask us to come. Then when we're at their door, their servant says they can't see us. And she doesn't know why. I couldn't make out one word that girl was trying to say!
ROSINA They ought to have given us some explanation. That servant was so pleasant when she asked us to come. You wouldn't think it was the same girl the way she muttered at us under her breath.

CHECCA They're either complete boors and don't know any better – or they've a very high opinion of themselves.

ROSINA Yet they seem to have plenty of friends.

CHECCA Friends! Acquaintances, you mean! That sort of person doesn't have friends. The young woman's been married only a fortnight and she's already got one of those so-called gentlemen dancing attendance on her.

ROSINA What about the young girl! D'you think she really is kept shut up, like a nun in a convent?

CHECCA That's what our cousin Lorenzino told me. She wears a black cloak down to her heels when she does go out. But apparently she doesn't behave quite so circumspectly when she's on the balcony outside her room.

ROSINA Didn't he tell you that was where they used to make love?

CHECCA You know what these young girls are nowadays. Don't model yourself on them, Sister. For myself, I can truthfully say that my husband was the first young man who ever spoke to me. You must always remember the precepts of our dear mother. And now that you live with me …

ROSINA My dear Sister, I have no need of your sermons. You should know that.

CHECCA Why do you think these people downstairs didn't want to receive us?

ROSINA Well, of course, they've only arrived today. Perhaps their apartment isn't finished yet. All the furniture may not have come.

CHECCA Yes, you may be right. But still that wouldn't excuse their behaviour. Though to tell the truth, I must admit we were a little hasty ourselves. We could have waited till tomorrow. But I am so very curious to see this young woman.

ROSINA I saw her when she arrived. To me she didn't seem anybody extraordinary.

CHECCA They say she likes having her own way.

ROSINA Yes, she looked as though she probably did.

CHECCA But how will Signor Anzoletto be able to afford a wife like that?

ROSINA He certainly won't on the dowry she brought him.

CHECCA Yes, that's what Lorenzino said. She hardly brought Signor Anzoletto anything. And he's such a spendthrift himself. Simply throws his money away.

ROSINA Yes, just think what that apartment must be costing him. Those men have been working on it for two months now.

CHECCA And yet all the old junk that's been arriving! Did you see that old mirror with the black border?

ROSINA Yes! Those things went out with the Ark!

CHECCA And the big leather armchair?

ROSINA That monstrosity! It must have belonged to his great-great-grandfather!

CHECCA They squander money on painters, carpenters, upholsterers – yet they can't have one room furnished in good taste.

ROSINA Yes, I must say I'd like to see it.

CHECCA I've simply got to see it! Perhaps I could slip in one day when they're out.

ROSINA What about Lorenzino? He did ask us to speak to the young girl for him.

CHECCA Yes, that young man doesn't know what to do with himself. Now that he can't look at her all day from his window.

ROSINA Then you will speak to Signorina Meneghina?

CHECCA Yes, to please him, I'll speak to her. Not that it will do any good.

ROSINA Why not?

CHECCA Well, what dowry d'you think that brother of hers will be able to give her?

ROSINA But Lorenzino's so much in love with her!

CHECCA Then he'll have to content himself with being in love. That young man's another spendthrift. It's not love that pays the bills, my dear Sister.

ROSINA Somebody's knocking.

CHECCA Yes, and nobody's answering it.

ROSINA I'll go and see who it is.

CHECCA Don't let anybody see you on the balcony.

ROSINA Oh, we're so high up here, who d'you think could see me? *(exit Rosina)*

Scene 2

Checca, followed by Rosina.

CHECCA Oh, I wish my husband would hurry his return to Venice. I must get him to arrange a good marriage for Rosina. The poor girl deserves a good husband.

ROSINA Do you know who it is?

CHECCA Who?
ROSINA It's that servant from downstairs!
CHECCA Did you pull the cord to open the door?
ROSINA Yes.
CHECCA Good. I'm glad she's come. Now we'll hear something.
ROSINA Yes, servants always tell everything.
CHECCA Leave it to me. I'll get her to tell me all she knows. But I know how to do it discreetly.
ROSINA Here she is.
CHECCA Come in, my child.

Scene 3

Enter *Lucietta.*

LUCIETTA Thank you, Signora.
CHECCA What a lovely girl! What is it, my dear? Have your mistresses sent you?
LUCIETTA The young one sent me, Signora.
ROSINA Signorina Meneghina?
LUCIETTA Yes, Signorina. I expect you know I'm her maid, not the married one's. I've been with her quite a time and I'm very fond of her and I'd like to stay with her. But if I have to wait on that other one, I won't stay in that house another hour, even though I've nowhere to go.
CHECCA That's right, my dear, you can tell me all about it. What is she like, the young married one?
LUCIETTA I don't know what to say. I'm not one of those who talk, Signora. If I can't say anything good, I don't say anything bad. Besides I've hardly seen her. But from the little I've seen, I don't believe there can possibly be, in the whole world, a more horrible woman than she is.
ROSINA *(aside)* If she were one who talked, what would we hear!
CHECCA Yes, but in what way? Is she a snob? A boor?
LUCIETTA With her servants and with her sister-in-law, she's bad-tempered and rude. But she's not like that with everybody. There's a certain Count …
CHECCA Come, come, no more of that. *(she motions her to be quiet on account of her sister)*

LUCIETTA I understand.

CHECCA Tell me, my dear, why did they treat us so ill-manneredly?

LUCIETTA Oh, that wasn't my mistress's fault. It was that other one.

CHECCA What? You mean, the young married one didn't want to see us?

LUCIETTA I'll tell you … really, it's enough to make you die laughing! When she thought you were visiting her, she said yes. But when she found out you were visiting both of them, she got in such a temper and refused to see you!

ROSINA What a thing to do!

CHECCA How absurd!

LUCIETTA So then my young mistress got annoyed as well.

CHECCA Well!

ROSINA Oh, my goodness, I *am* enjoying this!

LUCIETTA So you see, it's my young mistress who's just sent me to beg your forgiveness, and to say that if it's convenient she'll come herself and pay her respects.

CHECCA Oh, she mustn't put herself to that trouble …

ROSINA *(softly, to Checca)* Yes! Yes! Let her come!

LUCIETTA Truly, Signora, she is really very sorry.

CHECCA That's enough. If she's merely being polite, tell her there is no need to disturb herself. We do not let such things upset us. However, if she really wishes to make herself pleasant, tell her we shall be pleased for her to visit us whenever she wishes.

LUCIETTA Thank you, Signora. My mistress really is the most kind-hearted young lady. But you will see that for yourself.

CHECCA And I can see that you are very kind-hearted yourself, my dear. And that you are very fond of your mistress.

LUCIETTA Oh, yes, indeed, Signora. I couldn't do more for her if she were my own sister.

ROSINA It is good to find a servant who speaks well of her mistress. Most usually find fault with something.

LUCIETTA Oh, there's no danger of that with me. You'll never hear me speaking badly of her.

CHECCA That is how it should be!

ROSINA How old is your mistress?

LUCIETTA She's quite young, Signorina. I don't think she can be eighteen yet.

ROSINA Do you want to make her younger, too? Isn't that too much?

LUCIETTA Do you think she's older than that?

CHECCA Can't you see that she's way over twenty?

LUCIETTA I don't know, I am just saying what she says. If she hides her age, I don't know what to say.
ROSINA Isn't she in love with someone?
LUCIETTA A little.
CHECCA You know my cousin?
LUCIETTA Who is that, Signora?
CHECCA Signor Lorenzino Bigoletti.
LUCIETTA Good gracious, yes! I know him, of course!
CHECCA Do you think she would like to meet him?
LUCIETTA Wouldn't she just!
CHECCA I believe it was because of him she didn't want to leave the other house?
LUCIETTA Yes, it's really upset her, that has.
CHECCA She often speaks of him?
LUCIETTA Good heavens! All day long!
ROSINA I do think it's rather hard on her …
LUCIETTA Yes, isn't it, Signorina? If there's one thing I can't stand it's snobbishness.
CHECCA But what will she do now?
LUCIETTA Signor Lorenzino really is your cousin?
CHECCA Certainly. He is the son of one of my aunts.
LUCIETTA Then, don't you see, Signora, you can help her!
CHECCA How dare you suggest such a thing! Ladies do not involve themselves in intrigues. Of course, if she were seriously considering marriage with the young man, that would be quite another matter.
LUCIETTA But she is, Signora, she is! Only the poor girl hasn't any dowry. Her father was a grocer. Her uncle used to sell butter. Her brother's been able to live in such fine style on the money his father left him. But that'll soon be all gone. You know what they say: Easy come, easy go. There now, I'm boring you with my chatter. I'll go and tell my mistress she may come and visit you. Your servant, Signore. *(exit Lucietta)*

Scene 4

Checca and Rosina.

CHECCA What a chatterbox!
ROSINA But she is very attached to her mistress.

CHECCA The attachment of a servant.

ROSINA Why did you say you didn't want to concern yourself over our cousin?

CHECCA Because I most certainly don't want to become the talk of the neighbourhood.

ROSINA I suppose you are right.

CHECCA My dear Sister, I know I am.

Scene 5[7]

Enter *Lorenzino.*

LORENZINO [*(from inside)*] Hello? Anybody at home?[8]

ROSINA Oh, good gracious, here he is!

CHECCA Come in! We're in here, Lorenzino.

LORENZINO *(entering)* Most illustrious cousins, my deepest, my humblest respects to you both!

ROSINA Oh, fie, Cousin!

CHECCA You are not usually so polite!

LORENZINO I do my best.

ROSINA Didn't you sleep well last night?

LORENZINO No, very little.

ROSINA Never mind, there'll be nothing to disturb you tonight, will there?

LORENZINO Curses on this house!

CHECCA Now why should you curse this house?

LORENZINO Well, curses on that apartment downstairs, then.

ROSINA What! Even though your dearest one is there?

LORENZINO I can't even find her balcony. For three hours I've been walking up and down out there, coughing like a madman to attract her attention. But there's not been a sign of her.

CHECCA I could have told you that. Her room is at the back. It looks on to a courtyard where nobody passes.

LORENZINO And you wonder why I curse this house! And that fool of a brother of hers. He pays sixty ducats more than he needs to – and then lodges his sister in some old cubby-hole. Anyway, how does he manage it? How is he going to pay the rent? With his wife's dowry?

CHECCA You think Signor Anzoletto is in that sort of trouble?

LORENZINO I know nothing. All I know is he's had that apartment for two months now and he hasn't paid the rent for the first month yet.
ROSINA And you're well-off enough to get entangled with his sister?
LORENZINO She has an uncle who will give her a dowry.
CHECCA Yes, I've heard of this rich uncle of hers, but thought he had fallen out with his nephew.
LORENZINO But not with his niece.
CHECCA My dear Cousin, I think you should consider well before you do anything rash. You haven't money to throw away.
LORENZINO With a dowry of two or three thousand ducats I could buy a position of office, and with the little bit I have I'd be able to live.
ROSINA You certainly wouldn't be able to let your wife live in the style that Signor Anzoletto lets his.
LORENZINO How d'you mean?
ROSINA Oh, you should have seen her!
CHECCA A crinoline, my dear, all flounced out from here to there!
ROSINA The most extraordinary dress you could imagine!
CHECCA *(to Rosina)* Silk, embroidered with real gold by the look of it.
ROSINA Frills all round it!
CHECCA And her hair! Oh, the latest style, of course!
ROSINA With diamonds even!
CHECCA Murano glass, more likely!
ROSINA Well, they certainly glittered and shone like anything.
CHECCA So do cat's eyes!
LORENZINO And the young girl? You've seen her?
CHECCA Oh, we've seen her.
LORENZINO What do you think of her?
CHECCA Mmm ... so-so.
ROSINA She's not one of these beauties.
CHECCA She's well-made.
ROSINA But she's got quite a good figure.
CHECCA Oh, I wouldn't say so.
LORENZINO Then you can't have seen her very well.
ROSINA We aren't blind, you know!
LORENZINO Well, where did you see her?
ROSINA On her balcony.
LORENZINO You mean – it is possible to see her on her balcony?
CHECCA Our dining-room overlooks the courtyard, just opposite the balcony outside her room.
LORENZINO My dear Cousin, may I go into your dining-room?

CHECCA Now don't start your comedy here!
LORENZINO But you did promise me you'd speak to the Signorina Meneghina for me. So why won't you let me have a look at her balcony?
CHECCA Pardon me, young man, but you've got things the wrong way round. It's one thing for me to speak to her; it's quite another thing for you to make a fool of yourself on my balcony.
LORENZINO But no one will see me. I promise I won't let anyone see me.
CHECCA If you go on to the balcony, of course someone will see you!
LORENZINO I'll just peep over. No one will see me.
CHECCA Everybody opposite will see you.
LORENZINO But I'll be hidden by the shutters. I'll only open them a little.
ROSINA Please, Sister! Let the poor boy go.
LORENZINO Dear Cousin! Just a little peep!
CHECCA You certainly are in a bad way. Go on, then. But mind you take care and don't make yourself ridiculous.
LORENZINO Blessed woman. *(Lorenzino goes out)*

Scene 6

Checca and Rosina, followed by servant.

ROSINA Checca, dear! Let me go as well! I won't stay a moment.
CHECCA What on earth for?
ROSINA Only to have a little look.
CHECCA Well! I like that! What would the neighbours think!
ROSINA All right, if you don't want me to, I won't. But I only wanted to hear what the Signorina Meneghina speaks like.
CHECCA You can hear her speak when she comes here.
ROSINA But we may have to wait ages for that.
CHECCA What was that? Wasn't it somebody at the door?
ROSINA Yes, I thought I heard something myself. *(she goes to the door and looks out)* Oh! D'you know who I think it is? Good heavens, yes! I do believe it's her! The Signorina Meneghina!
CHECCA No!
ROSINA There's somebody on the stairs speaking to our servant. I didn't want to let myself be seen, so as not to appear …
CHECCA Quite right.
ROSINA Here's Toni. Now we'll know.
SERVANT Signora, the lady from downstairs wishes to see you.

CHECCA Is it the young girl, or the married one?
SERVANT I couldn't say, Signora. I don't know them.
ROSINA Does she wear a crinoline?
SERVANT No, Signorina.
ROSINA It's the young one.
CHECCA Tell her we shall be happy to receive her.
SERVANT Yes, Signora. *(exit servant)*
ROSINA What about Lorenzino? He'll be waiting on the balcony.
CHECCA Let him wait, then. He can't hear us from there. We'll play a joke on him and not tell him.
ROSINA Suppose he comes back in here?
CHECCA Well, what if he does?

Scene 7

Enter *Meneghina, followed by servant.*

[MENEGHINA Signore.
CHECCA Signora.
ROSINA Signora.]
MENEGHINA Please excuse the liberty I am taking.
CHECCA Not at all. We think it most courteous of you.
ROSINA We so much wanted to welcome you as our neighbour.
MENEGHINA Thank you. As we are so near, perhaps you will not mind if I come occasionally to call on you?
CHECCA Why, of course. You must come whenever you wish.
ROSINA And we will come and call on you.
MENEGHINA On me? … Oh, dear … I don't know how to tell you. But I will. Yes, I will tell you. Everything.
CHECCA Won't you sit down?
MENEGHINA Thank you.
CHECCA Hey, bring some chairs. (*servant brings some chairs*)
ROSINA Aren't you happy in your new apartment?
MENEGHINA Oh, the apartment's all right. It is simply that there are – well, some things about it I don't like.
ROSINA For example … the view from your balcony?
MENEGHINA How could anybody like it? Nothing but an old courtyard!
CHECCA And yet … perhaps it could be arranged that the view from your balcony did not displease you.

MENEGHINA No, Signora. That's impossible.

ROSINA For example … if you were on your balcony at this very moment – the view might not displease you.

MENEGHINA Oh, you mean the sun shines on the courtyard at this time of day? But I never look.

CHECCA If you were there – at this very moment – you would see the sun shining full on to your balcony.

MENEGHINA Oh, I can't bear the sun full on me.

ROSINA It depends on which sun you mean.

MENEGHINA You are making fun of me. Yes, I see you enjoy making jokes.

CHECCA When you were on the balcony at your old house, was there not a sun whose rays you could bear to fall on you?

MENEGHINA I'm afraid it's no use trying to make me laugh.

ROSINA Tell me, Signorina Meneghina, hasn't Lucietta said anything to you?

MENEGHINA About what?

ROSINA About a certain cousin of ours.

MENEGHINA No, she hasn't said anything.

CHECCA But you do know our cousin?

MENEGHINA No, who is he?

CHECCA Why, Lorenzino.

MENEGHINA Lorenzino Bigoletti?

CHECCA Lorenzino Bigoletti.

MENEGHINA What? You really mean it? He's your cousin?

ROSINA He is our cousin.

MENEGHINA Then … you know …

CHECCA We know all.

MENEGHINA *(sighs)* Oh, dear!

ROSINA What a horrible time you must be having in that awful apartment down there.

MENEGHINA Terrible!

CHECCA That horrible balcony!

MENEGHINA It's like being in hell!

ROSINA And all you can see is a glimpse of the sky!

CHECCA You might as well be in a prison cell.

MENEGHINA I might indeed! But now I begin to hope! That I may after all see him here as well sometimes.

CHECCA Really?

MENEGHINA Who would have thought I should be so fortunate as to find two such understanding ladies as yourselves?

ROSINA Cousins of Signor Lorenzino.

MENEGHINA It really is incredible.

CHECCA Yes, wouldn't it be incredible if he should come in now and find you here?

MENEGHINA Oh, if only he would!

ROSINA I have a feeling he may not be far away.

MENEGHINA You really think so?

CHECCA Doesn't your heart tell you?

MENEGHINA My heart tells me that if he should come I would see him willingly.

ROSINA And yet if you were at home you would be seeing him at this very moment.

MENEGHINA Where?

ROSINA From the balcony of your room.

MENEGHINA But nobody can pass through that courtyard! It's enclosed on every side by warehouses.

CHECCA I believe he's thinking of renting one of the warehouses.

MENEGHINA Oh, you're laughing at me again – and you're quite right to.

ROSINA Seriously, would you really like to see him?

MENEGHINA With all my heart I would.

CHECCA Signorina Rosina, have a look outside and see if there is anybody coming. I think there is somebody at the door.

MENEGHINA Oh, if only it were he!

ROSINA *(going to the door)* We'll see. You never know who it might be.

SERVANT Signora, the other lady from downstairs, the young married one, asks if she may, with your permission, also come to pay you her respects.

CHECCA Most willingly. Ask her to come in. *(the servant goes out)*

MENEGHINA Oh, damn the woman!

ROSINA It annoys you that she should come?

MENEGHINA That's putting it mildly. We simply can't agree. I bet anything she's only come just to annoy me.

CHECCA But why?

MENEGHINA There isn't time to tell you all about it now. But I will later. *(to Rosina)* Dear Signorina, please do go and see if Signor Lorenzino may be coming.

ROSINA But your sister-in-law will be here any moment.

MENEGHINA If only I could avoid her. Please, will you do me a favour?

CHECCA Of course. You have only to ask.

MENEGHINA Since my sister-in-law is here, allow me to go through there.

CHECCA Why through there?

MENEGHINA So I may leave through another door.

CHECCA But all our rooms communicate with each other. There is no other way out.

MENEGHINA Then let me stay in your dining-room.

CHECCA Really?

ROSINA You poor girl! In the dining-room of all places!

MENEGHINA Would it be worse for me there?

ROSINA Oh, no! You'd be all right there! Yes, indeed!

MENEGHINA Then let me go in there!

CHECCA No, no, you will have to excuse me. I'll have no more of this nonsense. You'll just have to be patient with her this time.

MENEGHINA *(to Rosina)* But you'll let Signor Lorenzino know, won't you?

ROSINA I'll send someone to tell him at once.

CHECCA No, no, wait! I'll send someone. *(she goes to the door)* Where are you, Toni?

SERVANT *(entering)* Yes, Signora?

CHECCA Is the lady from downstairs coming?

SERVANT Yes, she's coming now, Signora.

CHECCA *(softly to the servant)* Listen! Go to the dining-room and tell Signor Lorenzino he's to go at once. If he doesn't know the Signorina Meneghina is here, don't say anything. If he does, tell him he's still to go, because Signorina Meneghina's sister-in-law's coming and I don't want any trouble. You understand? Do your best.

SERVANT Leave it to me. *(exit servant)*

MENEGHINA You've sent him to look for him?

CHECCA Yes, Signorina.

MENEGHINA And what about my sister-in-law?

CHECCA He won't come in as long as he knows she is here.

ROSINA *(aside)* My sister's so sensible, she's probably told him to go.

CHECCA *(to Meneghina)* Does your sister-in-law know about Lorenzino?

MENEGHINA I don't think so. Unless my brother has told her.

Scene 8

Enter *Lorenzino.*

LORENZINO *(indignantly)* Thank you very much, Cousin!

CHECCA Go away at once!

LORENZINO I've been standing in there in the cold, getting a crick in my neck while …

CHECCA Go away! D'you hear me!
ROSINA D'you want to cause trouble?
MENEGHINA Where were you getting a crick in the neck?
LORENZINO In there, in the dining-room. Waiting to see if you came out on your balcony. And you've been here all the time!
MENEGHINA Well! Thank you very much, Signora Checca! You've been most kind!
CHECCA My dear child, can't you take a joke? That is all that was intended.
ROSINA But your sister-in-law coming like this spoilt the joke, you see?
LORENZINO Well, I'm not going, that's certain.
CHECCA Go away, I tell you!
LORENZINO I can't!
MENEGHINA Poor boy, he can't!
ROSINA If he goes down the stairs now, he'll meet her.
CHECCA They both want to drive me mad. A lot of help I'd be to them then. *(to Lorenzino)* Get back in there where you were.
LORENZINO Yes, Signora. But I beg you, allow me to say two words to her first. *(to Meneghina)* Dear Meneghina, if you love me, wait for me. *(to Rosina)* Dear little Cousin, help us also, I beg you. *(to Meneghina)* My sweet darling!
MENEGHINA *(wiping her eyes)* You poor boy!
CHECCA For heaven's sake, get out!
LORENZINO I go! I go! *(to Meneghina)* Bless you! *(exit)*
MENEGHINA *(aside)* The darling! Oh, I'm not going now! My sister-in-law can say what she likes. I'm my old self again now!
ROSINA *(to Meneghina)* My goodness, but you two have certainly got it badly!
CHECCA A great pity, if you ask me. Here she is, confound it.
MENEGHINA Make way for the princess!
ROSINA You call her princess?
MENEGHINA What else would you call such a conceited prig?
ROSINA Oh, Signorina Meneghina!

Scene 9

Enter *Cecilia, followed by servant.*

CECILIA Signora, your most humble servant conveys to you her most respectful greetings!

CHECCA Signora!

ROSINA Signora!

CECILIA My greetings to you, Sister-in-law.

MENEGHINA Signora.

CHECCA It is indeed most kind of you to favour us like this.

CECILIA I have come to pay my respects in order that I may gain the honour of your acquaintance and to thank you for already doing me the honour of inconveniencing yourselves by coming to see me and to beg that you will pardon me for having had to deprive myself of the pleasure of your gracious company.

MENEGHINA *(aside to Rosina)* You'd think sugar wouldn't melt in her mouth!

CHECCA My dear Signora, pray do not overwhelm me with ceremony. I am accustomed to speaking plainly, so if there is anything I can do for you, you have only to ask. We are neighbours, so we ought to be good friends. You will find me most willing.

CECILIA *(making an exaggerated curtsey)* Your kindness overwhelms me.

MENEGHINA *(aside to Rosina)* She'll fall over if she's not careful.

ROSINA *(aside to Meneghina)* She does put it on a little, doesn't she?

CHECCA *(to Cecilia)* Won't you sit down?

CECILIA After you, please.

CHECCA We'll all sit down, then.

MENEGHINA *(aside, to herself)* Yes, let's get this over with.

[SERVANT *(brings the chairs and leaves)*]

CECILIA My dear Sister-in-law, if you intended coming to pay your respects to these ladies, you might have let me know so that I could have accompanied you. But perhaps your intention was to make me appear lacking in good manners?

MENEGHINA My dear Sister-in-law, I thought you were waiting until they had made up their minds who was the mistress.

CECILIA *(to Checca)* You must excuse our little jokes. We are always teasing each other, my sister-in-law and I.

CHECCA You must be very fond of one another.

MENEGHINA Oh, we are!

ROSINA Yes, I can see you are.

CECILIA *(aside)* If you only knew!

CHECCA *(to Cecilia)* You are pleased with your new apartment?

CECILIA Well, to tell the truth, it does not displease me. But, of course, I cannot forget my old house.

MENEGHINA Nor I, mine.

CECILIA Oh, really now, when all's said and done, your house was only an old shack. I can assure you the house I was brought up in was very different. As a matter of fact, we often used to have a prince staying with us. There were four of us brothers and sisters, you know. And of course we each had our own suite of rooms. But I quite like it here. Oh, yes, indeed I do. Only when one's been accustomed to something better, if you understand … you do understand? …

CHECCA Oh, I understand … perfectly.

MENEGHINA *(to Rosina)* Now you see what I mean?

ROSINA *(aside to Meneghina)* I'm going to enjoy this!

CHECCA What a beautiful dress you are wearing. You have good taste.

CECILIA You think so? They're merely some old things I used to wear when I was a young girl.

ROSINA You used to go about dressed like that when you were a girl?

CECILIA Why not? Surely you know that the fashion nowadays is set by the young? Why, nowadays fashion no longer allows any distinction between a young girl and a married woman.

ROSINA In our house it does!

MENEGHINA And between my sister-in-law and me, it seems.

CECILIA My dear Signorina Meneghina, if one wishes to appear well-dressed, one needs to have the means to be so.

MENEGHINA Yes, it's quite obvious I haven't the means, isn't it? But if I had I'd save it up for a dowry instead of wasting it on clothes and new apartments. Then people wouldn't say I'd married without a penny to my name! *(aside)* And you can make what you like of that!

CECILIA *(aside)* The little wretch. I'll make her pay for that! *(to Checca)* How do you amuse yourselves? Do you go to the theatre? Do you entertain much?

CHECCA When my husband is in Venice we go to the Opera or to see a comedy once or twice a week. But as he is not here at the moment, we stay at home.

CECILIA If you would care to use one of my boxes, do let me know and I will let you have the keys. I have a box at all the theatres, you know. And please do borrow my gondola, if you wish.

CHECCA Thank you very much! But I really do not go anywhere when my husband is not here.

CECILIA And when your husband is here, you always want him with you?

CHECCA If he wishes.

CECILIA But how embarrassing for the poor man. One should have a little pity on one's husband, I always think. Let him do what he wants and go where he wants, that's what I say. I mean to say – if one can't even go to the theatre without one's husband – well! What can one do!

CHECCA Oh, I do not mind. If my husband cannot come with me, I had just as soon stay at home.

CECILIA *(aside)* What a fool!

MENEGHINA *(aside to Rosina)* Did you ever hear such cant and humbug?

ROSINA *(aside to Meneghina)* Yes, I do see what you mean now.

MENEGHINA *(aside to Rosina)* Yet my brother doesn't seem to notice such things.

ROSINA *(aside to Meneghina)* If her husband puts up with it, good luck to her.

CECILIA And at home here, what do you do? Play games?

CHECCA Occasionally we amuse ourselves.

CECILIA What do you play?

CHECCA Cards. Snap and beggar-my-neighbour.[9]

CECILIA But how boring. We play bridge of course. You must come and join us one evening. You will find the company and the conversation quite distinguished. We are never less than fourteen to sixteen at table. Oh, yes, we have people in to dine nearly every evening. Four or five chickens, salted tongue, or some truffles, or some good fish. Of course I have a wine cellar, which you will find is something quite, quite out of the ordinary.

ROSINA *(aside to Meneghina)* Divide all that by three!

MENEGHINA *(aside to Rosina)* By five at least!

CHECCA You enjoy yourself most fashionably.

CECILIA What can you expect? It is how I was brought up.

ROSINA Now that she is with you, the Signorina Meneghina must be enjoying herself as well.

MENEGHINA Oh, yes, I enjoy myself. Confined to my room.

CECILIA I'm sorry your room here doesn't provide what your room at your old house did.

MENEGHINA What d'you mean by that?

CECILIA Oh, nothing! Did you think I don't know? That my husband hasn't told me everything?

MENEGHINA Well, what about it? Why shouldn't I want to get married?

CHECCA Dear Signora Cecilia, if she is in love, she deserves our sympathy. After all, you have yourself, and so have I.

CECILIA Being in love is one matter; being in love with a good-for-nothing wastrel is quite another matter. My husband has told me she is infatuated with some loathsome creature who has neither rank nor position. A certain Lorenzino Bigoletti. Some foppish little upstart with no money and no education. Can you really imagine that I, a person such as I am, could put up with a relation of that sort?

MENEGHINA *(aside to Rosina)* Well! Did you hear that!

ROSINA *(aside to Meneghina)* If Lorenzino hears her, heaven help us!

CHECCA Tell me, Signora Cecilia, are you acquainted with him? With this Lorenzino Bigoletti?

CECILIA I most certainly am not. From what I have been told, he is completely undeserving of the hand of my husband's sister.

CHECCA Well, I do not claim he is wealthy. But he is certainly a gentleman. He comes from a family whose reputation is quite irreproachable. Nor have any of his relatives ever worn a tradesman's apron.

CECILIA What *are* you talking about, Signora Checca? I think my family is well enough known in this city.

CHECCA Oh, did you think I was meaning you?

CECILIA Who did you mean then?

CHECCA Shall we let sleeping dogs lie?

CECILIA Why are you getting so heated about this disgusting person?

CHECCA In what way is he a disgusting person? If I am getting heated, as you put it, it is because he is a respectable young man who is as well-educated as you, and who, moreover, happens to be my cousin.

CECILIA *(rising)* Your cousin?

ROSINA Yes, Signora, he is our cousin. And he is a good young man, and we don't like anybody saying such things about him.

MENEGHINA *(aside)* Brava!

CECILIA Now I see why you've been making up to me! Why you were in such a hurry to visit me! *(to Meneghina)* This young man has found a fine go-between for you, Sister-in-law!

CHECCA Just what does that mean? Who do you think you are speaking to?

CECILIA Not having met you before, I took you to be persons of some respectability. I am sorry to find myself mistaken. I bid you good day. As for you, I can't order you to come home, but I'll have you told to by somebody who can. And you can get out of your head all idea of marrying this blackguard. Because I won't have it! And when I say I won't have a thing that's final! I happen to be somebody in this city and I have influence. Do you understand me? Goodbye. *(exit Cecilia)*

Scene 10[10]

Checca, Meneghina, and Rosina, followed by Lorenzino.

MENEGHINA Did you ever hear such a tongue!

ROSINA But she must be quite mad!

CHECCA I don't know how I contained myself. If she hadn't been in my house, she would never have got away with that!

LORENZINO Cousin, for your sake, I've kept quiet till I was nearly bursting. But, by heavens, nobody's going to call me names like that!

ROSINA You heard her, then?

LORENZINO I'm not deaf, am I?

MENEGHINA But it doesn't worry me, my dear.

CHECCA Nevertheless, you will oblige me, Signorina Meneghina, if you will kindly go home. Never before has there been such a scene in my house. And I do not want it ever to happen again.

LORENZINO But it's not her fault!

CHECCA And you get out of here as well.

LORENZINO That's just what I'm going to do! To find this Signor Anzoletto and beat him to pulp!

MENEGHINA *(loudly)* Oh, what shall I do!

ROSINA Are you mad?

CHECCA That's enough. Stop your nonsense and get out.

LORENZINO *(striding up and down furiously)* Me, loathsome! Me, disgusting! Me, an upstart! Upstart herself! That's all she is! What's that husband of hers? What was his family? Grocers! Greasy-handed grocers!

MENEGHINA Oh, please – may I have a glass of water?

ROSINA Of course! I'll get a glass at once. *(to herself, as she goes to the door)* Poor girl, she'll have me crying too. *(exit Rosina)*

LORENZINO *(also going towards the door)* Yes, I'll go out on the balcony, and if I see her I'll tell her what I think of her!

MENEGHINA Don't!

CHECCA Come back here!

MENEGHINA Please!

CHECCA Listen to me!

LORENZINO I'm warning you, Cousin, you see what a state I'm in. Don't push me to something desperate.

MENEGHINA Please, Signora Checca, have pity on him.

CHECCA But what is it you want me to do? Do you want me to expose myself to more insults? Do you want my husband to come home and find me quarrelling with my neighbours?

MENEGHINA But you're different. You're sensible and kind. Oh, please try and think of something.

ROSINA *(entering carrying a glass of water)* Here is some water.

MENEGHINA Thank you.

CHECCA *(to Meneghina)* But how can you marry without a dowry?

ROSINA Do you want this water?

MENEGHINA *(to Rosina)* Just a minute. If you would speak to my uncle, I'm sure he would help us.

LORENZINO *(to Meneghina)* Why don't you go and see him yourself?

ROSINA Do you want this water?

MENEGHINA *(to Rosina)* In a moment. My brother won't let me go, and I'm frightened of what he might do.

CHECCA Very well, my dear. I know Signor Cristofolo. You would like me to ask him to come and see me, is that it?

MENEGHINA Oh, if you only would!

ROSINA Do you want it or don't you?

MENEGHINA *(distractedly)* Want what? Oh, I am so sorry: I don't know what I'm doing. *(she takes the glass in her hand)* Dear Signora Checca, that would be marvellous! Oh, it would be wonderful! *(as she speaks she begins to upset the water)* Ask him to call. You speak to him. Then you can send for me as well.

CHECCA My dear girl, you are spilling that water all over my dress!

MENEGHINA *(gulping the water while speaking)* Oh dear! I just don't know what I'm doing.

ROSINA *(aside)* She *is* in a bad way!

MENEGHINA Listen ... his house is ... on the other side of the Canal ... on the Gaffaro ... three bridges away ... near San Pantaleone.

CHECCA I know very well where he lives. He is a friend of my husband's. I will send a message asking him to call.

MENEGHINA Now – right away?

CHECCA I shall send at once. And now you can thank me by getting back downstairs again.

MENEGHINA Of course, Signora! I do thank you! And you, Signorina Rosina. Goodbye, Lorenzino. You will tell him everything, won't you? That I'm quite desperate? And you won't forget to ask him to call? Goodbye, dear Lorenzino. *(exit Meneghina)*

ROSINA Well, Cousin, you've cooked your goose now!

LORENZINO My dear Cousin ...

CHECCA You ought at least to offer to go yourself and ask Signor Cristofolo to call here.

LORENZINO Good heavens, yes! I'll run all the way!
CHECCA You know where he lives?
LORENZINO Do I? What d'you think!
CHECCA Off with you, then.
LORENZINO Right away!
ROSINA What a child he is!
CHECCA What a nuisance.
ROSINA Love can make a fool of anybody! *(exit Rosina)*
CHECCA Only if one's a fool to begin with!

Scene 11

Anzoletto's new apartment, as in Act One. Anzoletto enters, followed by Sgualdo with his workmen.

ANZOLETTO All my property at the old house sequestrated! Everything seized until I find the money to pay all these debts. Nobody will lend me any money. Nobody will even act as guarantor. I'm smothered in debts, and I've not one person to turn to. And now here are these workmen wanting their money. Not to mention a wife who thinks I can afford to buy her the whole world. If only I hadn't upset my uncle, I wouldn't be in this situation! He wouldn't lift his little finger to help me now, even if I were dying. And all because I got married. What on earth did I want to get married for! What a fool I was! What an absolute idiot! Yet who'd have thought you could regret it so soon? It's only a fortnight …
SGUALDO Right, Signore! I've come for the money.
ANZOLETTO Didn't I tell you tomorrow?
SGUALDO Yes, you told me tomorrow, but the men say now. *(aside)* Now I know the trouble he's in.
ANZOLETTO But you've done nothing to this room. It's the same as it was before. You haven't even moved the bed in.
SGUALDO The bed's not here because I was told not to move it.
ANZOLETTO *(furiously)* Who the devil told you that?
SGUALDO Her Excellency your wife did.
ANZOLETTO Oh … well … as long as I know.
SGUALDO So you'd best settle these bills now.
ANZOLETTO I'll settle them tomorrow.
SGUALDO These men won't wait.

ANZOLETTO Won't they, by heavens! They will when I get my stick to them!

SGUALDO There's no need to lose your temper. These men have carried out your orders. And they don't expect blows from your stick as their wages.

ANZOLETTO All right, I'll pay you before this evening. Is that good enough for you?

SGUALDO Very good. As long as you do.

ANZOLETTO You have my word.

SGUALDO Be sure you keep it. Because you don't get rid of us this evening if you don't. Come on. *(they go out)*

Scene 12

Anzoletto and Prosdocimo.

ANZOLETTO If I have them stuck here it will be the end. I can't even raise any money now on all my things at the old house.

PROSDOCIMO Anybody there?

ANZOLETTO Who is it? What d'you want?

PROSDOCIMO I am looking for Signor Anzoletto [Semolini.]

ANZOLETTO I am he. What is it you want?

PROSDOCIMO I pay my most humble respects to your Illustrious Excellency on behalf of my master the Count [Argagni], who has asked me to inform your Illustrious Excellency that you owe two months' rent on this apartment, that he has already made six applications for payment – this being the seventh – that you agreed to pay the first quarter in advance, and that he requests you to pay this immediately, at once, and without further delay. Otherwise, he regrets that he will be obliged to take certain steps of which Your Excellency will be notified in due course.

ANZOLETTO Illustrious Signore, I find you most tedious.

PROSDOCIMO It is too kind of your Illustrious Excellency to say so.

ANZOLETTO Tell your master that I will have the matter attended to tomorrow.

PROSDOCIMO If your Illustrious Excellency will pardon me, may I ask something? This "tomorrow" of which Your Excellency speaks, how many times does it come in a month?

ANZOLETTO Very funny! Come tomorrow, and you will be paid.

PROSDOCIMO If your Illustrious Excellency will pardon me, does your Excellency remember how many times he has said to me: "tomorrow"?

ANZOLETTO You have my word you will be paid.

PROSDOCIMO If your Illustrious Excellency will ...

ANZOLETTO Will you and your Illustrious Excellency get the hell out of here!

PROSDOCIMO *(going towards the door)* I am your Illustrious Excellency's most humble servant.

ANZOLETTO At your service.

PROSDOCIMO *(as above)* My salutations to Your Excellency.

ANZOLETTO Yours to command.

PROSDOCIMO Your Excellency's most humble servant. *(exit Prosdocimo)*

ANZOLETTO That makes everything perfect! Never a dull filament! I only need my wife and my sister to come in now. Yes, where can they be? Oh, well, they'll come when they will. If only they wouldn't!

Scene 13

Enter *Lucietta.*

LUCIETTA Oh, good heavens, he's back already!

ANZOLETTO What d'you want?

LUCIETTA When's all this moving going to finish? When will the things be here?

ANZOLETTO They're coming. Be patient and they'll be here.

LUCIETTA It's dinner-time now!

ANZOLETTO What's that to do with it?

LUCIETTA Well, d'you want to sit down at table with no table linen?

ANZOLETTO *(aside)* Here we go again. *(to Lucietta)* Can't you manage somehow or other just for today?

LUCIETTA I suppose I could use some hand towels.

ANZOLETTO But you can't make tablecloths out of hand towels, can you?

LUCIETTA They're all very worn and torn but I suppose that doesn't matter.

ANZOLETTO Well, can't you cut them up and make them into table napkins?

LUCIETTA Are you trying to make a fool of me, as well? Your wife's got to be pleased at all costs! That's it, isn't it? Well, I'm sorry for my young mistress, but I can't do more than I am doing. You just give me the seven months' wages you owe me and try managing without me. *(exit Lucietta)*

ANZOLETTO *(to himself)* What did I say? They're all at it. I mention napkins and she flies into a temper and demands her wages. Everybody's allowed to be sensitive and thin-skinned except me! I've got to put up with being treated any way they please! But everybody else – oh, no, *they* can't put up with the least little thing!

Scene 14

Enter *Cecilia, followed by Meneghina, followed by Fabrizio.*

CECILIA Husband, I've news for you.
ANZOLETTO Now what's happened?
CECILIA That sister of yours is a little liar!
MENEGHINA Brother, this wife of yours is an almighty snob!
CECILIA Either she leaves this house or I do! *(exit Cecilia)*
MENEGHINA It's I who'll be leaving! And when you least expect it! *(exit Meneghina)*
ANZOLETTO They're all at it! Of all the back-biting, beastly, vixenish …
FABRIZIO Here I am! In time for dinner!
ANZOLETTO And to hell with you as well! *(exit Anzoletto)*
FABRIZIO Thank you. It is really most kind of you. Most kind … *(exit Fabrizio)*

ACT THREE

Scene I

A room in Signora Checca's apartment. Enter *Checca, followed by Rosina.*

CHECCA It's what I've always said, the least spark can set the whole house aflame. Some people just can't help making mountains out of molehills. My harmless curiosity about these people and their new apartment has caused all this trouble. Well, they won't find me bothering myself over them again, that's certain. All the same I can't help feeling sorry for my cousin. And for that poor girl as well.
ROSINA Sister!
CHECCA Now what is it?

ROSINA That servant from downstairs, Lucietta, has been making signs from her balcony. I think she wants to speak to me.

CHECCA Well?

ROSINA Well, I've pulled the cord to open the door and told her to come up.

CHECCA You shouldn't have! We're not having anything more to do with those people!

ROSINA But you said Signorina Meneghina could call again.

CHECCA If her uncle comes, I will let her come up just that once. But never again, you understand. I want no more trouble with those people. Is that quite clear?

ROSINA Why speak to me like this? It's nothing to do with me.

CHECCA And I don't want any more familiarity from that servant.

ROSINA But what can I do now? I've opened the door. I won't open it another time. Do you want me to send her away?

CHECCA No, no. We'll hear what she wants.

ROSINA I did hear some shouting. I am curious to know what it was about.

CHECCA My dear Sister, you must moderate this curiosity. What good is it to you to know what others do? If Lucietta is coming here merely to gossip, let us cut her short and not allow ourselves to listen to her.

ROSINA Very well. I will do as you wish.

Scene 2

Enter *Lucietta, followed by Toni.*

LUCIETTA Good evening, Signore!

CHECCA Good evening.

ROSINA Good evening, Lucietta.

LUCIETTA I've managed to escape for a moment. Nobody knows. I simply had to tell you. Things are happening down there!

ROSINA Yes, go on!

CHECCA *(to Rosina)* Remember what I told you!

ROSINA *(to Checca)* But what have I said now?

LUCIETTA Have you something against me? What have I done?

CHECCA I don't want any gossiping here.

LUCIETTA I'm sorry, I only came to tell you … but if you don't want to hear … *(she goes towards the door.)*

CHECCA Come here. What is it you want to tell me?

ROSINA *(aside)* My sister's even more curious!

LUCIETTA I only wanted to tell you in confidence what's just happened, but if you think I've only come to gossip …

CHECCA Come, come, if you've anything to confide in me …

LUCIETTA Such things have been happening, you'd never believe!

CHECCA What things?

LUCIETTA My master's desperate! He can't move in from the old house. They've put seals on all his things there. He can't even pay the rent for the new apartment. And the workmen are demanding their money. And I've seen nothing myself of my wages for the last seven months. Oh, things are in a bad way all right.

CHECCA They are indeed!

ROSINA This is terrible!

CHECCA What has that fool of a wife of his got to say about it?

ROSINA And his poor sister.

LUCIETTA My mistress is crying. The new wife's raging like a fury.

CHECCA Tell me: how has he got into debt like this?

LUCIETTA Through trying to show off and by indulging the whims of that precious wife of his.

CHECCA But he's been married only a fortnight …

LUCIETTA Oh, Signora, you don't know the half of it. He was running after her for two years, ruining himself trying to please her.

ROSINA Yet she brought him no dowry?

LUCIETTA Absolutely nothing.

CHECCA So that's the sort of fine lady she is, then?

LUCIETTA She is that. Do you know, a servant who used to work in her parents' house told me she often had to pawn their gold bracelets to buy food for them.

ROSINA This servant left them?

LUCIETTA Yes, because they weren't even paying her. Oh, servants are not all like me, Signora. I haven't been paid for seven months but I've not said a word.

ROSINA *(aside)* Oh, yes, you're a pearl you are!

TONI Signora, somebody is asking for you.

CHECCA Who is it?

TONI It's an old man. Signor Lorenzino is with him.

ROSINA It must be Signor Cristofolo.

LUCIETTA My mistress's uncle?

CHECCA Yes, that's who it must be. Now listen carefully. Go downstairs, take Signorina Meneghina on one side, and tell her to come up here to me.

LUCIETTA Yes, Signora, I'll go at once.

CHECCA But take great care nobody hears you.

LUCIETTA *(going towards the door)* Leave it to me.

ROSINA And don't tell anyone else, either!

LUCIETTA *(as above)* What a thing to say! As if I'd breathe a word!

CHECCA Make sure you don't. This is something very important.

LUCIETTA Well, really, Signora. You're mistaken if you think I'm some sort of gossiping tittle-tattler. I know how to keep my mouth shut, when needed. Nobody will get a word out of me. *(exit Lucietta)*

CHECCA *(to Toni)* Ask this gentleman to come in. And tell Signor Lorenzino to wait outside.

TONI Yes, Signora. *(exit Toni)*

Scene 3

Checca and Rosina, followed by Cristofolo.

CHECCA And you, also, if you don't mind. While I am speaking to Signor Cristofolo, it will be best if you are not here.

ROSINA But I'd so much like to listen!

CHECCA I can see that. You're bursting with curiosity.

ROSINA And I suppose you're not?

CHECCA I listen only to what I ought to listen to.

ROSINA Well, I certainly don't want to hear what I oughtn't to hear. *(exit Rosina)*

CRISTOFOLO Pleasure to meet you again, Signora.

CHECCA And for me to meet you, Signor Cristofolo. Yes, indeed!

CRISTOFOLO Now, now, none of that. No need for flatteries with me, dear lady.

CHECCA Surely I may welcome you here?

CRISTOFOLO You may. But there's no need for lah-di-dah compliments. Can't stand 'em. I'm a straightforward man. Say what I think. Always have done. As for all these modern compliments, you can have 'em, as far as I'm concerned.

CHECCA As you wish. *(aside)* He's certainly one of the old school. *(aloud)* I hope I have not put you to any inconvenience?

CRISTOFOLO Well, I'm here, aren't I? At your service, ma'am. Command me, and if I'm able, it'll be done.

CHECCA Sit down, then.

CRISTOFOLO Certainly. How's your husband, Signor Fortunato? When d'you expect him back?

CHECCA I received a letter from him only yesterday. He should be here by the end of the week.

CRISTOFOLO Yes, he could arrive on Friday by the Bologna coach.

CHECCA If you only knew how I miss him. I can't wait to see him again.

CRISTOFOLO Ay, those who've got good husbands always want them with them, don't they, eh?

CHECCA I seem lost without him. I have no desire to go anywhere or do anything.

CRISTOFOLO Just as it should be. Respectable married ladies don't go gadding about without their husbands.

CHECCA *(aside)* How on earth am I to begin?

CRISTOFOLO Well then, Signora Checca, what can I do for you?

CHECCA My dear Signore, I beg that you will pardon me if you should consider I am taking a liberty, or that I am presuming upon our friendship.

CRISTOFOLO There's no need to stand on ceremony with me. I'm a good friend of your husband's. Ask me whatever it is you want and don't beat about the bush.

CHECCA Will you permit me to speak to you about a certain person?

CRISTOFOLO Who?

CHECCA A certain person.

CRISTOFOLO So long as it's not my nephew, you can speak of whom you please.

CHECCA Oh, I don't concern myself with your nephew's affairs!

CRISTOFOLO Well, how was I to know? I know the young scoundrel's come to live below you here. It seemed quite likely you wanted to speak to me about him, and thought I mightn't come if I knew.

CHECCA Oh, a gentleman such as yourself would never do that.

CRISTOFOLO That's what you think. I've had more than I can stomach of that damn fool.

CHECCA And his sister, poor child?

CRISTOFOLO His sister's as big a fool as he is. When her mother died I offered to give her a home with me, and she wouldn't come. Preferred to stay with her brother. Thought she'd have more freedom. Thought she'd have to go to bed too early at her old uncle's. No, that young scatterbrain deserves all she gets. She's made her bed, so let her lie on it.

CHECCA But if you only knew what trouble the poor girl's in!

CRISTOFOLO I know all about it. You think I don't, eh? Let me tell you there's nothing I don't know about those two. I know her brother's in debt up to his eyes. I know that in two years he's got through ten thousand ducats running after that precious wife of his. She's the one who's ruined him. Ever since he started going to that blasted house of hers he's never been the same. He had no time for me any more. Couldn't even come and see me. If he saw me in the street he'd go out of his way to avoid me. I wasn't well enough dressed for him. I didn't wear lace on my cuffs. Oh, I know it all. I even know what that trumped-up aristocrat of a strumpet of his says about me. I upset her stomach! I'm a disgrace to her! She couldn't bear to call me Uncle! Let her wait till I call her my niece! That'll be the day! The little shrew! Scum! Riff-raff! That's all she is!

CHECCA *(aside)* I'd have done better to have said nothing!

CRISTOFOLO I beg your pardon. I get a little annoyed when I think of it. What was it you were wanting to say to me?

CHECCA But my dear Signor Cristofolo, how is that poor young girl to blame for it all?

CRISTOFOLO Look, my dear Signora Checca, suppose you put your cards on the table? What is it you want to see me about?

CHECCA A certain matter.

CRISTOFOLO Concerning yourself?

CHECCA You could say so. It concerns a cousin of mine.

CRISTOFOLO So long as it concerns you or one of your family, you've only to ask. As long as it's nothing to do with that nephew of mine.

CHECCA And his sister?

CRISTOFOLO *(loudly and angrily)* And her as well!

CHECCA *(aside)* Oh, dear! *(aloud)* Well, as I was saying, I wanted to speak to you about my cousin.

CRISTOFOLO Who is he?

CHECCA He is the young man who went to call on you for me.

CRISTOFOLO Oh, him!

CHECCA You know him?

CRISTOFOLO Never set eyes on him before.

CHECCA He has not long been out of college.

CRISTOFOLO Well he must know me. Found me in the Rialto, stopped me, and brought me along here.

CHECCA Oh, yes, he certainly knows you.

CRISTOFOLO Well, what's he after? What's he want?

CHECCA What did you think of him?

CRISTOFOLO Seemed quite a respectable young fellow.

CHECCA Oh, he is! He's a fine young man!

CRISTOFOLO Yes, quite a pleasant young fellow. What's he do? Got a job?

CHECCA He's looking for one.

CRISTOFOLO Well, I've some influence. Friends, you know. Could be of use to him.

CHECCA Oh, that would be wonderful!

CRISTOFOLO Is this what you asked me to call for?

CHECCA Yes, it was for this as well.

CRISTOFOLO And for what else?

CHECCA Well, I'll tell you. The young man wants to marry.

CRISTOFOLO What is he? An infant prodigy? He's not stopped growing yet, and he wants to get married? He's got no job, yet he wants to raise a family? No, no! I don't think much of him, then. He's gone down in my estimation.

CHECCA *(aside)* Now I'm in a real pickle! *(aloud)* But supposing he finds a young lady with a good dowry?

CRISTOFOLO They take some finding …

CHECCA And is able to buy himself a good position somewhere?

CRISTOFOLO In that case …

CHECCA In that case he wouldn't be doing badly.

CRISTOFOLO In that case he'd have no need of me.

CHECCA But that's just why he would have need of you.

CRISTOFOLO Of me? I don't understand you.

CHECCA *(aside)* This is where I put my foot in it!

CRISTOFOLO *(aside)* She's got me so mixed up I don't know what the hell she's talking about.

CHECCA Signor Cristofolo, don't you really think my cousin might be able to find a respectable young girl with a reasonable dowry?

CRISTOFOLO Has he got any income of his own?

CHECCA He has a little – and then if he obtained a good position …

CRISTOFOLO All right, Signora, I'll agree with you. He's a presentable young fellow and he'll find a young lady.

CHECCA Tell me, dear friend, if you yourself had a daughter, would you give her to him?

CRISTOFOLO I'm not married; I've got no daughter; so there's no point in answering a damn silly question.

CHECCA Then tell me, dear friend – your niece, would you give her to him?

CRISTOFOLO Signora Checca, I'm not blind and I'm not deaf. I see what you're after. And I must say I'm surprised at you. I told you I didn't want to hear or to speak about those two. And so if there's nothing more I can do for you, I'll say good day! *(he gets up)*

CHECCA But listen.

CRISTOFOLO I don't want to hear any more!

CHECCA I'm not saying any more.

CRISTOFOLO I don't want to hear or speak another word about those two.

CHECCA Not even about your niece?

CRISTOFOLO I have no niece!

Scene 4

Enter *Meneghina.*

MENEGHINA Oh, Uncle!

CRISTOFOLO *(to Meneghina)* What d'you mean by this! *(to Checca)* What way's this to trick me?

CHECCA Trick you? What way's that to speak? Anybody would think you were being robbed! Whether you like it or not, this young lady is your niece. She's been let down badly by her brother, and she's very very miserable about it all. And when a young girl becomes desperate there's no knowing what she might do. When she has a rich uncle like you, he should feel honour bound to find her a husband and help her to live in a manner commensurate with his own dignity. If you don't like hearing the truth, that's too bad. Out of kind-heartedness I have tried to help this poor child. As for you – you can do as you please![11]

CRISTOFOLO Have you quite finished?

CHECCA I'll finish when I want to! If I want to go on I could tell you a few more home truths.

CRISTOFOLO You needn't trouble. I've heard enough, and I've understood enough. *(to Meneghina)* Well, Miss, what is it you expect from me?

MENEGHINA Dear Uncle, I don't expect anything from you! Why should I? I'm only a poor girl who's had a lot of bad luck. By ruining his own life, my brother has also ruined mine.

CRISTOFOLO Then why didn't you come and live with me?

MENEGHINA Because I acted foolishly. Because I let myself be influenced by my brother. Dear Uncle, I ask your forgiveness!

CHECCA Well? You must be made of stone if you're not moved by that.

CRISTOFOLO *(to Checca)* Pity, Signora, is a good thing, a fine thing. But you should keep it for those who deserve it. And not waste it on those who abuse it.

MENEGHINA Oh, what will become of me? If you don't help me I'll find myself without a roof over my head one of these days. I won't even have a pillow to lie on!

CRISTOFOLO What are you talking about? Are you out of your mind? Hasn't your brother just rented this exclusive apartment downstairs? And paying sixty ducats more than he need for it?

MENEGHINA Yes, you are right to shame me so. The apartment is far beyond what he can afford. And he hasn't paid any of the rent yet. And tomorrow they're putting all our things out into the street!

CRISTOFOLO So that's what it's come to, is it?

MENEGHINA And they've put seals on the furniture that is still in the other house! And I haven't even a dress to go out in!

CHECCA Did you ever hear anything more pitiful?

CRISTOFOLO What's that wife of your brother's got to say about all this?

MENEGHINA I've no idea, Signore. I only know that on top of everything else I've to endure her wicked jibes and insults.

CRISTOFOLO What's that? She's had the damned nerve to insult you?

CHECCA I can vouch for that! She treats her most unkindly.

CRISTOFOLO *(aside)* Blood's thicker than water, after all. I'm sorry for the girl. *(aloud)* Well, Miss, what d'you think you can do about it?

MENEGHINA Whatever you wish, Uncle. Here I am, kneeling to you. Please help me.

CRISTOFOLO *(takes out his handkerchief and wipes his eyes)*

CHECCA *(aside)* At last we're getting somewhere!

CRISTOFOLO Get up, get up! You don't deserve it, but I'll see if I can help you. Well? What were you thinking of doing?

MENEGHINA Oh, thank you, thank you! I'll do anything you say!

CHECCA My dear Signor Cristofolo, she wants to get married. So why don't you help her to marry the young man?

CRISTOFOLO Who is he?

CHECCA He is my cousin.

CRISTOFOLO Can he support her?

CHECCA He has a little money of his own – enough to buy himself a position.

CRISTOFOLO All right, but I'll have to have a talk with him first.

CHECCA Would you like us to call him in?

CRISTOFOLO Why, where is he?

CHECCA Outside.

CRISTOFOLO I see! He's outside, is he? He comes to fetch me here and now he's hiding outside waiting to be called in. So that's been your little game! Everything all arranged to trick me into doing what you want me to do! All right! I've heard enough. You'll get nothing from me. I don't want to hear another word about it! *(exit Cristofolo)*

CHECCA We'll see about that! He's not leaving here until he agrees to help you! *(exit Checca)*

Scene 5

Meneghina, followed by Rosina.

MENEGHINA Oh, poor me!

ROSINA Don't give up hope, Signorina Meneghina.

MENEGHINA But what can I do?

ROSINA I heard everything you said, and if you keep on at him I know you'll be all right. Throw yourself on your knees, weep, show him you're desperate. Lorenzino begs you. He's nearly dying, poor boy, because he can't do anything!

MENEGHINA Oh, poor Lorenzino! Yes! I'll do anything for him. I'll go and plead and plead with my uncle! I'll throw myself on the ground at his feet! *(exit Meneghina)*

ROSINA That's more like it! When we women really want something we don't do things by halves! And tears are our best weapon! *(exit Rosina)*

Scene 6

Anzoletto's new apartment. Cecilia, Count, and Fabrizio.

COUNT Come, Signora, one must not abandon oneself to melancholy like this!

CECILIA Oh, yes, Count! It's easy enough for those who are not in trouble to be full of polite, consoling words! Have patience! Don't worry! But this time it's I who's got to have patience! *(she throws herself into a chair)*

FABRIZIO The proverb says: there's a remedy for everything except a broken neck.

CECILIA Oh, what a fool I've been! What an idiot! I could have married into the best families in the town. I could have been covered with gold from head to foot. And here I am burdened with a man who wants to drag me down into the mud!

COUNT You will see, things aren't as bad as they seem.

FABRIZIO Yes, I am quite sure everything will be all right.

COUNT After all, a few debts! What are they?

CECILIA *(she gets up)* And yet I can almost pity that poor husband of mine. He lets his friends eat him out of house and home, yet when he's in trouble not one of them will help him. *(walking up and down)*

FABRIZIO *(softly to the Count)* That's one for you.

COUNT *(softly to Fabrizio)* For you, you mean.

CECILIA For this to happen to a woman like me! Brought up in luxury as I was! Waited on like a princess! Respected like a queen! *(she throws herself into another chair)*

COUNT The Signora Cecilia will always be respected and waited upon.

CECILIA *(she gets up)* Ah, my dear Count, when you can no longer offer them a meal, few people will put themselves to the trouble of visiting you. *(walks up and down)*

COUNT *(aside, to Fabrizio)* It's you she means now.

FABRIZIO *(aside, to the Count)* Both of us, more likely.

CECILIA But where the devil is Signor Anzoletto? Is he keeping out of the way and leaving me to face everything on my own? By heavens, I'll see they don't touch a thing of mine! *(walks up and down)*

COUNT Signora, I would advise you to take out an insurance on your dowry.

CECILIA How does one do that?

FABRIZIO We will arrange it if you wish.

COUNT Yes, we will go and do what is necessary.

CECILIA All right. You can at least do this little thing for me.

FABRIZIO We will need to show the legal document concerning your dowry.

CECILIA Is that necessary?

COUNT Certainly. One always has to produce the contract. Whatever the circumstances.

CECILIA No, I don't want it to be said I helped to ruin my husband. And anyway, nobody in my family ever stooped to do such a thing, and I won't either. *(walks up and down)*

FABRIZIO *(aside to the Count)* Didn't you know she had no dowry?

COUNT *(aside to Fabrizio)* I knew it better than you!

CECILIA And where's my sister-in-law got to? Has she gone? Has she abandoned me as well? Where are they all? Why are they leaving me here all on my own? Are they trying to make me do something desperate? *(she sits)*

COUNT But, Signora, we are here!

FABRIZIO We are both here! Whatever happens, we will not abandon you.

COUNT For heaven's sake, Signora, take courage.

FABRIZIO It's three hours past dinner time. Don't you think you should eat something?

CECILIA I've other things to think of than eating. The thought of food's enough to poison me.

COUNT Very well. Eat something a little later. When you feel like it.

FABRIZIO But we will stay. We will not leave you. Not like all those others who came to dine with you and left as quick as they could when they heard how things were. Ah, no! We are true friends of the Signora Cecilia.

COUNT But dear lady, I urge you not to let your health suffer by not partaking of a little nourishment.

FABRIZIO Would you like me to tell the cook to prepare a little chocolate?

CECILIA *(getting up irritably)* I don't want anything! How could my husband treat me like this! Hiding everything from me! Pretending he was rolling in money! Making himself out to be what he wasn't! How dare he treat me like this! The lying villain! *(she throws herself into a chair)*

COUNT Do not distress yourself too much, Signora.

FABRIZIO Our presence perhaps is disturbing you?

Scene 7

Enter *Anzoletto.*

ANZOLETTO *(aside)* Oh, my poor wife!

CECILIA *(jumping to her feet and rushing furiously towards Anzoletto)* Get out of here! Don't come anywhere near me!

ANZOLETTO *(holding out a knife to her)* Take it! Go on! Take this knife and kill me!

CECILIA *(taking the knife and hurling it from her)* You brainless – irresponsible – fool!

ANZOLETTO Oh, my dear Wife, you see what a state I'm in! Everybody is against me, but surely you will have pity on me. If I've got into debt, you know it was for your sake …

CECILIA What's that? You dare to say you've got into debt on my account! What have you ever spent on me? What jewels have you ever given me? What've you ever bought for me except a few dresses – and this cursed apartment on which you've not even paid any rent yet? Come on! Tell me! Just what have you spent on me? What debts have I made you make?

ANZOLETTO None, none, you are quite right, my dear. I've done nothing for you. I've spent nothing on you. I've simply been throwing all my money into the canal just for the fun of it.

CECILIA And don't you take that tone to me! Don't say another word, d'you hear?

ANZOLETTO No, my dear, I won't say another word. *(aside)* What's the use?

COUNT *(aside to Fabrizio)* He'll need all the patience he's got, poor fellow.

FABRIZIO *(aside to the Count)* He must know what she's like by now.

ANZOLETTO Where is my sister?

CECILIA How should I know? I've not set eyes on her for two hours.

ANZOLETTO I only hope she hasn't gone there.

CECILIA Gone where?

ANZOLETTO To my uncle's.

CECILIA If that's where she's gone, then she's shown some sense. And you'd better go as well.

ANZOLETTO I? That's one thing I'll never do! Even if I have to go to prison.

CECILIA Anybody in your position has to learn to swallow his pride.

COUNT The Signora is right you know!

CECILIA *(to the Count)* Will you shut up and stop interfering in what doesn't concern you!

FABRIZIO But we are your friends.

CECILIA At times like this one finds out who one's real friends are. Deeds speak louder than words!

COUNT If my presence disturbs you, that can soon be remedied. Signora, Signore, your humble servant. *(exit Count)*

FABRIZIO Yes, indeed. Your most humble and devoted servant. *(exit Fabrizio)*

Scene 8

Cecilia and Anzoletto.

CECILIA You see what sort of friends they are!

ANZOLETTO Why say that to me? It was you brought them here.

CECILIA Don't change the subject! So you're not going to ask your uncle to help you?

ANZOLETTO Ask him? Not likely! Even if I'd the courage, I know what would happen. He'd only fly into a rage and call me all the names he can think of.

CECILIA Perhaps I could speak to him?

ANZOLETTO That wouldn't do any good.

CECILIA Why wouldn't it?

ANZOLETTO Because he can bear the sight of you – even less than he can of me.

CECILIA Oh, I'd be able to calm him down.

ANZOLETTO You calm him down! When you can't even calm yourself down!

CECILIA At least I've enough sense to realize this isn't the time to lose one's head and get all heated.

ANZOLETTO You can get heated with me all right …

CECILIA There you go again! As if things aren't bad enough without you keeping changing the subject, twisting everything so that everybody's to blame except you! Get out of my sight, you cruel beast!

ANZOLETTO All right! I'll not say another word! Go on, then! Do what you like! Go and see him and come to what arrangements you please with him!

CECILIA You come as well.

ANZOLETTO Oh, no! Not me!

CECILIA What a coward you are! Well, make your sister come with me.

ANZOLETTO She may not want to.

CECILIA She'll have to.

ANZOLETTO Well, where is she? Lucietta!

Scene 9

Enter *Lucietta.*

LUCIETTA [*(from inside)*] Yes, Signore?

ANZOLETTO Come here!

LUCIETTA Coming, Signore.

CECILIA It will be best if your sister does come with me because Signor Cristofolo does not know me. He's never seen me. And besides, she can do her bit as well. Leave it to me, I'll tell her what to say on the way.

ANZOLETTO Where is my sister?

LUCIETTA *(confused)* I don't know ...
CECILIA What d'you mean – you don't know?
LUCIETTA *(as above)* No, really, I don't.
ANZOLETTO Look! I want to know where she is!
LUCIETTA All right, I'll tell you, Signore. But don't say that it was me who told you.
ANZOLETTO No, no, I won't say anything.
CECILIA This is going to be interesting.
LUCIETTA She's with the ladies in their apartment upstairs.
CECILIA What's she gone there for?
ANZOLETTO Has she gone to babble everything to them?
LUCIETTA I'll tell you all, Signore, but please don't say anything.
ANZOLETTO Go on, I won't say a word.
LUCIETTA Well! D'you know who's up there?
CECILIA Ah! That lout Lorenzino!
LUCIETTA That's right. But there's somebody else as well.
ANZOLETTO Who?
LUCIETTA Signor Cristofolo.
ANZOLETTO My uncle?
CECILIA His uncle is up there?
LUCIETTA Yes, Signora, but don't let on I told you!
CECILIA *(to Anzoletto)* Quick! Come with me!
ANZOLETTO Where?
CECILIA Come with me, I tell you!
ANZOLETTO I don't want to go up there.
CECILIA Come along, you big baby. And you'll see what sort of a wife you've married. *(she takes him by the arm and pulls him out with her)*
LUCIETTA Now I've gone and done it! But why should I miss all the fun? I'm going up as well. *(exit Lucietta)*

Scene 10

A room in Signora Checca's apartment. Checca, Meneghina, Cristofolo, and Lorenzino.

CHECCA Long life to you, Signor Cristofolo! A long life to your kind heart and your good nature. And may heaven reward you for your goodness to this poor young girl.
MENEGHINA I shall never be able to repay his kindness to me.

LORENZINO Nor I! Everything I value in this world, I shall owe to our dear uncle.

CRISTOFOLO *(to Lorenzino)* Not so fast, young man. I'm not your uncle yet, remember.

CHECCA Oh, come now! They'll be married tomorrow. And then you'll be his uncle.

MENEGHINA Oh, please don't frighten me!

LORENZINO His word is enough for me. A man such as he doesn't go back on his word.

CHECCA Perhaps it might be best to have it all down in black and white?

CRISTOFOLO What I've said, I've said; and what I've said, I keep to. The girl's his. And I'll buy him a position. But before I sign the contract I want to know what's happened to all that her father left. *(to Meneghina)* Your part of your father's estate should have come to you. If your brother's mortgaged it, we'll take him to court if necessary. I'll do all I can. I'll help you with my own money if I've got to. But I don't want to be taken for a fool.

CHECCA I don't know enough about these things to give my opinion, but I'm sure you must be right.

MENEGHINA Oh, dear, what a lot of things have to be done yet!

LORENZINO Can't everything wait until after the marriage?

CRISTOFOLO You're young; you know nothing. Leave it to me.

Scene 11

Enter *Rosina.*

ROSINA Signora Checca, may I have a word with you?

CHECCA Yes, I'll come, my dear. Excuse me, please. *(she goes over to Rosina and they talk in low voices; Checca makes gestures of astonishment)*

MENEGHINA Uncle, where shall I live in the meantime?

CRISTOFOLO You can come to me.

LORENZINO May I come and see her?

CRISTOFOLO You may – when I am there.

MENEGHINA *(aside)* Oh, dear, I'll be too scared to open my mouth in his house.

CHECCA *(aside)* What shall I do? I've succeeded so far, I might as well try and get them settled as well. I feel so sorry for her I couldn't say no. *(aloud)* Signorina Meneghina, do me the kindness to go out to my sister for a little while, will you? I have a matter to discuss with Signor Cristofolo.

MENEGHINA Certainly. *(aside, to Checca)* Make him arrange everything now! *(aside, to herself)* I'm sure she'll do it! *(exit Meneghina with Rosina)*

CHECCA Signor Lorenzino, will you do me a favour?

LORENZINO Of course. At your service, Signora.

CHECCA Go to the post and see if there are any letters from my husband.

LORENZINO You want me to go now?

CHECCA Yes, run along. It's only round the corner. Go, and come back at once.

LORENZINO But won't our uncle be going soon?

CHECCA He won't have gone before you get back.

LORENZINO I'll be back as quick as I can, then. *(exit Lorenzino running)*

Scene 12

Checca and Cristofolo.

CRISTOFOLO Well, I'd better be on my way. I'm not as young as I used to be, and I like having my meals at regular times. Because of all this I haven't had my dinner yet.

CHECCA Dear Signor Cristofolo, since you have been so kind, will you bear with me a little longer? Will you do me a very great favour and listen to somebody who would like to say a few words to you?

CRISTOFOLO Devil take it, if it's my nephew, I won't listen.

CHECCA It is not your nephew.

CRISTOFOLO Who is it then?

CHECCA Now don't get into a temper. It's the young wife of your nephew.

CRISTOFOLO *(irritably)* What does she want with me?

CHECCA I'm afraid I don't know.

CRISTOFOLO All right, damn it, I'll see her. But I won't be held responsible for what I say. If anybody gives me a pain in the neck, she does. So if I tell her what I think of her, don't complain I'm not behaving as I should in your house.

CHECCA In that case, please behave entirely as if you were in your own house. Speak to her just as you please. *(exit Checca)*

Scene 13

Cristofolo, followed by Cecilia.

CRISTOFOLO So! This – lady, who says I upset her stomach, condescends to speak to me! Well, she'll get none of my money, if that's what she's after. A piece of my mind is what she'll get.
CECILIA *(aside)* How I hate having to do this! But it's got to be done!
CRISTOFOLO *(aside)* Ay, ay! Battle stations it is!
CECILIA Your humble servant, Signore.
CRISTOFOLO Y' servant, Signora.
CECILIA Would you do me the honour of allowing me to pay you my respects?
CRISTOFOLO Y' servant, Signora.
CECILIA Would you do me the great honour of allowing me to seat myself by you?
CRISTOFOLO Ay, sit, if you wish. *(jumps to his feet and moves away)*
CECILIA Why do you move away?
CRISTOFOLO Because you don't like the smell of the bacon from my shop.
CECILIA Dear sir, please do not make me drain my cup of misery to the dregs. Be kind enough to sit here.
CRISTOFOLO No. You see, I don't want to upset your stomach.
CECILIA Oh, my dear Uncle …
CRISTOFOLO Where d'you get this "dear Uncle" from? *(turns as if bitten by a snake)*
CECILIA Don't raise your voice; we mustn't make fools of ourselves here. I have not come here to make trouble. I have not come here to ask you for anything. I have come to humiliate myself in front of you. And even if you think such a gesture cannot be disinterested – and despite all the reasons you can have for disliking me – when a lady humiliates herself, pleads, and begs for forgiveness, any gentleman would subdue his resentment and listen to her. I ask nothing from you – I deserve nothing – only that you listen to me. Will you show me that courtesy?
CRISTOFOLO You can talk your head off, Signora, for all I care. Go ahead. I can wait. *(aside)* Then I can take her to pieces bit by bit.
CECILIA I shan't beat about the bush because it's getting late. Besides, when one is in trouble, every minute is precious. I am your nephew's wife. Your nephew is your brother's son. In other words, you and I are closely related. I know you feel badly disposed towards my husband, and to me. And you've just cause to be. That's right, have a good look at me. I'm young, and I'm not ashamed to say that up till now I've

behaved with all the foolishness of the young. It's been my misfortune never to have had anybody to give me good advice or to correct me. As a child I was spoilt and given everything I wanted. My husband, whom you know better than I, the poor man, has a kind and generous nature. And because of that, he has ruined himself. Without realizing what I was doing, I have kept asking more from him than he could afford. And it's true I have spoken badly about you. I have spoken very badly about you. But try to put yourself in my position. I was brought up to a certain way of life, to wear these foolish clothes, to behave in a way completely opposed to all your principles. And if my father wore the sort of clothes that you do, I would even have spoken badly of my own father. And now I am reaping the reward of the ignorant way in which I was brought up. I am finding it very hard to hold back my tears at the situation my poor husband is in. All our possessions impounded. Our furniture to be moved out into the street. My poor husband faced with arrest and imprisonment. Tomorrow morning we shall be on the street without food or home. Everybody mocking us. Everybody scorning and despising us. My husband become the laughing-stock of the town. And yet who is my husband? He is Signor Anzoletto Argagni. He is the nephew of Signor Cristofolo. And I am his niece. It is our own fault that we have ruined ourselves. But we have learnt from our mistakes. We have been taught our lesson and we would like to live better lives. And that we may do so, we ask the forgiveness of a compassionate uncle. We ask his pity and his help, and we ask it humbly and sincerely.

CRISTOFOLO *(aside)* What the devil can I say now!

CECILIA And now that you have been so good as to listen to me, speak, say what you think of me, take your revenge. You have every right to.

CRISTOFOLO I should be scolding you … I have the right to … at least you know I have the right to.

CECILIA *(aside)* He is talking to me, that's a good sign.

CRISTOFOLO If all you have said is true …

CECILIA Don't you believe we are in trouble, terrible trouble …?

CRISTOFOLO I didn't say that. I said if it's really true that your husband and you are sorry and want to change your way of living, then, though I'm not obliged to do anything – what I've got I've earned through hard work – I've a good heart and I might be able to do something for you.

CECILIA I'm not asking you to believe me. I'm a woman, I'm young. I know I've all these silly ideas now, but I could change. Listen – hear what my husband has to say. Take his word. And I will help him to keep it. Do you think I would be so unworthy as to try to ruin him a second time?

CRISTOFOLO *(aside)* She could twist anybody round her little finger! *(aloud)* Where is he, then, this good-for- nothing husband of yours?
CECILIA Come in, Husband. Providence is being kind to us.
CRISTOFOLO *(aside)* So he's here as well! This place is Liberty Hall.

Scene 14

Enter *Anzoletto.*

ANZOLETTO I hardly dare face you, Uncle.
CRISTOFOLO Get to the point. Make out a list of your debts. A transfer of your assets. A resolution to alter your ways. And I'll do what my heart tells me to – and which you don't deserve, you worthless young good-for-nothing.
ANZOLETTO I promise, I swear, I will always do as you wish.
CRISTOFOLO I will pay the rent you owe on this new apartment you've taken. But you will give notice that you're giving it up. It's not the sort of place for you.
CECILIA Dear Uncle, give us just one little room in your house.
CRISTOFOLO There isn't one.
CECILIA Dear Uncle, please. Just while we find somewhere else to go.
CRISTOFOLO Well, for no longer then, you cunning little minx. While you're in my house you'll both behave yourselves. And mark well, I'll have none of those friends of yours in my house either.
CECILIA Believe me, I'm so disgusted with those people there's no danger of that.

Scene 15

Enter *Checca, Meneghina, Rosina, Lorenzino, followed by Lucietta.*

CHECCA Well? Is everything arranged?
ANZOLETTO Everything! Thanks be to heaven and to my dear uncle.
MENEGHINA And I will come and stay with you, Uncle.
CECILIA And I'm going to stay with him as well.
MENEGHINA *(annoyed)* You are?
CRISTOFOLO *(aside)* These two together would drive me mad. One'll be more than enough. *(aloud)* Signora Checca, if I have done something for you, would you do me a kindness in return?

CHECCA Of course. You have only to ask.

CRISTOFOLO Would it inconvenience you if we arranged the marriage of my niece from your apartment?

CHECCA But that would be wonderful!

LORENZINO *(jumping with joy)* The wedding! The wedding!

MENEGHINA *(jumping with joy)* My wedding!

CHECCA Let us do it now!

CRISTOFOLO Now, if you wish.

CHECCA Take each other's hand.

MENEGHINA Do you agree, Uncle?

CRISTOFOLO I'm agreeable. But what about your brother. Is he?

MENEGHINA *(to Anzoletto)* Are you pleased? Do you agree to our marriage?

ANZOLETTO Of course. Whatever pleases my uncle will please me.

CECILIA *(aside to Anzoletto)* He is not as bad as you made him out to be, then!

ANZOLETTO *(aside to Cecilia)* My dear, I was saying that because I didn't know how to pay for her dowry.

CHECCA Good. Then give each other your hand. *(they take each other's hand)*[12]

LORENZINO This is my wife.

MENEGHINA This is my husband.

ROSINA I am so very happy for you, Signorina Meneghina.

MENEGHINA Thank you [Signorina Rosina.]

CRISTOFOLO *(to Cecilia and Anzoletto)* That leaves you two. You'd both better come home with me. And from now on, start showing some sense. Or it will be the worse for you.

ANZOLETTO Dear Wife, I owe all this to you.

CECILIA I was the cause of your troubles, so it is only right that I should know how to put them right. I wanted a new house and it was my fault that you took this apartment. Yet even from that has come good. For if we had not taken this new house, we should never have found the friendship of these two ladies. All this would never have happened. But it is not for us to sing the praises of The New House. *(she turns and addresses the audience)* Let us leave praise and blame to those who are qualified to give it, to those who have the right to give it – to all who, through us, may now feel their hearts full of kindness, gentleness, and love.

CURTAIN

NOTES TO THE NEW HOUSE

Notes by Brittany Asaro are indicated with the initials BA.

Notes by Gianluca Rizzo are indicated with the initials GR.

Notes adapted from the Mondadori editon of *La casa nova* (*Tutte le opere di Carlo Goldoni,* vol. 7, a cura di Giuseppe Ortolani [Milan: Arnoldo Mondadori Editore, 1959]) are indicated with the letter M.

1 While we believe that this translation by Frederick Davies is the best one available in English, we found a few places in which it could be improved: Mr Davies omitted a few lines here and there and changed the division in scenes and the stage directions. In reprinting his translation we made all necessary adjustments so that the final English text better reflects Goldoni's original Venetian. Out of respect for his work, we marked all our edits by enclosing them in brackets. The names of two characters, Sgualdo and Meneghina, have been restored to the original Italian. Mr Davies had rendered them as Oswald and Domenica. Toni is not listed in the original Dramatis Personae but he appears instead of Servant in act 3, scene 2 (p. 54). Parentheses in the original are here given as "aside"; "da se" is translated "to himself, to herself"; "piano" is translated as "softly." All interlinear indications of characters entering have been replaced by descriptions of which characters are in each scene, and that description has been placed at the beginning of each scene, to reflect the original. "Ottavio" is replaced with "Count," as in the original. (GR and BA)

2 It is difficult to assess the value of a three- to four-thousand-ducat salary in modern terms. As a point of reference, Frederic Chapin Lane writes in his *Venice: A Maritime Republic* (Baltimore and London: Johns Hopkins University Press, 1973) that by the sixteenth century, "Writers who boasted of Venice's wealth considered nobles as well off only if they had an income of 1,000 ducats a year and counted as really rich those with 10,000 a year" (333) (BA).

3 One Venetian ducat was worth approximately 124 soldi (BA).

4 Naturally, the north-facing rooms of a house almost never receive direct sunlight, and are thus always the coldest (BA).

5 Count Ottavio is an example of a *cicisbeo,* a professed gallant and lover of a married woman in eighteenth- and nineteenth-century Italy. He served as her companion when she went on various outings, such as to church or the opera. This practice was done with the knowledge and consent of the

husband, and was widely accepted among the nobility in Venice and other cities at this time. Several critics have studied Goldoni's treatment of *cicisbei* in his works; see, for instance, M. Merlato, *Mariti e cavalieri serventi nelle commedie del Goldoni* (Florence: Carnesecchi, 1906) (GR and BA).

6 The various floors that make up an Italian palazzo reflect not only the different functions to which each part of the building is assigned but also a strict social hierarchy: the ground floor is where the kitchens, the stables, and the shops are located; the first floor is where the richest families in the building live; after this, the higher the floor the poorer the inhabitant, all the way to the attic, where the servants had their rooms (GR).

7 According to Guido Mazzoni, this scene is one of the best examples of Goldoni's art of dialogue; *La casa nova* in *Tutte le opere di Carlo Goldoni*, vol. 7, a cura di Giuseppe Ortolani (Milan: Arnoldo Mondadori Editore, 1959), 1403 (M).

8 In his edition of *La casa nova*, Edmondo Rho writes, "The figure of Lorenzino is purely comical. He is a typical Goldonian youth, naïve and a bit of a simpleton. The playwright is the first one to smile at his fumbling, his anger, and his spite"; *La casa nova: Con prefazione e note di Edmondo Rho* (Florence: La Nuova Italia, 1930) (M).

9 Snap and beggar-my-neighbour are two card games related to Egyptian ratscrew that have been translated from the three popular Italian card games listed in the original text, *tresette*, *cotecchio*, and *mercante in fiera* (BA).

10 Edmondo Rho insists that act 2, scene 10, is the most vibrant in the whole comedy: "It is moving and dramatic, and yet the lasting impression that it makes is a comical one"; *La casa nova: Con prefazione e note di Edmondo Rho* (Florence: La Nuova Italia, 1930) (M).

11 Giuseppe Ortolani writes, "Few pages in all of Italian literature can compete with these dialogues with respect to their realism and psychology. Note Checca's hesitation in the previous scene and this outburst that seems to compromise the conversation with Cristofolo, while it instead decides the lady's victory"; *La casa nova* in *Tutte le opere di Carlo Goldoni*, vol. 7, a cura di Giuseppe Ortolani (Milan: Arnoldo Mondadori Editore, 1959), 1404 (M).

12 In the notes to his translation, Frederick Davies writes, "Apart from the priest's blessing which would be given later, the holding of hands was a common way of performing a marriage in Venice in the eighteenth century – granted that both parties had given their free consent and that there were at least two witnesses" (61).

The Coffee House

TRANSLATED BY JEREMY PARZEN

Prose comedy in three acts
Performed for the first time in Mantua on 2 May 1750

Figure 5 *The Coffee House* (La bottega del caffè)

Figure 6 *The Coffee House* (La bottega del caffè), act 1, scene 7

Figure 7 *The Coffee House* (La bottega del caffè), act 2, scene 23

Figure 8 *The Coffee House* (La bottega del caffè), act 3, scene 24

The Author to the Reader

When I first wrote the present comedy, I used the characters Brighella and Arlecchino and, to tell the truth, it enjoyed success everywhere. In spite of this, in giving it to the press, I believed that I could better serve the public by rendering it more universal. I thus changed to Tuscan not only the language of the two characters mentioned above but also that of three others who spoke in the Venetian dialect.

Another comedy ran in Florence with a similar title and various incidents which, having been copied from my comedy, made it similar to mine. A talented and witty friend of mine put his memory to the test: but having seen my comedy performed in Milan only once or twice, he inevitably mixed in many things of his own invention. I have attributed the prank to friendship and praised its ingenuity. Nonetheless, I do not want to take credit for the worthy parts which are not mine, nor do I want something I find distasteful to pass for something of mine.

I wish, therefore, to inform the public of the matter so that when my comedy – which I am now publishing – is compared with that of my abovementioned friend, the truth may be evident and each of us profit from his portion of praise and content himself with his portion of criticism.

The characters of this comedy are so familiar that, wherever it has been performed, they have been thought to be drawn from recognizable originals. The Scandalmonger, in particular, found his prototype everywhere, and, despite my innocence, I have at times been forced to suffer the accusation of having maliciously copied it – something I am certainly not capable of doing.

My characters are human, lifelike, and maybe even real. The fact is that I draw them from the universal throng of men, and it so happens that some people recognize themselves in them. When this occurs, it is not my fault that the wretched character resembles a certain depraved person. It is that depraved person's fault that, to his misfortune, he finds himself lambasted by the character that I portray.

Dramatis Personae

RIDOLFO	*owner of the coffee house*
DON MARZIO	*a Neapolitan gentleman*

EUGENIO	*a merchant*
FLAMINIO	*under the name of Count Leandro*
PLACIDA	*Flaminio's wife, dressed as a wayfarer*
VITTORIA	*Eugenio's wife*
LISAURA	*dancer*
PANDOLFO	*owner of the gambling house*
TRAPPOLA	*Ridolfo's boy*
A BOY	*from the Wig-maker, who speaks*
ANOTHER BOY	*from the Coffee House, who speaks*
A WAITER	*from the Inn, who speaks*
A POLICE SERGEANT	*with his men, who speaks*
OTHER POLICEMEN,	*who do not speak*
OTHER WAITERS	*from the Inn, who do not speak*
OTHER BOYS	*from the Coffee House, who do not speak*

The permanent scene is a small square in Venice, or an equally spacious street, with three shops: the one in the middle used as a cafe, the one on the right used as a wig-maker and barbershop, the one on the left used as a gambling house or card room. Above the shops some accessible rooms, which belong to the gambling house, its windows overlooking the street. The dancer's house is on the side of the barbershop (with a street in between), and the inn, with functioning doors and windows, is on the side of the gambling house.

ACT ONE

Scene 1

Ridolfo, Trappola, and other boys.

RIDOLFO Come on, lads. Be good. Be quick and ready to serve our customers politely, with civility. Because the reputation of a shop often rests on the good manners of its servants.[1]

TRAPPOLA My dear Master, to tell the truth, this early rising isn't any good for my constitution.

RIDOLFO Nonetheless, we have to get up early. We have to serve everyone. At this hour travellers, workmen, boatmen, and sailors come, all the people who rise with the dawn.[2]

TRAPPOLA It's really enough to make one die laughing, to see even the porters come to have their coffee.

RIDOLFO Everybody tries to do what everyone else does. There was a time when brandy was the rage; now it's coffee.

TRAPPOLA And that lady, where I bring the coffee every morning, she almost always asks me to buy her a measly four-farthings' worth of firewood. Yet even she wants to have her coffee.

RIDOLFO Gluttony is a never-ending vice, and it grows with age.

TRAPPOLA I don't see anyone coming to our shop. We could have slept for another hour.

RIDOLFO People will come soon enough. It's not so early. Don't you see? The barber's open. He's in his shop working on his wigs. Look, the gambling house is open, too.

TRAPPOLA Oh, that card room's been open for a while. They made a night of it.

RIDOLFO Well, then. Things must be good for Master Pandolfo.

TRAPPOLA Things are always good for that dog. He profits in cards, he profits in sponging, he profits in the understandings he has with the cardsharps. Every penny that goes in there is his.

RIDOLFO Don't ever fall in love with such profit, for you know that the devil's meal is half bran.

TRAPPOLA And poor Signor Eugenio's been ruined.

RIDOLFO There's a fool for you. He doesn't have any sense! He's married to a charming and sensible young lady, yet he runs after every woman in sight. And besides that, he gambles like a madman.

TRAPPOLA Gallantries of modern youth!

RIDOLFO He's playing with that Count Leandro, and he's lost his money for sure.

TRAPPOLA Oh, that Count Leandro is a rare flower of virtue!

RIDOLFO Well, run along. Go roast the coffee, and make a fresh pot.

TRAPPOLA Shall I use yesterday's leftovers?

RIDOLFO No. Make it fresh.

TRAPPOLA Dear Master, I have a poor memory. How long have you been open here?

RIDOLFO You know perfectly well. About eight months.

TRAPPOLA Then it's time to change our ways.

RIDOLFO What is that supposed to mean?

TRAPPOLA When you first open a shop, you make perfect coffee. But after six months – at the most – lots of hot water and the soup lasts longer! *(exit Trappola)*

RIDOLFO Witty, that fellow. I hope he'll be good for business. For wherever there's someone to play the fool, the crowd will gather.

Scene 2

Ridolfo, followed by Master Pandolfo from his gambling house, rubbing his eyes as if sleepy.

RIDOLFO Master Pandolfo, would you like a coffee?

PANDOLFO If you would be so obliging.

RIDOLFO Boys, give Master Pandolfo his coffee. Sit down. Make yourself comfortable.

PANDOLFO No, no. I have to drink it in a hurry and get back to my work. *(a boy brings Pandolfo his coffee)*

RIDOLFO Are they still playing at your place?

PANDOLFO Two looms are working.

RIDOLFO This early?

PANDOLFO They've been playing since yesterday.

RIDOLFO What are they playing?

PANDOLFO An innocent little game of faro.[3]

RIDOLFO And how are things going?

PANDOLFO Well enough, for me.

RIDOLFO Have you been playing, too?

PANDOLFO Yes, I cut the cards a few times as well.

RIDOLFO Bear with me, my friend – it's not my place to meddle in your affairs – but it doesn't look good when the owner of the house plays as well, because if he loses, he's laughed at, and if he wins he's suspect.

PANDOLFO As long as they don't make fun of me. Anyhow, let them suspect as much as they want. It doesn't bother me.

RIDOLFO My dear friend, you and I are neighbours, and I wouldn't want anything bad to happen to you. You know that you've been arrested more than once for this gambling of yours.

PANDOLFO I'm not greedy. I pocketed two sequins,[4] and that was enough for me.

RIDOLFO Good man. You pluck the fowl without making it squawk. Who'd you win them from?

PANDOLFO A goldsmith's apprentice.

RIDOLFO Bad, bad indeed. That's how boys are inspired to steal from their masters.

PANDOLFO Oh, spare me your morals. Let the dunces stay at home. I'll keep play for whoever wants to gamble.

RIDOLFO Running card games is bad enough, but you'll be marked as someone who's not above cheating, and in that sort of thing, one is quick to fall.

PANDOLFO I play no tricks. I know how to play. I'm lucky, and so I win.

RIDOLFO Very well, do things your way. Did Signor Eugenio play last night?

PANDOLFO In fact, he's still playing. He had no supper, nor did he sleep. And he's lost all his money.

RIDOLFO *(aside, to himself)* Poor fellow! *(to Pandolfo)* How much could he have lost?

PANDOLFO A hundred sequins in cash. And now he's losing on his word.

RIDOLFO Who's he playing with?

PANDOLFO With the Count.

RIDOLFO With someone like that?

PANDOLFO With him, precisely.

RIDOLFO And with who else?

PANDOLFO Just those two, head to head.

RIDOLFO Poor devil! He's really in for it!

PANDOLFO So what! As long as they keep on shuffling the cards.

RIDOLFO I wouldn't run such games, even if I believed it would make me rich.

PANDOLFO No? Why not?

RIDOLFO It seems to me that a gentleman couldn't just stand by, watching people be killed.

PANDOLFO Well, my friend, if you are as soft-hearted as that, you'll never make much money.

RIDOLFO I couldn't care less. Up to now, I've been a servant and fulfilled my task with honour. I saved a few pennies, and with some help from my former master – who, as you know, was Signor Eugenio's father – I opened this shop and I want to make an honourable living with it, without discrediting my profession.

PANDOLFO Well, even in your profession there are some true gems.

RIDOLFO There are in all professions. But the distinguished people who come to my shop don't mix with them.

PANDOLFO You too have your private rooms.

RIDOLFO True. But I don't shut the doors.

PANDOLFO You can't refuse coffee to anyone.

RIDOLFO Coffee cups aren't market.

PANDOLFO Oh, come! You look the other way.

RIDOLFO I do no such thing. In this shop you'll find only respectable people.

PANDOLFO Yes, yes. You're still green.

RIDOLFO What's that supposed to mean? *(people call from the gambling house: Cards!)*

PANDOLFO *(towards his gambling house)* Right away.

RIDOLFO For heaven's sake, get poor Eugenio away from that table!

PANDOLFO He can lose the shirt off his back for all I care. *(starts to walk towards his gambling house)*

RIDOLFO My friend, the coffee? Shall I put it on your bill?

PANDOLFO No. We'll play for it at primero.[5]

RIDOLFO I'm no dunce, friend.

PANDOLFO Why talk like that? You know full well that my customers come to your shop, too. I'm surprised that you bother with such trifles. *(starts to walk) (more calls from the gambling house)*

PANDOLFO Here I am. *(enters the gambling house)*

RIDOLFO A fine profession! To live on the misfortunes and ruination of youth. As for me, there's no chance that I'll ever allow gambling. One begins with party-games and ends with basset.[6] No, no, coffee, coffee. It brings in fifty per cent. What more can we ask?

Scene 3

Don Marzio and Ridolfo.

RIDOLFO *(aside, to himself)* Here's the one who never shuts up, and insists on being right all the time.

DON MARZIO Coffee.[7]

RIDOLFO Right away, at your service.

DON MARZIO Haven't you seen anyone yet in this shop of yours?

RIDOLFO It's still very early.

DON MARZIO Early? It's well past nine.

RIDOLFO Oh, no, your grace, it's not yet seven o'clock.

DON MARZIO Oh come, joker.

RIDOLFO I assure you that it hasn't yet struck seven.

DON MARZIO Oh come, you ass.

RIDOLFO You're getting rough with me for no reason.

DON MARZIO I've counted the bells to this point, and I'm telling you that it's nine o'clock. And anyway, look at my watch: it's never wrong. *(shows him the watch)*

RIDOLFO Well, if your watch is never wrong, look at this: your own watch reads six and three quarters.

DON MARZIO Oh, that can't be. *(takes out his lorgnette and looks)*

RIDOLFO What does it say?

DON MARZIO My watch isn't right. It's nine o'clock. I heard the tolls myself.

RIDOLFO Where did you buy that watch?

DON MARZIO I sent for it from London.

RIDOLFO They swindled you.

DON MARZIO They swindled me? Why do you say that?

RIDOLFO *(ironically)* They sent you a bad watch.

DON MARZIO What do you mean, bad? It's one of the most perfect Quares[8] ever made.

RIDOLFO If it were good, it wouldn't be off by two hours.

DON MARZIO This watch always runs well. It's never wrong.

RIDOLFO But if it reads a quarter till seven, and you say that it's nine …

DON MARZIO My watch runs fine.

RIDOLFO Then it's just about seven, as I was saying.

DON MARZIO You fool. My watch runs fine. Watch your tongue or I'll smack you on the head. *(a boy brings his coffee)*

RIDOLFO *(with disdain)* Here's your coffee, sir. *(aside)* Oh, what a block-head.

DON MARZIO Have you seen Signor Eugenio?

RIDOLFO No, your grace.

DON MARZIO *(drinking his coffee)* He's probably at home petting his wife. What an effeminate man! Always his wife! It's always his wife! He doesn't show himself around here any more. He's becoming ridiculous. What a bore. He doesn't know what he's doing. Always his wife, always his wife.

RIDOLFO It's everything but his wife! He was here all night playing cards at Master Pandolfo's.

DON MARZIO As I was saying. It's always gambling! Always gambling! *(gives Ridolfo the cup, and stands)*

RIDOLFO *(aside)* It's always gambling. It's always his wife. It's always the devil: the devil take him.

DON MARZIO He came to me the other day, in great secrecy, begging me to lend him ten sequins on a pair of his wife's earrings.

RIDOLFO You see, all men may find themselves in need, but for this need to be known, none of them like it. That's probably why he came to you, sure that you wouldn't say anything to anyone.

DON MARZIO Oh, I don't gossip. I'm happy to be of service to everyone, and I don't brag about it. Here they are. These are his wife's earrings. I lent him ten sequins. Do you think I'm covered? *(shows him the earrings in a case)*

RIDOLFO I'm no expert, but it seems so.
DON MARZIO Do you have your boy here?
RIDOLFO He should be here.
DON MARZIO Call him. Hey, Trappola.

Scene 4

Enter *Trappola from the back of the shop.*

TRAPPOLA Here I am.
DON MARZIO Come here. Go to the jeweller nearby. Show him these earrings that belong to Signor Eugenio's wife, and ask him, on my behalf, if I'm covered for the ten sequins that I lent him.
TRAPPOLA At your service, sir. Let's see. These earrings belong to Signor Eugenio's wife?
DON MARZIO Yes, in a little while he won't have anything left. He's down on his uppers.
RIDOLFO *(aside, to himself)* Poor fellow, what hands he's fallen into!
TRAPPOLA And doesn't Signor Eugenio mind making his affairs known to all?
DON MARZIO I'm someone you can trust with a secret.
TRAPPOLA And I'm someone not to be trusted at all.
DON MARZIO Why?
TRAPPOLA Because I have a vice: I repeat everything freely.
DON MARZIO Bad, bad indeed. If you act like that, you will lose credit, and no one will trust you.
TRAPPOLA But just as you told it to me, likewise I can tell it to someone else.
DON MARZIO Go see if the barber is ready to give me a shave.
TRAPPOLA Right away, sir. *(aside, to himself)* For ten farthings he wants to have his coffee, and he wants a servant at his command. *(enters the barbershop)*
DON MARZIO Tell me, Ridolfo, what does she do, that dancer who lives around here?
RIDOLFO To be honest, I don't know anything about her.
DON MARZIO I've been told that Count Leandro keeps her under his tutelage.
RIDOLFO Please excuse me, sir, the coffee is about to boil. *(aside)* I mind my own business. *(enters the shop)*

Scene 5

Trappola and Don Marzio.

TRAPPOLA The barber has someone in his chair. As soon as he's finished skinning him, he'll be with your grace.

DON MARZIO Say, do you know anything about that dancer who lives around here?

TRAPPOLA Signora Lisaura?

DON MARZIO Yes.

TRAPPOLA I do, and I don't.

DON MARZIO Tell me something.

TRAPPOLA If I tell about other people's affairs, I'll lose my credit, and no one will trust me any more.

DON MARZIO You can tell me. You know me. I don't gossip. Does Count Leandro call on her?

TRAPPOLA When it's convenient, he calls on her.

DON MARZIO What does convenient mean?

TRAPPOLA It means when it doesn't create embarrassment.

DON MARZIO Good man. Now I understand. He's a dear friend of hers, and he doesn't want to wrong her.

TRAPPOLA Just the opposite: he wishes her to do well so that he too can share in her precious charms.

DON MARZIO Better yet! Oh, aren't you malicious, Trappola! Off with you, go and have the earrings looked at.

TRAPPOLA May I tell the jeweller that they belong to Signor Eugenio's wife?

DON MARZIO Yes, go ahead and tell him.

TRAPPOLA *(aside)* Don Marzio and myself, what a fine pair of confidants we make. *(exit Trappola)*

Scene 6

Don Marzio, followed by Ridolfo.

RIDOLFO Sir.

DON MARZIO Since you don't know anything about the dancer, I'll tell you.

RIDOLFO To tell you the truth, I don't care for other people's business.

DON MARZIO But it's good to know something so that one knows how to act. She is protected by that scoundrel Count Leandro. And from her earnings as a dancer, he rakes the price of his protection. Instead of spending money on her, he eats up everything that poor wretch has. And because of him she's perhaps forced to do what she wouldn't otherwise do. What a rascal!

RIDOLFO But I'm here all day, and I can assure you that I've seen no one but Count Leandro go into her house.

DON MARZIO She has a back door, you idiot! In they come and out they go. She has a back door, you idiot!

RIDOLFO I mind my shop. Why should it matter to me if she has a back door? I don't stick my nose in anyone else's affairs.

DON MARZIO Scoundrel! You speak like this to someone of my station? *(stands)*

RIDOLFO I beg your pardon. Can't I make a joke?

DON MARZIO Give me a glass of rosolio.

RIDOLFO *(aside)* This joke is going to cost me a couple of farthings. *(gestures to the boys to pour Don Marzio the rosolio)*

DON MARZIO *(aside)* Oh, my! I'll let everyone know about the dancer.

RIDOLFO Here is your rosolio.

DON MARZIO *(drinking his rosolio)* In they come and out they go, through the back door.

RIDOLFO She must not be well with all this coming and going through the back door.

Scene 7

Enter *Eugenio from the gambling house, in evening dress and dazed, looking at the sky and stomping his feet.*

DON MARZIO Your servant, Signor Eugenio.

EUGENIO What time is it?

DON MARZIO It's nine o'clock.

RIDOLFO And his watch runs fine.

EUGENIO Coffee.

RIDOLFO Right away, sir. *(enters the shop)*

DON MARZIO Friend, how did it go?

EUGENIO *(paying no attention to Don Marzio)* Coffee.

RIDOLFO *(from afar)* Right away.

DON MARZIO *(to Eugenio)* Did you lose?
EUGENIO *(yelling loudly)* Coffee.
DON MARZIO *(aside)* I understand. He lost everything. *(goes to sit down)*

Scene 8

Enter *Pandolfo from the gambling house.*

PANDOLFO Signor Eugenio, a word with you. *(takes him aside)*
EUGENIO I know what you want to tell me. I lost thirty sequins on my word. I'm a gentleman. I'll pay.
PANDOLFO But the Count is waiting. He says that he risked his money, and he wants to be paid.
DON MARZIO *(aside)* I'd give anything to hear what they're saying!
RIDOLFO *(to Eugenio)* Here's your coffee.
EUGENIO *(to Ridolfo)* Go away. *(to Pandolfo)* He won a hundred sequins in cash. It seems to me that he didn't waste the night.
PANDOLFO These are not the words of a gambler. You know the rules of gambling better than I, my lord.
RIDOLFO *(to Eugenio)* Sir, the coffee is getting cold.
EUGENIO *(to Ridolfo)* Leave me alone.
RIDOLFO If you didn't want it …
EUGENIO Go away.
RIDOLFO Then I'll drink it. *(goes inside with the coffee)*
DON MARZIO *(to Ridolfo, who doesn't answer)* What are they saying?
EUGENIO *(to Pandolfo)* I know full well that when you lose, you pay. But when you've run out, you can't pay.
PANDOLFO Listen. I'm the type of man who can find thirty sequins and save your reputation.
EUGENIO Great! *(calling out loudly)* Coffee.
RIDOLFO *(to Eugenio)* Oh, dear, now I need to make it.
EUGENIO It's been three hours that I've been asking for coffee. And you still haven't made it?
RIDOLFO I brought it, and you chased me away.
PANDOLFO Order it from him nicely, and he'll make it like no one else.
EUGENIO *(to Ridolfo)* Tell me, can you find it in your heart to make me a good cup of coffee? There's a good fellow.
RIDOLFO If you give me a moment, I'll get it for you. *(goes into the shop)*
DON MARZIO *(aside)* Some important affair. I'm curious to find out what.
EUGENIO Come, come, Pandolfo. Find me the thirty sequins.

PANDOLFO I have a friend who can give you the money, but against security and with interest.

EUGENIO Don't talk to me about security, or we won't get anywhere. I have that cloth at the Rialto, as you know. I'll put it up for sale, and when I sell it, I'll pay.

DON MARZIO *(aside)* "I'll pay." He said, "I'll pay." He lost on his word.

PANDOLFO Very well. How much interest do you want to pay?

EUGENIO You decide how much you believe is appropriate.

PANDOLFO Listen, it'll take at least a sequin a week.

EUGENIO A sequin of usury a week?

RIDOLFO *(with the coffee, to Eugenio)* Here's your coffee.

EUGENIO *(to Ridolfo)* Go away.

RIDOLFO And now a secondary exchange.

EUGENIO *(to Pandolfo)* A sequin a week?

PANDOLFO For thirty sequins, it seems fair to me.

RIDOLFO *(to Eugenio)* Do you want it, or don't you?

EUGENIO *(to Ridolfo)* Go away before I throw it in your face.

RIDOLFO *(aside)* Poor devil! He's drunk with gambling. *(takes the coffee into the back)*

DON MARZIO *(gets up and goes towards Eugenio)* Signor Eugenio, is there some misunderstanding? Do you want me to take care of it?

EUGENIO It's nothing, Signor Don Marzio. I beg you to leave me alone.

DON MARZIO If you are in need, feel free to call on me.

EUGENIO I tell you, I don't need anything.

DON MARZIO Master Pandolfo, what is your business with Signor Eugenio?

PANDOLFO A small matter that we prefer not to make known to the whole world.

DON MARZIO I am a friend of Signor Eugenio's. I know all about his affairs, and he knows that I don't gossip with anyone. I myself lent him ten sequins on a pair of earrings. Isn't that so? And I didn't tell anyone.

EUGENIO You didn't have to say so now.

DON MARZIO Oh, we can speak freely here with Master Pandolfo. Did you lose on your word? Are you in need of something? Here I am.

EUGENIO To tell the truth, I lost thirty sequins on my word.

DON MARZIO Thirty sequins, and ten that I gave you. That's forty. The earrings can't be worth that much.

PANDOLFO I'll find you the thirty sequins.

DON MARZIO Very well. Get him forty sequins. You'll give me my ten, and I'll give you his earrings.

EUGENIO *(aside)* Curse the hour that I got mixed up with this fellow!

DON MARZIO *(to Eugenio)* Why not take the money that Signor Pandolfo is offering you?

EUGENIO Because he wants a sequin a week.

PANDOLFO I don't want anything for myself. It's my friend who performs the service that wants it.

EUGENIO Do this: speak with the Count. Tell him to give me twenty-four hours. I'm a gentleman. I'll pay him.

PANDOLFO I'm afraid that he needs to be leaving, and he wants the money right away.

EUGENIO If I could only sell a piece or two of that cloth, I could get out of this predicament.

PANDOLFO Do you want me to see if I can find a buyer?

EUGENIO Yes, dear friend, do me this favour, and I will pay you for your brokerage.

PANDOLFO Let me have a word with the Count. I'll go right away. *(enters the gambling house)*

DON MARZIO *(to Eugenio)* Did you lose much?

EUGENIO One hundred sequins that I cashed yesterday, and then thirty on my word.

DON MARZIO You could have brought me the ten that I lent you.

EUGENIO Come on, don't make it worse than it already is. I'll give you your ten sequins.

PANDOLFO *(enter Pandolfo with cloak and hat, from his gambling house)* The Count has fallen asleep with his head on the table. In the meantime, I'll go see about this service. If he wakes up, I left orders with the boy to tell him to wait. You mustn't leave, my lord.

EUGENIO I'll wait for you right here.

PANDOLFO *(aside)* This cloak is old. Now it's time for me to get a new one for free. *(exit Pandolfo)*

Scene 9

Don Marzio and Eugenio, followed by Ridolfo.

DON MARZIO Come, sit down. Let's drink some coffee.

EUGENIO Coffee. *(they sit)*

RIDOLFO What game are we playing, Signor Eugenio? Do you find this amusing?

EUGENIO Dear friend, bear with me. I'm in a daze.

RIDOLFO Ah, dear Signor Eugenio, if you would listen to me, you wouldn't be in such a predicament.

EUGENIO I don't know what to say. You're right.

RIDOLFO I'm going to make you another coffee, and then we'll discuss it. *(enters the shop)*

DON MARZIO Have you heard about that dancer who seemed not to be interested in anyone? The Count looks after her.

EUGENIO I surely believe he can take care of her. He wins sequins by the hundreds.

DON MARZIO I found out all about it.

EUGENIO How did you find out, dear friend?

DON MARZIO Me? I know everything. I'm very well informed. I know when he goes there, when he leaves. I know what he spends, what he eats. I know everything.

EUGENIO So it's only the Count?

DON MARZIO Oh, come, there's a back door.

RIDOLFO *(with the coffee, to Eugenio)* Here's your third coffee.

DON MARZIO Ah! What do you say, Ridolfo? Don't I know everything about the dancer?

RIDOLFO I told you once already that I'm not getting mixed up in this.

DON MARZIO I am quite a man for finding out everything. Whoever wants to know what goes on in the homes of actresses and dancers must come to me.

EUGENIO So, this dancer is a true gem.

DON MARZIO I've discovered what really goes on. It's quite refined stuff. Ridolfo, do I know or don't I?

RIDOLFO When you call me as witness, my lord, I have to tell the truth. All the neighbourhood thinks her a respectable woman.

DON MARZIO A respectable woman? A respectable woman?

RIDOLFO I tell you that no one goes to her house.

DON MARZIO Through the back door, in they come and out they go.

EUGENIO And yet she seems a rather sensible girl.

DON MARZIO Sensible all right! Count Goodheart looks after her, and whoever wants to, goes there.

EUGENIO I've tried once or twice to have a little word with her, and I didn't get anywhere.

DON MARZIO Do you have a farthing to bet? Let's go and see.

RIDOLFO *(aside)* Oh, what a gossip!

EUGENIO I come here to have coffee every day, and, to tell the truth, I've seen no one go in there.

DON MARZIO Don't you know that she has a secret door on the street in back? That's how they get in.
EUGENIO If you say so.
DON MARZIO Of course it is.

Scene 10

Enter *the barber's boy.*

BOY *(to Don Marzio)* Your grace, if you want to have a shave, my master is ready for you.
DON MARZIO I'm coming. It's as I tell you. I'm going to have a shave, and when I come back, I'll tell you the rest. *(enters the barbershop)*
EUGENIO What do you say, Ridolfo? The dancer has given herself away.
RIDOLFO Do you believe Signor Don Marzio? Don't you know what a gossip he is?
EUGENIO I know that he has a sharp and cutting tongue. But he speaks with such frankness that you have to assume he knows what he's talking about.
RIDOLFO Look. That's the alley door. From here you can see it, and I swear – as a man of honour – that no one goes into the house from there.
EUGENIO But is she kept by the Count?
RIDOLFO The Count goes to her house, but they say he wants to marry her.
EUGENIO If it were so, there wouldn't be anything wrong. But Signor Don Marzio says that whoever wants goes to her house.
RIDOLFO And I tell you that no one goes there.
DON MARZIO *(comes out of the barbershop with a towel around his neck and lather on his face)* I tell you that they go through the back door.
BOY Your grace, the water is getting cold.
DON MARZIO Through the back door. *(enters the barbershop with the boy)*

Scene 11

Eugenio and Ridolfo.

RIDOLFO You see? That's the kind of man he is. With lather on his face.
EUGENIO Yes, when he gets something stuck in his head, there's no stopping him.

RIDOLFO And he bad-mouths everyone.

EUGENIO I don't know how he can always speak of other people's affairs.

RIDOLFO I'll tell you. He has few concerns. He spends little time thinking about his own affairs, and so he's always thinking about other people's.

EUGENIO You're really better off not knowing him.

RIDOLFO Dear Signor Eugenio, how could you get mixed up with him? Wasn't there anyone else who could lend you ten sequins?

EUGENIO You know about it, too?

RIDOLFO He said so publicly, here in the shop.

EUGENIO Dear friend, you know how it goes: a man in need will lay hold on anything.

RIDOLFO And this morning, from what I hear, my lord, you didn't hold on too well.

EUGENIO Do you believe that Master Pandolfo wants to take me in?

RIDOLFO You'll see what kind of terms he'll propose.

EUGENIO But what am I to do? I need to pay thirty sequins that I lost gambling on credit. I'd like to free myself from Don Marzio's clutches.

I have some other pressing matters. If I can sell two bolts of cloth, all my affairs will be in order.

RIDOLFO What quality of cloth is it that you'd like to dispose of?

EUGENIO Paduan cloth, worth fourteen lire a yard.

RIDOLFO Do you want me to see if I can sell it for you for a respectable sum?

EUGENIO I would be much obliged to you.

RIDOLFO Give me a little time, and let me work on it.

EUGENIO A little time? Gladly. But he's waiting on thirty sequins.

RIDOLFO Come here, please. Have two bolts of cloth delivered to me, and I'll personally lend you the thirty sequins.

EUGENIO Yes, dear friend, I will be obliged to you. I shall honour my obligations.

RIDOLFO You surprise me. I'm not asking for a penny. I'm indebted to the memory of your worthy father, who was my good master, and to whom I owe my good fortune. I don't have the heart to see you killed by these dogs.

EUGENIO You are a true gentleman.

RIDOLFO Please draft me an order in writing.

EUGENIO I'm ready. You dictate, and I'll write.

RIDOLFO What's the name of the chap in charge of your store?

EUGENIO Pasquino de' Cavoli. *(Ridolfo dictates and Eugenio writes)*

RIDOLFO Pasquino de' Cavoli ... Deliver to Master Ridolfo Gamboni ... two bolts of Paduan cloth ... as he may select, in order that he may sell them for profit on my behalf ... having advanced to me without charge the sum of thirty sequins ... Put the date there and your signature.

EUGENIO It's done.

RIDOLFO Do you trust me?

EUGENIO Good heavens! Shouldn't I?

RIDOLFO And I trust you. Here, take these thirty sequins. *(counts out thirty sequins)*

EUGENIO Dear friend, I am obliged to you.

RIDOLFO Signor Eugenio, I'm giving you the money so that you can pay your debt on time and maintain your honour. I'll sell the cloth for you so that it won't be squandered, and I'll do it right away so as not to waste time. But permit me to speak a loving word to you as an old servant of your house. The road you're travelling, my lord, is the true road to ruin. Soon enough you'll lose your credit and you'll go bankrupt. Forget gambling. Forget your bad habits. Take care of your store and of your family, and act with prudence. Just a few words of advice from an ordinary yet good-hearted man. Heed these words, and you'll be better off. *(exit Ridolfo)*

Scene 12

Eugenio alone, followed by Lisaura at the window.

EUGENIO He's right. I have to admit that he's right. My wife, poor wretch, what will she say? Last night she didn't see me. It must have made her crazy. Women. When their husbands don't come home, they think a hundred different things, each worse than the next. She probably thinks that I was with other women, or that I fell into some canal, or that I fled since I owe so much money. I know that she worries because she loves me. I love her, too, but I like my freedom. I see, however, that it brings me more bad than good and that if I did what she says, things at home would get better. I've got to be resolute and set this right. Oh, how many times have I said this! *(enter Lisaura at the window) (Eugenio sees Lisaura at the window) (aside)* Faith! My stars! Yes,

I'm afraid that there is a little trick door. *(to Lisaura)* My most reverend lady.

LISAURA Your most humble servant.

EUGENIO Has it been long, Signora, since you got up?

LISAURA I got up just this moment.

EUGENIO Have you had your coffee?

LISAURA Not yet. It's still early.

EUGENIO May I see to it that you are served?

LISAURA Much obliged, but don't trouble yourself.

EUGENIO It's no trouble at all. Boys, bring the lady coffee, chocolate, all that she wants. I'm paying.

LISAURA Thank you. Thank you, but I make my coffee and chocolate at home.

EUGENIO You must have good chocolate.

LISAURA To tell the truth, it couldn't be better.

EUGENIO It's good, eh?

LISAURA My maid has a real knack for it.

EUGENIO Do you want me to come up and give it a little stir.

LISAURA You needn't trouble yourself.

EUGENIO With your permission, I'll come up and have some with you.

LISAURA It's not for you, sir.

EUGENIO I should be pleased to accept anything at all. Come now, open the door, and we'll spend a little while together.

LISAURA Forgive me, but I don't open the door so easily.

EUGENIO Well, tell me. Do you want me to come through the back door?

LISAURA People who come to my house have nothing to hide.

EUGENIO Come now, open the door. Let's not make a scene.

LISAURA Be so gracious as to tell me, Signor Eugenio, have you seen Count Leandro?

EUGENIO I only wish I hadn't!

LISAURA Perhaps you played together last night?

EUGENIO Unfortunately. What good does it do us to make our affairs known to everyone? Open the door, and I'll tell you everything.

LISAURA I tell you, sir, that I don't open the door to anyone.

EUGENIO Perhaps you need the Count to give you permission? I'll call him.

LISAURA When I look for the Count, I have my own reasons for doing so.

EUGENIO I'll get him for you right away. He's here in the gambling house, sleeping.

LISAURA If he's sleeping, let him sleep.

Scene 13

Enter *Leandro from the gambling house.*

LEANDRO I'm not sleeping. No, I'm not sleeping. I'm admiring Signor Eugenio's savoir-faire.

EUGENIO What do you say of this lady's arrogance? She doesn't want to open the door for me.

LEANDRO Who do you think she is?

EUGENIO According to Don Marzio, in they come and out they go.

LEANDRO Don Marzio is a liar, and so is whoever believes him.

EUGENIO Well, maybe it's not so, but shall I not be able, through your good offices, to pay her my respects?

LEANDRO You'd be better off paying me my thirty sequins.

EUGENIO I'll give you the thirty sequins. When you lose on credit, you have twenty-four hours to pay.

LEANDRO Do you see, Signora Lisaura? He's one of those characters who claim to be honourable. He doesn't have a penny and still thinks he's a charmer.

EUGENIO Young men of my kind, my dear Count, are not capable of assuming an obligation without having the means of discharging it with honour. Had she opened her door to me, I wouldn't have wasted her time, and you wouldn't have remained down here with your uncertainties. This is money. This is thirty sequins, and these faces, when they're not to be had, they're to be found. Take your thirty sequins and learn how to speak with a gentleman like me. *(goes to sit in the coffee house)*

LEANDRO *(aside)* He paid me. Let him say what he wants. I don't care. *(to Lisaura)* Open the door.

LISAURA Where were you all last night?

LEANDRO Open the door.

LISAURA Go to the devil.

LEANDRO Open the door. *(pours the sequins in his hat so that Lisaura sees them)*

LISAURA Just this once I'll open the door for you. *(goes inside and opens the door)*

LEANDRO She does me the favour – thanks to these bright coins. *(enters the house)*

EUGENIO Why him and not me? I'll show her what sort of man I am.

Scene 14

Placida dressed as a wayfarer and Eugenio.

PLACIDA Charity for a poor wayfarer.
EUGENIO *(aside)* There you go. Wayfarers are in fashion.
PLACIDA *(to Eugenio)* Sir, for the love of heaven, couldn't you give me a little something?
EUGENIO What do you mean by that, Signora? Are you merely amusing yourself, or have you come up with another excuse?
PLACIDA Neither the one, nor the other.
EUGENIO So what is it that makes you roam the world?
PLACIDA Because I need to.
EUGENIO What do you need?
PLACIDA Everything.
EUGENIO Even company?
PLACIDA I would have no need of that if my husband hadn't abandoned me.
EUGENIO The same old song: My husband abandoned me. Where are you from, Signora?
PLACIDA From Piedmont.
EUGENIO And your husband?
PLACIDA He, too, is from Piedmont.
EUGENIO What did he do there?
PLACIDA He was a merchant's bookkeeper.
EUGENIO And why did he leave?
PLACIDA Little desire to do good.
EUGENIO I've suffered from this disease as well, and I'm not yet cured.
PLACIDA Sir, help me, in pity's name. I've just arrived in Venice. I don't know where to go. I don't know anyone. I don't have any money. I'm desperate.
EUGENIO Why did you come to Venice?
PLACIDA To see if I can find that no-good husband of mine.
EUGENIO What's his name?
PLACIDA Flaminio Ardenti.
EUGENIO I've never heard that name.
PLACIDA I'm afraid he's changed his name.
EUGENIO As you go about the city, if he's here, maybe you'll find him.
PLACIDA If he sees me, he'll flee.

EUGENIO Since it's now carnival, you should do this: wear a mask, and that way it will be easier to catch him.

PLACIDA But how can I do that if I don't have anyone to help me? I don't even know where I can find lodgings.

EUGENIO *(aside)* I understand. I'm about to do some way-faring of my own. *(to Placida)* If you'll permit me, this is a good inn.

PLACIDA How can I be so bold as to show myself at an inn if I don't have enough to pay for a bed?

EUGENIO My dear wayfarer, if you want a half-ducat, I can give it to you. *(aside)* It's all I have left from last night's game.

PLACIDA I thank you for your charity. But more than a half-ducat, more than any money, I would value your protection.

EUGENIO *(aside)* She doesn't want my half-ducat. She wants something more.

Scene 15

Enter *Don Marzio from the barbershop.*

DON MARZIO *(aside)* Eugenio with a wayfarer! This has got to be good! *(sits down at the cafe, looking at the wayfarer with his lorgnette)*

PLACIDA Do me this favour. Introduce me to the innkeeper. Speak a good word for me to him so that when he sees me like this, by myself, he won't chase me away or mistreat me.

EUGENIO Gladly. Let's go. I'll accompany you. The innkeeper knows me, and out of regard for me, I hope that he will extend you every courtesy.

DON MARZIO *(aside)* It seems to me that I've seen her before. *(looks on with the lorgnette)*

PLACIDA I will be eternally indebted to you.

EUGENIO I help everyone when I can. Should you not find your husband, I'll take care of you. I'm a good-hearted person.

DON MARZIO *(aside)* I'd pay something good to hear what they're saying.

PLACIDA Dear sir, you comfort me with your kind offer. But I wouldn't want the charity of a young man to be misinterpreted. After all, I am not yet an old woman.

EUGENIO Let me tell you, Signora. If everyone had such misgivings, a man's freedom to perform acts of kindness would be taken away. If a rumour is founded upon an apparent impropriety, the fault of the rumourmonger is diminished. But if bad people find reason to suspect a good or indifferent action, the fault is totally theirs, and the merit is not taken away from those who act well. I confess that I'm no saint, but at the same time I pride myself on being a decent and honourable man.

PLACIDA These are the sentiments of an honest, noble, and generous soul.

DON MARZIO *(to Eugenio)* Friend, who is this pretty wayfarer?

EUGENIO *(aside)* Here he goes again. He wants to stick his nose into everything. *(to Placida)* Let's go inside.

PLACIDA I'll follow you. *(enters the inn with Eugenio)*

Scene 16

Don Marzio, followed by Eugenio from the inn.

DON MARZIO Oh, isn't he kind, Signor Eugenio! He gets involved in everything, even that wayfarer. She certainly seems to be the one from last year. I bet that she's the one who used to come every evening to the cafe begging alms. But I never gave her any! Hah. What little money I have, I want to spend well. Boys, has Trappola come back yet? Hasn't he brought back the earrings that Signor Eugenio gave me as security for the ten sequins?

EUGENIO What are you saying about my affairs?

DON MARZIO Well. So now it's the wayfarer!

EUGENIO Can't I help a poor creature who finds herself in need?

DON MARZIO Yes. Indeed, you do well to help her. Poor wretch! Hasn't she found someone to give her shelter since last year?

EUGENIO What do you mean, since last year? Do you know that wayfarer?

DON MARZIO Do I know her? I know her and how! It's true that I'm short-sighted, but I have a good memory.

EUGENIO Dear friend, tell me who she is.

DON MARZIO Last year she used to come to this cafe every evening to cozen one man or another.

EUGENIO And she told me that she had never been to Venice before.

DON MARZIO And you believe her? You poor simpleton!

EUGENIO The one from last year, where was she from?

DON MARZIO Milan.

EUGENIO This one is from Piedmont.

DON MARZIO Oh, yes, you're right. From Piedmont.

EUGENIO She's the wife of a certain Flaminio Ardenti.

DON MARZIO Last year as well she had someone with her who passed for her husband.

EUGENIO Now she doesn't have anyone.

DON MARZIO What a life they lead! They change husbands every month.

EUGENIO But how can you say that it's the same one?

DON MARZIO I know her!

EUGENIO Did you get a good look at her?

DON MARZIO My lorgnette is never mistaken, and I also heard her speak.

EUGENIO What was the name of the one from last year?

DON MARZIO I don't remember her name.

EUGENIO This one is called Placida.

DON MARZIO That's right. She was called Placida.

EUGENIO If I were sure of this, I'd really like to tell her what she deserves.

DON MARZIO When I say something, you can believe it. She's a wayfarer all right, not so much seeking to be put up for the night as to put one over on you.

EUGENIO Wait. I'll be right back. *(aside)* I want to find out the truth. *(enters the inn)*

Scene 17

Don Marzio, followed by Vittoria, masked.

DON MARZIO It can't be anyone else but her, absolutely: her air, her stature, even her dress seem the same. I didn't see her face very well, but it's her without a doubt. And then, when she saw me, she hid herself right away in the inn.

VITTORIA Signor Don Marzio, my respects. *(takes off her mask)*

DON MARZIO I'm your servant, my sweet mask.

VITTORIA By chance, have you seen my husband?

DON MARZIO Yes, Signora, I've seen him.

VITTORIA Could you tell where he is at present?

DON MARZIO I certainly could.

VITTORIA I pray that you will have the kindness to tell me.

DON MARZIO Listen. *(takes her aside)* He's here at the inn with quite some wayfarer. Oh, boy! With all the trimmings.

VITTORIA How long has he been in there?

DON MARZIO He just now arrived. A wayfarer was passing through. He saw her. He liked her, and he went straight into the inn.
VITTORIA What a reckless man! He wants to ruin his good name.
DON MARZIO Last night you must have waited for him for a good while.
VITTORIA I was afraid some misfortune had befallen him.
DON MARZIO Do you call losing a hundred sequins in cash and thirty on credit a misfortune?
VITTORIA He lost all that money?
DON MARZIO Yes! And more, too! What do you expect if he plays all day and all night like a scoundrel?
VITTORIA *(aside)* Woe is me! I feel my heart breaking.
DON MARZIO Now he'll have to sell off at a sacrifice what little cloth he has, and that's the end of him.
VITTORIA I hope that he isn't about to go bankrupt.
DON MARZIO Well, he's pawned everything.
VITTORIA Pardon me, but it's not true.
DON MARZIO You're telling me?
VITTORIA I ought to know better than you.
DON MARZIO If he's pawned things with me … Enough of this. I am a gentleman. I won't say any more.
VITTORIA I beg you to tell me what he's pawned. It might be something I don't know.
DON MARZIO Go on now. You have a fine husband.
VITTORIA Do you care to tell what it is that he has pawned?
DON MARZIO I'm a gentleman. I don't have anything more to tell you.

Scene 18

Enter *Trappola with the earring-case.*

TRAPPOLA Oh, here I am. The jeweller said … *(aside)* Oh! What do I see? Signor Eugenio's wife. I don't want her to hear me.
DON MARZIO *(quietly to Trappola)* Well, what did the jeweller say?
TRAPPOLA *(quietly to Don Marzio)* He says that you may have paid more than ten sequins for them, but he'd never pay that much.
DON MARZIO *(to Trappola)* So I'm not covered?

TRAPPOLA *(to Don Marzio)* I'm afraid not.

DON MARZIO *(to Vittoria)* Do you see your husband's fine roguery? He pawns these earrings to me for ten sequins, and they're not even worth six.

VITTORIA These are my earrings.

DON MARZIO Give me ten sequins, and I'll give them to you.

VITTORIA They're worth more than thirty.

DON MARZIO Thirty figs! You must be in league with him.

VITTORIA Keep them until tomorrow, and I'll find the ten sequins.

DON MARZIO Until tomorrow? Don't mock me. I want to have them appraised by all the jewellers in Venice.

VITTORIA At least don't say that they are mine, for my reputation's sake.

DON MARZIO What do I care about your reputation? If you don't want such things known, don't pawn your valuables. *(exit Don Marzio)*

Scene 19

Vittoria and Trappola.

VITTORIA What an inconsiderate, uncouth man! Trappola, where is your master?

TRAPPOLA I don't know. I just got to the shop.

VITTORIA So my husband gambled the whole night long?

TRAPPOLA I found him this morning where I left him last night.

VITTORIA Accursed vice! And he lost one hundred and thirty sequins?

TRAPPOLA That's what they say.

VITTORIA Abominable plague! And now he's amusing himself with a stranger?

TRAPPOLA Yes, ma'am. He's probably with her. I've seen him around her a good deal of late. Likely he's at her house.

VITTORIA They tell me that this stranger arrived not long ago.

TRAPPOLA No, ma'am. She's been here for maybe a month.

VITTORIA She's not a wayfarer?

TRAPPOLA What? A wayfarer? I don't know how you could get it wrong. "Wayfarer" and "dancer" don't sound at all alike. She's a dancer.

VITTORIA And she's staying here at the inn?

TRAPPOLA No, ma'am. *(indicating the house)* She stays in this house.

VITTORIA Here? But Signor Don Marzio told me that he's at the inn with the wayfarer!

TRAPPOLA Fine! A wayfarer, too?

VITTORIA Besides the wayfarer there's a dancer? One here and one there?

TRAPPOLA Yes, ma'am. Probably to keep sailing before the wind. Windward to leeward, depending on whether the wind is north or south.

VITTORIA Must he always lead a life like this? Does a spirited and talented man like that have to waste his time so miserably, sacrifice his possessions, wreck his house? And do I have to suffer this? And am I to let myself be mistreated without resenting it? I want to be good, but not stupid. I don't want my silence to encourage his misbehaviour. I'll talk to him. I'll tell him what I think. And if words aren't enough, I'll go to court.

TRAPPOLA Quite so. Quite so. Here he comes from the inn.

VITTORIA Dear friend, leave me.

TRAPPOLA Be my guest, as you like. *(enters the back of the shop)*

Scene 20

Vittoria, followed by Eugenio from the inn.

VITTORIA I will increase his surprise by putting the mask on again. *(puts the mask on)*

EUGENIO I don't know what to say. She denies it, and he stands firm. I know Don Marzio is a scandalmonger, and these women who travel are not to be trusted. A mask! Good morning! Are you a mute? Would you like a coffee? If you'd like something, I'm at your service.

VITTORIA I don't need coffee, but I do need bread. *(takes off her mask)*

EUGENIO How in the world? What are you doing here?

VITTORIA I came out of sheer desperation.

EUGENIO What's this all about? Masked so early in the day?

VITTORIA What do you think of that? Some fun! A mask so early!

EUGENIO Go home right away.

VITTORIA I'll go home, and you'll stay here and amuse yourself.

EUGENIO You go home, and I'll stay where I like.

VITTORIA Nice life, my dear spouse!

EUGENIO Enough nonsense, Signora. Go home, and you'll be better off.

VITTORIA Yes, I'll go home, but I'll go to my house, not to your house.

EUGENIO Where do you intend to go?

VITTORIA To my father's house. He'll be sick when he hears how you've mistreated me. He'll know how to deal with your doings and my dowry.

EUGENIO Well, well, Signora. This shows your great love for me. This is how you care for me and my reputation.

VITTORIA I've always heard that cruelty is the death of love. I've suffered so much. I've cried so much. But now I can't take any more.

EUGENIO Really, what have I done to you?

VITTORIA All night gambling.

EUGENIO Who told you that I was gambling?

VITTORIA Signor Don Marzio told me. And he also told me that you lost a hundred sequins in cash and thirty on credit.

EUGENIO Don't believe him. It's not true.

VITTORIA And then, amusing yourself with the wayfarer.

EUGENIO Who told you this?

VITTORIA Signor Don Marzio.

EUGENIO *(aside)* Curse you, Don Marzio! *(to Vittoria)* Believe me. It's not true.

VITTORIA And what's more, you pawned my things. Take my earrings without telling me? Is this the way you treat a loving, civil, and honest wife?

EUGENIO How did you find out about the earrings?

VITTORIA Signor Don Marzio told me.

EUGENIO He ought to have his tongue cut out!

VITTORIA Signor Don Marzio is saying it already, and so will everyone: one of these days you'll be completely ruined. And before that happens, I want to make sure my dowry is safe.

EUGENIO Vittoria, if you loved me, you wouldn't talk like that.

VITTORIA I love you too much, and if I hadn't loved you so much, I would have been better off.

EUGENIO Do you intend to go to your father's house?

VITTORIA Yes, I certainly do.

EUGENIO You don't want to be with me any more?

VITTORIA I'll be with you when you get some sense into your head.

EUGENIO *(angry)* Oh, spare me, Signora Know-it-all.

VITTORIA Be quiet. Let's not make a scene in the street.

EUGENIO If you cared for your reputation, you wouldn't come to chide your husband in a coffee house.

VITTORIA Don't worry, I won't come again.

EUGENIO Come on. Off with you.

Vittoria I'll go. I'll obey you because an honest wife must obey even a wayward husband. But maybe you will long for me when you can't see me any more. You'll invoke the name of your dear wife when she won't be able to answer you and help you. But yet you won't be able to complain about my love. I've done everything a wife who loves her husband can do. You've responded with ingratitude. So be it. I will cry away from you, but I can't conscience all the wrong that you do me. I will always love you, but you won't see me ever again.
(exit Vittoria)

Eugenio Poor woman! She's touched my heart. I know that she says she will, but she's not capable of doing it. I'll follow after her and wheedle her till I bring her around. If she takes away the dowry, I'm ruined. But she won't have the heart to do it. When your wife is vexed, a few caresses are enough to console her. *(exit Eugenio)*

ACT TWO

Scene 1

Enter *Ridolfo from the street, followed by Trappola from the back of the coffee house.*

Ridolfo Boys, where are you?

Trappola Here I am, Master.

Ridolfo So, you leave the shop all alone?

Trappola I was there with ears open and eyes peeled. And what is there to steal anyway? No one goes behind the counter.

Ridolfo They can steal the coffee cups. I know for sure that there's someone collecting cups, pinching them one by one from poor shop owners.

Trappola Like those who go to parties to keep up their supply of cups and saucers.

Ridolfo Has Signor Eugenio left?

Trappola If you only knew! His wife came by. Oh, how she cried and complained! Barbarian! Cruel traitor! With a little affection and a little anger she managed to soften him up.

Ridolfo And where did he go?

Trappola What kind of question is that! Last night he didn't go home, his wife comes here looking for him, and you ask where did he go?

RIDOLFO Did he leave any instructions?

TRAPPOLA He came back through the back door and told me to remind you about the cloth deal because he's flat broke.

RIDOLFO I sold the two bolts of cloth for thirteen lire a yard, and I got the money. But I don't want him to know. I don't want to give it all to him because if he gets his hands on it, he'll spend it in one day.

TRAPPOLA When he finds out that you have it, he'll want it right away.

RIDOLFO I won't tell him that I got it all. I'll give him what he needs, and then I'll see what happens.

TRAPPOLA Here he comes. *Lupus est in fabula.*

RIDOLFO What's it mean, this Latin of yours?

TRAPPOLA It means: the wolf pestles the lava. *(withdraws to the shop laughing)*

RIDOLFO He's a strange one. He thinks he speaks Latin, and he doesn't even know how to speak his native tongue.

Scene 2

Ridolfo and Eugenio.

EUGENIO So, my friend Ridolfo, have you been able to do anything?

RIDOLFO I managed to do something.

EUGENIO I heard that you got the two bolts of cloth. The boy told me. Did you sell them?

RIDOLFO I sold them.

EUGENIO For how much?

RIDOLFO Thirteen lire a yard.

EUGENIO Not bad. Did you get all the money?

RIDOLFO Some in hand, some in time.

EUGENIO Oh, no! How much in hand?

RIDOLFO Forty sequins.

EUGENIO Well, that's not bad. Give it to me. It's just in the nick of time.

RIDOLFO Slow down, Signor Eugenio. My lord, you know full well that I lent you thirty sequins.

EUGENIO Very well. You'll get your money when the balance is paid.

RIDOLFO This sentiment, I'm sorry to say, does not become you. You know how I have served you: promptly, quickly, and without self-interest. And you want to make me wait? I, too, sir, have my obligations.

EUGENIO Well, you're right. Bear with me. You're right. Keep the thirty sequins, and give me ten.

RIDOLFO Don't you want to pay Signor Don Marzio with these ten sequins? Don't you want to get that devil off your back?

EUGENIO He's got his security. He'll wait.

RIDOLFO My lord, is this all you care for your reputation? Why should you let yourself be bullied by that gossipmonger and his chatter, by one who helps others just so he can brag about it, and who has no other pleasure in life than discrediting true gentlemen?

EUGENIO You're right. I've got to pay him. But must I remain penniless? How much time did you give the buyer?

RIDOLFO How much do you need?

EUGENIO I don't know. Ten or twelve sequins.

RIDOLFO Right away, sir. Here are ten sequins, and when Signor Don Marzio comes by, I'll get the earrings back.

EUGENIO This money you're giving me, what is to be the understanding about it?

RIDOLFO Keep it, and don't worry any more. In time we'll settle.

EUGENIO But when will we cash in on the rest of the cloth?

RIDOLFO Don't worry about it. Spend the money, and then we'll see. But be sure to spend it wisely. Don't throw it away.

EUGENIO Yes, friend, I am obliged to you. Don't forget your brokerage fee in the bill for the cloth.

RIDOLFO I don't understand. I'm a coffeemaker, not a broker. If I go out of my way for my master, for a friend, I don't expect anything out of it. Every man is obliged to help another when he can, and I am obliged to do so with you principally, my lord, in gratitude for the good I have received from your father. I'll consider myself compensated if this money – that I have honourably procured for you – is used to profit your household, so that your dignity and honour will be restored.

EUGENIO You are a very upright and decent man. It's a pity that this is your profession. You deserve a higher station and a better lot than this.

RIDOLFO I am happy with what heaven gives me, and I wouldn't trade places with many others who have more show but less substance. I lack nothing in my station. I have a respectable profession in the order of trades. It's honest, dignified, and decent. It's a profession that serves all classes of men when it's done rightly and nobly. It's a profession necessary to the dignity of the city, for the health of men, and for the wholesome amusement of all those who need some respite. *(enters the shop)*

EUGENIO There goes a gallant man. I wouldn't want anyone to think him too smart, however. In fact, for a coffee house owner, it seems he talks too much. But in every profession there are talented and upright men. At least he doesn't talk of philosophy or mathematics. He speaks like a man of sound judgment. If heaven only willed that I were as wise as he is.

Scene 3

Enter *Leandro from Lisaura's house and Eugenio.*

LEANDRO Signor Eugenio, here's your money, right here in this purse. If you want it back, let's go.

EUGENIO I'm out of luck. I'm not gambling any more.

LEANDRO You know the proverb: sometimes the hound wins, sometimes the hare.

EUGENIO But I'm always the hare, and you're always the hound.

LEANDRO I'm so sleepy, I can't see straight. I'm sure I wouldn't even be able to hold my cards. Yet thanks to this accursed habit, I don't care if I lose – as long as I play.

EUGENIO I'm sleepy myself. I'm certainly not playing today.

LEANDRO If you don't have any money, it doesn't matter. I'll take your word.

EUGENIO You think I don't have any money? Here are ten sequins, but I don't want to play. *(showing him his purse)*

LEANDRO Let's just play for a cup of chocolate.

EUGENIO I don't feel like it.

LEANDRO A cup of chocolate a hand.

EUGENIO But I told you …

LEANDRO Just one little cup of chocolate. Whoever suggests we play for anything more loses a ducat.

EUGENIO All right. For a cup of chocolate. Let's go. *(aside)* Ridolfo won't see me.

LEANDRO *(aside)* The bird is in the snare. *(enters the gambling house with Eugenio)*

Scene 4

Don Marzio, followed by Ridolfo from the back of the shop.

Don Marzio All the jewellers tell me that they're not worth ten sequins. All of them are amazed that Eugenio cheated me. That's what you get when you do someone a favour. I'm never giving a penny to anyone again, even if he's dying. Where the devil could he be? He's probably hiding so he doesn't have to pay me.

Ridolfo Sir, do you have Signor Eugenio's earrings?

Don Marzio Here they are. Fine earrings, not worth a straw. He tricked me, that cheater! He's hiding so he doesn't have to pay me. He's ruined. He's ruined.

Ridolfo Here, sir. Don't make any more ruckus. Here are ten sequins. Please give me the earrings.

Don Marzio *(examining the sequins with his lorgnette)* These coins, solid gold?

Ridolfo I guarantee them. If they're not, I'm to blame.

Don Marzio Are you putting them up for sale?

Ridolfo It has nothing to do with me. This is Signor Eugenio's money.

Don Marzio Where on earth did he find this money?

Ridolfo That is his affair, not mine.

Don Marzio Did he win it gambling?

Ridolfo I'm telling you, I don't know.

Don Marzio Now that I think about it, he probably sold the cloth. Yes, yes. He sold the cloth. He had Master Pandolfo sell it for him.

Ridolfo Have it your way, but take the money, and please give me the earrings.

Don Marzio Did Signor Eugenio give it to you himself, or did Pandolfo give it to you?

Ridolfo What difference does it make? Do you want the money or not?

Don Marzio Give it here. Give it to me. Mistreated cloth. I'm sure he gave it away.

Ridolfo Are you going to give me the earrings?

Don Marzio Are you supposed to take them to him?

Ridolfo Yes, to him.

Don Marzio To him, or his wife?

Ridolfo *(impatiently)* To him or to his wife.

Don Marzio Where is he?

Ridolfo I don't know.

DON MARZIO So you'll take them to his wife?
RIDOLFO I'll take them to his wife.
DON MARZIO I'm coming, too.
RIDOLFO Give them to me, and don't worry. I'm a gentleman.
DON MARZIO *(leaving)* Let's go, let's go. We'll take them to his wife.
RIDOLFO I know how to get there by myself.
DON MARZIO I want to do her this favour. Let's go. Let's go. *(exit Don Marzio)*
RIDOLFO When he wants something, there's no two ways about it. Lads, watch the shop. *(he follows Don Marzio)*

Scene 5

Boys in the coffee house, enter Eugenio from the gambling house.

EUGENIO Curse my luck! I lost it all. For a cup of chocolate, I lost ten sequins. But the way he treated me is harder to bear than the loss. Drag me in there and win all that money, and then refuse to credit my word? Now that's going too far. It really is. Now I'll play until tomorrow even if it kills me. Let Ridolfo say what he wants. He's got to give me more money. Boys, where's your master?
BOY He just left.
EUGENIO Where did he go?
BOY I don't know, sir.
EUGENIO Accursed Ridolfo! Where the devil could he have gone? *(towards the gambling house)* Signor Count, wait for me. I'll be right back. *(about to leave)* I want to see if I can't find that devil Ridolfo.

Scene 6

Enter *Pandolfo from the street.*

PANDOLFO Where, where are you going, Signor Eugenio, so worked up?
EUGENIO Have you seen Ridolfo?
PANDOLFO No, I haven't.
EUGENIO Have you done anything about the cloth?
PANDOLFO Yes, sir, I have.
EUGENIO Great! What have you done?

PANDOLFO I found a buyer, but it wasn't easy! I showed it to more than ten people, and none of them thought much of it.

EUGENIO How much is this buyer willing to give?

PANDOLFO I talked him in to giving me eight lire a yard.

EUGENIO What the devil are you saying? Eight lire a yard? Ridolfo sold two bolts of it at thirteen lire.

PANDOLFO Cash down?

EUGENIO Part of it right away, and the rest in time.

PANDOLFO Some good deal! In time! I'm getting you all the money up front. The more yards of cloth, the more ducats of Venetian silver.

EUGENIO *(aside)* Ridolfo's not around! I could use the money. This has gone too far.

PANDOLFO Had I wanted to sell the cloth on credit, I could have sold it for sixteen lire. But with the money up front, these days, you've got to take what you can get.

EUGENIO But the cloth cost me ten lire.

PANDOLFO What does it matter if you lose two lire a yard as long as you have the money to take care of your affairs, and to make up what you've lost?

EUGENIO Wouldn't it be possible to get a better deal? Couldn't we sell it at cost?

PANDOLFO We can't hope to get a penny more.

EUGENIO *(aside)* I've no other choice. *(to Pandolfo)* All right, do what you need to right away.

PANDOLFO Make me an order for two bolts of cloth, and in half an hour I'll bring you the money.

EUGENIO I'm right with you. Boys, bring me something to write on. *(boys bring a small writing table and writing implements)*

PANDOLFO Write an order for your boy to give me the two bolts of cloth I picked out.

EUGENIO *(writing)* Very well. It's all the same to me.

PANDOLFO *(aside)* Oh, what a fine suit I'm going to have made!

Scene 7

Enter *Ridolfo from the street.*

RIDOLFO *(aside)* Signor Eugenio is writing an agreement with Master Pandolfo. Something must have happened.

PANDOLFO *(aside, watching Ridolfo)* I wouldn't want him to spoil what I've got going.

RIDOLFO Signor Eugenio, your servant.

EUGENIO *(continues to write)* Oh, how are you?

RIDOLFO Deep in business, Signor Eugenio? Deep in business?

EUGENIO *(writing)* Oh, just a small deal.

RIDOLFO Would you care to enlighten me?

EUGENIO You see what it means to sell the goods on credit? I can't avail myself of my own property. I need money, and so I'll have to sacrifice another two bolts of cloth.

PANDOLFO Don't say sacrifice two bolts of cloth when you're getting what you can for them.

RIDOLFO How much are they giving you a yard?

EUGENIO I'm ashamed to tell you. Eight lire.

PANDOLFO But all of his money up front.

RIDOLFO Why, my lord, do you want to unload your goods so cheaply?

EUGENIO But I have no choice! I need the money.

PANDOLFO It wasn't easy, but in an hour I found him the money he needs.

RIDOLFO *(to Eugenio)* How much do you need?

EUGENIO What? Do you have some to give me?

PANDOLFO *(aside)* I'll bet he's going to queer the deal yet.

RIDOLFO If all you needed was six or seven sequins, I'd find them.

EUGENIO Are you joking? I need real money. *(writes)*

PANDOLFO *(aside)* I'm glad we settled that.

RIDOLFO Wait. How much will the two bolts bring at eight lire a yard?

EUGENIO Let's see. There are sixty yards in each roll. Two times sixty is one hundred and twenty. One hundred and twenty silver ducats.

PANDOLFO But there's the brokerage to pay.

RIDOLFO *(to Pandolfo)* To whom does he pay the brokerage?

PANDOLFO *(to Ridolfo)* To me, sir, to me.

RIDOLFO Very well. One hundred and twenty silver ducats, at eight lire each. How many sequins does that make?

EUGENIO For every eleven, four sequins. Ten times eleven is one hundred and ten. Plus eleven is one hundred and twenty-one. Four times eleven is forty-four. Forty-four sequins, less a ducat. Forty-three, and fourteen lire, Venetian coin.

PANDOLFO Let's say forty sequins. I keep the small change for my brokerage.

EUGENIO Are three sequins small change?

PANDOLFO Certainly, but you get the money right away.

EUGENIO All right. All right. It doesn't matter. I'll give it to you.

RIDOLFO *(aside)* What a thief! *(to Eugenio)* Now let's see, Signor Eugenio. How much do the two bolts bring at thirteen lire?

EUGENIO They bring a lot more!

PANDOLFO But paid over time: you can't take care of your affairs.

RIDOLFO Figure it out.

EUGENIO Now I'll do it in pen. One hundred and twenty yards, at thirteen a yard. Three times zero. Two times three is six. One times three. One times zero. One times two. One times one. The total is: zero; six; two and three makes five; one. One thousand, five hundred, sixty lire.

RIDOLFO How many sequins does that make?

EUGENIO I'll tell you right away. *(counts)* Seventy sequins and twenty lire.

RIDOLFO Without the brokerage.

EUGENIO Without the brokerage.

PANDOLFO But who knows how long you'll have to wait. A bird in the hand is worth two in the bush.

RIDOLFO I gave you: first thirty sequins, and then ten. That makes forty, and ten for the earrings that I got back. That's fifty. Well, then, I've given you now ten sequins more than you get right away in cash, up front, from him, this most honourable Signor Broker.

PANDOLFO *(aside)* Curse you!

EUGENIO It's true. You're right. But I need the money now.

RIDOLFO You're in need of money? Here it is: here are twenty sequins and twenty lire that make up the rest of the seventy sequins and twenty lire, price of the one hundred and twenty yards of cloth at thirteen lire a yard, without paying any brokerage. Right away, in hand, up front, without thievery, without sponging, without any cheater's tricks.

EUGENIO When you put it that way, dear Ridolfo, I can't thank you enough. I'll rip up this order. *(to Pandolfo)* And I won't be needing anything from you, Signor Broker.

PANDOLFO *(aside)* The devil himself must have brought him here. There goes my new suit. *(to Eugenio)* Very well, it doesn't matter. The only thing I wasted was time.

EUGENIO I'm sorry for the trouble.

PANDOLFO At least a glass of brandy.

EUGENIO Wait. Take this ducat. *(takes out a ducat from the bag that Ridolfo gave him)*

Pandolfo Much obliged. *(aside)* Well, I'll catch him yet. *(to Eugenio)* Is there anything else that you need?

Eugenio Just your good will.

Pandolfo *(to Eugenio, making a gesture inviting him to play cards, unseen by Ridolfo)* What do you say?

Eugenio *(secretly to Pandolfo)* You go ahead. I'll follow.

Pandolfo *(aside)* I'll have him at it again before dinner. *(enters the gambling house)*

Eugenio How did it go, Ridolfo? Have you already seen the debtor? Did he already give you the money?

Ridolfo To tell you the truth, I had the money in my pocket from the beginning. But I didn't want to give it to you right away, so that you wouldn't squander it so quickly.

Eugenio You are wrong to speak to me like that. I'm not a child any more. Enough … Where are the earrings?

Ridolfo After I gave him the ten sequins, the ever-kind Signor Don Marzio insisted on taking the earrings to Signora Vittoria personally.

Eugenio Did you speak with my wife?

Ridolfo Of course I did. I went along with Signor Don Marzio.

Eugenio What did she say?

Ridolfo All she did was cry. Poor dear! It makes you feel sorry for her.

Eugenio You should have seen how mad she was! She wanted to go back to her father. She wanted her dowry back. She wanted to stir things up in grand fashion.

Ridolfo How did you calm her down?

Eugenio With a hug and a kiss.

Ridolfo You can tell that she loves you. She's a good-hearted woman.

Eugenio But when she gets angry, she's a fury.

Ridolfo You shouldn't mistreat her so. She was born a lady, well-bred. She told me that if I saw you, I should tell you to get home early for dinner.

Eugenio Yes, yes. I'm on my way.

Ridolfo Dear Signor Eugenio, I beg you: stand firm. Forget gambling. Stop chasing after women. My lord, you already have a young and beautiful wife who loves you. What more could you want?

Eugenio You're right. I am very grateful to you.

Pandolfo *(from his gambling house, coughs so that Eugenio looks at him; Eugenio turns around; Pandolfo gestures that Leandro is waiting to play cards; Eugenio gestures by hand that he'll go; Pandolfo goes back inside; Ridolfo doesn't notice)*

RIDOLFO I'd advise you to go home now. It's almost noon. Go and take care of your dear wife.

EUGENIO Yes. I'll go right away. I'll see you later.

RIDOLFO Whenever I may be of service, you have only to call on me.

EUGENIO *(wanting to gamble, but fearful that Ridolfo might see him)* I am much obliged to you.

RIDOLFO May I do something for you? Do you need anything?

EUGENIO No, no. See you later.

RIDOLFO Your servant. *(turns towards his coffee house)*

EUGENIO *(seeing that Ridolfo is not watching him, enters the gambling house)*

Scene 8

Ridolfo, followed by Don Marzio.

RIDOLFO Bit by bit I hope to get him on the right path. They'll say to me: Why do you want to break your back for a young man who isn't even a relative of yours, who has nothing to do with you? Well? Can't I care for a friend? Can't I help a family to which I am indebted? This profession of ours allows for plenty of leisure time. Many spend the extra time gambling, or gossiping. I use it to help others when I can. *(enter Don Marzio)*

DON MARZIO Oh, what a blockhead! Oh, what a blockhead! Oh, what an ass!

RIDOLFO With whom are you cross, Signor Don Marzio?

DON MARZIO Listen to this, Ridolfo, if you want to laugh. I know a doctor who maintains that hot water is healthier to drink than cold water.

RIDOLFO Don't you share his opinion?

DON MARZIO Hot water weakens the stomach.

RIDOLFO It certainly relaxes the fibre.

DON MARZIO What is this fibre?

RIDOLFO I've heard that there are two fibres in our stomach, almost like two nerves, that grind food. And when these fibres slow down, it causes bad digestion.

DON MARZIO Yes, sir. Yes, sir. Hot water relaxes the ventricle, and the systole and the diastole can't chop the food.

RIDOLFO What do the systole and the diastole have to do with it?

DON MARZIO What do you know, you jackass? Systole and diastole are the names of the two fibres that do the grinding of the digestive food.

RIDOLFO *(aside)* Oh, what nonsense! He's worse than my Trappola!

Scene 9

Enter *Lisaura at the window.*

DON MARZIO *(to Ridolfo)* Look! It's our friend from the back door.

RIDOLFO With your permission, I'm going to see to the coffee. *(enters the shop)*

DON MARZIO He's an ass. He won't stay in business very long. *(to Lisaura, watching her now and then with his lorgnette)* Your servant, my lady.

LISAURA Your most humble servant.

DON MARZIO Are you well?

LISAURA At your service.

DON MARZIO When did you last see Count Leandro?

LISAURA About an hour ago.

DON MARZIO The Count is a friend of mine.

LISAURA Glad to hear it.

DON MARZIO A true gentleman!

LISAURA It's very kind of you to say so.

DON MARZIO Say, is he your husband?

LISAURA I don't discuss my affairs at the window.

DON MARZIO Open the door. Open the door, and we'll talk.

LISAURA I beg your pardon. I don't receive guests.

DON MARZIO Oh, come!

LISAURA No, really.

DON MARZIO I'll come through the back door.

LISAURA So, you've dreamt up a back door, too? I open my door for no one.

DON MARZIO You don't have to talk to me that way. I know full well that you receive people through there.

LISAURA I am a respectable woman.

DON MARZIO May I offer you some dried chestnuts? *(takes them out from his pocket)*

LISAURA I'm deeply grateful.

DON MARZIO They're good, you know. I dry them myself on my estate.

LISAURA I can see that you've a good hand for drying.
DON MARZIO Is that so?
LISAURA Why don't you go dry up yourself!
DON MARZIO I like a spirited woman! Since you like frolicking so much, you must be a good dancer.
LISAURA It's no concern of yours, whether I'm a good dancer or not.
DON MARZIO To tell the truth, I couldn't care less.

Scene 10

Enter *Placida, dressed as a wayfarer, at the window of the inn.*

PLACIDA *(aside)* I don't see Signor Eugenio.
DON MARZIO *(to Lisaura, after looking at Placida with his lorgnette)* Say, have you seen the wayfarer yet?
LISAURA Who is she?
DON MARZIO One of those women of pleasure.
LISAURA Does the innkeeper take in people like that?
DON MARZIO She's kept.
LISAURA By whom?
DON MARZIO By Signor Eugenio.
LISAURA A married man? Better yet!
DON MARZIO Last year she made the rounds.
LISAURA *(going back inside)* Your servant.
DON MARZIO Are you leaving?
LISAURA I don't want to be at the window when there's a woman of that sort across the way. *(goes back inside)*

Scene 11

Placida at the window, Don Marzio in the street.

DON MARZIO Oh, oh, oh, this is grand! The dancer retires for fear of compromising her respectability! *(with his lorgnette)* Signora, my respects.
PLACIDA Your obedient servant.
DON MARZIO Where is Signor Eugenio?
PLACIDA Do you know Signor Eugenio?
DON MARZIO Oh, we're very good friends. I just went to call on his wife.

PLACIDA So, Signor Eugenio has a wife?

DON MARZIO Sure he has a wife. But that doesn't mean he doesn't like a pretty face. Did you see that lady at that window?

PLACIDA I saw her. She had the courtesy to close the window in my face, without a word, after she took a good look at me.

DON MARZIO She passes for a dancer, but … You understand.

PLACIDA Is she a loose woman?

DON MARZIO And Signor Eugenio is one of her protectors.

PLACIDA And he has a wife?

DON MARZIO And a pretty one at that.

PLACIDA The world is full of reckless youths.

DON MARZIO Perhaps he gave you reason to believe that he wasn't married?

PLACIDA I couldn't care less whether he is or not.

DON MARZIO You're indifferent. You take him as he is.

PLACIDA Insofar as it concerns me, I don't care one way or the other.

DON MARZIO Yes, of course. One today, tomorrow another.

PLACIDA How do you mean? Explain yourself.

DON MARZIO Would you care for some dried chestnuts? *(takes them out of his pocket)*

PLACIDA Much obliged.

DON MARZIO Really, if you like, I'll give them to you.

PLACIDA You're too generous, sir.

DON MARZIO You're really worth more than a couple of chestnuts. If you want, I'll throw in a few lire.

PLACIDA You ill-mannered ass. *(closes the window) (exit Placida)*

DON MARZIO She's too good for a couple of lire … And to think last year she didn't mind less. *(calling out loudly)* Ridolfo!

Scene 12

Enter *Ridolfo*..

RIDOLFO Sir?

DON MARZIO There's a shortage of women. They think they're too good for my money.

RIDOLFO What makes you think they're all the same?

DON MARZIO Just riff-raff that roams the world. It makes me laugh.

RIDOLFO Respectable people roam the world, too.

Don Marzio A wayfarer! Ah, you fool!
Ridolfo No one knows who that wayfarer is.
Don Marzio I do. She's the one from last year.
Ridolfo I've never seen her before.
Don Marzio Because you're a numbskull.
Ridolfo Thanks for your kindness. *(aside)* I'd like to give that wig of his a brush or two.

Scene 13

Enter *Eugenio from the gambling house.*

Eugenio *(happy and laughing)* Your servant, dear sirs and masters.
Ridolfo How can it be! What's Signor Eugenio doing here?
Eugenio *(laughing)* Of course I'm here.
Don Marzio Did you win?
Eugenio Yes, sir, I won. Yes, sir.
Don Marzio It's a miracle!
Eugenio What's the big deal? Can't I win, too? Who do you think I am? A complete idiot?
Ridolfo Signor Eugenio, is this your resolution to stop gambling?
Eugenio Why don't you shut up. I won.
Ridolfo What if you had lost?
Eugenio I couldn't lose today.
Ridolfo No? Why?
Eugenio When I'm going to lose, I can feel it.
Ridolfo And when you feel it, why do you play?
Eugenio Because I've got to lose.
Ridolfo And when are we going home?
Eugenio Come off it. You're getting on my nerves.
Ridolfo I've nothing more to say. *(aside)* Wasted words.

Scene 14

Enter *Leandro from the gambling house.*

Leandro Congratulations. You've won my money. And if I hadn't quit when I did, you would have cleaned me out.

EUGENIO Huh? That's the kind of man I am. I skinned you in three cuts.

LEANDRO You gamble like a madman.

EUGENIO I gamble like a skilled player.

DON MARZIO *(to Leandro)* How much did he win from you?

LEANDRO A lot.

DON MARZIO *(to Eugenio)* But really, how much did you win?

EUGENIO *(happily)* Six sequins.

RIDOLFO *(aside)* Accursed fool! Since yesterday he's lost one hundred and thirty, and he thinks he's won a fortune by earning six.

LEANDRO *(aside)* Every once in a while, you've got to let yourself be beaten to keep their hopes up.

DON MARZIO *(to Eugenio)* What are you going to do with these six sequins?

EUGENIO If you'd like to eat them, I'm for it.

DON MARZIO Let's eat them.

RIDOLFO *(aside)* All my efforts wasted.

EUGENIO Shall we go to the tavern? Everyone can pay for himself.

RIDOLFO *(quietly to Eugenio)* Don't go. They'll try to get you to play some more.

EUGENIO *(quietly to Ridolfo)* Let them try. I'm feeling lucky today.

RIDOLFO *(aside)* He's beyond all help.

LEANDRO Instead of going to the tavern, we could have them prepare something for us at Master Pandolfo's.

EUGENIO Fine, wherever you please. We'll order the dinner from the inn, and we'll have it brought upstairs.

DON MARZIO I'm with you, gentlemen, all the way.

RIDOLFO *(aside)* Poor simpleton! He doesn't know what he's getting into.

LEANDRO Hey, Master Pandolfo.

Scene 15

Enter *Pandolfo from the gambling house.*

PANDOLFO Here I am, at your service.

LEANDRO Would you mind lending us your rooms for dinner?

PANDOLFO At your service, but, you see, I, too … I pay rent …

LEANDRO Yes, of course. We'll pay you for your trouble.

EUGENIO Who do you think you're dealing with? We'll pay for everything.

PANDOLFO Very well, be my guest. I'll go have them prepared. *(enters the gambling house)*
EUGENIO So, who'll go order?
LEANDRO *(to Eugenio)* You should, since you know the town.
DON MARZIO *(to Eugenio)* Yes, you do it.
EUGENIO What shall I order?
LEANDRO You decide.
EUGENIO How does the song go? Merriment is second-class, when a lad's without a lass.
RIDOLFO *(aside)* And he wants a woman, too!
DON MARZIO The Count could have the dancer come.
LEANDRO Why not? I don't see any problem with her coming since we're all friends here.
DON MARZIO *(to Leandro)* Is it true that you want to marry her?
LEANDRO Now's not the time to speak of these things.
EUGENIO And I'll see if I can get the wayfarer to come.
LEANDRO Who is this wayfarer?
EUGENIO A decent and respectable lady.
DON MARZIO *(aside)* Yes, yes. I'll fill him in later.
LEANDRO Off with you. Go order the dinner.
EUGENIO How many are we? The three of us, and two women: that makes five. Signor Don Marzio, do you have a lady?
DON MARZIO Not me. I'm with you.
EUGENIO Ridolfo, would you come have a bite to eat with us?
RIDOLFO Thank you. I have to look after my shop.
EUGENIO Come on, don't be shy.
RIDOLFO *(quietly to Eugenio)* I'm astonished you have such a big heart.
EUGENIO What do you want me to do? I won, and I want to enjoy it.
RIDOLFO And then?
EUGENIO And then, sweet dreams. Let the astrologers worry about the future. *(enters the inn)*
RIDOLFO *(aside)* Oh, well! I wasted my time. *(withdraws)*

Scene 16

Don Marzio and Count Leandro.

DON MARZIO Hurry up. Go fetch the dancer.
LEANDRO When everything's ready, I'll have her come.

DON MARZIO Let's sit down. What's new in the world?

LEANDRO I don't bother with the news. *(they sit)*

DON MARZIO Did you hear that the Muscovite troops went to their winter quarters?[9]

LEANDRO Good for them. The season called for it.

DON MARZIO No, sir. It was a mistake. They shouldn't have given up the place they had occupied.

LEANDRO It's true. They should have suffered the cold rather than lose the conquered territory.

DON MARZIO No, sir. They didn't have to risk staying there with the danger of freezing to death.

LEANDRO So they had to move on.

DON MARZIO No, sir. Oh, you're a true war expert! To march in the winter season!

LEANDRO So, what should they have done?

DON MARZIO Let me see a map, and then I'll tell you exactly where they should have gone.

LEANDRO *(aside)* What a fool!

DON MARZIO Have you been to the opera?

LEANDRO Yes, sir.

DON MARZIO Do you like it?

LEANDRO Very much so.

DON MARZIO You have bad taste.

LEANDRO Oh, well.

DON MARZIO Where are you from?

LEANDRO Turin.

DON MARZIO An awful city.

LEANDRO On the contrary, it's one of Italy's most beautiful.

DON MARZIO I am Neapolitan. See Naples, and then you can die.

LEANDRO I'd like to tell you what a Venetian would say.

DON MARZIO Do you have any snuff?

LEANDRO Here. *(opens the box for him)*

DON MARZIO Oh, what bad snuff!

LEANDRO I like it like this.

DON MARZIO You don't know snuff. Rappee is real snuff.[10]

LEANDRO I like Spanish snuff.

DON MARZIO Spanish snuff is rubbish.

LEANDRO And I tell you it's the best snuff you can get.

DON MARZIO *(yelling loudly)* What? You want to teach me what snuff is? I make snuff. I have it made. I buy it here, I buy it there. I know what this kind is, and I know what the other kind is, too. Rappee, rappee, it has to be rappee.

LEANDRO *(also yelling loudly)* Yes, sir. Rappee, rappee. It's true. The best snuff is rappee.

DON MARZIO No, sir. The best snuff is not always rappee. You need to be discriminating. You don't know what you're talking about.

Scene 17

Enter *Eugenio from the inn.*

EUGENIO What's all this ruckus?

DON MARZIO On the subject of snuff, I yield to no one.

LEANDRO *(to Eugenio)* How's dinner coming?

EUGENIO It'll be ready soon.

DON MARZIO Is the wayfarer coming?

EUGENIO She doesn't want to come.

DON MARZIO Go on, Signor Snuff-amateur, go fetch your lady.

LEANDRO I'm going. *(aside)* If he does this at dinner, I'm going to throw a plate at that mug of his. *(knocks on the dancer's door)*

DON MARZIO Don't you have the keys?

LEANDRO No, sir. *(the door is opened and Leandro enters)*

DON MARZIO *(to Eugenio)* He probably has the keys to the back door.

EUGENIO It's too bad that the wayfarer doesn't want to come.

DON MARZIO She just wants to hear you beg.

EUGENIO She says that she's absolutely never been to Venice.

DON MARZIO She wouldn't say that to me.

EUGENIO Are you sure it's her?

DON MARZIO Positive. And what's more, I spoke with her a while ago and she wanted me to come up ... Of course, I didn't go, for friendship's sake.

EUGENIO You talked to her?

DON MARZIO Did I ever!

EUGENIO Did she recognize you?

DON MARZIO Who doesn't recognize me? My name is a household word.

EUGENIO So you do it; go and get her to come.

DON MARZIO If I go, it might cause her embarrassment. Do this: wait until the food's on the table; go get her, and without saying anything, bring her up.

EUGENIO I did all I could, and she told me, frankly, that she doesn't want to come.

Scene 18

Enter *waiters from the inn carrying into Pandolfo's a table-cloth, napkins, plates, utensils, wine, bread, glasses, and food; they go back and forth a number of times; enter Leandro and Lisaura.*

WAITER Gentlemen, the soup is served. *(enters the gambling house with the others)*

EUGENIO *(to Don Marzio)* Where's the Count?

DON MARZIO *(knocking hard on Lisaura's door)* Come, come. The soup's getting cold. *(enter Leandro and Lisaura)*

LEANDRO *(giving Lisaura his hand)* Here we are. Here we are.

EUGENIO *(to Lisaura)* My esteemed lady.

DON MARZIO *(to Lisaura, looking at her with his lorgnette)* Your servant.

LISAURA Your servant, gentlemen.

EUGENIO *(to Lisaura)* I'm happy that you find us worthy of your presence.

LISAURA Anything to please the Count.

DON MARZIO And nothing for us?

LISAURA Certainly not, especially not for you.

DON MARZIO Likewise, I'm sure. *(quietly to Eugenio)* I'm above all this.

EUGENIO Come, let's go. The soup's waiting. *(to Lisaura)* After you.

LISAURA With your permission. *(enters the gambling house with Leandro)*

DON MARZIO *(to Eugenio, with his lorgnette)* Can you believe this? I've never seen anything worse. *(enters the gambling house)*

EUGENIO Like the fox that didn't want the cherries, I, for one, wouldn't mind having them. *(also enters the gambling house)*

Scene 19

Enter *Ridolfo from the shop.*

RIDOLFO There he is, crazier than ever. Making merry with women while his wife worries and suffers. Poor woman. I really feel sorry for her.

Scene 20

Eugenio, Don Marzio, Leandro, and Lisaura in the rooms of the gambling house where their meal has been prepared; they open the windows above the three shops and lean out. Ridolfo is in the street, followed by Trappola.

EUGENIO *(at the window)* What wonderful air! What sunshine! Today it isn't cold at all.

DON MARZIO *(at another window)* It really feels like spring.

LEANDRO *(at another window)* From up here you certainly can enjoy the people passing by.

LISAURA *(near Leandro)* After dinner we'll see the masks.

EUGENIO Dinner is served, dinner is served. *(they sit, with Eugenio and Leandro near the windows)*

TRAPPOLA *(to Ridolfo)* Master, what's all this ruckus?

RIDOLFO That crazy Eugenio, Don Marzio, and the Count with the dancer are having dinner up there in Master Pandolfo's rooms.

TRAPPOLA *(comes out and looks up)* How nice! *(towards the window)* Bon appetit to all!

EUGENIO *(from the window)* Here's to Trappola.

TRAPPOLA Here's to you. Do you need any help?

EUGENIO Would you like to come up and serve the wine?

TRAPPOLA I'll serve the wine if you give me something to eat.

EUGENIO Come up, come up, and get some food.

TRAPPOLA *(to Ridolfo)* Master, with your permission. *(tries to enter the gambling house, and a waiter stops him)*

WAITER *(to Trappola)* Where are you going?

TRAPPOLA To serve wine to my masters.

WAITER They don't need you. We're here.

TRAPPOLA Someone once told me that "host" means enemy in Latin. Hostelry people certainly are hostile when it comes to the common man!

EUGENIO Trappola, come up.

TRAPPOLA Coming. *(to waiter)* With all due disrespect. *(enters the gambling house)*

WAITER Careful with the plates, and don't let him get his hands on our leftovers. *(enters the inn)*

RIDOLFO I don't know how there can be such senseless people in the world. Signor Eugenio is headed for ruin. He's bent on destroying himself. How can he talk like that to me, someone who's done so much for him, who treats him with a big heart and a lot of love? How can he laugh at me and make fun of me? I've had enough. I did what I did for the sake of good. And I'll never be sorry for that.

EUGENIO *(drinking, loudly)* Signor Don Marzio, here's to the lady.

ALL Cheers!

Scene 21

Enter *Vittoria, masked, walking in front of the coffee house, looking for her husband.*

RIDOLFO What's the matter, masked lady? What can I do for you?

EUGENIO *(drinking)* Here's to good friends.

VITTORIA *(hears the voice of her husband, moves towards the gambling house, looks up, sees him, and becomes enraged)*

EUGENIO *(with a glass of wine at the window, makes a toast to Vittoria, not recognizing her)* Masked lady, here's to your health.

VITTORIA *(trembles with rage and shakes her head)*

EUGENIO *(to Vittoria as above)* Would you like to join us? My lady, we are all gentlemen here.

LISAURA *(from the window)* Who is this mask that you want to invite?

(Vittoria more and more agitated)

Scene 22

Waiters arrive from the inn with more food and enter the gambling house.

RIDOLFO And who's paying? The simpleton.

EUGENIO *(to Vittoria)* Masked lady, if you don't want to come up, it doesn't matter. We've something better than you here.

VITTORIA Oh, my! I feel sick. I can't take it any more.

RIDOLFO *(to Vittoria)* Masked lady, do you feel unwell?

VITTORIA Ah, Ridolfo, help me for pity's sake. *(takes off the mask)*

RIDOLFO You? Here?

VITTORIA It's me, unfortunately.

RIDOLFO Have a little rosolio.

VITTORIA No, give me some water.
RIDOLFO No, not water. It has to be rosolio. When your spirits are down, you need something to lift them. Please, come inside.
VITTORIA I want to go up there where that dog is. I want to kill myself in front of his very eyes.
RIDOLFO For heaven's sake, come here. Be calm.
EUGENIO *(drinking)* Here's to the lovely lass and her lovely eyes!
VITTORIA Do you hear the rogue? Do you hear him? Let me go.
RIDOLFO *(holding her back)* I would never let you do such a rash thing.
VITTORIA I can't take it. Help me. I'm dying. *(faints)*
RIDOLFO Now, that's all I need. *(holds her up as best he can)*

Scene 23

Enter *Placida at the door of the inn.*

PLACIDA Good heavens! I thought I heard my husband's voice from the window. If he's here, I've come at the right moment to shame him. *(enter waiter from the gambling house) (to waiter)* Young man, please tell me. Who's up there in those rooms?
WAITER Three gentlemen. One is Signor Eugenio, the other Signor Don Marzio from Naples, and the third is Count Leandro Ardenti.
PLACIDA *(aside)* Flaminio isn't among them, unless he changed his name.
LEANDRO Here's to Eugenio's good fortune.
ALL *(drinking)* Hurrah!
PLACIDA *(aside)* That's my husband for sure. *(to waiter)* Dear sir, do me a favour. Take me up to these gentlemen. I'd like to play a trick on them.
WAITER Right away, my lady. *(aside)* That's what waiters are for. *(he leads her into the gambling house)*
RIDOLFO *(to Vittoria)* Come, now, be brave. It's nothing serious.
VITTORIA *(wakes up)* I feel I'm dying. *(Leandro looks surprised when he sees Placida and acts like he's going to kill her; through the windows all can be seen getting up from the table in confusion)*
EUGENIO No, stop!
DON MARZIO Don't do it.
LEANDRO Get out of here!

PLACIDA Help, help! *(flees down the stairs; Leandro tries to follow her with his sword; Eugenio holds him back; Trappola with a plate of food wrapped in a napkin jumps out of a window and runs into the coffee house; Placida exits the gambling house and runs into the inn; Eugenio, with weapon in hand, defends Placida against Leandro, who's following her)*

DON MARZIO *(exits quietly from the gambling house and flees) Rumores fuge.*

(waiters pass from the gambling house to the inn and close the door; Vittoria remains in the coffee house with Ridolfo)

LEANDRO *(with sword in hand, against Eugenio)* Make way. I want to enter the inn.

EUGENIO No, it shall never be. You've been terrible to your wife, and I will defend her to the death.

LEANDRO In the name of heaven, you'll regret this. *(pressing Eugenio with his sword)*

EUGENIO I'm not afraid of you. *(advances on Leandro and forces him to draw back, so much so that when he finds the dancer's door open, he enters and saves himself)*

Scene 24

Eugenio, Vittoria, and Ridolfo.

EUGENIO *(towards the dancer's door)* You vile coward, why do you flee? Why do you hide? Come out, if you dare.

VITTORIA *(approaches Eugenio)* If you want blood, then shed mine.

EUGENIO Get out of here, you stupid, crazy woman.

VITTORIA As long as I live, I will never leave your side.

EUGENIO *(threatening her with his sword)* Confound you, get out of my way before I lose my temper.

RIDOLFO *(runs to Vittoria's defence with weapon in hand and challenges Eugenio)* What do you think you're doing, Master? What are you doing? Do you think you can terrorize the world because of that sword? This poor, innocent woman may not have anyone to defend her, but I'll defend her to the death. How dare you threaten her, after the way you've treated her? How dare you? *(to Vittoria)* Signora, come with me and fear nothing.

VITTORIA No, dear Ridolfo. If my husband wants me dead, let him have his satisfaction. So then, kill me, you dog, assassin, traitor. Kill me, you scoundrel. You have neither honour, heart, nor conscience.

EUGENIO *(mortified, puts the sword back into its sheath without a word)*

RIDOLFO *(to Eugenio)* Ah, Signor Eugenio, I see that you are sorry, and I beg your pardon if I spoke too harshly. My lord, you know that I love you, and you know what I've done for you. Even this outburst of mine was the effect of love. I pity this poor woman. How can it be that her tears do not touch your heart?

EUGENIO *(dries his eyes and doesn't speak)*

RIDOLFO *(quietly to Vittoria)* Look, Signora Vittoria, look at Signor Eugenio. He's crying. He's calmed down. He will repent and mend his ways. Rest assured that he loves you.

VITTORIA Crocodile tears. How many times has he promised me that he would mend his ways? How many times has he fooled me with his tears? I won't believe him any more. He's a traitor. I won't believe him any more.

EUGENIO *(trembles, visibly moved and shaken; he throws his hat on the ground like a desperate man, and without a word he enters the back room of the coffee house)*

Scene 25

Vittoria and Ridolfo.

VITTORIA *(to Ridolfo)* What's the meaning of this silence?

RIDOLFO He's confused.

VITTORIA How can he have changed in one minute?

RIDOLFO I believe he has. Let me tell you something: if both of us had done nothing but cry and beg, he would have become more enraged. But we were a little hardheaded, and we did some swaggering, and this embarrassed him, and it made him change. He recognizes his mistake, and now he'd like to be forgiven, but he doesn't know how.

VITTORIA Dear Ridolfo, let's go and console him.

RIDOLFO That's something your ladyship must do without me.

VITTORIA You go first, and find out how I should behave.

RIDOLFO Gladly. I'll go and see, but I expect to find that he's repented. *(enters the shop)*

Scene 26

Vittoria, followed by Ridolfo.

VITTORIA This is the last time that he'll see me cry. Either he'll repent, and he'll be my dear husband again, or he'll keep this up, and I won't be able to bear it any longer.
RIDOLFO Signora Vittoria, bad news. He's not here any more! He left through the back door.
VITTORIA Didn't I tell you that he's treacherous, that he's stubborn?
RIDOLFO I believe that he left out of shame. He's confused, since he didn't have the courage to say he's sorry and ask for your forgiveness.
VITTORIA Yes, he knows how easy it is to be forgiven by a loving wife like me.
RIDOLFO Look. He left without his hat. *(picks up the hat)*
VITTORIA Because he's crazy.
RIDOLFO Because he's confused. He doesn't know what he's doing.
VITTORIA . But if he's sorry, why doesn't he say so?
RIDOLFO He doesn't have the courage.
VITTORIA Ridolfo, I almost want to believe you.
RIDOLFO Do this: go to the back room. Let me go find him, and hopefully I'll bring him back here like a little puppy.
VITTORIA It would be much better for me to forget about him!
RIDOLFO Do what I say one more time, and you won't regret it.
VITTORIA Yes, I'll do what you say. I'll wait for you in the back room. I'd like to be able to say that I've done everything I can for my husband. But if he takes advantage of me, I swear that my love will surely turn to scorn. *(enters the back of the shop)*
RIDOLFO I couldn't feel more sorry for him if he were my own son. *(exit Ridolfo)*

ACT THREE

Scene 1

Enter *Leandro, kicked out of Lisaura's house.*

LEANDRO How dare you treat me so?
LISAURA *(at the door)* Because you're a liar, an impostor.

LEANDRO What have I ever done wrong to you? Do you call abandoning my wife for you something wrong?

LISAURA If I had known you were married, I wouldn't ever have received you in my home.

LEANDRO I wasn't the first to come here.

LISAURA But you'll be the last.

Scene 2

Enter *Don Marzio looking on with his lorgnette and laughing to himself.*

LEANDRO You didn't waste your time with me.

LISAURA Yes, I, too, enjoyed your tawdry profits. I'm ashamed just to think of it. Go to hell and don't come around here any more.

LEANDRO I'll come by to collect my things.

DON MARZIO *(laughs and makes fun of Leandro behind his back)*

LISAURA My servant will bring you your things. *(enters the house and closes the door)*

LEANDRO How dare you insult me so? You'll pay for this.

DON MARZIO *(laughs, and when Leandro turns around, assumes a serious air)*

LEANDRO Friend, did you see that?

DON MARZIO See what? I just got here.

LEANDRO You didn't see the dancer at the door?

DON MARZIO I certainly did not.

LEANDRO *(aside)* Thank God.

DON MARZIO Come here. Speak to me as a true gentleman. Confide in me and rest assured that no one whosoever will find out about your affairs. You're a stranger, as I am, but I've been around here longer than you. Should you need protection, assistance, advice, and above all secrecy, you can count on me. You can trust me. From the heart: a caring and good friend. No one will ever find out anything.

LEANDRO Since you show such goodness towards me, I will open my heart to you. But for heaven's sake, secrecy is of the utmost importance.

DON MARZIO Go on.

LEANDRO I want you to know that the wayfarer is my wife.

DON MARZIO Good Lord!

LEANDRO The wife I abandoned in Turin.

DON MARZIO *(aside, looking at him through his lorgnette)* Oh, what a rogue!

LEANDRO Besides this, I'll have you know that I am not Count Leandro.

Don Marzio *(aside, as above)* Better yet!

Leandro I was not born of noble blood.

Don Marzio You wouldn't happen to be the son of a dirty policeman, would you?

Leandro You surprise me, sir. I was born poor, but to respectable people nonetheless.

Don Marzio Yes, yes. Go on.

Leandro I was a clerk …

Don Marzio Hard work, eh?

Leandro And since I wanted to see the world …

Don Marzio At the expense of simpletons.

Leandro I came to Venice.

Don Marzio To be a knave.

Leandro You're being too rough on me. That's no way to treat a friend.

Don Marzio Listen, I promised to protect you, and I will. I promised you secrecy and that you will have. This is between you and me, but you must allow me to tell you – from the heart – what I think.

Leandro You see my predicament. If my wife finds me out, I'll be in a lot of trouble.

Don Marzio What do you think you'll do?

Leandro We could try to have her chased out of Venice.

Don Marzio Oh, come, come. It's obvious that you're a rogue.

Leandro Sir, how you speak!

Don Marzio Between you and me, from the heart.

Leandro Then I'll be the one to leave. The important thing is that she not learn of it.

Don Marzio She certainly won't find out from me.

Leandro Is your advice that I leave?

Don Marzio Yes, this is the best remedy. Leave right away. Take a gondola. Have them take you to Fusina. Take the coach to Ferrara.

Leandro I'll leave tonight. It's almost dark. I want first to get what few things I have here at the dancer's house.

Don Marzio Hurry and leave right away. Don't let yourself be seen.

Leandro I'll leave by the back door so as not to be seen.

Don Marzio *(aside)* I knew it. He uses the back door.

Leandro Above all, I implore you to keep it a secret.

Don Marzio You can be sure of that.

Leandro I beg you to do me a favour: give her these two sequins. Then send her away. Write to me, and I'll return right away. *(gives him two sequins)*

DON MARZIO I'll give her the two sequins. Leave.
LEANDRO But make sure that she leaves …
DON MARZIO Leave, damn you.
LEANDRO Are you chasing me away?
DON MARZIO I'm telling you, from the heart, for your own good: get the devil out of here.
LEANDRO *(aside)* What kind of man is he? If he's this rough with his friends, I wonder how he treats his enemies! *(enters Lisaura's house)*
DON MARZIO Signor Count! What a rogue! Signor Count! If he hadn't sought my protection, I'd have his bones broken with a cudgel.

Scene 3

Enter *Placida from the inn.*

PLACIDA Yes, come what may, I want to find that no-good husband of mine.
DON MARZIO Wayfarer, how's it going?
PLACIDA If I'm not mistaken, you were among those who dined with my husband.
DON MARZIO Yes, I'm the one with the dried chestnuts.
PLACIDA I beg you, tell me where I can find that traitor.
DON MARZIO I don't know. And even if I did, I wouldn't tell you.
PLACIDA For what reason?
DON MARZIO Because you're better off not finding him. He'll murder you.
PLACIDA That doesn't matter! At least my suffering will have ended.
DON MARZIO What nonsense! That's sheer idiocy! Go back to Turin.
PLACIDA Without my husband?
DON MARZIO Yes, without your husband. What's left for you to do now? He's a rogue.
PLACIDA That doesn't matter! I'd like to see him, at least.
DON MARZIO Oh, you won't see him any more.
PLACIDA Please tell me, if you know. Could it be that he's left?
DON MARZIO He did, and he didn't.
PLACIDA It seems to me, my lord, that you know something about my husband.
DON MARZIO Who? Me? I know, and I don't know. But I don't gossip.
PLACIDA Sir, have pity on me.

Don Marzio Go back to Turin and forget about it. Here, I'll give you two sequins.

Placida Bless you for your kindness. But won't you tell me about my husband? So be it! *(starts to leave crying)* I'll leave. It's hopeless.

Don Marzio *(aside)* Poor woman! *(calling Placida)* I say!

Placida Sir.

Don Marzio Your husband is here in the dancer's house getting his things, and he'll leave through the back door. *(exit Don Marzio)*

Placida He's in Venice! He hasn't left! He's in the dancer's house! If I could find someone to help me, I'd like to hazard it again. But all alone, I'm afraid I'll get nothing but insults.

Scene 4

Enter *Ridolfo and Eugenio.*

Ridolfo Oh, come on, what's so difficult about that? We're all human, all liable to make mistakes. When a man repents, the goodness of his repentance cancels the shame of his shortcomings.

Eugenio That's all very well, but my wife wouldn't believe me any more.

Ridolfo Come with me. Leave the talking to me. Signora Vittoria loves you. Everything will work out.

Placida Signor Eugenio.

Ridolfo Be good enough to leave Signor Eugenio in peace. He has other things to do besides taking care of you.

Placida I don't expect him to neglect his affairs for me. I'm begging both of you to help me out of the miserable state in which I find myself.

Eugenio Believe me, Ridolfo, this poor woman deserves sympathy. She's most honest, and her husband's a rogue.

Placida He abandoned me in Turin. I find him in Venice. He tries to kill me. And now he's planning to slip through my hands once again.

Ridolfo Do you know where he is?

Placida He's here at the dancer's house getting his things together, and he'll be leaving before long.

Ridolfo When he leaves, you'll see him.

Placida He'll leave through the back door, and I won't see him. And if he discovers me, he'll kill me.

Ridolfo Who said that he'll leave through the back door?

PLACIDA That gentleman named Don Marzio.

RIDOLFO The town-crier. Do this: go inside the barbershop. From there you can see the secret door. As soon as you see him leave, tell me and leave the rest to me.

PLACIDA They may not want me in that shop.

RIDOLFO Now they will. *(calling)* Master Agabito?

Scene 5

Enter *the barber's boy from the barbershop.*

BOY What do you want, Master Ridolfo?

RIDOLFO Tell your master to take in this wayfarer for a little while, until I come back to fetch her – as a favour to me.

BOY Gladly. Come along, your ladyship. You'll learn how to shave. Although, when it comes to fleecing, you could probably teach us barbers something. *(re-enters the shop)*

PLACIDA I have to suffer all this because of that scoundrel. Poor women! We'd be better off drowning than landing a bad husband. *(enters the barbershop)*

Scene 6

Ridolfo and Eugenio.

RIDOLFO If I can, I'd like to try to help this poor wretch, too. At the same time, if I get her to leave with her husband, Signora Vittoria won't be jealous any more. She's already said something to me about the wayfarer.

EUGENIO You're a good-hearted man. In case of need, a hundred friends will offer their service to you.

RIDOLFO I pray to heaven that I won't need anyone. In such a case, I wouldn't know what to expect. There's plenty of ingratitude in the world.

EUGENIO You can count on me as long as I live.

RIDOLFO I'm eternally thankful. But let's get back to us. What are you planning to do? Do you want to go in the back room with your wife, or do you want her to come into the shop? Do you want to go alone? Do you want me to come, too? Just give the word.

EUGENIO The coffee house won't do. If you come, she'll be embarrassed. If I go alone, she'll tear my eyes out … It doesn't matter. Let her get it off her chest. Her anger will pass. I'll go alone.
RIDOLFO Go, then, and may heaven protect you.
EUGENIO If I need to, I'll call you.
RIDOLFO Remember. You don't need a witness.
EUGENIO *(about to leave)* Oh, you're quite a fellow, Ridolfo! I'll go.
RIDOLFO Get on with it.
EUGENIO How do you think it will go?
RIDOLFO Well.
EUGENIO Crying or scratching?
RIDOLFO A little bit of everything.
EUGENIO And then?
RIDOLFO Every man for himself.
EUGENIO Don't come unless I call.
RIDOLFO Understood.
EUGENIO I'll tell you everything.
RIDOLFO Go on, be on your way.
EUGENIO *(aside)* What a great man this Ridolfo! A great friend! *(enters the back of the shop)*

Scene 7

Ridolfo, followed by Trappola and boys.

RIDOLFO Husband and wife? I'll let them be alone as long as they need. Trappola, boys, where are you?
TRAPPOLA Here I am.
RIDOLFO Mind the shop. I'm going to the barber's. If Signor Eugenio wants me, call me and I'll come right away.
TRAPPOLA May I go keep Signor Eugenio company?
RIDOLFO No, sir. You mustn't go back there. And make sure that no one goes back there.
TRAPPOLA But why not?
RIDOLFO Because I say so.
TRAPPOLA I'll go see if he needs anything.
RIDOLFO Don't go unless he calls. *(aside)* I want to hear more from the wayfarer and see how her affairs are going … see if I can be of assistance. *(enters the barbershop)*

Scene 8

Trappola, followed by Don Marzio.

TRAPPOLA I'm eager to go back there precisely because he told me not to.
DON MARZIO Trappola, were you scared?
TRAPPOLA A little.
DON MARZIO Have you seen Signor Eugenio since?
TRAPPOLA Yes, sir, I've seen him: he's back there. But … be quiet.
DON MARZIO Where?
TRAPPOLA Be quiet. In the back room.
DON MARZIO What's he doing there? Is he gambling?
TRAPPOLA *(laughing)* Yes, sir, he's gambling.
DON MARZIO With whom?
TRAPPOLA *(sotto voce)* With his wife.
DON MARZIO Is his wife there?
TRAPPOLA She's there. But be quiet.
DON MARZIO I want to go see him.
TRAPPOLA You can't.
DON MARZIO Why not?
TRAPPOLA My master won't allow it.
DON MARZIO Get out of here, you buffoon. *(tries to go in)*
TRAPPOLA *(stopping him)* I'm telling you that you're not going back there.
DON MARZIO I'm telling you that I will.
TRAPPOLA And I'm telling you that you won't.
DON MARZIO I'll shower you with blows.

Scene 9

Enter *Ridolfo from the barbershop.*

RIDOLFO What's going on?
TRAPPOLA He insists on playing the third wheel in the game of marriage.
RIDOLFO Content yourself, sir, that nobody is going there.
DON MARZIO But I insist on going there.
RIDOLFO In my shop, I'm in charge, and you won't be going back there. Have some respect, if you don't want me to resort to drastic measures.

(to Trappola and the boys) And you, until I get back, don't let anyone go back there, no matter who. *(knocks on the dancer's door and enters)*

Scene 10

Don Marzio, Trappola, and boys, followed by Pandolfo.

TRAPPOLA Did you hear that? Marriage is to be respected.

DON MARZIO *(aside, pacing)* To someone of my station? You won't be going …? To someone of my station? Have some respect …? And I remain silent? And I say nothing? And do I not beat him up? Scoundrel! Boorish upstart! To me? To me? *(to Trappola)* Coffee. *(sits down)*

TRAPPOLA Right away. *(goes to get him the coffee and brings it to him)*

PANDOLFO Your grace, I am in need of your protection.

DON MARZIO What's the matter, gambler?

PANDOLFO Something bad.

DON MARZIO What's wrong? Confide in me, and I'll help you.

PANDOLFO I'll have you know, sir, that there are some evil, envious people who don't like to see a poor man do well. These rogues see that I honestly strive to maintain my family with dignity, and they have charged me with cheating at cards.

DON MARZIO *(ironically)* What rogues! A gentleman like you! How did you find out?

PANDOLFO A friend told me. I trust, however, that they don't have proof because all those who frequent my gambling house are gentlemen, and no one can speak ill of me.

DON MARZIO Oh, if only I were called as witness, I know all about your finer abilities.

PANDOLFO Your grace, for heaven's sake, don't ruin me. I appeal to your mercy for help, on account of my little ones.

DON MARZIO All right, yes, I'll help you. I'll protect you. Leave it to me. But be careful. Do you have any marked cards in there?

PANDOLFO I don't mark them … but some of the players may have indulged …

DON MARZIO Hurry. Burn them right away. I won't talk.

PANDOLFO I'm afraid that I won't have time to burn them.

DON MARZIO Hide them.

PANDOLFO I'll go to my shop and hide them right away.

DON MARZIO Where do you intend to hide them?

Pandolfo I have a secret place under the rafters where the devil himself couldn't find them. *(enters the gambling house)*
Don Marzio Go on, you crafty fellow!

Scene 11

Don Marzio, followed by a police sergeant, masked, and other policemen also disguised, followed by Trappola.

Don Marzio He's jail-bound for sure. Even if they discover only half of his tricks, they'll take him to prison straight away.
Sergeant *(to his men on the corner of the street)* Have a look around here, and when I call, come. *(his men break up)*
Don Marzio *(aside)* Marked cards! Such thieves!
Sergeant Coffee. *(sits down)*
Trappola At your service. *(goes for the coffee and brings it)*
Sergeant Fine weather we're having.
Don Marzio The weather won't last.
Sergeant Oh, well. Let's enjoy it while it's good.
Don Marzio We won't enjoy it for long.
Sergeant When the weather's bad, people go to a casino and gamble.
Don Marzio You just have to go to the places where they don't rob you.
Sergeant This gambling house nearby seems respectable.
Don Marzio Respectable? It's a den of thieves.
Sergeant I believe Master Pandolfo is the owner.
Don Marzio Indeed he is.
Sergeant To tell the truth, I've heard that he stacks the deck.
Don Marzio He's an egregious cheat.
Sergeant Has he perhaps swindled you, too?
Don Marzio Not me. I'm no simpleton. But you wouldn't believe how many he manages to lure into his trap.
Sergeant He must be afraid of something. He's nowhere to be found.
Don Marzio He's inside the gambling house hiding the cards.
Sergeant Why ever would he hide the cards?
Don Marzio Because they've been tampered with, I imagine.
Sergeant Of course. And where could he hide them?
Don Marzio You want a good laugh? He hides them in a nook under the rafters.
Sergeant *(aside)* That's all I need to know.

DON MARZIO You, sir, do you enjoy gambling?
SERGEANT Sometimes.
DON MARZIO I don't believe I know you.
SERGEANT You'll know who I am before long. *(gets up)*
DON MARZIO Are you leaving?
SERGEANT I'll be right back.
TRAPPOLA *(to the sergeant)* Sir! Your coffee.
SERGEANT I'll pay for it in just a second. *(the sergeant goes out to the street and whistles; his men enter Pandolfo's gambling house)*

Scene 12

Don Marzio and Trappola.

DON MARZIO *(gets up and carefully looks around without speaking)*
TRAPPOLA *(looks around carefully as well)*
DON MARZIO Trappola …
TRAPPOLA Signor Don Marzio …
DON MARZIO Who are they?
TRAPPOLA The city's finest, I believe.

Scene 13

Enter *Pandolfo, bound at the wrists, and the sergeant's men.*

PANDOLFO Signor Don Marzio, I'm obliged to you.
DON MARZIO To me? I don't know what you're talking about.
PANDOLFO Perhaps I'll be going to jail, but you and your big mouth deserve the stocks. *(exit Pandolfo with the sergeant's men)*
SERGEANT *(to Don Marzio)* Yes, sir. I caught him hiding the cards. *(exit sergeant)*
TRAPPOLA I want to follow him to see where he's going. *(exit Trappola)*

Scene 14

Don Marzio alone.

DON MARZIO Oh, what the devil! What have I done? The one I believed a reputable gentleman was a policeman in disguise. He betrayed me. He fooled me. I'm a good-hearted person – I tell everything freely.

Scene 15

Enter *Ridolfo and Leandro from the dancer's house.*

RIDOLFO *(to Leandro)* Good man. This is more like it. He who understands reason proves himself an admirable man. After all, the only things we have in the world are our good name, honour, and reputation.

LEANDRO There he is. The one who advised me to leave.

RIDOLFO Wonderful, Signor Don Marzio. Is this your idea of advice? Instead of trying to unite him with his wife, you persuade him to abandon her and go away?

DON MARZIO Unite him with his wife? It's impossible. He doesn't want her with him.

RIDOLFO It was possible for me. With a word or two, I persuaded him. He'll go back to his wife.

LEANDRO *(aside)* Of course, so as not to be ruined.

RIDOLFO Let's go get Signora Placida who's waiting in the barbershop.

DON MARZIO *(to Leandro)* Go find that high-class wife of yours.

LEANDRO Signor Don Marzio, let me tell you in confidence, between you and me, that you've got a big mouth. *(enters the barbershop with Ridolfo)*

Scene 16

Don Marzio, followed by Ridolfo.

DON MARZIO They complain about my tongue, but it seems to me that I speak well. It's true that sometimes I talk about this or that. But since I tell the truth, why should I refrain from speaking? I freely say what I know. But I do it because I'm a good-hearted person. *(enter Ridolfo from the barbershop)*

RIDOLFO Well, that's the end of that. If he's telling the truth, he's repented. If he's pretending, it'll be the worse for him.

DON MARZIO The great Ridolfo! So you're the one who brings marriages together.

RIDOLFO And you're the one who tries to take them apart.

DON MARZIO I did it to do good.

RIDOLFO He who thinks the worst, can never hope to do good. You mustn't ever fool yourself that a good thing can derive from a bad one. Separating a husband from his wife is a deed against all laws, and the only things that will come of it are misunderstanding and confusion.

DON MARZIO *(with disdain)* What a philosopher!

RIDOLFO You certainly understand more than I. But, pardon me, my tongue works better than yours.

DON MARZIO You speak like a reckless man.

RIDOLFO Bear with me, if you can, and if you can't, take your patronage elsewhere.

DON MARZIO I will take it elsewhere, I will. I'll never come back to this shop of yours.

RIDOLFO *(aside)* Would to God it were true!

Scene 17

Enter *boy from the coffee house.*

BOY Master, Signor Eugenio is calling you. *(withdraws)*

RIDOLFO I'll be right there. *(to Don Marzio)* With your permission.

DON MARZIO My respects to the master. What do you gain from this politicking with people?

RIDOLFO I earn the merit of having done good. I earn people's friendship. I earn a mark of honour that I value above all things in the world. *(enters the shop)*

DON MARZIO What a fool! He talks like a minister or a secretary. A coffee-maker acting as a broker. And how tiring it must be! And how long it takes him! I could have taken care of everything in a quarter of an hour.

Scene 18

Enter *Ridolfo, Eugenio, and Vittoria from the coffee house, and Don Marzio.*

DON MARZIO *(aside)* Here are the three fools. The mischievous fool, the jealous fool, and the glorious fool.

RIDOLFO *(to Vittoria)* In truth, this is a great blessing.

VITTORIA Dear Ridolfo, I thank you for my peace, my tranquillity, and – I can truly say – my life.

EUGENIO Believe me, my friend, I was tired of leading that life, but I didn't know how to break away from my vices. You – bless your soul – have opened my eyes. And with a little coaxing and a little criticism, with a little charm and a little kindness, you have enlightened me, you have humbled me. I'm a new man, and I hope that my change will endure: here's to our blessing, to your glory, and to the example of wise, respectable fine men like you.

RIDOLFO You're too kind, sir. I don't deserve it at all.

VITTORIA As long as I live, I will remember the good that you have done for me. You've returned to me my dear husband, the only good thing I have in the world. It cost me as many tears to get him as it did to lose him. And it costs still more to get him back. But these are tears of sweetness, tears of love and tenderness that fill my soul with joy, that make me forget any pain from the past. I give thanks to heaven and praise your mercy.

RIDOLFO Such consolation makes me cry.

DON MARZIO *(looking on with his lorgnette)* Accursed fools!

EUGENIO Should we go home?

VITTORIA I'm sorry, but I'm still all misty, messy, and flustered. My mother's probably there with some other relative of mine waiting for me. I wouldn't want them to see me with tears in my eyes.

EUGENIO All right, pull yourself together. We'll wait a little.

VITTORIA Ridolfo, do you have a mirror? I'd like to see how I look.

DON MARZIO *(aside, continuing to look on with the lorgnette)* Her husband must have messed up her perruque.

RIDOLFO If you want to use a mirror, let's go up to the rooms above the gambling house.

EUGENIO No, I'm not setting foot in there.

RIDOLFO Haven't you heard the news? Pandolfo's gone to prison.

EUGENIO Really? He deserves it. That rogue! He's raked in plenty of my money.

VITTORIA Let's go, my dear Husband.

EUGENIO When no one's there, we'll go.

VITTORIA I'm so messy; I can't stand to see myself like this. *(enters the gambling house happily)*

EUGENIO Poor dear! Jubilant with bliss. *(also enters the gambling house happily)*

RIDOLFO I'll come as well to serve you. *(also enters the gambling house happily)*

Scene 19

Don Marzio, followed by Leandro and Placida.

DON MARZIO I know why Eugenio has made peace with his wife. He's ruined, and he hasn't anything left to live on. His wife is young and pretty ... He's thought this one out, and Ridolfo will be his go-between.

LEANDRO *(coming out of the barbershop)* So let's go to the inn and fetch your little baggage.

PLACIDA Dear Husband, how could you have found it in your heart to leave me?

LEANDRO Enough. Let's not speak of it any more. I promise you that I'll change my ways.

PLACIDA The Good Lord willing. *(approaches the inn)*

DON MARZIO *(to Leandro, teasing him)* Your humble servant, my lord, Signor Count.

LEANDRO My respects, Lord Protector, Master of the Good Tongue.

DON MARZIO *(to Placida, making fun of her)* I kneel before the Countess.

PLACIDA Your servant, Signor Knight of the Dried Chestnuts. *(enters the inn with Leandro)*

DON MARZIO So they'll wander about together playing their knavish tricks. Their whole income consists in a deck of cards.

Scene 20

Lisaura at the window and Don Marzio.

LISAURA The wayfarer's gone back to the inn with that no-good Leandro. If she's there too long, I'm leaving this house for good. I can't tolerate the sight of either of them.

DON MARZIO *(with his lorgnette)* Your servant, Signora Ballerina.

LISAURA *(brusquely)* My respects.

DON MARZIO What's wrong? You seem upset.

LISAURA I'm amazed that the innkeeper takes such people at his inn.

DON MARZIO Whom do you mean?

LISAURA I mean that wayfarer, the tart. We've never had such riff-raff in our neighbourhood.

Scene 21

Placida at the window of the inn.

PLACIDA Signorina, what are you saying about me? I'm a respectable woman. I'm not sure I can say the same for you.
LISAURA If you were a respectable woman, you wouldn't go around the world playing knavish tricks on people.
DON MARZIO *(listens and looks on now and then with his lorgnette and laughs)*
PLACIDA I came in search of my husband.
LISAURA Really. And last year, who were you in search of?
PLACIDA I have never been to Venice before.
LISAURA You're a liar. Last year you cut a rather bad figure in this city. *(Don Marzio looks on with his lorgnette and laughs)*
PLACIDA Who told you that?
LISAURA There he is. Signor Don Marzio told me.
DON MARZIO I didn't say anything.
PLACIDA He couldn't have told such a lie. But he did tell me about your life and fine manners. He informed me about your ways, and he told me that you secretly receive people through the back door.
DON MARZIO *(continues to look on with his lorgnette)* I didn't say that.
PLACIDA You did too.
LISAURA Is it possible that Signor Don Marzio said such bad things about me?
DON MARZIO I'm telling you that I didn't say that.

Scene 22

Eugenio at a window of the gambling house, followed by Ridolfo, opening another, followed by Vittoria, opening another.

EUGENIO He did too, and he said it to me as well, about each of them: the wayfarer was in Venice last year playing knavish tricks, and the dancer receives visitors through the back door.
DON MARZIO I heard it from Ridolfo.
RIDOLFO I wouldn't dream of saying such a thing. Just the opposite: we argued over this. I defended Signora Lisaura's honour, and you, good sir, held that she was a bad woman.
LISAURA You wretch!

DON MARZIO You're a liar.

VITTORIA And he told me that my husband was intimate with both the dancer and the wayfarer. He portrayed them as two very wicked women.

PLACIDA Oh, you wicked man!

LISAURA Accursed one!

Scene 23

Enter *Leandro at the door of the inn.*

LEANDRO Yes, sir, yes, sir. You, my good sir, gave rise to a thousand misunderstandings. With that tongue of yours you ruined the reputation of two respectable ladies.

DON MARZIO You think the dancer's respectable?

LISAURA Respectable and proud of it. My friendship with Signor Leandro was directed towards nothing less than marriage with him – not knowing that he had a wife.

PLACIDA A wife he has, and it's me.

LEANDRO And if I had done what Signor Don Marzio said, I would have fled from her again.

PLACIDA You despicable man!

LISAURA Impostor!

VITTORIA Scandalmonger!

EUGENIO Blabber!

DON MARZIO Me? Me, the most respectable man in the world?

RIDOLFO To be respectable, it's not enough not to steal. You have to be kind as well.

DON MARZIO I have never done a bad deed.

Scene 24

Enter *Trappola.*

TRAPPOLA Signor Don Marzio's done it this time.

RIDOLFO What did he do?

TRAPPOLA He betrayed Master Pandolfo's confidence. They tied him up, and they say that tomorrow they're going to whip him.

RIDOLFO He's an informer! Get out of my shop. *(leaves the window)*

Scene 25

Enter *Barber's boy.*

BOY Signor Squealer, don't come to our shop any more for a shave. *(enters his shop)*

Scene Last

Enter *waiter from the inn.*

WAITER Signor Squealer, don't come to our inn any more for dinner. *(enters the inn)*

LEANDRO Signor Protector, between you and me, in confidence, such a betrayal is the act of a rogue. *(enters the inn)*

PLACIDA You and your dried chestnuts! Signor Tattletale. *(leaves the window)*

LISAURA Put him in the stocks, in the stocks. *(leaves the window)*

VITTORIA Oh, what a dear you are, Signor Don Marzio! You were probably using those ten sequins that you lent my husband as a bribe for information. *(leaves the window)*

EUGENIO My respects to Signor Informer. *(leaves the window)*

TRAPPOLA I kneel to the Reverend Signor Referendary. *(enters the shop)*

DON MARZIO I'm overwhelmed. I'm a broken man. What kind of world is this? Me, an informer? An informer? I'm accused of being a tattletale just for having accidentally revealed Pandolfo's evil ways? I didn't know the policeman. I didn't foresee his trickery. I'm not guilty of such a despicable crime. And yet they all insult me. They all slander me.

Nobody wants me. Everyone chases me away. Oh, I guess they're right. My loose tongue had to lead me to this fall, sooner or later. It's brought me disgrace, something worse than any ill. There's no excuse. I've lost my good name, and I'll never get it back again. I'll leave this city. I'll leave in spite of myself, and because of this awful tongue of mine, I'll give up a city where all live well, all have freedom, peace, and joy as long as they know how to be cautious, careful, and honourable.

CURTAIN

NOTES TO THE COFFEE HOUSE

Notes by Brittany Asaro are indicated with the initials BA.

Notes adapted from Jeremy Parzen's edition of *The Coffee House* are indicated with the initials JP.

1 In the first performances of *La bottega del caffè*, taking place in 1750, the character of the coffee house owner, Ridolfo, was played by Brighella, a classic character of commedia dell'arte (JP).

2 Parzen credits Goldoni as being the first writer to bring the coffee house into Italian theatre and literature. He also explains the varying nature of coffee houses in Goldoni's day: "[...] in the eighteenth century, coffee houses were popular and versatile establishments, whose greater or lesser respectability stretched on a wide range. At the lowest level were the *Caffè degli Italiani* in London, where shady adventurers used to meet, and away from which the knowledgeable Casanova advised Da Pointe to remain. [...] More intellectual were certain coffee houses in Paris, such as the *Procope*, where, as Montesquieu jokingly says, 'they make coffee in such a way, that it gives wit to all those who drink it: or at least there isn't anyone, among those who leave the house, who is not convinced that he is four times wittier than when he came in'; or the *Régence*, meeting place for the strongest chess players in town, and theatre of the immortal dialogue between Diderot and the Neveu de Rameau" (xii–xiii).

3 For an explanation of faro, see note 12 to *Off to the Country*, below page 215.

4 A sequin, or *zecchino* in Italian, is a Venetian gold ducat (BA).

5 Primero is the predecessor of modern-day poker. Its origins are unclear, but it was most likely developed in Italy or in Spain. In any case, there is evidence of its being popular throughout Europe by the seventeenth century (BA).

6 In Goldoni's day, basset (in Italian, *basetta*) was considered among the "most polite" card games. Its players were necessarily of a high social and economic status because of the game's tendency to generate extreme financial gains and losses. This "polite" game originated in sixteenth-century Venice and, strangely enough, is most likely the descendant of an illegal version of Italian roulette (BA).

7 Don Marzio's coming out of the barbershop with a towel around his neck and lather on this face in this scene, as well as other instances – such as Placida's being disguised as a traveller, the duel between Leandro and

Eugenio, and Eugenio threatening his own wife with his sword – hark back to the tradition of old Italian comedy (JP).

8 Daniel Quare was an English clockmaker who made clocks and watches for an elite clientele in the late seventeenth and early eighteenth centuries. He is said to have designed a clock for King William III, and possibly a watch for King James II as well (BA).

9 Russia was involved in a series of conflicts throughout the eighteenth century, and so it is difficult to determine the precise event to which Don Marzio refers here (BA).

10 Rappee is a type of coarse, pungent snuff made from dark tobacco (BA).

THE HOLIDAY TRILOGY: THREE COMEDIES

TRANSLATED BY ANTHONY OLDCORN

Off to the Country

Prose comedy in three acts
Performed for the first time in Venice at the
Teatro San Luca on 5 October 1761

Figure 9 *Off to the Country* (Le smanie per la villeggiatura)

Figure 10 *Off to the Country* (Le smanie per la villeggiatura), act 1, scene 1

Figure 11 *Off to the Country* (Le smanie per la villeggiatura), act 2, scene 4

Figure 12 *Off to the Country* (Le smanie per la villeggiatura), act 3, final scene

The Author to the Reader

The innocent pastime of the country holiday has lately become a passion, a mania, a disorder. Virgil, Sannazaro,[1] and a host of other panegyrists of the country life gave Men a taste for the pleasant tranquillity of seclusion; but ambition has invaded the forests: people going to the country take with them the pomp and tumult of the City, and they have poisoned the pleasures of the shepherds and countrymen, who from the arrogance of their masters learn to despise their own penury. This topic is so fertile in ridicule and extravagance that it has furnished me with the material for five of my comedies, all of them founded upon the truth, and yet all different. After publishing I malcontenti [The Malcontents] and La villeggiatura (A Stay in the Country), the first in Volume III, the second in Volume IV of my Teatro comico [Comic Theatre] in the Pitteri edition,[2] I still managed to find satisfactory material, calculated to fuel shall I call it my whim or my zeal against such a fanatical practice. I conceived simultaneously the idea of three consecutive comedies: the first entitled Le smanie per la villeggiatura [Off to the Country], the second Le avventure della villeggiatura [Adventures in the Country], the third Il ritorno dalla villeggiatura [Back from the Country]. In the first we see the frantic preparations, in the second the absurd conduct, in the third the painful consequences arising therefrom. The chief characters of these three compositions, who are the same in each play, are from that walk of life that it was my precise intention to pillory, persons, that is to say, of civil rank, neither noble nor wealthy, since the noble and the wealthy are entitled by their rank and their fortunes to outdo the others. The ambition of the lowly goads them to figure alongside the great, and this is the ridiculous aspect I have tried to bring out, in order to correct it, should that prove possible.

These three comedies, all equally fortunate in their reception and in the universal approval of the public,[3] were performed separately at short intervals from one another, since they were composed in such a way that each of them can stand on its own, while all three fit together perfectly. I could therefore by the same token have published them separately in different volumes of the new edition of my works, being content to include only one of the unpublished Comedies in each tome, as I had promised.[4] But, after reviewing the archive of my unpublished works, I find myself in a position to be generous without fear of running out of material, and I am pleased to present the entire picture at once, convinced that it will give greater pleasure. In this way, the Reader will be better able to observe the continuity of consistent characters through three different plots; and, if one of the difficulties of writing plays lies in keeping the characters consistent within a single work, it will be that much more of a pleasure to see them consistent in three.

Dramatis Personae

FILIPPO	*a good-natured old city-dweller*
GIACINTA	*Filippo's daughter*
LEONARDO	*in love with Giacinta*
VITTORIA	*Leonardo's sister*
FERDINANDO	*a freeloader*
GUGLIELMO	*in love with Giacinta*
FULGENZIO	*an elderly friend of Filippo's*
PAOLO	*Leonardo's manservant*
BRIGIDA	*Giacinta's maidservant*
CECCO *and* BERTO	*Leonardo's other servants*

The action takes place in Leghorn,[5] *partly in Leonardo's house, partly in Filippo's.*

ACT ONE

Scene 1

A private room in Leonardo's house. Paolo, Leonardo's manservant, is packing clothes and linens into a trunk. Enter *Leonardo.*

LEONARDO (*to Paolo*) What the devil are you doing in here? There are hundreds of things that need doing, and here you are wasting time, and nothing's getting accomplished!

PAOLO Begging your pardon, sir, but I believe packing the trunk is one of the things that need doing.

LEONARDO I've got more important work for you. Have the women take care of the trunk.

PAOLO The women are waiting on my mistress, sir. She's keeping them busy. Nobody else can so much as get near them.

LEONARDO That's the trouble with my sister. She's never satisfied. She'd like to have all of the servants catering to her every minute of the day. She needs a whole month and more to get ready for a little trip to the country. Two maids tied up for a month just for her! It won't bear thinking about!

PAOLO You might add, sir, that, as if the two maids weren't enough, she's called in two more women to help them.

LEONARDO What does she do with all this help? Is she having some new dress made on the premises?

PAOLO Oh, no, sir. The new dress is being made at the tailor's. These women have come in to restyle her old dresses. She's having mantillas made, and capes, nightcaps, daycaps, masses of lace, ribbons, frills, and flounces, a regular arsenal of frippery. And all of this just to go to the country! It's getting so that people care more about the way they look in the country than they do in town.

LEONARDO Yes. I'm afraid you're right. If a person wants to cut a decent figure in society, he has to keep up with his neighbours. Montenero,[6] where our country place is, is one of the most popular resorts, and it's even more demanding than the others. The company one keeps there takes some keeping up with. Even I feel obliged to make more of an effort than I would really like to. That's what I need you for. Time waits for no man. We must leave Leghorn before nightfall. I want everything ready. I don't want to forget anything.

PAOLO Just give me my orders, sir, and I'll do my level best.

LEONARDO First of all, let's take a quick inventory of what we have and what we still need. I'm afraid we're going to be short of silverware.

PAOLO Two dozen settings should be enough!

LEONARDO Ordinarily, I'd agree with you. But who's to say we won't be overrun by troops of friends? People staying in the country usually keep open house. It's just as well to be on the safe side. Place settings have to be changed constantly, and two boxes of cutlery just won't be enough.

PAOLO Forgive me, sir, if I'm speaking too freely. But your honour is not obliged to do everything those aristocrats from Florence do, with their landed properties, their enormous estates, their court appointments, and their fancy titles.

LEONARDO I don't need my manservant to give me lessons in social deportment.

PAOLO Forgive me. I'll say no more.

LEONARDO My situation compels me to spare no expense. My place in the country is next door to Signor Filippo's. He's accustomed to treating himself well. He's a splendid man, a generous man. His country holidays are always magnificent. I don't want to suffer by comparison. I don't want to be outdone.

PAOLO Go right ahead, sir. I know we can count on your common sense!

LEONARDO Go to Monsieur Gurland's and ask him for me if he would be so kind as to lend me two boxes of silverware, four silver trays, and six silver candlesticks.

PAOLO At your service, sir.

LEONARDO Then go to the grocer's and have him give you ten pounds of coffee, fifty pounds of chocolate, twenty pounds of sugar, and an assortment of spices for the kitchen.

PAOLO Would you like me to pay?

LEONARDO No. Tell him I'll pay when I get back.

PAOLO Forgive me for speaking out, sir, but the other day he told me he hoped you'd pay what you already owe before you left for the country.

LEONARDO There's no point in paying now. Tell him I'll pay when I get back.

PAOLO Very well.

LEONARDO Make sure we have enough playing cards for six or seven tables, and above all that we're not short of wax candles.

PAOLO The shop that sells the candles from Pisa would also like your old account paid, before they open a new one.

LEONARDO Buy candles from Venice. They cost more, but they last longer and the quality's better.

PAOLO Shall I pay cash?

LEONARDO Have them give you what you need on credit. They'll be paid when I get back.

PAOLO When you get back, sir, you're going to have a regular horde of creditors to annoy you.

LEONARDO You annoy me more than anyone else! You've been with me for ten years, and every year you get more insolent. One of these days I'm going to lose my patience.

PAOLO There's nothing to stop you dismissing me. But remember, if I speak out, it's only because I have your best interests at heart.

LEONARDO Use your concern to serve me properly, not to annoy me. Do as I told you, and send in Cecco.

Paolo At your service, sir. *(aside)* It won't be long now before his prodigality in the country makes him a pauper in town! *(exit Paolo)*

Scene 2

Leonardo, followed by Cecco.

Leonardo I know as well as anyone that I'm overextending myself. But everyone else does it, and I don't want to be looked down on. That old skinflint of an uncle of mine[7] could help me out, but he won't. Still, unless my calculations are completely off, he is due to kick the bucket before I do, and, unless he plans to do an injustice to his own flesh and blood, I'll be the one to inherit his property.

Cecco You sent for me, sir?

Leonardo Go to Signor Filippo Ghiandinelli's.[8] If he's home, give him my respects, and tell him I have ordered the carriage horses, and that we'll leave together a couple of hours before sunset.[9] Then go to his daughter Signora Giacinta's room. Tell her, or have her maid tell her, that I send her my compliments, and would like to know if she got a good night's sleep, and that in a few hours I shall be coming by to pick her up. And, while you're there, keep a weather eye open, to see if Signor Guglielmo is there by any chance. Find out from the servants if he's been there, if he's sent any messages, if they think he's likely to visit. Be sure you do everything I say, and come back with an answer.

Cecco At your service, sir. *(exit Cecco)*

Scene 3

Leonardo, followed by Vittoria.

Leonardo I can't stand Signora Giacinta seeing Guglielmo. She claims she has to put up with him to please her father, that he's a friend of the family, that she doesn't find him in the least bit attractive. But I don't have to believe everything she says, and I don't like these meetings of theirs one bit. I'd better finish packing the trunk myself. *(enter Vittoria)*

Vittoria Is it true, Brother, that you've ordered the carriage horses and that we're to leave this evening?

LEONARDO Yes, of course. Isn't that what we decided yesterday?

VITTORIA Yesterday I said that I hoped to be ready to leave, but now I must inform you I'm not. Please send someone to cancel the horses, since it is quite out of the question for us to leave today.

LEONARDO And why can't we leave today?

VITTORIA Because the tailor has not finished my "mariage."[10]

LEONARDO And what the devil is a "marriage"?

VITTORIA It's a dress in the very latest fashion.

LEONARDO If it's not finished yet, he can send it on to you in the country.

VITTORIA Certainly not. I want to have it tried on, and I want to see it finished.

LEONARDO But we can't put off leaving. We agreed to leave with Signor Filippo and Signora Giacinta, and we said we were leaving today.

VITTORIA That's too bad. I know that Signora Giacinta is a woman of taste, and I don't want to go and risk making a bad impression in comparison with her.

LEONARDO You have all the dresses you could possibly want. You don't have to be afraid of comparison with anyone.

VITTORIA All of mine are antiques.

LEONARDO Didn't you have a new dress made only last year?

VITTORIA From one year to the next a dress can no longer be said to be in fashion. It's true that I have had almost all of my dresses restyled, but one has to have one new dress, one new dress is an absolute must, one simply can't do without one.

LEONARDO And this year the "mariage" is all the rage. Is that it?

VITTORIA Yes, precisely. Madame Granon brought one back from Turin. So far I don't believe any have been seen in Leghorn. I hope to be one of the first.

LEONARDO But what kind of a dress is it? Does it take so long to make one?

VITTORIA No time at all. It's a silk dress, all one colour, with braided trimming in two colours. The secret is in having the good taste to choose the right colours, colours that go well together, and at the same time stand out, colours that don't get confused.

LEONARDO Well, I don't know what to say. I'd be very sorry to see you disappointed. But, whatever happens, we must leave.

VITTORIA I absolutely refuse to come.

LEONARDO If you won't come, I'll go by myself.

VITTORIA What? Without me? You'd have the courage to leave me behind in Leghorn?

LEONARDO I'll come back for you later.

VITTORIA No, I don't trust you. Heaven knows when you'd come, and if I stay here without you, I'm afraid that miserable uncle of ours will oblige me to stay in Leghorn with him. If I were forced to stay here, when everyone else is going to the country, I'd be sick with rage and despair.

LEONARDO So, make your mind up and come.

VITTORIA Go to the tailor's and make him put everything else aside and finish my "mariage."

LEONARDO I have no time to waste. I have a hundred and one things to do.

VITTORIA Oh! Curse my misfortune!

LEONARDO *(ironically)* A fine misfortune indeed! One less dress to your name! What a lamentable, unbearable, uttermost misfortune!

VITTORIA Indeed, sir. To be without a fashionable dress can cause a person with a reputation for good taste to lose all face.

LEONARDO But, when all is said and done, you are still a single woman; and single women are not judged by the same standards as married women.

VITTORIA Signora Giacinta is a single woman, too, and she keeps up with all the fashions, all of the latest frippery married women wear. In any case, today no one distinguishes any more between single women and married women, and a young woman who doesn't keep in step with the rest is considered a clodhopper or an antique. What's more, I am surprised to hear such an opinion coming from you. How could you stand by and see me humiliated and abused to such a degree?

LEONARDO So much fuss about a dress?

VITTORIA Rather than stay here, or go away without my dress, I'd prefer to come down with an illness.

LEONARDO Then, may your wish be granted.

VITTORIA *(scornfully)* You mean, for me to get sick?

LEONARDO No, for you to get your new dress, and be happy.

Scene 4

Enter *Berto, another of Leonardo's servants.*

BERTO Sir, Signor Ferdinando is here to pay his respects.

LEONARDO Show him in, show him in. He's most welcome.

VITTORIA Listen. Go to my tailor's immediately, to Monsieur de la Rejouissance, and tell him he must finish my dress right away, because

I want it before I leave for the country. Otherwise, he'll have me to reckon with, and his days as a tailor in Leghorn will be numbered.

BERTO At your service, madam. *(exit Berto)*

LEONARDO Come along, now, Sister, calm down. Don't let Signor Ferdinando see you this way.

VITTORIA What do I care about Signor Ferdinando? I am not afraid of him. I suppose he'll be coming to the country with us again this year and pitching his tent in our living room.

LEONARDO Certainly, he has led me to hope that he may come along with us. He believes he is doing us a favour. But, since he is one of those people who stick their noses into everything and distinguish themselves by reporting back here and there on other people's business, it's a good idea to play it safe and not tell him everything. If he knew, for instance, what a fuss you are making over a dress, he would be quite capable of making you look foolish at every social gathering and every conversation in town.

VITTORIA Then how can you insist on taking this pest along with us, if you know what kind of a person he is?

LEONARDO Oh, come on, now. In the country one just has to have company. Everybody does his best to have as many guests as possible. All you hear is: So-and-so has ten house guests, someone else six, someone else eight. And whoever has the most is the most highly regarded. What's more, Ferdinando is an extremely useful person to have around. He can play all the card games, he's always in good spirits, he tells funny stories, he eats hearty, he does honour to any table, he can take a joke, and he never takes things the wrong way.

VITTORIA Yes, yes, you're right. In the country, one needs people like him. But what can he be up to? Why doesn't he come in?

LEONARDO Ah, there he is, coming out of the kitchen.

VITTORIA What do you suppose he was doing in the kitchen?

LEONARDO Curiosity! He has to know everything. He has to know what people are up to, what they're eating, and then he spreads the news everywhere he goes.

VITTORIA Fortunately, he won't have any tales of misery to tell about us!

Scene 5

Enter *Ferdinando.*

FERDINANDO My honoured friends. My respects to Signora Vittoria.

VITTORIA Your servant, Signor Ferdinando.

LEONARDO Well, friend, will you be one of us?

FERDINANDO Yes, I'll be joining your party. I managed to shake off that bore Count Anselmo,[11] who was insisting on my going with him at all costs.

VITTORIA Are Count Anselmo's trips to the country so miserly?

FERDINANDO On the contrary, he treats himself very well, he keeps a good table; but at his place the life one leads is too cut and dried. Supper at ten-thirty, off to bed at half-past eleven.

VITTORIA Oh! I couldn't put up with a life like that if you paid me! If I go to bed before dawn, I can't sleep.

LEONARDO You know how it goes at our place. We play cards, we dance, we never go in to supper before two-thirty in the morning, and then, with a nice little game of faro,[12] more often than not we are still up to see the sun rise.

VITTORIA That's what I call living.

FERDINANDO And that's why I chose your country place over Count Anselmo's. What's more, that old relic of a wife of his is positively insufferable.

VITTORIA Yes, yes. She insists on acting like a young girl still.

FERDINANDO Last year, for the first few days, I was her beau. Then, along came a young fellow of twenty-two, and she threw me over and went and set her cap at him.

VITTORIA Oh, you don't say! Not with a boy of twenty-two?

FERDINANDO Yes, would I tell you a lie? He was a blond chap, not a curl out of place, all peaches and cream, like a rose.

LEONARDO I am surprised at the boy. I wonder that he could put up with it.

FERDINANDO You know how it is. He was one of those fellows who don't have the wherewithal, who hang on here and there, wherever they can. They attach themselves to some aging female. She pays for their trips and provides them with a little extra pocket money for gambling.[13]

VITTORIA *(aside)* He certainly has a good word for everybody!

FERDINANDO What time are we leaving?

VITTORIA We don't know yet. The time has still to be arranged.

FERDINANDO I suppose you'll be going in a four-seater carriage.

LEONARDO I ordered a calèche for my sister and myself,[14] and a horse for my servant.

FERDINANDO And how am I going to get there?

LEONARDO Whatever way you choose.

VITTORIA *(to Leonardo)* Come, come. Signor Ferdinando will come with me; you can go in the open carriage with Signor Filippo and Signora Giacinta. *(aside)* I stand to cut a better figure in the calèche with him than if I go with my brother.

LEONARDO *(to Vittoria)* But are you quite sure you want to leave?

FERDINANDO Why? Is there some problem?

VITTORIA There may be a small problem.

FERDINANDO If you aren't sure you're leaving, feel free to say so. If I can't go with you, I'll go with someone else. Everybody is going to the country, and I wouldn't want people to say that I'm staying behind to mount guard over Leghorn.

VITTORIA *(aside)* That would be a terrible mortification for me, too.

Scene 6

Enter *Cecco.*

CECCO *(to Leonardo)* Here I am, sir …

LEONARDO *(to Cecco)* Come over here. *(to Ferdinando)* Please excuse me.

CECCO *(aside)* Signor Filippo sends his respects, and says that he is counting on you for the horses. Signora Giacinta is well. She's waiting for you, and she begs you to hurry, because she doesn't like travelling at night.

LEONARDO *(aside)* And have you nothing to tell me about Guglielmo?

CECCO *(aside)* They assured me he hadn't put in an appearance this morning.

LEONARDO *(aside)* Good, good; I'm delighted. *(aloud)* Now, go and inform the livery stables that I would like the horses ready at three-thirty.

VITTORIA But what if that other business isn't settled? …

LEONARDO Whether it's settled or not, whether you come or you don't, I am determined to leave at three-thirty …

FERDINANDO And I'll be here and ready at three-thirty.

VITTORIA I'd just like to see …

LEONARDO *(to Vittoria)* I've given my word, and you are not going to make me break it for something and nothing. If there were a good reason, all well and good; but we are not going to stay behind on account of a silly dress. *(exit Leonardo)*

Scene 7

Vittoria, Ferdinando, and Cecco.

VITTORIA *(aside)* Alas, poor me! What a miserable position to be in! I'm not my own mistress; I'm dependent on my brother! I can't wait to be married, if for no other reason than to be able to do as I please.

FERDINANDO Tell me, madam, if you can, just between you and me; why is it you're not sure whether you'll leave or not?

VITTORIA *(to the servant)* Cecco!

CECCO Madam?

VITTORIA Have you been round to Signora Giacinta's?

CECCO Yes, madam.

VITTORIA Did you see her?

CECCO Yes, I saw her.

VITTORIA What was she doing?

CECCO She was trying on a dress.

VITTORIA A new dress?

CECCO Brand new.

VITTORIA *(aside)* Oh, curses! If I don't have mine, I absolutely refuse to leave.

FERDINANDO *(aside)* So that's it! She'd like a new dress, too, but she doesn't have the money to buy one. It's just as they say: brother and sister are both crazy. They spend more than they can afford. In one month at Montenero they squander enough to last them a year in Leghorn.

VITTORIA Cecco!

CECCO Madam?

VITTORIA What's this dress of Signora Giacinta's like?

CECCO To tell the truth, I didn't pay much attention, but I think it was a wedding dress.

VITTORIA A wedding dress? Did anyone say she was getting married?

CECCO I didn't hear anyone say that exactly. But I did hear the tailor say a word in French, and I thought I understood it.

VITTORIA I understand French, too. What did he say?

CECCO He said "mariage."

VITTORIA *(aside)* Oh, now I get it. She's having a "mariage" made, too. I would have been surprised if she hadn't. *(to Cecco)* Where's Berto? See if you can find Berto. If he isn't in, run over to my tailor's and tell him I insist that he bring me my "mariage" within three hours without fail.

CECCO Doesn't "mariage" mean "wedding"?
VITTORIA Go to the devil! Now go at once, and get a move on. Do as I tell you, and don't talk back.
CECCO Yes, madam. Off I go, at once. *(exit Cecco)*

Scene 8

Vittoria and Ferdinando.

FERDINANDO Madam, tell me the truth. Is it because you don't have the dress that you're not sure about leaving?
VITTORIA And what if it were? Would you blame me?
FERDINANDO No! You couldn't be more right. A new dress is absolutely essential. All the ladies have one, even the ones who can't afford it. Do you know Signora Aspasia?
VITTORIA Yes, I know her.
FERDINANDO She had one made, too. She bought the cloth on credit, and she's paying it off at so much a month. And Signora Costanza? In order to buy a new dress, Signora Costanza sold two pairs of sheets and a Flanders linen tablecloth and twenty-four linen napkins.
VITTORIA What was the occasion? What was the emergency? Why did they do it?
FERDINANDO To go to the country.
VITTORIA What can I say? The country is a real passion. I sympathize. If I were in their shoes, I don't know what I wouldn't do. In town, I don't care what kind of impression I make, but in the country I'm always afraid of not making a good impression. Will you do me a favour, Signor Ferdinando, will you come with me?
FERDINANDO And where are we supposed to go?
VITTORIA To the tailor's, to give him a good scolding.
FERDINANDO No, madam. Shall I tell you how to make him hurry?
VITTORIA What would you suggest?
FERDINANDO Forgive me for being indiscreet, but do you plan to pay him right away?
VITTORIA I will pay him when I get back.
FERDINANDO Pay right away, and you'll be served right away.
VITTORIA I'll pay him when I feel like paying him, and I expect to be served when I feel like being served. *(exit Vittoria)*

FERDINANDO Good for her! A fine way to behave! To cut a fine figure in the country, she's prepared to be the talk of the town! *(exit Ferdinando)*

Scene 9

A room in Filippo's house. Filippo and Guglielmo meet each other.

FILIPPO Oh, Signor Guglielmo, you're too kind. To what do I owe the honour of this visit?

GUGLIELMO My duty, Signor Filippo, nothing more than my duty. I know you are leaving for the country today, so I came to wish you a pleasant journey and a pleasant stay.

FILIPPO My dear friend, I'm grateful for your affectionate concern. Yes, today we're finally off to the country. If it had been up to me, I would have been there a good month ago. In my day, when I was a lad, we went to the country earlier, and we came back earlier, too. As soon as the wine was pressed, we would come back to town. In those days, we went for the grape harvest; nowadays, people go for amusement. And they stay in the country even after it turns cold; they stay long enough to see the leaves turn brown on the trees.[15]

GUGLIELMO But surely you're your own master? Why don't you go when you feel like going, and come back when you feel like coming back?

FILIPPO Yes, you're right. I could do that. But I've always been a good sport; I've always liked company; and, at my age, I like to live it up a little, have people around. If I suggest going to the country in September, there's not even a dog to go with me, no one is willing to put himself out. Even my daughter pulls a long face. And my little Giacinta's all I have in the world, and I'm determined to humour her. You just have to go when everyone else goes, and I let myself be ruled by the others.

GUGLIELMO In fact, you have to agree that what most people do is what's best.

FILIPPO Not always, not always. That's open to discussion. Where will you be spending your holidays this year?

GUGLIELMO I don't know. I haven't decided yet. *(aside)* Oh, if only I could go with him. If only I could spend my vacation with his delightful daughter!

FILIPPO Your father used to go to the Pisan hills for his holidays.

GUGLIELMO True, true. That is where our country properties are, and there is a decent enough house there. But I'm all alone now, and I couldn't agree with you more: to be alone in the country is to die of melancholy.

FILIPPO Would you like to come with us?

GUGLIELMO Oh, Signor Filippo, I've done nothing to deserve it, I wouldn't dare to impose such a burden on you.

FILIPPO I'm not one for ceremony. I go along with your modern ways in most things, but I have no time for ceremony. If you want to come with us, I can offer you a comfortable bed and a tolerable table, a heart that always has a welcome for friends, and makes no distinctions among them.

GUGLIELMO I don't know what to say. You are so obliging. How can I refuse your kindness?

FILIPPO That's the way! Come, and stay as long as you like. Don't neglect business, but stay as long as you like.

GUGLIELMO What time were you planning on leaving?

FILIPPO I don't know. Make arrangements with Signor Leonardo.

GUGLIELMO Is Signor Leonardo coming with you?

FILIPPO Yes, of course. We agreed to go together with him and his sister. We are close neighbours in the country, we are friends, and we're going together.

GUGLIELMO *(aside)* I don't relish this company one bit. But it's certainly not going to make me pass up the chance to spend some time with Giacinta.

FILIPPO Is there a problem?

GUGLIELMO No, sir. I am just wondering whether I should take a calèche, or, since I'm alone, a saddle horse.

FILIPPO Let's do it this way. There are three of us and we have a four-seater carriage, so come with us.

GUGLIELMO Who's the fourth, may I ask?

FILIPPO My widowed sister-in-law,[16] who's coming with us as a chaperone for my daughter. Not that she needs a chaperone, she has judgment enough of her own, but for appearance's sake, since she lost her mother, she needs the company of an older woman.

GUGLIELMO Excellent. *(aside)* I'll do all I can to win the old biddy over.

FILIPPO Well, then? Does it suit you to come along with us?

GUGLIELMO Indeed, I couldn't imagine a greater kindness.

FILIPPO Go to Signor Leonardo's, then, and tell him not to give your place to anyone else.

GUGLIELMO Could you do me a favour and send someone else over?

FILIPPO All my servants are busy. In any case, if I may say so, I really don't think it's too much to ask.

GUGLIELMO You're absolutely right. It's just that I had a little business to attend to. But … no more of that … I'll go and let him know. *(aside)* Leonardo can say what he likes, he can take it however he chooses, what does it matter to me? I don't have to answer to him. Signor Filippo, I look forward to seeing you later.

FILIPPO Don't keep us waiting.

GUGLIELMO I'll be on time, don't you worry. I have my reasons for being punctual. *(exit Guglielmo)*

Scene 10

Filippo, followed by Giacinta and Brigida.

FILIPPO Come to think of it, I wouldn't want to be criticized for inviting a young man to come with us, and me with a daughter of marriageable age. But, dammit, these days so many other people do the same thing, why should they pick on me? They might just as well talk about Signor Leonardo, who is coming with us. Or about me, since I'll be going with his sister! True, I'm not as young as I was, but I'm not old enough yet to be above suspicion! Oh, well! Nowadays there's no such thing as malice aforethought. It's as if the innocence of the country were catching! In the country, people don't expect the same strict standards they look for in town. And besides, it's my house, and I give the orders. My daughter's a good girl, and she's been properly brought up. Ah, here she comes now, God bless her!

GIACINTA Father, could I have another six florins?[17]

FILIPPO What for, my dear girl?

GIACINTA To pay for a silk travelling cape to keep off the dust on the road.

FILIPPO *(aside)* My God, will it never end? *(to Giacinta)* Does it have to be silk?

GIACINTA Absolutely. It would be too common for words to wear a linen dust coat. It has to be silk, with a hood.

FILIPPO And what's the hood for?

GIACINTA For the night, for the air, for the damp, for when it gets cold.

FILIPPO But don't people wear hats? Don't hats provide better protection?

GIACINTA Oh, hats!

BRIGIDA Ha, ha, ha, hats!

GIACINTA Did you hear that, Brigida? Hats!

BRIGIDA The master is so droll! Hats!

FILIPPO What's the matter? Did I say something wrong? Did I say something foolish? What's all the amazement about? Didn't people use to wear hats?

GIACINTA How gauche, how gauche!

BRIGIDA Hats are old hat!

FILIPPO Since when did people stop wearing hats?

GIACINTA Oh, at least two years ago.

FILIPPO Only two years … and they're already outmoded?

BRIGIDA But don't you know, sir, that what one wears one year, one can't wear the next.

FILIPPO It's true. In the space of a few years, I have seen caps, bonnets, little hats, big hats; now hoods are all the rage. Next year I suppose you'll all be wearing shoes on your heads.

GIACINTA But what's all this fuss about women? Tell me, aren't men worse than we are? Once, when they travelled to the country, they wore heavy jackets, woollen leggings, and heavy boots; now they wear dust coats, too, and patent leather shoes with diamond buckles, and they ride in their gigs wearing silk knee socks.

BRIGIDA And they don't carry sticks any more.

GIACINTA And they wear little curved swords.

BRIGIDA And they carry umbrellas to keep off the sun.

GIACINTA And they talk about us!

BRIGIDA When they're worse than we are!

FILIPPO I know nothing about that. All I know is that the way I dress today is the way people dressed fifty years ago.

GIACINTA All this talk is wasting time. Please let me have the six florins.

FILIPPO That's it! Let's get to the point! Spending has always been in style.

GIACINTA I think I'm one of the more careful spenders.

BRIGIDA Oh, sir, you just don't know. Take a look around you in the country at what the rest of the women are up to, and then come and tell me.

FILIPPO So that's it. I'm supposed to be thankful to my daughter for being good enough to save me so much money!

BRIGIDA I assure you, sir, you won't find a thriftier girl anywhere.

GIACINTA I only want the bare essentials, and no more.

FILIPPO My dear Daughter, essential or unessential, you know that all I want is to make you happy. You can come to my room for the six florins, and they'll be there waiting. But, while we're on the subject of economy, please give it a little more study, because, if you do get married, it's not going to be easy to find a husband as generous as your father.

GIACINTA What time are we leaving?

FILIPPO *(aside)* Not to change the subject! *(to Giacinta)* About three-thirty, I believe.

GIACINTA Oh! I think we'll leave earlier. And who's coming in the carriage with us?

FILIPPO I'm coming, your aunt is coming, and the fourth is a gentleman, a friend of mine whom you've already met.

GIACINTA An older man, I suppose?

FILIPPO Would you be upset if he were an older man?

GIACINTA Oh! No, sir. It doesn't matter to me, so long as he isn't a bore. Even if he's old, so long as he's good company, I couldn't be happier.

FILIPPO He's a young man.

BRIGIDA Better yet.

FILIPPO Why, better yet?

BRIGIDA Because young people are naturally livelier, wittier. He'll keep you amused. You won't fall asleep on the way.

GIACINTA And who is this gentleman?

FILIPPO Signor Guglielmo.

GIACINTA Oh yes! He's a talented young man.

FILIPPO I imagine Signor Leonardo will go by calèche with his sister.

GIACINTA Probably.

BRIGIDA How about me, sir, who will I go with?

FILIPPO You'll go the way you always go, by sea, in a felucca,[18] with the rest of my servants, and Signor Leonardo's.

BRIGIDA But sir, I always get seasick, and last year I almost got drowned. I don't want to go by sea this year.

FILIPPO Would you like me to hire a calèche especially for you?

BRIGIDA Who is Signor Leonardo's manservant going with, if I may ask?

GIACINTA A good point. He usually takes his servant by land. Poor Brigida! Let her go with him.

FILIPPO With the manservant?

GIACINTA Yes, what are you afraid of? We'll be there; and you know that Brigida is a good girl.

BRIGIDA For my part, I swear, the minute I get into the coach, I'll go to sleep, and I won't even look at him.

GIACINTA It's only fair that I should have my maid with me.
BRIGIDA All the ladies take their maids with them.
GIACINTA I may need a hundred and one things on the trip.
BRIGIDA At least I'll be there, ready to help, ready to serve my mistress.
GIACINTA Dear, dear Father.
BRIGIDA Dear, dear Master.
FILIPPO What can I say? I don't know how to say no, I'm incapable of saying no, I'll never say no. *(exit Filippo)*

Scene 11

Giacinta and Brigida.

GIACINTA Are you satisfied?
BRIGIDA What a clever mistress I have!
GIACINTA Oh! If I have one quality, it's the ability to get people to do anything I want.
BRIGIDA But how is this going to sit with Signor Leonardo?
GIACINTA What are you talking about?
BRIGIDA About Signor Guglielmo. You know how jealous he is. If he sees him in the carriage with you …
GIACINTA He'll just have to lump it.
BRIGIDA I'm afraid he'll be angry.
GIACINTA With whom?
BRIGIDA With you.
GIACINTA Precisely! I've put him through worse trials than this.
BRIGIDA Forgive me, mistress, but the poor fellow's too fond of you.
GIACINTA I have nothing against him.
BRIGIDA He hopes to make you his wife someday.
GIACINTA And that just might happen.
BRIGIDA But if his intentions are honest, why don't you try a bit harder to please him?
GIACINTA On the contrary. Precisely because he may be my husband one day, I intend to train him in good time not to be jealous, not to be constantly critical, not to deprive me of my honest freedom. If he starts laying down the law and giving me orders already, if he succeeds in humiliating me and getting the upper hand at this stage, it's all over: I'll be a slave forever. Either he loves me, or he doesn't. If he loves me, he must trust me; if he doesn't, he can leave.

BRIGIDA On the other hand, you know what the proverb says: A man in love lives in fear. If Leonardo's suspicious, he's suspicious because he's in love.

GIACINTA That kind of love is not for me.

BRIGIDA Just between you and me: you don't love Signor Leonardo very much, do you?

GIACINTA I don't know how much I love him, but I do know that I love him more than I ever loved anyone else, and I'd have no trouble marrying him; but not if it means a life of torment.

BRIGIDA Forgive me, but that's not real love.

GIACINTA What do you want from me? It's the best I can do.

BRIGIDA I think I hear someone coming.

GIACINTA Go and see who it is.

BRIGIDA Oh, it's him. It's Signor Leonardo.

GIACINTA Well, why doesn't he come in?

BRIGIDA I know! What if he's found out about Signor Guglielmo?

GIACINTA He has to find out sooner or later.

BRIGIDA He's not coming in. Something's wrong. Do you want me to go and see?

GIACINTA Yes, go and see. Send him in.

BRIGIDA *(aside)* Heavens! I couldn't care less about him! The one that interests me is his servant. *(exit Brigida)*

Scene 12

Giacinta and Leonardo.

GIACINTA True, I love him, I respect him, I want to marry him, but I can't stand jealousy!

LEONARDO *(stiffly)* Your servant, Signora Giacinta.

GIACINTA *(stiffly)* Your servant, Signor Leonardo.

LEONARDO Forgive me if I'm disturbing you.

GIACINTA *(ironically)* Oh! Come now, Mr Formality, spare me such ceremony!

LEONARDO I came to wish you a pleasant journey.

GIACINTA Where to?

LEONARDO To the country.

GIACINTA But aren't you coming with us?

LEONARDO No, madam.

GIACINTA Why not, may I ask?

LEONARDO Because I don't wish to incommode you.

GIACINTA *(ironically)* But you never incommode me; it's always a delight to have you. You're so charming, it's always a delight to have you!

LEONARDO I'm not the charming one. Prince Charming will be with you in your carriage.

GIACINTA I don't make the decisions, sir. My father's in charge, and he's free to invite whomever he chooses.

LEONARDO But his daughter goes along with it quite happily.

GIACINTA Happily or not, sir, I suggest you stop trying to interpret my feelings.

LEONARDO Let me come to the point, Signora Giacinta: I do not approve of your companion.

GIACINTA It's no good telling me.

LEONARDO Who am I supposed to tell?

GIACINTA My father.

LEONARDO But I'm not free to speak frankly to him.

GIACINTA Nor do I have the authority to make him do as I wish.

LEONARDO But, if my friendship meant anything to you, you would find a way not to displease me.

GIACINTA How? Why don't you make a suggestion?

LEONARDO Oh! Pretexts are not hard to find. Where there's a will there's a way.

GIACINTA For instance?

LEONARDO For instance, you could say something has come up to postpone your departure; that way you gain time; or, if it can't be postponed, you could give up going altogether, rather than hurt someone you respect.

GIACINTA You're right. That is the best way … to make myself look like a fool!

LEONARDO Go ahead! Say you don't care about me.

GIACINTA I think very highly of you, I care about you a great deal: but I have no intention of cutting a sorry figure in public for your sake.

LEONARDO Would it be such a tragedy not to go to the country for one year?

GIACINTA A year without going to the country? What would they say about me in Montenero? What would they say about me in Leghorn? I wouldn't dare look anyone in the face ever again!

LEONARDO If that's the way things stand, I'll say no more. Go ahead, have a good time, and I hope you're satisfied.

GIACINTA But you're coming, too?

LEONARDO No, madam. I'm not coming.
GIACINTA *(cajolingly)* Oh, yes, you are.
LEONARDO I'm not coming if he's coming.
GIACINTA What harm has he done you?
LEONARDO I can't stand the sight of him.
GIACINTA So, you hate him more than you love me.
LEONARDO You are the reason I hate him.
GIACINTA But why?
LEONARDO Because … Because … Don't make me say it.
GIACINTA Because you're jealous of him?
LEONARDO Yes, because I'm jealous of him.
GIACINTA Now I've got you where I wanted you. Your jealousy of him is an insult to me. If you're jealous of him you must think me fickle, a flirt, a coquette. Someone who really respects someone else couldn't possibly harbour such feelings, and where there's no respect, there can be no love; and if you don't love me, then leave me, and if you don't know how to love, then learn. I love you, and I'm faithful, and I'm sincere, and I know my duty, and I won't have jealousy, and I don't want scenes, and I'm not about to make myself look foolish for anyone … And I'm going to go to the country, I must go, and I will go. *(exit Giacinta)*
LEONARDO Go, and be damned. But no; maybe you won't go. Maybe I'll see to it that you don't go. Damn the country! Their friendship began in the country. She met this fellow in the country. We'll give everything up! So what if people talk. So what if my sister has a fit. There'll be no more vacation! There'll be no more trip to the country! *(exit Leonardo)*

ACT TWO

Scene 1

Leonardo's room. Vittoria and Paolo.

VITTORIA Come along, come along. Don't just stand there complaining. Let the women get done what they have to do. I'll help you finish packing my brother's trunk.
PAOLO What can I say? There's a whole houseful of people, but it still seems I have to do everything myself.

VITTORIA Quickly now, quickly. Let's get it over with, so that when Signor Leonardo gets back, he'll find everything ready. I couldn't be happier now: at noon my new dress will be here.

PAOLO Did the tailor finish it?

VITTORIA Oh, yes, he finished it all right. But I'm never going to use him again.

PAOLO Why not, madam? Did he do a bad job?

VITTORIA No, to tell the truth, it came out beautifully. It looks well on me, it's in excellent taste, there probably won't be another dress like it. It's going to make one or two people green with envy.

PAOLO So, why are you upset with the tailor?

VITTORIA Because he was rude. He wanted to be paid on the spot for the material and the work.

PAOLO Pardon my saying so, but I don't see what was so wrong with that. He told me more than once that your account hasn't been paid for ages, and he wanted it settled.

VITTORIA Well, he ought to have added this last at the end of the list. That way he would have been paid for everything all at once.

PAOLO And when would he have been paid?

VITTORIA When we get back from the country.

PAOLO Do you think you'll come back from the country with money to spare?

VITTORIA Nothing simpler! We play cards in the country. I am rather lucky at cards, and I could probably have paid him without having to dip into the pittance my brother gives me for clothes.[19]

PAOLO Well, anyway, this dress is paid for, and you don't have to worry about it any more.

VITTORIA Yes, but now I don't have any money.

PAOLO What does that matter? For the moment you have nothing to spend it on.

VITTORIA But what am I supposed to play cards with?

PAOLO It doesn't cost much to play for low stakes.

VITTORIA Oh! I never play for low stakes. That's no fun, I just can't be bothered. In town I occasionally play to oblige; but in the country my only pastime, my passion, is faro.

PAOLO Well, this year you'll just have to go without playing.

VITTORIA Oh! No, no, no, no, no! I will play, because I like to play, because I need to win, and I have to play, or else people will wonder why not. In any case, I'm relying, I'm counting on you.

PAOLO On me?

VITTORIA Yes, on you. Would it be so difficult for you to lend me a little something to be paid back out of my next year's clothing allowance?

PAOLO Excuse me, but as far as I can see you've already spent half of it.

VITTORIA What does that matter? When I've spent it, I've spent it. I'm sure you're not going to make me go down on my knees!

PAOLO If it were up to me, I'd be more than happy to oblige, but I don't have the cash. True – though my title and wages are only those of a servant – I have the honour of serving my master as his steward and bursar. However, the cash I administer is so tight that I can't even keep up with our everyday expenses; and, if the truth were known, I'm six months behind in pay myself!

VITTORIA I'll ask my brother. He'll give me what I need.

PAOLO Madam, bear in mind that he is in direr straits now than he ever was; don't count on him, because he can't give you anything.

VITTORIA We must have wheat in the country.

PAOLO Not even enough for the bread we need.

VITTORIA The grape harvest hasn't been sold.

PAOLO The grapes are all spoken for.

VITTORIA The grapes, too!

PAOLO And if we go on like this, madam ...

VITTORIA But my uncle doesn't have the same problems.

PAOLO Oh, he has grain, he has wine, he has money.

VITTORIA And don't we have a claim on any of it?

PAOLO No, madam. The inheritance was divided. Each of the heirs got what was coming to him. The estates are separate. There's nothing to hope for from that quarter.

VITTORIA So my brother is headed for ruin.

PAOLO Unless he does something about it.

VITTORIA And what could he do?

PAOLO Control his expenditures. Change his way of living. Above all, give up these trips to the country.

VITTORIA Give up our trips to the country! You're obviously worthless! Let him cut down on the household expenses, give less lavish dinners in town, fire some of the servants, pay them less wages. Let him dress with less flair, and save what he squanders in Leghorn. But we simply must have our trips to the country! And they must do us credit, in the style we're accustomed to, with our usual "noblesse oblige."

PAOLO Do you imagine this can go on much longer?

VITTORIA It can go on as long as I'm around. My dowry is safe in the bank, and I hope it won't be long before I'm married.

PAOLO And in the meantime?

VITTORIA In the meantime, let's get on with the trunk.

PAOLO Here comes the master.

VITTORIA Let's not say anything to him for now. Let's not upset him. I want him in a good mood, so we can all leave in good spirits. Let's get on with the trunk. *(they stuff things hurriedly into the trunk)*

Scene 2

Enter *Leonardo.*

LEONARDO *(aside)* Oh! If I could only hide what I'm feeling, but I don't know if I can. I'm just too upset.

VITTORIA Here we are, dear Brother, here we are, working for you.

LEONARDO There's no need to hurry. Our departure may be postponed.

VITTORIA No, no. Leave as soon as you like. I'm ready, my "mariage" is finished. I couldn't be happier, I can't wait to get going.

LEONARDO I thought I was doing you a favour. I changed the arrangements. We're not leaving today.

VITTORIA Would it be so hard to get ready to leave again?

LEONARDO For today it's impossible, I tell you.

VITTORIA All right, too bad about today. But we'll leave first thing in the morning when it's cool, won't we?

LEONARDO I don't know. I'm not sure.

VITTORIA Are you trying to drive me to despair?

LEONARDO Despair all you like. There's nothing I can do.

VITTORIA You must have a very good reason.

LEONARDO Something more than a missing dress.

VITTORIA Is Signora Giacinta leaving tonight?

LEONARDO She may not leave either.

VITTORIA So that's the good reason! That's the great motive! Because the fair lady's not leaving, her admirer isn't leaving either. She's no concern of mine, we can leave without her.

LEONARDO We can leave when I feel like leaving.

VITTORIA You're doing me wrong, you're being unjust. I can't stay in Leghorn when everyone else is going to the country. Signora

Giacinta will get a piece of my mind if I have to stay in Leghorn on account of her.

LEONARDO This is no way for a polite and well-bred young lady like you to talk. *(to Paolo)* And what do you think you're doing, standing there as if you were made out of wood?

PAOLO I'm waiting for my orders, I'm watching, I'm listening. I don't know whether I'm supposed to keep on packing or start unpacking.

VITTORIA Keep on packing.

LEONARDO Start unpacking.

PAOLO Packing or unpacking, whichever way you look at it, it's still work. *(he begins to unpack)*

VITTORIA I'd like to throw everything out of the window!

LEONARDO You can start by throwing out your "mariage"!

VITTORIA You're right. If I don't go to the country, I shall tear it into a hundred thousand pieces.

LEONARDO *(to Paolo)* What's in this box?

PAOLO The coffee, the chocolate, the sugar, the candles, and the spices.

LEONARDO I suppose none of it's paid for.

PAOLO What was I supposed to pay for it with? All I know is that I had to sweat bullets to get all this stuff on credit. And the shopkeepers insulted me as if I had stolen it.

LEONARDO Take it all back where it came from, and have it struck off our account.

PAOLO Yes, sir. I say, is anyone there? Help me. *(aside)* Right away.

VITTORIA *(aside)* Oh, poor me! Our trip to the country is over.

PAOLO Well done, Master! That's the way! Make as few debts as you can.

LEONARDO Go to the devil. Don't try to lecture me, or I'll lose my temper.

PAOLO *(aside)* Let's get out of here, before he changes his mind. He's obviously not doing it to save money. He must have some other bee in his bonnet. *(exit Paolo, carrying the box)*

Scene 3

Vittoria and Leonardo.

VITTORIA May we know what got you into this desperate state?

LEONARDO I don't even know myself.

VITTORIA Did you and Signora Giacinta have a row?

LEONARDO Giacinta is not worthy of my love, she is unworthy of the friendship of my household. I am telling you, I am ordering you, I don't want you seeing her ever again.

VITTORIA There you are! When I get an idea, I'm never wrong. It's just as I said. It's on account of that baggage that we're not going to the country. She's going, and I'm not. I'll be everyone's laughing stock!

LEONARDO Oh, no! She can go to the devil. She's not going either. I'll see to it that she doesn't.

VITTORIA If Giacinta doesn't go either, I think I'd be less upset about not going myself. But what if she goes, and I don't? Is she going to strut about in the country, while I stay in town? It would be enough … It would be enough to make me beat my head against the wall.

LEONARDO She won't go, just wait and see. Anyway, I cancelled the horses.

VITTORIA *(ironically)* Oh, splendid! They'll have no end of trouble sending out for horses themselves!

LEONARDO Ha! That's not all I did. I sent someone to tell Signor Filippo a thing or two. If he isn't a fool, if he isn't a complete blockhead, he'll think twice about taking his daughter to the country just now.

VITTORIA I love it. Then she'll have to show off her fine dress in Leghorn as well. I can just see her pacing the ramparts. If I meet her, you can bet I'll make her feel small.

LEONARDO I don't want you speaking to her.

VITTORIA I won't say a word, I won't say a word. I can make people feel small without speaking.

Scene 4

Enter *Ferdinando in his travelling outfit.*

FERDINANDO Here I am, here I am ready, here I am dressed for the trip.

VITTORIA Oh! You did well to come early!

LEONARDO My dear friend, I regret to inform you that, because of some urgent business that just came up, I can't leave today after all.

FERDINANDO Oh, curses! When are you leaving? Tomorrow?

LEONARDO I don't know. I may have to put off leaving for several days. It may even turn out that my business will prevent me going to the country at all this year.

FERDINANDO *(aside)* Poor fellow. He's probably run out of cash.

VITTORIA *(aside)* I'm breaking out in a cold sweat just thinking about it.

LEONARDO You can go with Count Anselmo.

FERDINANDO Oh, I'm not short of places to go! I've already sent Count Anselmo packing. I have a mind to go with Signor Filippo and Signora Giacinta.

VITTORIA Oh, this year Signora Giacinta may just have to eat her heart out in town.

FERDINANDO But I just came from their house, and I saw they were ready to leave; I heard they'd ordered the horses for three-thirty.

VITTORIA Did you hear that, Signor Leonardo?

LEONARDO *(aside)* Signor Fulgenzio can't have talked to Signor Filippo yet.

FERDINANDO Ha, they're not afraid of spending money in that family. Signor Filippo lives like a lord. He doesn't have problems in Leghorn that prevent him going off for a splendid stay in the country.

VITTORIA Did you hear that, Signor Leonardo?

LEONARDO I heard, I heard; and I've heard and put up with quite enough. I know your satirical style. You've been a guest in my house, both in town and out, any number of times, and you never died of starvation. If I am not going to the country, I have my good reasons for not going, and I don't have to account to anyone. Go with whomever you like, and don't ever darken my doorstep again. *(aside)* Insolent spongers! Nosy meddlers! *(exit Leonardo)*

Scene 5

Vittoria and Ferdinando.

FERDINANDO Has your brother gone mad? What does he have against me? Have I ever given him cause for complaint?

VITTORIA Well, to tell you the truth, you did seem to be implying that we can't go to the country for lack of the wherewithal.

FERDINANDO Me? I'm amazed. I would die for my friends. I would defend your reputation sword in hand. If he has business in Leghorn, who's going to force him to go to the country? If I said that Signor Filippo has no interests to keep him in town, what I meant was that Signor Filippo is an old fool who neglects his business for the sake of a good time; and a squanderer to boot; and his daughter has even less sense than her father. She makes him spend his last penny on one knick-knack after another. I have the highest regard for Signor Leonardo's common sense, as I have for yours, and the way you adapt to events. We do what we can. Let those who are determined to ruin themselves go right ahead.

VITTORIA You do get some funny ideas! My brother isn't staying in Leghorn out of need.

FERDINANDO I know. He's staying here out of necessity.

VITTORIA What necessity?

FERDINANDO The necessity of attending to his business.

VITTORIA And do you think Signora Giacinta will be going to the country?

FERDINANDO For sure.

VITTORIA For certain?

FERDINANDO Without a doubt.

VITTORIA *(aside)* I'm afraid my brother may be trying to pull the wool over my eyes. He says he's not going, but he may be planning to leave me behind and go off on his own.

FERDINANDO I saw Signora Giacinta's new dress.

VITTORIA Was it pretty?

FERDINANDO Magnificent.

VITTORIA Prettier than mine?

FERDINANDO I wouldn't say prettier than yours, but it is quite lovely, and it's sure to make a big splash in the country.

VITTORIA *(aside)* And in the meantime I have to stay behind and sweep the streets of Leghorn with my fine dress?

FERDINANDO This year I think the season in Montenero will be superb.

VITTORIA What makes you think so?

FERDINANDO There will be more ladies this year, newlyweds, splendidly turned out, dressed to kill, and where there are women, the men soon follow, and everyone flocks where the young people are. There'll be plenty of card games, fantastic balls. We'll have a truly marvellous time.

VITTORIA *(aside)* And I have to stay behind in Leghorn?

FERDINANDO *(aside)* She's squirming, she's eating her heart out. I love it!

VITTORIA *(aside)* No! I won't stay. What if I were to force myself on one of my friends?

FERDINANDO Signora Vittoria, I look forward to the pleasure.

VITTORIA My respects, sir.

FERDINANDO Can I do anything for you in Montenero?

VITTORIA Oh, we may see each other there yet.

FERDINANDO If you come, we'll see each other there. If you don't come, we'll drink to your health.

VITTORIA Don't put yourself out.

FERDINANDO Long live fine weather! Long live light hearts! Long live the country! Your most humble servant, madam.

VITTORIA My profoundest respects.

FERDINANDO *(aside)* If she can't go to the country, she'll croak before the month's out! *(exit Ferdinando)*

Scene 6

VITTORIA *(alone)* Well! Unfortunately, that's the way it goes. Once you're in the public eye, once you start trying to keep up with society, the minute you can no longer do it, you become an object of scorn and derision. If only I'd never got started! Oh! It's hard to have to come down in the world. I don't have the courage to bear it. I'm in a terrible state, and my chief torment is envy. If the women I know weren't going to the country, there'd be no question of my being sorry for not going. But who knows whether Giacinta is going or not? She's more important to me than the others. I want to be sure. I want to know for certain. I shall go and see her myself. My brother can say whatever he likes. I'm determined to settle this doubt. I'm a woman, I'm young. They've always let me do as I liked. It's hard for me to change my ways and my character at one fell swoop.

Scene 7

A room in Filippo's house. Filippo and Brigida.

BRIGIDA So! Signor Leonardo has sent round to say he's unable to leave for the moment?

FILIPPO Yes, of course. That's what he sent round for. But that's nothing. Some important business may have come up. There's nothing surprising about that. What does surprise me is that he also sent round to the stables to cancel the horses, for him and for me. As if he were afraid I wouldn't pay, and he'd end up paying for both of us.

BRIGIDA *(aside)* I knew it, I knew it. My mistress is going to get her own way, God bless her.

FILIPPO I didn't expect this insult from him.

BRIGIDA So what have you decided to do, Master?

FILIPPO I've decided that I'm quite capable of ordering the horses without him, and I've sent a man out to order them for today.

BRIGIDA How many horses did you order, may I ask?

FILIPPO Four, as usual, for my carriage.

BRIGIDA And what about poor little me?

FILIPPO You're going to have to get used to the idea of going by sea.

BRIGIDA Oh! I absolutely refuse to go by sea.

FILIPPO But what do you expect me to do? Order a carriage especially for you? As long as Signor Leonardo's valet was coming with you, I was ready to pay half the cost, but the full price would be too much. In fact I'm surprised you still have the nerve to insist!

BRIGIDA I'm not insisting. I'll put up with anything. But bear with me a little. Isn't Signor Ferdinando coming with you, too?

FILIPPO Yes, that's right. He was supposed to stay with Signor Leonardo, but he came around a few minutes ago to say he was coming to stay with me.

BRIGIDA Then you have to take care of his trip.

FILIPPO Why should it be my responsibility?

BRIGIDA Because he thinks he is coming as a favour to you. Because he's accustomed to going to the country as a profession, not for amusement. If you were to take along an architect, or a painter, or a surveyor, to employ in your service, wouldn't you have to pay for his trip? Then you must do the same for Signor Ferdinando, who is coming with you to grace your table and to amuse your guests. And as long as you're taking him, you may as well take me. If I don't go in the calèche with Signor Leonardo's servant, I can go in the calèche with the Knight of the Errant Tooth![20]

FILIPPO Clever girl! I never knew you were such a wit. That was a fine eulogy you composed for Signor Ferdinando. That does it! If I'm going to be obliged to pay for the trip of the Knight of the Errant Tooth, I shall also take care of the Countess of the Quick Tongue.

BRIGIDA It would be a tribute to your graciousness, and not to my merits.

FILIPPO Who's that in the drawing room?

BRIGIDA Some people.

FILIPPO Take a look.

BRIGIDA *(after taking a look)* It's Signor Fulgenzio.

FILIPPO Is he looking for me?

Brigida Probably.

Filippo Go and see what he wants.

Brigida Right away. Who knows but what it's another ceremonious guest come to pledge his humble respects in the country?

Filippo He's welcome. I'd be delighted. I owe him a number of favours, and, in any case, in the country I turn no one away.

Brigida Don't worry, master, you'll never want for company. The birds go where the grain is, and freeloaders flock to a well-stocked table. *(exit Brigida)*

Scene 8

Filippo, followed by Giacinta.

Giacinta At this late hour, Father, they could spare you these tiresome intrusions. It's getting late, we're supposed to leave at three-thirty. I have to change completely for the trip, and we still have to eat dinner.

Filippo But I must hear what Signor Fulgenzio wants.

Giacinta Have the servants tell him you're busy, you're rushed, you can't …

Filippo You don't know what you're talking about. He's done me a number of favours. I can't treat him rudely.

Giacinta Get it over with quickly, then.

Filippo I'll be as quick as I can.

Giacinta He's a buttonholer. You won't get rid of him so easily.

Filippo Here he comes.

Giacinta I'm going, I'm going. *(aside)* I can't stand him! Every time he comes here, he always has something to say about the way we live, the way we spend our money, or the way we behave. I'll eavesdrop and see if he has anything to say about me. *(exit Giacinta)*

Scene 9

Filippo, followed by Fulgenzio.

Filippo These young girls are really something! When they're about to go to the country, they've no idea what they're doing, they've no idea what they're saying, they're beside themselves.

FULGENZIO Good day, Signor Filippo.

FILIPPO Ah! Dear, dear Fulgenzio, greetings. What lucky chance brings you this way?

FULGENZIO Our friendship, and my wish to see you before you go to the country, to wish you a pleasant trip.

FILIPPO I'm very grateful for your concern and goodwill. You'd be doing me a great honour if you would accept my invitation to come with me.

FULGENZIO No, dear friend, but I thank you. I went to the country for the harvest, I went at seedtime, I went back to check on the growing crops, and I'll go for the vintage. But I'm accustomed to going alone and staying as long as my business warrants, and no longer.

FILIPPO As far as my own interests in the country go, I keep the same eye on them, more or less, as you do. It's just that I can't bear to stay there alone. I love company, and I like to combine business with pleasure.

FULGENZIO Excellent, excellent. Everyone should follow his bent. Me, I like to be alone, but I don't disapprove of those who love company. As long as it's good company, that is, as long as it's above board, as long as it gives no ground for scandal.

FILIPPO From the way you say that, Signor Fulgenzio, it sounds as if you're trying to tell me something.

FULGENZIO My dear friend, we've been friends for years. I don't have to remind you what a good friend I've been, or how many times you've had proof of my friendship.

FILIPPO Yes, I haven't forgotten, and I'll be in your debt for as long as I live. Whenever I needed cash, you always came up with it without any fuss. And for my part, I always repaid it. As for the thousand crowns you lent me the other day,[21] you can count on having them back in three months, as promised.

FULGENZIO I am quite certain of that. Lending a thousand crowns to a man of honour I consider a thing of no consequence. But allow me to mention something I've noticed. I have observed that you come to ask for a loan practically every year, just as it gets to be time to go to the country. A clear sign that these trips to the country are a strain on your purse. It's a pity that a gentleman like yourself, someone comfortably off, a man of means with everything it takes to get by, should overextend himself and borrow money he intends to spend badly. Yes, sir, spend badly. Because the very people who come to devour your capital are the first to disparage you, and, among those you treat with such affection, there are one or two who detract from your good name and reputation.

FILIPPO Dammit, sir, now you've really upset me. As for spending a little excessively and letting myself be taken advantage of, I grant you that, it's true, but it's what I've always been used to, and, after all, I only have the one daughter. I'm in a position to give her a good dowry, and I'll still have enough to live well on for the rest of my life. What I really object to is your suggestion that there's someone who might damage my good name and reputation. How can you say a thing like that, Signor Fulgenzio?

FULGENZIO Not without good reason, and if I do say it, it is precisely with the fact in mind that you have a marriageable daughter. I know of someone who would like to make her his wife, but he's reluctant to ask because you allow her too much familiarity with young men, and think nothing of admitting young dandies to your house, and even of travelling with her in their company.

FILIPPO Are you referring to Signor Guglielmo?

FULGENZIO I am referring to everyone, and to no one in particular.

FILIPPO If you were referring to Signor Guglielmo, I assure you that he is the most respectful, best-intentioned young man in the world.

FULGENZIO She's young.

FILIPPO Oh, my daughter is a sensible young woman.

FULGENZIO She's a woman.

FILIPPO And my sister is with her; she's an elderly lady.

FULGENZIO There are plenty of old women even more foolish than the young ones.

FILIPPO I did have some doubts of my own on this matter, but then I thought, so many other people do the same thing …

FULGENZIO My dear friend, have you never seen things happen? All those people who behaved as you say, were they pleased in the long run with the way they'd behaved?

FILIPPO To tell you the truth, some were and some weren't.

FULGENZIO And are you quite certain you'll be pleased? You have no fear that you won't?

FILIPPO You are putting doubts in my head. I can't wait to get rid of this daughter! My dear friend, who is the person you mentioned, the one who wants to make her his bride?

FULGENZIO I can't tell you that for the moment.

FILIPPO Why not?

FULGENZIO Because for the moment he doesn't want his name known. Change your style of living, and he'll declare himself.
FILIPPO And what am I supposed to do? Give up going to the country? I can't. It's too much of a habit.
FULGENZIO Do you have to take your daughter along?
FILIPPO Heaven help us! If I didn't take her, there'd be the devil to pay.
FULGENZIO Your daughter's allowed to express her opinions?
FILIPPO She has always expressed them.
FULGENZIO And who's to blame for that?
FILIPPO I am, I admit it. It's all my fault. I'm too kind-hearted.
FULGENZIO An overly generous father makes for ungenerous daughters.
FILIPPO What do you advise me to do now?
FULGENZIO A little discipline. If not across the board, in some areas at least. Keep the young man away from her.
FILIPPO If I only knew how to get rid of Signor Guglielmo!
FULGENZIO Let's get to the point! This Signor Guglielmo is about to be your ruin. It's on his account that the gentleman who wishes to marry her won't declare himself. He's an excellent match, and if you want us to parley, if you want us to discuss the matter, see to it that we see the last of this monstrosity – a daughter who has more say than her father!
FILIPPO But she has nothing to do with it. It was I who invited him to come.
FULGENZIO Better yet! You get rid of him, then!
FILIPPO Worse yet! I don't know how to get rid of him.
FULGENZIO Are you a man, or what are you?
FILIPPO When it comes to being rude, I'm simply not up to it.
FULGENZIO You'd better watch out, or somebody else may give you a lesson in rudeness!
FILIPPO Well, then, I suppose I'll just have to get it over with.
FULGENZIO Get it over with once and for all, you'll never regret it.
FILIPPO You could at least tell me the name of this friend who aspires to the hand of my daughter.
FULGENZIO I can't, for the time being. Forgive me. I have to go now – an urgent matter of business.
FILIPPO By all means, as you wish.
FULGENZIO Forgive me if I've been too outspoken.
FILIPPO On the contrary, you've done me a favour.
FULGENZIO I hope we'll meet again soon.
FILIPPO With the greatest of pleasure.

FULGENZIO *(aside)* I believe I have served Signor Leonardo well. But my true intention was to serve truth, reason, and Signor Filippo's own reputation and interest. *(exit Fulgenzio)*

Scene 10

Filippo, followed by Giacinta.

FILIPPO Fulgenzio told me a number of undeniable home truths, and I'm not so foolish as not to recognize them. To tell the truth, I knew them already. But what can I say? Society has a glamour all of its own, which makes people do things against their better judgment. But if one's conduct is in danger of attracting unfavourable attention, one must be more careful. All right, then, I had better get rid of Signor Guglielmo, any way I can, even if it means not going to the country. *(enter Giacinta)*

GIACINTA Thank heavens, sir, that tiresome bore has gone.

FILIPPO Call one of the servants.

GIACINTA If you want dinner served, I can tell them myself.

FILIPPO Call one of the servants. I have to send him on an errand.

GIACINTA Where do you plan to send him?

FILIPPO You ask too many questions. I shall send him wherever I please.

GIACINTA On some errand Signor Fulgenzio suggested?

FILIPPO You take too many liberties with your father.

GIACINTA Who told you that, sir? Signor Fulgenzio?

FILIPPO That's enough. Leave me alone, I tell you.

GIACINTA Is this how you talk to your daughter? Your darling Giacinta?

FILIPPO *(aside)* I'm not used to playing the ogre, and I can't keep it up.

GIACINTA *(aside)* I'll bet my boots Leonardo has used Signor Fulgenzio to get the upper hand ... But he won't get away with it.

FILIPPO Isn't there anybody there? Where are the servants?

GIACINTA Now, now, calm down a little. I'll go and call someone.

FILIPPO Hurry up, then.

GIACINTA May I know what you want the servant for?

FILIPPO What confounded curiosity! I intend to send him to Signor Guglielmo's.

GIACINTA Are you afraid Signor Guglielmo won't come? He'll come all right. I wish he wouldn't!

FILIPPO You wish he wouldn't!

GIACINTA Yes, sir, I wish he wouldn't. We'd be freer without him, and poor Brigida, who wants to come with us, could come with us.

FILIPPO But wouldn't you like to have someone to talk to on the trip, someone to keep you amused?

GIACINTA It doesn't matter to me, and it never has. Wasn't it you who invited him? Did I ever say anything to persuade you to have him come with us?

FILIPPO *(aside)* My daughter is more sensible than I am! *(calling offstage)* Hello! A servant! Is there anyone there?

GIACINTA I'll go call the servant at once. What is he supposed to say to Signor Guglielmo?

FILIPPO Not to bother coming round, we can't take him.

GIACINTA *(ironically)* Oh! A fine scene that will be! A fine scene! A fine scene indeed!

FILIPPO I'll tell him politely.

GIACINTA And what reason will you give him?

FILIPPO What shall I say? … I could say, for instance … that your maid is coming in the carriage, and there's no room for him.

GIACINTA *(ironically, as before)* Better and better! Better by the minute!

FILIPPO Are you making fun of me, young lady?

GIACINTA I am certainly surprised at you, surprised to find you capable of such weakness. What do you expect him to say? What do you expect people to say? Do you want them to call you a bad-mannered boor?

FILIPPO Do you think it correct for a young man to ride in the carriage with you?

GIACINTA You're right, it's wrong, it couldn't be more wrong; but you should have thought of that sooner. If I'd invited him, you could have said: I don't want him; but you invited him yourself.

FILIPPO Very well. I did the damage and I'll fix it.

GIACINTA As long as the fixing's not worse than the damage! When all's said and done, even if he does come along, my aunt will be there, you will be there. It's a mistake, but it's not an important mistake. But if you say now you don't want him, if you insult him by sending him packing, within twenty-four hours you and I will be on everyone's lips in Leghorn and Montenero. We'll be the subject of absurd speculation, of the wildest conjectures. Some people will say: they were lovers, and they got tired of each other. Others will say: the father caught on. Some will speak ill of you, some will speak ill of me. And, for not going through with something perfectly innocent, our reputations will suffer!

Filippo *(aside)* I'd give anything for Signor Fulgenzio to be here to hear her! *(to Giacinta)* Wouldn't we be better off giving up the idea of going to the country altogether?

Giacinta Better off from one point of view, but from the other, worse. Just imagine what those busybodies in Montenero would say about our situation! Signor Filippo has stopped coming to the country, he can't afford it any more. His daughter, poor thing, didn't last many seasons! Her dowry has gone up in smoke. Who will have her? Who will want her? They should have given fewer dinners, they should have stayed home. What we saw was all smoke, without fire. I can hear them now. It sends cold shivers down my spine.

Filippo What can we do, then?

Giacinta Whatever you like.

Filippo If I jump out of the frying pan, I'm afraid I'll land in the fire!

Giacinta And fire burns, and we must protect our reputations.

Filippo Then, do you think the best thing to do is to have Signor Guglielmo come with us?

Giacinta This one time, anyway, since it's all been arranged. But never again, mind you, never again! Let this be a lesson to you, and don't let it ever happen again!

Filippo *(aside)* Oh, what a clever girl!

Giacinta So, do you want me to call the servant, or don't you?

Filippo Let's leave things as they are, since it's all been arranged.

Giacinta That's the best thing to do. Let's go in to dinner.

Filippo And, in the country, should he stay at our house?

Giacinta What arrangements did you make with him?

Filippo Well, to tell the truth, I did invite him.

Giacinta Then how can you send him away?

Filippo He'll have to stay, then.

Giacinta But never again, mind you, never again!

Filippo Never again, Daughter, bless you, never again! *(exit Filippo)*

Scene 11

Giacinta, followed by Brigida.

Giacinta I couldn't care less about Signor Guglielmo. But I am not going to have Leonardo boasting he won. I'm sure he'll get over it anyway, I'm sure he'll come round, he'll realize that this is not something to get so worked up over. And if he really loves me, as he says he does, he'll have to learn to behave more discreetly in future, because I wasn't born a slave, and I have no intention of becoming one.

BRIGIDA Madam, you have a visitor.

GIACINTA Who can it be, at this hour?

BRIGIDA Signora Vittoria.

GIACINTA Did you tell her I was in?

BRIGIDA What was I supposed to tell her? That you were out?

GIACINTA She chose a fine time to come! Where is she?

BRIGIDA She sent her servant on ahead. She's on her way over.

GIACINTA Go and show her in here. I'll have to put up with her. I'm curious anyway to know whether or not she's coming to the country, and whether anything new has come up. For her to come here at this hour, there has to be something.

BRIGIDA I did hear one thing.

GIACINTA What was that?

BRIGIDA That she had a new dress made, too, and she couldn't get it back from the tailor, because I think the tailor insisted on being paid; and there was a real to-do, and if she hadn't gotten the dress, she wasn't going to go to the country. *(exit Brigida)*

Scene 12

Giacinta, followed by Vittoria.

GIACINTA She's as vain as they come! If she sees somebody wearing something new, she can't wait to have one like it. She must have heard that I got a new dress, and she wanted one, too. But she won't know it's a "mariage." I never told anyone. She can't have had time to find out.

VITTORIA Giacinta, my dear, dear friend.

GIACINTA Good day to you, my darling, my sweet. *(they embrace)*

VITTORIA I know what you're thinking. A fine time to come bothering you.

GIACINTA Bothering me! When I heard you were coming, my heart swelled with happiness.

VITTORIA How are you? Are you well?

GIACINTA I couldn't be better. And you? But there's no point in asking, you look so plump and fresh, bless you, it's a treat to look at you.

VITTORIA And you look so well! You're a sight for sore eyes.

GIACINTA Oh! What on earth are you saying? I got up too early this morning, I didn't sleep a wink, I have a pain in the stomach, a pain in the head; imagine how well I must look!

VITTORIA I don't know what's wrong with me, either. It's been days since I've eaten. Not a bite to eat for days! Really, practically nothing! I don't know how I survive. I ought to be thin as a rake!

GIACINTA Yes, indeed. Thin as a rake! These plump little arms are not rake handles!

VITTORIA You're not exactly skin and bone yourself!

GIACINTA No, you're right. Thank heavens, I do get what little I need.

VITTORIA Oh! Dear, dear Giacinta!

GIACINTA Oh! Bless you, Vittoria! *(they embrace)* Sit down, my dearest. Please sit down.

VITTORIA I was dying to see you. But you can never spare me a visit. *(they sit)*

GIACINTA Oh, my angel, I never go anywhere. I stay home all the time.

VITTORIA Me, too. I go out for a moment on Sunday, then the rest of the week I'm at home.

GIACINTA I don't know how they do it, those women who parade about town all the livelong day.

VITTORIA *(aside)* What I really want to know is whether or not she's going to Montenero, but I don't know how to get it out of her.

GIACINTA *(aside)* I'm surprised she hasn't mentioned our trip to the country.

VITTORIA Is it long since you last saw my brother?

GIACINTA I saw him this morning.

VITTORIA I don't know what's the matter with him. He's so restless and tiresome.

GIACINTA But surely you know that we all have our good days and bad days.

VITTORIA I was beginning to think you and he might have quarrelled.

GIACINTA With me? Why should he quarrel with me? I admire and respect him, but he hasn't acquired the right to quarrel with me just yet. *(aside)* I bet her brother sent her round.

VITTORIA *(aside)* She's proud as a peacock!

GIACINTA Vittoria, dear, would you like to stay to dinner?

VITTORIA Oh, no, my precious, I couldn't. My brother's waiting.

GIACINTA We'll send someone to tell him.

VITTORIA No, no. I can't, absolutely.

GIACINTA Won't you please be our guest, they'll be serving dinner any minute now.

VITTORIA *(aside)* I get it. She wants to get rid of me. *(to Giacinta)* Are you dining so early?

GIACINTA Well, you see, we're off to the country, we're leaving soon, so we're pressed for time.

VITTORIA *(aside)* Oh! Curse my bad luck!

GIACINTA I have to get completely changed; I have to get dressed for the trip.

VITTORIA *(mortified)* Yes, yes, you're right. It will be dusty. No use spoiling a nice dress.

GIACINTA Oh, don't worry about this one. I'll be wearing a better one. I'm not afraid of the dust. I had a silk flannel riding cape made, with a hood, so there's no way that the dust can bother me.

VITTORIA *(aside)* A riding cape, too, with a hood! I want one, too, even if it means selling some of my dresses.

GIACINTA Don't you have a riding cape, with a hood?

VITTORIA Yes, yes, I have one, too. I had it made last year.

GIACINTA I didn't see it last year.

VITTORIA I never wore it, because, if you remember, it wasn't dusty.

GIACINTA Oh, yes, you're right, it wasn't dusty. *(aside)* How absurd can you get!

VITTORIA This year I had a dress made.

GIACINTA Oh? I had a gorgeous one made.

VITTORIA You'll see mine. I think you'll like it.

GIACINTA Well, talk about dresses! You are going to see something special.

VITTORIA Mine has no silver or gold, but, if I say so myself, it's stupendous.

GIACINTA Oh, fashion's the thing. It must be in fashion.

VITTORIA Oh, if it's fashion you want, you can't say mine's not in fashion.

GIACINTA *(snickering)* Oh, yes, I'm sure it's in fashion.

VITTORIA Don't you believe me?

GIACINTA Of course I believe you. *(aside)* She'll die when she sees my "mariage."

VITTORIA When it comes to fashion, I think I've always been in the vanguard.

GIACINTA And what kind of dress do you have?

VITTORIA A "mariage!"

GIACINTA *(astonished)* A "mariage!"

VITTORIA Yes, of course. You don't think it's in fashion?

GIACINTA How did you find out the "mariage" was the latest fashion from France?

VITTORIA Probably the same way you did.

GIACINTA Who made it for you?

VITTORIA The French tailor, Monsieur de la Rejouissance.

GIACINTA Now I get it! The scoundrel! He'll pay for this. I sent for him, I gave him the "mariage" fashion. I had Madame Granon's dress in the house.

VITTORIA Oh! Madame Granon came to pay me a visit the day after she arrived in Leghorn.

GIACINTA That's it, make excuses for him. But he'll pay for it just the same.

VITTORIA Does it upset you that I have a "mariage?"

GIACINTA Not at all, I'm delighted.

VITTORIA Did you want to be the only person to have one?

GIACINTA Why? Do you think I'm jealous? I think you're aware that I don't envy anyone. I mind my own business, I do as I please, and I let other people do as they please. A new dress every year, granted. And I insist on being served right away, and served properly, because I pay, I pay on time, and I don't make the tailor come back over and over again.

VITTORIA I thought everyone paid.

GIACINTA No, not everyone pays. Not everyone has the breeding and consideration we have. There are people who keep him waiting for years; and then, when they try to hurry him up, the tailor baulks. He wants his money, or else … Then the fun starts! *(aside)* Take that, then! And tell me if it's in fashion!

VITTORIA *(aside)* She can't be talking about me. If I thought the tailor had said something, I'd give him a piece of my mind!

GIACINTA And when do you plan to wear this wonderful dress?

VITTORIA I don't know, I may never wear it. That's how I am. I'm happy to have things; I'm not concerned about showing them off.

GIACINTA If you go to the country, that would be the ideal time to wear it. Poor thing, what a shame you're not going this year!

VITTORIA Who told you I wasn't going?

GIACINTA I don't know. Signor Leonardo sent to cancel the horses.

VITTORIA What does that mean? Couldn't he change his mind any time? Do you think I can't go without him? Do you think I've no friends or relatives I could go with?

GIACINTA Would you like to come and stay with me?

VITTORIA No. No, thank you.

GIACINTA Are you sure? I'd be happy to have you.

VITTORIA I'll tell you what. If I can convince one of my cousins to come with me to Montenero, maybe we'll see each other there.

GIACINTA Oh! I'd be so glad to see you.

VITTORIA What time are you leaving?

GIACINTA Three-thirty.

VITTORIA Oh! Then there's time. I can stay here a bit longer. *(aside)* I'd love to see this dress, if I could.

GIACINTA *(into the wings)* Yes. Yes, I hear you. Can't you wait a few minutes?

VITTORIA If you have things to do, go ahead.

GIACINTA No, it's nothing. They were telling me dinner is ready, and my father would like to start eating.

VITTORIA I'll be running along, then.

GIACINTA Why, no! If you'd like to stay, please feel free to stay.

VITTORIA I wouldn't want your father to worry.

GIACINTA It's true, he is a bit tiresome.

VITTORIA I'll make myself scarce, then. *(she gets up)*

GIACINTA If you'd like to join us, I'd be delighted. *(she gets up)*

VITTORIA *(aside)* I'm really tempted to stay, I'm so curious about this dress.

GIACINTA *(into the wings)* I heard you the first time. Can't you see? Have some manners!

VITTORIA Who are you talking to?

GIACINTA To the servant who's telling me to hurry. These people have no manners whatsoever.

VITTORIA I didn't see anyone.

GIACINTA Well, I saw him all right.

VITTORIA *(aside)* I get it! *(to Giacinta)* Signora Giacinta, I look forward to seeing you again.

GIACINTA Goodbye, my dear. Wish me well when we're apart, as I always wish you well.

VITTORIA Count on me. With all my heart!

GIACINTA A little kiss at least?

VITTORIA Of course, my dearest. *(they kiss)*

GIACINTA My precious darling!

VITTORIA Goodbye.

GIACINTA Goodbye.

VITTORIA *(aside)* I'm trying so hard to pretend, I could burst! *(exit Vittoria)*

GIACINTA I can't abide envious women! *(exit Giacinta)*

ACT THREE

Scene 1

Leonardo's room. Leonardo and Fulgenzio.

LEONARDO Signor Fulgenzio, your news is a tremendous relief. So Signor Filippo has promised to get out of his commitment to Signor Guglielmo?

FULGENZIO Yes, of course. He gave me his word.

LEONARDO Are you sure he'll keep it?

FULGENZIO I couldn't be surer. We have business together that makes me certain I can depend on him.[22] And in any case I've usually found him reliable when it came to matters of importance. I've no doubt he'll be the same in this case.

LEONARDO So Signor Guglielmo won't be going to the country with Signora Giacinta.

FULGENZIO Nothing could be surer!

LEONARDO And I couldn't be happier! Now I'll be delighted to go myself.

FULGENZIO After everything I said and did, the good fellow came to his senses. He's kindhearted to a fault. Don't get the idea he does wrong out of malice aforethought; if he errs on occasion it's out of an excess of goodness.

LEONARDO I expect his daughter leads him by the nose.

FULGENZIO No, she's not a bad girl. Signor Filippo confessed that she had nothing at all to do with inviting Signor Guglielmo. He was the one who asked him to join them, because of his passion for company and for having his capital devoured.

LEONARDO I'm glad Signora Giacinta had nothing to do with it. I could hardly credit it, considering everything that's happened between us.

FULGENZIO And just what has happened between you?

LEONARDO Words that assure her I love her, and make me hope she loves me.

FULGENZIO And her father knows nothing?

LEONARDO As far as I'm concerned, he knows nothing.

FULGENZIO I have to conclude that he doesn't know anything, because, when I spoke of a match for his daughter, it never occurred to him to ask about you.

LEONARDO He can't know; that's for sure.

FULGENZIO But he should know.

LEONARDO One day we'll tell him.

FULGENZIO Why not now?

LEONARDO Now, we're about to leave for the country.

FULGENZIO My friend, let's be perfectly frank. I was only too happy to help you out with Signor Filippo, and persuade him to rescue his daughter from dangerous company, because I thought I was serving the cause of decency, and because you assured me of your good intentions towards her, that, once you obtained what you wanted, you'd ask for her hand in marriage. Now I don't want this affair going on without being nipped in the bud, making me the cause of a worse evil. To put it bluntly, maybe in Signor Guglielmo's case there was no malice aforethought, but that can't be said of you. From what you tell me, you two are deeply involved, and, now you've brought me into it, too, I don't intend to get out with dishonour. So it's fish or cut bait: either you declare your intentions to Signor Filippo, or I'll give him the same advice I gave him about Signor Guglielmo. Only this time it'll be about you!

LEONARDO What do you advise me to do?

FULGENZIO Either you ask for her hand, or you stop seeing her.

LEONARDO And how am I supposed to ask for her hand in the short time available?

FULGENZIO It can be done in no time! I'd be happy to be of service myself.

LEONARDO Couldn't we wait till we get back from the country?

FULGENZIO Who knows what may happen in the country? I was young myself once. I was never foolish, thank heavens, but I've seen my share of foolishness. My responsibility to my friend requires me to speak to him clearly: either to ask for the hand of his daughter, or to warn him to watch out for you.

LEONARDO If you put it like that, let's ask for her hand.

FULGENZIO On what terms do you want me to ask for it?

LEONARDO As far as the dowry goes, it's common knowledge that he means to give her eight thousand crowns plus her trousseau.

FULGENZIO Are you happy with that?

LEONARDO I couldn't be happier.

FULGENZIO How soon do you want to get married?

LEONARDO Four, six, eight months; I leave it up to Signor Filippo.

FULGENZIO Very good. I'll speak to him.

LEONARDO But bear in mind that we must leave for Montenero today.

FULGENZIO Couldn't you put it off for a day or two?

LEONARDO There's no chance, it can't be put off.

FULGENZIO But the business at hand is worth some sort of sacrifice.

LEONARDO If Signor Filippo stays behind, I'll stay behind, too, but you'll see it's not possible.

FULGENZIO Not possible, why?

LEONARDO Because everyone's leaving, and Signor Filippo will want to leave too, and Signora Giacinta will want to leave today without fail. My sister has been tormenting me no end, she's so impatient to go. And, for a hundred and one reasons, there's no way I can stay.

FULGENZIO Bah! Look how far the passion for country vacations has gone! A day seems like a century! Serious business takes a back seat! Very well, I'll go at once, I'll do what I can, I'll get you what you want. But, my dear friend, allow me to say a couple of words from the bottom of my heart. If you marry, marry to turn over a new leaf, not to get yourself into a worse fix than ever. I know your affairs are not going too well. A dowry of eight thousand crowns could just bail you out. But don't spend it all on your wife, don't throw it away in the country. Prudence, thrift, common sense! A peaceful night's sleep, without worry, is worth more than all the pleasures in the world. As long as the money lasts, everyone's with you. When there's no more left: jeers, derision, hisses. Now excuse me. I'm off at once to do my bit on your behalf. *(exit Fulgenzio)*

Scene 2

Leonardo, followed by Cecco.

LEONARDO He's right. I can do it. I'll turn over a new leaf. I say, is anyone there?

CECCO You called, sir?

LEONARDO Go to Signor Filippo's and Signora Giacinta's right away. Tell them I got my business out of the way and that I'll be honoured to be one of their party for Montenero today. Tell them I've found someone to send with my sister in the calèche, and that, if they'll allow me, I'll go in the carriage with them. Hurry up and bring me an answer.

CECCO Right away, sir.

LEONARDO And tell my man Paolo to come here at once.

CECCO Yes, sir. *(aside)* Did you ever see so many changes in one day? *(exit Cecco)*

Scene 3

Leonardo, followed by Paolo.

LEONARDO Now that Guglielmo is not going in their carriage, they won't turn down my company. It would be an outright insult. And then, if Signor Fulgenzio speaks to him, and if Signor Filippo is willing to give me his daughter, as I have no doubt he will be, things will be just as they should be: I'll go in their carriage. I'll have Signor Ferdinando go in the calèche with my sister. I know how he is, he won't remember a word of what I said earlier.

PAOLO At your orders, sir.

LEONARDO Quick, get together everything we need, and send out for the horses; we leave at three-thirty.

PAOLO Splendid!

LEONARDO And look sharp about it.

PAOLO What about dinner?

LEONARDO What do I care about dinner? All I care about is being ready to leave.

PAOLO But I unpacked everything I'd packed.

LEONARDO Pack it again!

PAOLO That's impossible!

LEONARDO It has to be possible, and it has to be done!

PAOLO *(aside)* Curse being a servant, if it means being treated like this.

LEONARDO And I want the coffee, the candles, the sugar, and the chocolate.

PAOLO I returned everything to the shopkeepers.

LEONARDO Go and get everything back again.

PAOLO They won't want to give me a thing.

LEONARDO Don't try my patience.

PAOLO But, sir …

LEONARDO There's nothing more to be said. Look sharp about it!

PAOLO You know what I say? Get whomever you like to wait on you, because I'm no longer up to it.

LEONARDO No, dear Paolo, don't leave me in the lurch. After so many years of service, don't leave me now. There's too much at stake. I'll let you in on a secret, not as your master but as your friend. Signor Filippo may be about to give me his daughter's hand in marriage, with a dowry of twelve thousand crowns.[23] Do you want me to lose face? Do you want to see me a pauper? Don't you see that I must make one last effort to impress? Can you really have the heart to tell me that it can't be done, that it's impossible, that you can't go on in my service?

PAOLO My dear Master, thank you for taking me into your confidence. I'll do what I can. You'll be served. Even if I have to put up the money myself; never fear, you'll be served. *(exit Paolo)*

Scene 4

Leonardo, followed by Vittoria.

LEONARDO He's a good man, he's devoted and faithful. He says I'll be served, even if he has to put up the money himself. But, if I'm not mistaken, what is his now, was once mine. In the meantime, let me get my trunk packed again.

VITTORIA *(heatedly)* Listen here, Brother dear; I've come here to tell you quite frankly that I've never stayed in Leghorn this time of year before, and I don't intend to stay now. I intend to go to the country. Signora Giacinta is going, everyone else is going, and I intend to go too.

LEONARDO What brings you here so hot and bothered?

VITTORIA If I'm hot and bothered, I have every reason to be hot and bothered. I shall go to the country with my cousin Lucrezia and her husband.

LEONARDO Why don't you want to come with me?

VITTORIA When?

LEONARDO Today.

VITTORIA Where?

LEONARDO To Montenero.

VITTORIA You?

LEONARDO Me.

VITTORIA Oh!

LEONARDO Yes, on my word of honour.
VITTORIA Are you making fun of me?
LEONARDO I'm telling the truth.
VITTORIA The truth? Are you sure?
LEONARDO Can't you see I'm repacking the trunk?
VITTORIA Oh, Brother, dear Brother, what happened?
LEONARDO I'll tell you. You know that Signor Fulgenzio …
VITTORIA Yes, yes, you can tell me later. Quick, servants! Oh, where are you? Servants! My boxes, my linen, my bonnets, my dresses, my "mariage"! *(exit Vittoria)*

Scene 5

Leonardo, followed by Cecco.

LEONARDO She's beside herself with relief. It's a fact that there could have been no greater humiliation for her than staying on in Leghorn. And what about me? I might have gone crazy. Oh! What we won't do in defence of our honour! Love makes us do the most extravagant things! For a point of honour, out of pure pique, I was ready to give up our stay in the country!
CECCO Here I am back.
LEONARDO So, what did they say?
CECCO I found them both together, father and daughter. They send their respects. They said they'll be glad of your company on the trip, but, as for the seat in the carriage, to be patient and try and understand. They can't accommodate you, because they've promised the seat to Signor Guglielmo.
LEONARDO To Signor Guglielmo!
CECCO That's what they said.
LEONARDO Are you sure you understood? To Signor Guglielmo?
CECCO To Signor Guglielmo.
LEONARDO No, it can't be. You're a dolt, you're an idiot.
CECCO But I tell you, I understood perfectly, and to prove I was right, as I came downstairs, Signor Guglielmo was going up, with his servant and his suitcase.
LEONARDO Oh, poor me! I don't know if I'm coming or going! Fulgenzio has betrayed me, they're all making fun of me. I'm going out of my mind. I'm desperate! *(he sits down)*

CECCO Sir?

LEONARDO Bring me some water.

CECCO To wash your hands?

LEONARDO A glass of water, damn you. *(he gets up)*

CECCO Right away. *(aside)* Well, so much for the trip to the country! *(exit Cecco)*

LEONARDO But how could the old man double-cross me, damn him? They must have put one over on him. But he told me that he and Filippo had business together that would prevent Filippo deceiving him. So he's the culprit. But he can't be the culprit. It must be her. But it can't be her either. It must be her father. But her father promised … It must be his daughter. But his daughter does what she's told. It must be Fulgenzio, then. But what reason could Fulgenzio have for betraying me? I don't understand anything. It's me who's the jackass, the madman, the booby.

CECCO *(enters with the water)*

LEONARDO *(aside, not noticing Cecco)* Madman! Jackass!

CECCO Hey, what do you mean "jackass"?

LEONARDO Yes, that's right. Jackass! Jackass! *(takes the water)*

CECCO Sir, I'm not a jackass.

LEONARDO No! I am! I'm the jackass! *(he drinks)*

CECCO *(aside)* He's right, a jackass drinks water, and I drink wine.

LEONARDO Go to Signor Fulgenzio's right away. See if he's in. Ask him if he would be so good as to come over, or should I come to his place?

CECCO To Signor Fulgenzio's? Across the street?

LEONARDO Of course, you ass. Where else?

CECCO Are you talking to me this time?

LEONARDO Yes, you.

CECCO *(aside)* Ass … Jackass … There's not a whole lot of difference. *(exit Cecco)*

Scene 6

Leonardo, followed by Paolo.

LEONARDO I'll make no allowance for his age, I'll make no allowance for anyone.

PAOLO Cheer up, sir, don't worry. Everything's going to be ready.

LEONARDO Leave me alone.

PAOLO I beg your pardon, sir, I've done my duty, and more than my duty.
LEONARDO Leave me alone, I tell you.
PAOLO Has something new come up?
LEONARDO Yes, it certainly has!
PAOLO The horses are ordered.
LEONARDO Cancel the order.
PAOLO Again?
LEONARDO Oh! Curse my bad luck!
PAOLO What on earth has come over him?
LEONARDO For God's sake, leave me alone.
PAOLO *(aside)* Oh, poor me! Things are getting worse by the minute.

Scene 7

Enter *Vittoria carrying a folded dress.*

VITTORIA Brother, would you like to see my "mariage"?
LEONARDO Go away.
VITTORIA Is that any way to treat people?
PAOLO *(softly to Vittoria)* Leave him alone.
VITTORIA What the devil's the matter?
LEONARDO Yes, the devil's the matter. Go away.
VITTORIA My, you certainly are in a gay mood for going to the country!
LEONARDO Forget about the country, forget about our vacation, forget about everything!
VITTORIA You don't want to go to the country?
LEONARDO No, I'm not going. And you're not going either.
VITTORIA Have you taken leave of your senses?
PAOLO *(aside to Vittoria)* Don't upset him any more, for heaven's sake!
VITTORIA *(to Paolo)* Don't you come butting in, too!

Scene 8

Enter *Cecco.*

CECCO *(to Leonardo)* Signor Fulgenzio isn't home.
LEONARDO Where the devil has he gone?

CECCO They told me he'd gone to Signor Filippo's.
LEONARDO *(to Paolo)* My hat and my sword!
PAOLO Sir?
LEONARDO *(louder, to Paolo)* My hat and my sword!
PAOLO Right away, sir. *(he goes to get Leonardo's hat and sword)*
VITTORIA *(to Leonardo)* What on earth ...?
LEONARDO My hat and my sword.
PAOLO Here you are, sir. *(he gives him his hat and sword)*
VITTORIA *(to Leonardo)* What on earth's gotten into you?
LEONARDO You'll know soon enough. *(exit Leonardo)*
VITTORIA *(to Paolo)* What's the matter with him?
PAOLO I've no idea. I'll follow him at a safe distance. *(exit Paolo)*
VITTORIA *(to Cecco)* Do you know what's going on?
CECCO I know he called me a jackass. That's all I know. *(exit Cecco)*

Scene 9

Vittoria, followed by Ferdinando.

VITTORIA I'm stunned. I'm all in a muddle. I come home, I find him in good spirits, he says: we're off to the country. I leave the room. Not three minutes pass. He's raving, he's sulking. Forget going to the country! I think something's wrong with his mind. If that's the case, I'm more desperate than ever. If my brother is sick, it's goodbye country, it's goodbye Montenero! As for you, you damned dress, you get away from me, too! Oh, I feel like slashing it to ribbons! *(throws the dress on a chair)*
FERDINANDO Here I am. I've come to congratulate Signora Vittoria.
VITTORIA Oh, so you're here, too, to annoy me?
FERDINANDO What, Signora? I come here on an errand of courtesy, and all you do is insult me?
VITTORIA What are you here for?
FERDINANDO To tell you how glad I am that you're going to the country, too.
VITTORIA Oh, if it weren't for the fact ... for the fact ... I would tell you how happy I'm feeling inside!
FERDINANDO Signora, you won't find anyone more willing to listen than me. When it comes to relieving people's spiritual burdens, all they have to do is open their hearts to me. They always have my permission.

VITTORIA Oh, I pity you, if you were to share the rage that's inside me.

FERDINANDO But what is it? What's the matter? What's upsetting you? Tell me all about it. You can speak freely with me. You can be sure I won't tell a soul.

VITTORIA Oh, yes. For sure. Tell your secrets to the town crier!

FERDINANDO You have a low opinion of me, and I don't believe I deserve it.

VITTORIA I'm only repeating what everyone else says.

FERDINANDO How can they say that I talk about other people's failings? Did I ever criticize anyone to you?

VITTORIA Thousands of times! What about Signora Aspasia, and Signora Flaminia, and Signora Francesca?

FERDINANDO Did I say something about them?

VITTORIA I'll say you did.

FERDINANDO Perhaps I let it slip out inadvertently.

VITTORIA Yes, that's probably it. The things people do out of habit, they don't even notice.

FERDINANDO In a word, you're angry, and you won't tell me why?

VITTORIA No, I won't tell you anything.

FERDINANDO Listen here. Either I am a gentleman or I'm a gossip. If I'm a gentleman, you can speak freely, you have nothing to fear. And if I'm a gossip, what's to stop me putting my own interpretation on your behaviour and making you look as foolish as I like?

VITTORIA *(ironically)* You want to know what I think? I think you're a very very witty young man!

FERDINANDO I am a gentleman, madam. And when speaking's in order, I speak. And when it's time to be silent, I'm silent.

VITTORIA Very well! So you don't jump to the wrong conclusions, and let your imagination run riot, I'll tell you. There's nothing the matter with me, but my brother is completely unstable, he's out of his mind, he's delirious; and he's making me worse than he is.

FERDINANDO Yes, he must be going crazy because of Signora Giacinta. She's a flirt, she's inconstant, she encourages all comers, she's ruining her reputation, she's a general laughing stock.

VITTORIA I see! Never an unkind word about anyone!

FERDINANDO Where is Signor Leonardo?

VITTORIA I believe he's gone to her house.

FERDINANDO By your leave, madam.

VITTORIA Where are you going?

FERDINANDO To join my friend, to assist, to advise him. *(aside)* To pick up some juicy gossip for Montenero! *(exit Ferdinando)*

VITTORIA And what am I supposed to do? Should I wait for my brother, or should I go to my cousin's? I'll just have to wait for him. I must see how this business comes out. But no! I can't wait! I have to know right away. I'll go back to Signor Filippo's. I'll go back to Giacinta's. How do I know this isn't a deliberate trick to keep me from going to the country? But I am dead set on going, whatever happens, and she's not going to stop me. *(exit Vittoria)*

Scene 10

A room in Filippo's house. Filippo and Fulgenzio.

FILIPPO For my part, I tell you, I couldn't be happier. Signor Leonardo is a proper young man, well born, well bred, and comfortably off. True, he's a liberal spender, especially in the country, but he'll come to his senses.

FULGENZIO You're hardly the one to criticize him on that score.

FILIPPO I'm as bad as he is, you mean. But there is a difference between him and me.

FULGENZIO That's enough! What more can I say? You know him, you know his background. Give him her hand, if you will. If not, not.

FILIPPO I would be happy to give him her hand; as long as she's agreeable.

FULGENZIO I'm sure she won't turn him down.

FILIPPO Oh? Do you know something I don't know?

FULGENZIO Yes, I know more than you know; I know what you ought to know better than anyone. A father's job is to keep an eye on his family, and, with only one daughter to watch, you should have found it easier than most. You don't let a daughter keep company with whomever she pleases. Do you hear? It just isn't done. Didn't I tell you before? She's a woman. Oh yes, you replied: she's sensible. And what did I say? She's a woman! And for all her common sense, for all her judgment, there have already been pledges of affection between her and Signor Leonardo.

FILIPPO Oh! There have been pledges of affection, have there?

FULGENZIO Yes, and thank heavens you're dealing with a gentleman. Give him her hand. You'll be doing the right thing.

FILIPPO Certainly, I'll give him her hand, and he'd better take it, and she'd better have him. The vixen! Pledges of affection, indeed!

FULGENZIO What do you think? That girls are made out of stone? When you let them keep company with whomever they please …

FILIPPO Did Signor Leonardo say he was coming over?

FULGENZIO No, I'll go over to his place, I'll bring him back here, and we'll get everything settled.

FILIPPO I am more and more obliged to your affection and friendship.

FULGENZIO You see, I was right to persuade you to get Signor Guglielmo away from your daughter.

FILIPPO *(aside)* Oh, my God! He's right here, in my house!

FULGENZIO Leonardo couldn't abide it, and he was right. If Signor Guglielmo had gone to the country with you, he wouldn't have wanted to marry her, that's for sure.

FILIPPO *(aside)* Oh, poor me! I've never been so embarrassed!

FULGENZIO And see to it that Signor Guglielmo is never seen again in your daughter's company.

FILIPPO *(aside)* If Giacinta can't come up with an explanation, I'll be damned if I can.

FULGENZIO Speak to your daughter. Meanwhile, I'll go get Signor Leonardo.

FILIPPO Very well … We'll have to see …

FULGENZIO Is there a problem?

FILIPPO No, no problem.

FULGENZIO *(preparing to leave)* Au revoir, then. I'll be right back.

Scene 11

Enter *Guglielmo.*

GUGLIELMO Gentlemen, it's almost three-thirty. If you like, I'll go check on the horses myself.

FULGENZIO What's this I see? Guglielmo?

FILIPPO *(aside)* Oh, damn you, Guglielmo. *(to Guglielmo)* No, no, that's all right. We won't be leaving so early after all. Something's come up … *(aside)* I don't even know what I'm saying.

FULGENZIO Are you off to the country, Signor Guglielmo?

GUGLIELMO Yes, sir.

FILIPPO *(aside)* I don't have the heart to say anything.

FULGENZIO And with whom are you going, may I ask?

GUGLIELMO With Signor Filippo.

FULGENZIO In his carriage?

GUGLIELMO Precisely.
FULGENZIO With Signora Giacinta?
GUGLIELMO Yes, sir.
FULGENZIO *(aside)* A fine state of affairs!
FILIPPO *(to Guglielmo)* You go ahead, then. Go hurry up the horses.
GUGLIELMO But you said there was plenty of time.
FILIPPO No, no. Go ahead, go ahead.
GUGLIELMO I don't get it.
FILIPPO Have them fodder the horses, and stay with them to make sure they eat it all up, and don't let the stable boys take it away again.
GUGLIELMO Will you pay for the fodder?
FILIPPO I'll pay. Now be off with you.
GUGLIELMO That's all, then. I'll see that it's done … *(exit Guglielmo)*

Scene 12

Fulgenzio and Filippo.

FILIPPO *(aside)* He's finally gone!
FULGENZIO Well done, Signor Filippo!
FILIPPO Well done … well done … When you give someone your word …
FULGENZIO Yes, you gave me your word, and you certainly kept it!
FILIPPO But, hadn't I given him my word first?
FULGENZIO If you had no intention of breaking your promise to him, why promise me?
FILIPPO Because I meant to do what you told me.
FULGENZIO So why didn't you?
FILIPPO Because … a lesser evil could have led to a worse evil; because people would have said … because people would have concluded … oh, dammit! If you'd heard my daughter's arguments, you'd have been convinced too.
FULGENZIO So that's it! This is no way to treat a gentleman like me. I'm not a puppet to be toyed with like this. I shall make my excuses to Signor Leonardo. I'm sorry I got mixed up in all this. I wash my hands of the whole business. I want nothing more to do with it. *(prepares to leave)*
FILIPPO No! Please listen.
FULGENZIO I've heard all I intend to hear.
FILIPPO Just one more word!
FULGENZIO What more can you say?

Filippo My dear friend, I'm so confused. I don't know if I'm standing on my head or my heels.

Fulgenzio Excuse me, a wrong is a wrong.

Filippo Let's correct it, for heaven's sake!

Fulgenzio And just how do you propose to correct it?

Filippo Isn't there still time to send Signor Guglielmo packing?

Fulgenzio Didn't you just send him to hurry up the horses?

Filippo What better excuse could I find to get him out of the way?

Fulgenzio And when he comes back with the horses?

Filippo Oh, I'm swimming in a sea of confusion.

Fulgenzio I'll tell you what to do. Why not give up the idea of going to the country altogether?

Filippo How can I do that?

Fulgenzio Say you're sick.

Filippo What should I say I have?

Fulgenzio *(angrily)* How does a plague on you sound?

Filippo Please don't lose your temper. *(enter Leonardo)*

Scene 13

Enter *Leonardo.*

Leonardo I'm delighted to find both of you here. Which of you is making a fool out of me? Who's been trifling with my affairs? Which of you insulted me?

Fulgenzio *(to Filippo)* You answer.

Filippo *(to Fulgenzio)* Oh, my dear friend! You answer.

Leonardo Is this any way to treat a gentleman? Is this any way to treat a man of my station? What kind of uncivil discourteous behaviour is this?

Fulgenzio *(to Filippo)* Go ahead, answer.

Filippo *(to Fulgenzio)* I don't know what to say.

Scene 14

Enter *Giacinta.*

Giacinta What's all this racket? Are we in a public square?

Leonardo Madam, I am not the one making a scene. The ones to blame are the ones who make fools of respectable people, and don't live up to their word, and betray the people who trust them.

GIACINTA *(dramatically)* And who is the culprit? Who is the guilty party?

FULGENZIO *(to Filippo)* Speak up!

FILIPPO *(to Fulgenzio)* Won't you please begin?

FULGENZIO Very well, then, I have a stake in this business. Since the devil got me into it, my reputation's at stake if I keep silent. So, if Signor Filippo is incapable of speaking up, I'll have to speak up for myself. Yes, madam. Signor Leonardo has every right to complain. After you had given him your word that Signor Guglielmo wouldn't come with you, to break your word, to have him come, to take him with you to the country, was not the right way to behave. It was an insult.

GIACINTA What do you have to say for yourself, father?

FILIPPO He was talking to you. You answer.

GIACINTA Be so good as to tell me, Signor Fulgenzio, what gives Signor Leonardo the right to lay down the law in someone else's house?

LEONARDO A suitor has the right …

GIACINTA *(to Leonardo)* I beg your pardon, I'm not talking to you at the moment. *(to Fulgenzio)* Let Signor Fulgenzio answer. How dare Signor Leonardo insist that my father and I refrain from seeing whomever we please, that we shouldn't take to the country a person he doesn't approve of?

LEONARDO You are perfectly well aware …

GIACINTA I'm not talking to you. Let Signor Fulgenzio answer.

FILIPPO *(aside)* What he said about pledges of affection can't be true. She wouldn't talk to him like that if it were.

FULGENZIO Since you insist on my speaking, I'll speak. Signor Leonardo would have no say in the matter, no claims to make, if he didn't plan to make you his wife.

GIACINTA *(to Fulgenzio)* What? Signor Leonardo intends to ask for my hand in marriage?

LEONARDO You mean you didn't know?

GIACINTA *(to Leonardo)* I beg your pardon. Let me talk to Signor Fulgenzio. *(to Fulgenzio)* Tell me, sir, what grounds do you have for that assertion?

FULGENZIO The grounds that I presented his proposal myself on Leonardo's behalf to your father a few minutes ago.

LEONARDO But, now that I find myself insulted …

GIACINTA *(to Leonardo)* For God's sake, be quiet! It's not your turn to speak yet. You can talk when your turn comes. *(to Filippo)* And what does my father have to say about all this?

FILIPPO What would you say?

GIACINTA No, tell me what you think first. Then I'll say what I think afterwards.

FILIPPO Well, what I say is this … As far as I'm concerned, I don't see any problem.

LEONARDO What I say at this point …

GIACINTA It's not your turn yet. At the moment it's my turn to speak. Be so good as to listen, and then, if you wish, you may answer. Ever since I had the honour of meeting Signor Leonardo, he cannot deny that I have always held him in the highest esteem; and I am fully aware that he has always considered me likewise. Little by little, esteem leads to love, and I am prepared to concede that he loves me, just as, to be perfectly honest, my feelings for him are not exactly indifferent. On the other hand, if a man is going to acquire authority over a woman, unavowed affection isn't enough, there has to be an open declaration. Once that has been made, it isn't enough for only the woman to know it, her father must know, people must know. The arrangements have to be discussed and agreed on with all of the usual stipulations. Then and only then must all of her cares, all her attention, be for her fiancé, and only then does he have the right, if not to insist and give orders, at least to speak his mind freely and expect to be listened to. Otherwise, an honest woman is entitled to keep whatever company she pleases, without distinction: she can see anyone, talk to anyone, as long as she treats them all alike. But she cannot and must not play favourites. That would attract negative attention and compromise her reputation. I have always behaved towards Guglielmo and others with the same honesty I have always used with you. My father was the one who invited him along, and I accepted his company as I would have anyone else's. You're wrong to complain, if you're critical of him or of me. But now you've declared yourself, now your affection for me has been made public, now you do me the honour of asking for my hand in marriage, now my father knows and has given his consent, let me tell you I'm flattered, I'm delighted you love me, and I thank you, sir, for your kindness. For the future, you are free to impose all the conditions you please, they're your right, you're entitled to insist and obtain what you want. I ask only one favour of you. On it may depend my good opinion of you, and my happiness in having you for a husband. Insist on my love, but don't insist on me being uncivil. Don't let the first signs of your love be base suspicions, offensive mistrust, and vulgar, plebeian behaviour. We're just about to leave. Do you want me to send the man uncivilly packing, to expose your suspicions to the world, and to make fools of ourselves in front of everybody? Let it go, this one time. Trust me. Don't insult me. That way I'll know if you love me, if you want my heart or my hand. My hand is ready and waiting, you have only to take it. But my heart must be earned, if you want to possess it.

FILIPPO *(to Fulgenzio)* What do you say to that?

FULGENZIO *(aside, softly to Filippo)* I wouldn't have her, not even if she had a dowry of a hundred thousand crowns!

FILIPPO *(aside, to himself)* What a fool!

LEONARDO What can I say? I love you. I want your heart more than anything else in the world. Your arguments are convincing. I don't want to be ungrateful. Do as you think best, and have pity on me.

FULGENZIO *(aside)* Oh, what a fool!

GIACINTA *(aside, to herself)* I don't care whether Guglielmo comes with me or not. As long as Leonardo doesn't contradict me.

Scene 15

Enter *Brigida.*

BRIGIDA Sir, your sister is here with your servant.

LEONARDO By your leave, sir? Show them in.

BRIGIDA *(soflty to Giacinta)* Are we leaving, or aren't we?

GIACINTA *(softly to Brigida)* We're leaving, we're leaving.

BRIGIDA *(aside)* I was terrified we wouldn't go! *(exit Brigida)*

Scene 16

Vittoria, Paolo, and Brigida.

VITTORIA *(in a melancholy tone)* May I?

GIACINTA Yes, my precious, come in.

VITTORIA *(aside)* There she goes: my precious, my precious! *(to Leonardo, in the same tone as above)* How do you do, Signor Leonardo?

LEONARDO Never better, thank heavens. Paolo, quickly, get everything ready. The trunk, the horses, everything we need. We're leaving soon.

VITTORIA *(happily)* We're leaving?

GIACINTA Yes, my precious, we're leaving. Are you happy?

VITTORIA Oh, yes, my dear heart, I couldn't be happier.
FILIPPO *(softly to Fulgenzio)* It's so nice to see the future sisters-in-law so loving.
FULGENZIO *(to Filippo)* If you ask me, they're as loving as the wolf and the lamb.
FILIPPO *(aside)* What an odd fellow he is!
PAOLO Thank heavens, he seems to have gotten over it. *(exit Paolo)*
VITTORIA Come, Brother, let us go, too.
LEONARDO You're extremely impatient.
GIACINTA The poor thing! She's dying to leave for the country.
VITTORIA Just like you, more or less.
FULGENZIO Do you plan to go off to the country without getting things settled and signing the contract?
VITTORIA What contract?
FILIPPO We could put it in writing before we leave.
VITTORIA Put what in writing?
LEONARDO I'm perfectly willing.
VITTORIA But what is it you have to do?
GIACINTA Send for two witnesses.
VITTORIA What do you want two witnesses for?
BRIGIDA *(to Vittoria)* Don't you know?
VITTORIA I haven't the faintest idea.
BRIGIDA If you don't know now, you'll know soon.
VITTORIA Brother, dear?
LEONARDO Yes, madam.
VITTORIA Are you planning to get married?
LEONARDO Yes, I am.
VITTORIA And nobody tells me anything?
LEONARDO Give me time and I'll tell you.
VITTORIA Is this your wife-to-be?
GIACINTA Yes, my dear, I'm the lucky woman. Will you have me?
VITTORIA Oh, how wonderful! How happy it makes me! My dear, dear Sister-in-law. *(they embrace) (aside)* That's all I needed! Her in the house!
GIACINTA *(aside)* Pray God we can get her off our hands soon!
FILIPPO *(aside to Fulgenzio)* Just look how affectionate they are!
FULGENZIO *(aside to Filippo)* I can see you know nothing about women.
FILIPPO *(aside)* Oh, he makes my blood boil!
GIACINTA Here they come, here they come, here come the two witnesses.

LEONARDO *(aside, to himself, observing from the wings)* Oh, here comes Guglielmo. He's a thorn in my side. I can't stand the sight of him.

VITTORIA *(aside)* What a kind, considerate brother! Taking a wife before he finds me a husband! He'll hear a thing or two from me, when I can get it off my chest.

Scene 17

Enter *Guglielmo and Ferdinando.*

GUGLIELMO The horses are ready.

FERDINANDO Come along, come along, it's getting late. And how is my friend Leonardo? Recovered from your fit of depression?

LEONARDO What do you know about my fit of depression?

FERDINANDO Oh, Signora Vittoria said something about it.

VITTORIA Not true! I said nothing of the kind.

FERDINANDO I can accept contradiction, as long as it comes from a woman.

FILIPPO Gentlemen, before we leave, there's one thing we must do. Signor Leonardo has done me the honour of asking for my daughter's hand in marriage, and I have promised her to him. The wedding will take place … *(to Leonardo)* When would you like to have the wedding?

LEONARDO I'd say, when we get back from the country.

FILIPPO Excellent. So it'll be when we get back from the country. In the meantime, we should put it in writing. I therefore invite you both to act as witnesses.

GUGLIELMO *(aside)* This is a development I wasn't expecting!

FERDINANDO At your service, sir, glad to oblige. Let's get it over with quickly, so we can leave for the country. Oh, by the way, gentlemen, is there a place left for me?

FILIPPO I don't know … What do you say, Giacinta?

GIACINTA It's up to you to decide.

FILIPPO And what about Signor Guglielmo? I'm sorry. What are we going to do?

VITTORIA *(to Filippo)* May I say something?

FERDINANDO You come up with an answer, Signora.

VITTORIA I say that if my brother is engaged to Signora Giacinta, then he should go in the carriage with his fiancée.

FULGENZIO That's what appearances would seem to require, Signor Filippo.

FILIPPO What does Giacinta have to say?

GIACINTA I'm inviting nobody, and I'm turning nobody down.

LEONARDO What does Signor Guglielmo have to say?

GUGLIELMO I say that, if I'm in the way, I can always stay behind.

VITTORIA No, no. You can come in the calèche with me.

GUGLIELMO *(aside)* It would be bad manners to stick to my guns. *(out loud)* With Signor Leonardo's permission, I accept Signora Vittoria's kind offer.

LEONARDO Of course, my dear friend. I am forever in your debt for being so understanding.

GIACINTA *(aside to herself)* Since he gave up his place of his own accord, I don't care. I made my point.

FILIPPO *(aside to Fulgenzio)* Well, what do you say? Is everything satisfactory now?

FULGENZIO *(aside to Filippo)* I have some reservations about Signora Vittoria's arrangements.

FILIPPO *(aside to Fulgenzio)* Ridiculous!

FERDINANDO And who am I supposed to go with?

GIACINTA Sir, would you be willing to travel with my maid?

FERDINANDO In a calèche?

GIACINTA In a calèche.

FERDINANDO *(to Brigida)* Very well, my fair maid, I shall have the pleasure of enjoying your delightful company.

BRIGIDA Oh, my cup of joy runneth over! *(aside to herself)* I'd rather have gone with the servant!

FULGENZIO Very well, then. You're all in agreement.

VITTORIA Oh, come on now, let's get this over with. Let's be off to the blessed country.

GIACINTA Yes, let's sign the contract and let's leave right away. The moment we've all been waiting for has finally arrived. We've all been on edge for fear of not going to the country. But that's only normal this time of year. A pleasant journey, then, to those who are off to the country, and a pleasant stay to those who are staying behind.

END OF THE COMEDY

NOTES TO OFF TO THE COUNTRY

All notes to *Off to the Country* are taken from the edition of the Holiday Trilogy translated by Anthony Oldcorn.

1 Goldoni is referring, naturally, to Virgil's *Eclogues* or Bucolics *(37 B.C.)*, and perhaps to his Georgics (30 B.C.). The first edition of the influential *Arcadia*, a pastoral romance in prose interspersed with verse lyrics, by the Neapolitan humanist Jacopo Sannazaro *(1457–1530)*, was published in 1504. Sannazaro's *Arcadia*, imitated in England by Sir Philip Sidney in 1590, was still setting the literary tone in Italy in the eighteenth century.

2 Goldoni is misremembering. *I malcontenti*, written in 1755, was first published in Volume IV, not III, of the Pitteri edition (Venice, 1758), while *La villeggiatura*, written in 1756, appeared in Volume V, not IV. The theme of the ritual stay in the country crops up in other comedies not mentioned in the preface: *Il prodigo* [*The Prodigal*] of 1739–40, *La castalda* [*The Maid Manager*] of 1751, *La cameriera brillante* [*The Witty Chambermaid*] of 1754. We encounter the aristocracy in the country in *Il feudatario* [*The Lord of the Manor*] of 1752, *L'amante di se medesimo* [*The Self-Lover*] of 1756, and *L'apatista o sia l'indifferente* [*The Apathist, or the Indifferent Man*] of 1758. A number of Goldoni's opera librettos echo the same themes: the intermezzo entitled *La vendemmia* [*The Grape Harvest*], for instance, or the comic operas *L'Arcadia in Brenta* [*Arcadia on the Banks of the Brenta*], *Il filosofo di campagna* [*The Country Philosopher*], and *Amor contadino* [*Love among the Peasants*].

3 In point of fact, the three plays were less successful when first performed, in October and November of 1761, than the author remembers: *Off to the Country* played for only five nights, *Adventures in the Country* for seven, and *Back from the Country* for four. Fifteen performances was considered a good run, twenty an outstanding success.

4 Goldoni is referring to one of the "promises" he made in the 1761 Manifesto for the Pasquali edition of his plays: "Each volume ... will include an unpublished comedy or tragedy."

5 One of the few Italian cities with a thriving entrepreneurial middle class actively engaged in trade and commerce, Leghorn (whose Italian name is Livorno) was a rival international seaport on the Tuscan coast, on the opposite side of the peninsula from Venice. Goldoni had already come under attack for his criticism of Venetian society, and his setting the action of the trilogy in Leghorn and nearby Montenero, far from Venice and

its mainland resorts of Strà, Mira, Dolo, etcetera, was a prudent gesture, though not about to fool anyone. The introduction to the 1761 fall season's offerings, recited by Goldoni's leading actress Caterina Bresciani, ironically reassured the members of her Venetian audience that the country follies described in our plays reflected the mores of other more reprehensible communities, and did not for one minute concern them! Indirect tongue-in-cheek criticism of one's own society by appearing to be talking about someplace else was a common ploy in eighteenth-century satirical literature.

6 Montenero, a small hill town a few kilometres to the south overlooking Leghorn, was a fashionable country resort. In the account he gives of the plot of this play in his *Mémoires*, Goldoni makes it clear that, although his friend Signor Filippo is the owner of a country property there, Leonardo and his sister are going to a place they have rented and obviously cannot afford.

7 Leonardo is referring to his wealthy but avaricious Uncle Bernardino, whom the reader will not meet until act 2 of *Back from the Country*. He is worth the wait!

8 In the last of the three plays, *Back from the Country*, Goldoni inadvertently alters Filippo's last name, chosen of course for its non-Venetian ring, to "Ganganelli."

9 The Italian text has "verso le ventidue," about 22:00 hours. It was, however, customary in eighteenth-century Italy, before the institution of Greenwich Mean Time, to begin and end the twenty-four hour day at sunset. One o'clock, then, would be one hour after sunset, 23:00 hours one hour before sunset, and so on. The translation takes this difference into account, sometimes, as here, using a circumlocution, sometimes giving the time according to our modern clock, assuming a 6:30 p.m. sunset as the basis of conversion. In modern terms, two hours before sunset is the equivalent of about 4:30 p.m. Today Montenero is a ten- to fifteen-minute bus ride from downtown Leghorn. The journey by horse-drawn carriage would, of course, have taken longer.

10 Goldoni explains in his *Mémoires* that the "mariage" style, fashionable in Italy and soon to be described by Vittoria, was in fact an invention of enterprising Italian tailors (who affected names like Monsieur de la Rejouissance!), and was quite unknown in France. Such was France's cultural preeminence that to give a French name to a dress was the equivalent of sewing a designer label in today's ready-to-wear.

11 It is worth noting that Count Anselmo, whom Ferdinando claims to have shaken off in favour of the bourgeois Leonardo, is one of those aristocrats with titles, etcetera, mentioned at the start of the play by Leonardo's manservant Paolo as being out of Leonardo's league.

12 Faro is a banking game played with a thirteen-card layout and a full pack of fifty-two cards. Players place their bets on the cards exposed in the layout, and are winners if the most recently exposed card in the dealing box matches the card or cards they have bet on. "This is strictly a gambling game. There is very little, if any, latitude for skill and strategy" (*Scarne's Encyclopedia of Games*). The reader will observe, especially in *Adventures in the Country*, that several of the characters are identified with their favourite card games. Filippo always wants to play piquet, Tognino can only play bezique, and so on. Faro is also Vittoria's game (see act 2, scene 1, p. 177), and her predilection is a measure of her reckless financial irresponsibility, second only to her brother's. For full descriptions of most of the card games alluded to in the plays, the reader may usefully consult Professor Louis Hoffmann's *Cyclopoedia of Card and Table Games* (London: George Routledge, 1891) and John Scarne's above-mentioned *Scarne's Encyclopedia of Games* (New York: Harpercollins, 1973).

13 The lifestyle that Ferdinando is ridiculing is that of the *cicisbeo,* a married woman's official beau or cavalier, tolerated by her husband, a common social type in the Italian society of the day. As the action progresses, however, it will become clear that he knows so much about it because it is his own lifestyle.

14 "Calèche" is the French name, naturalized in English, for a light two-wheeled carriage with a fold-down hood. A similar vehicle can also be called a "calash" (the word and the thing are Slavic in origin), or more simply a "two-wheeler."

15 In Goldoni's day, anybody who was anybody in Venice went to the country two times a year: the first time for the last two weeks of July, and the second time from the beginning of October until mid-November.

16 Filippo's widowed sister-in-law, Sabina, will appear as a character (or caricature), an easy mark for Ferdinando, in *Adventures in the Country.*

17 Though the play is supposed to be set in Tuscany, the fact that Goldoni had his native Venice in mind is corroborated by references here and elsewhere in the Italian text to the gold coin called the "zecchino" (more properly rendered as "sequin"), the highest unit of Venetian, not Tuscan, currency, worth (on the basis of Ferdinando's calculation of his winnings in *Adventures,* 1, 4, p. 232) about twelve Venetian liras. I have arbitrarily chosen to substitute "florins," the gold currency of Florence, not because the latter term is more appropriate to the Tuscan setting, though it is, but because I thought it would sound less odd to the English-speaking reader.

18 A felucca was a small sailing boat. It is unlikely, however, that anyone would go from Leghorn to Montenero by sea. Once again, Goldoni probably has Venice and its mainland in mind.

19 In the eighteenth century, a single woman like Vittoria, whose parents are presumably dead, would of course be entirely dependent on her brother for her living expenses until she got married, just as Giacinta is dependent on her father. Upon receipt of her dowry, her husband would take over her support.

20 "Knight of the Errant Tooth": in the only author's note to the entire trilogy, Goldoni explains that the Italian equivalent "is the name given to scroungers to chide them."

21 The decision to render Goldoni's "scudi" with "crowns" is again arbitrary and in keeping with the non-realistic treatment of questions of currency adopted elsewhere in the translation (see note 17 above). Like "florin" for "zecchino," the choice is dictated by the desire to find a term immediately recognizable as a monetary unit and acceptable to the anglophone ear. No reference is intended in either case to predecimal British currency. The "scudo" was a silver coin, and therefore worth less than the gold "zecchino." To date, the European Community's "ecu," a false cognate of "scudo" and a candidate for use in the translation, has not acquired general acceptance. Our unconcern for economic detail would certainly have upset Goldoni, who shares Fulgenzio's precision in such matters.

22 Presumably, Fulgenzio's mysterious influence with Filippo has to do with the debt of a thousand crowns Filippo owes him (previously mentioned in act 2, scene 9, p. 187), to be paid back in three months' time, after Filippo's trip to the country.

23 Giacinta's dowry is worth eight thousand crowns, not twelve thousand. Leonardo appears to be attempting to blackmail Paolo by exaggerating his own (and therefore his dependent Paolo's) future prospects.

Adventures in the Country

Prose comedy in three acts
Performed for the first time in Venice at the Teatro San Luca in the second half of October 1761

Figure 13 *Adventures in the Country* (Le avventure della villeggiatura)

Figure 14 *Adventures in the Country* (Le avventure della villeggiatura), act 1, scene 3

Figure 15 *Adventures in the Country* (Le avventure della villeggiatura), act 2, scene 10

Figure 16 *Adventures in the Country* (Le avventure della villeggiatura), act 3, scene 11

The Author to the Reader

The plot of the preceding Comedy concerns the departure for the country. The difficulties which came up delayed and almost prevented it; once these difficulties are overcome, the Characters have what they wanted, and the Comedy is over. In that play Guglielmo is a necessary character, since it is he who excites the jealousy of Leonardo and provides the motive force of the action, first postponing the departure and then hurrying it up at the end. But without a second Comedy, his cold and phlegmatic disposition would leave something to be desired. This character is given an opportunity to develop in this second Comedy, and the same cold and phlegmatic disposition produces the most important of the Adventures, in other words the principal action of this second drama.

This continuation produces several other positive effects. Giacinta' s self-assurance is mortified. Filippo's folly is ridiculed. Fulgenzio's forecasts come true. And finally the abuse of country holidays is proved, and its dangerous consequences exposed for the consideration and disenchantment of the audience. This Comedy, too, has closure. I will not say here how it ends, so as not to tip off the Reader and rob him of the pleasure of suspense; he will nevertheless realize, when he has done reading, that there is still something missing, and will be content, I trust, to read the third Comedy.

All the characters of the first play take part in the second, with the exception of Fulgenzio, who is however spoken of and will return in the third. In addition to the above-mentioned characters, four new ones are introduced, all of whom contribute to multiplying the Adventures in the Country, and all of whom serve to advance the main action. Unity of action is an indispensable precept, to be observed in dramatic compositions in which the plot chiefly concerns a single character. But when the collective title encompasses a number of persons, unity is itself found in the multiplicity of the actions. To the latter genre belong (speaking of my own comedies) Il teatro comico,[1] La bottega del caffè, I pettegolezzi delle donne, and precisely the present three Comedies. All of the characters act towards the same end, and all of their different actions serve to advance the plot.

Dramatis Personae

Characters from the Previous Play

Filippo	*a good-natured old city-dweller*
Giacinta	*Filippo's daughter*
Leonardo	*in love with Giacinta*
Vittoria	*Leonardo's sister*
Ferdinando	*a freeloader*
Guglielmo	*in love with Giacinta*
Brigida	*Giacinta's maidservant*
Paolino [Paolo]	*Leonardo's manservant*

New Characters

Sabina	*an elderly lady, Giacinta's aunt and Filippo's sister-in-law*
Costanza	*a country neighbour*
Rosina	*her niece*
Tognino	*a simple-minded young man, in love with Rosina*
Tita	*a manservant in Costanza's household*
Beltrame	*Tognino's father's manservant*
Another Servant	*of Filippo's*

The action takes place in Montenero, a country resort a few miles from Leghorn.

ACT ONE

Scene 1

A room on the ground floor of Filippo's country house, with card tables, chairs, love seats, etc. Large French doors at the back of the stage open onto the garden.
Brigida, Paolino, Tita, and Beltrame.

Brigida Come on in, come on in. Everybody's asleep.
Paolino Everyone went to bed at our house not so long ago, too.

TITA There's no chance of my mistresses waking up for at least another three hours.

BELTRAME If they're up all night, what else are they going to do besides sleep all day?

PAOLINO How did you manage to get up so early, Signora Brigida?

BRIGIDA Who, me? I couldn't have slept better. When they got together for the evening's entertainment, I went straight to bed. They played cards, had dinner, went back to playing cards, and all the while I was getting a good night's sleep. It was broad daylight by the time my mistress sent for me. I got out of bed, helped her undress, put her to bed, locked her door, and got dressed myself. I took a nice walk in the garden, I gathered some jasmine, I couldn't have had a better time.

PAOLINO Now you're talking. That's what I call a good time. But I ask you what fun do our masters ever have?

BRIGIDA None. For them the country's the same as the town. The life they lead is the same.

PAOLINO The only difference is that in the country they invite more guests over, and they spend more money.

BRIGIDA *(playfully)* Come, now. This morning, it's my turn to have the honour of entertaining my own beaux. What would you like? Coffee, hot whipped chocolate, something stronger? Speak up, now.

PAOLINO I believe I'll have a hot chocolate.

TITA Chocolate for me, too.

BELTRAME And I'll have a glass of the good stuff.

BRIGIDA *(getting ready to leave)* My pleasure, gentlemen. I'll be back right away.

TITA *(to Brigida)* Oh, and don't forget, I can't drink my chocolate without something sweet to go with it.

BRIGIDA That goes without saying.

PAOLINO Signora Brigida certainly knows how to take care of people.

BRIGIDA Well, there's no shortage of food; if they don't know how to make the most of it, we might as well take advantage ourselves. *(exit Brigida)*

Scene 2

Paolino, Tita, and Beltrame.

PAOLINO This time tomorrow morning I'll be expecting you over at my place.

TITA Excellent, and one of these mornings you'll be welcome at mine.
PAOLINO *(to Tita)* Did your master drive down to the country?
TITA My master's in Leghorn, my mistress is here enjoying herself. While her husband's working his fingers to the bone, his wife's in the country spending his money and having a good time!
PAOLINO Yes, Signora Costanza is making a splash all right! Somebody who didn't know her would never guess she was a shopkeeper's wife.
BELTRAME I'll say she makes a splash! In Montenero they've nicknamed her the "Governor's Lady."
PAOLINO And who's this young woman who's come to stay with her this year?
TITA A niece of hers, poor as a church mouse, without a penny in the world. My mistress has to lend her every stitch she puts on!
PAOLINO Why burden her husband with the added expense? Why bring a niece to the country, if you have to supply her with clothes?
TITA Well, between you and me, there is a reason. Granted, my mistress, Signora Costanza, is still a young woman; but these days there are women in Montenero younger than her. Society flocks to where the young people are; that's why she's fixed herself up with this sixteen-year-old niece, so as not to be left out in the cold.

Scene 3

Enter *Brigida and servants carrying hot chocolate, wine, etc.*

BRIGIDA I'm back, I'm back. Sorry to keep you all waiting.
PAOLINO Don't worry. We kept ourselves amused.
BRIGIDA How?
PAOLINO *(laughing)* Speaking well of our neighbours!
BRIGIDA Good for you, good for you, I know what you mean. If someone should decide to become a writer, and describe what goes on in the country, he could fill volumes. Playwrights rack their brains to write comedies. If they want to write a good play, all they have to do is to come here. This is for you, Signor Paolino. *(serving him his hot chocolate)* If they're looking for a good subject, they should come take a look at the old dowager. This is for you, Tita. *(giving him his hot chocolate)* Sixty-five years old, and still acting like she's the belle of the ball! *(she serves them both cookies)* And Signor Ferdinando is so good at leading her on, you'd think he was pining away with love, and the

old woman eats it up. If you ask me, the scoundrel's milking her dry! Signor Beltrame, I think you'll appreciate this. *(she pours wine into a glass and gives it to him)*

BELTRAME This is the best chocolate I've ever tasted!

BRIGIDA Here are a couple of cookies for you. What do you make of the latest topic of conversation – Signor Guglielmo declaring his love to Signora Vittoria? Is it true or not? You ought to know, Paolino.

PAOLINO They say that in the calèche, on the way here, there was some hint of that kind. The groom, who was in the rumble seat, says the calèche was open. They shut it, but he managed to catch some of what they said.

BRIGIDA Yes, indeed! Two young people alone in a calèche is a golden opportunity.

BELTRAME That was good, really good! *(handing the glass back)*

BRIGIDA Would you care for some more?

BELTRAME No, I'm fine.

BRIGIDA Go on, one more glass!

BELTRAME No, really, I'm fine.

BRIGIDA Come on, one more, for my sake!

BELTRAME Oh, my goodness, go on, then. How can I refuse if you put it like that?

BRIGIDA That's the way I like my men – easy to deal with!

PAOLINO Tomorrow morning, Signora Brigida, Signor Tita, Signor Beltrame, I'll be expecting you at my place.

TITA And the day after tomorrow at mine.

BELTRAME I'm afraid I'm not in a position to invite you. My master goes out for his coffee and chocolate; in the house we don't get so much as a whiff.

PAOLINO *(to Beltrame)* Isn't your master the physician, the local Montenero doctor?

BELTRAME Exactly. He has been a country doctor for years, he never made it to town.

PAOLINO He came over yesterday for a cup of hot chocolate.

BRIGIDA To your place? He had a cup with us, too.

TITA And what if I told you he had a cup with us, too?

BRIGIDA I hope all that chocolate was good for the doctor!

PAOLINO He'll probably make the same rounds this morning.

BELTRAME No, not this morning. He's not in Montenero. He's been called out to Maremma.[2] He won't be back till tomorrow.

BRIGIDA How come you didn't go with him?

BELTRAME They sent a carriage and a servant to pick him up; he left me to look after his son.

BRIGIDA That simpleton Signor Tognino?

TITA Simple is right! He must be simple-minded! He's fallen head over heels for Rosina!

BRIGIDA For Signora Costanza's niece?

BELTRAME Yes, it's true. They got their hooks into him. Taking advantage of the fact that his father the doctor is courting Signora Costanza, he took up with the niece.

BRIGIDA Really? Tell me more …

PAOLINO Someone's coming.

TITA Let's make ourselves scarce.

BRIGIDA Come on, let's go out in the garden. I can't wait to hear all about it.

PAOLINO A fine story! *(exit Paolino)*

TITA The same old story! *(exit Tita)*

BELTRAME The fruits of youth! *(exit Beltrame)*

BRIGIDA Country adventures! *(exit Brigida)*

Scene 4

Ferdinando in his house clothes, followed by servant.

FERDINANDO Hello, hello! Is anybody there? Where is everybody? Don't tell me they're all still asleep? Hello! Is anybody there?

SERVANT You called, sir?

FERDINANDO What the devil! … Do I have to shout myself hoarse to get waited on around here?

SERVANT Sorry, sir.

FERDINANDO Bring me my hot chocolate.

SERVANT Right away, sir. *(aside)* What a freeloader! And how well he gives orders! As though he were in his own home, or a paying guest at an inn! *(exit servant)*

FERDINANDO Signor Filippo couldn't be nicer, but he doesn't know how to handle the servants. Still, one is better off here than anyplace else. Here there's more freedom, better food, better company. Luckily for me I came down in the carriage with my lady's maid. So I had an excuse to stay here instead of going to Signor Leonardo's. Not that his place is that bad; but this is the best there is. In a word, things couldn't be working out better, and, to top it all, I'm doing quite well at cards this year. Let's do a little bookkeeping! Let's check our finances. *(he sits at the table and takes out a notebook)* At tarots, winnings: 18 liras; at primero, winnings: 62 liras; at "trentuno," winnings: 96 liras; at faro, winnings: 16 florins. That makes, altogether ... *(adding it up)* altogether, I'm up about 30 florins.[3] If things go on at this rate ... But what the devil are they up to? *(shouts)* Are you going to bring me my chocolate or aren't you? Are you ever going to get here, damn you?

Scene 5

Enter *Filippo.*

FILIPPO My dear friend, you'll oblige me by not raising your voice.
FERDINANDO But you never say a word, and the servants do just as they please.
FILIPPO I get excellent service; and I never raise my voice.
FERDINANDO I'm not thinking about myself. You do have other guests in the house, and they're not at all happy with the servants.
FILIPPO Let me tell you something, my friend. I pay my servants myself, and anybody who isn't happy with them is perfectly free to leave.
FERDINANDO Have you had your hot chocolate yet?
FILIPPO No, I haven't.
FERDINANDO What are you waiting for?
FILIPPO I'm waiting till I'm good and ready; when I want it I'll have it.
FERDINANDO I'd really like mine now.
FILIPPO Don't let me stop you.
FERDINANDO It's three hours since I ordered it. *(shouting into the wings)* Hello there! I say, is that hot chocolate coming or not?
FILIPPO Please, don't shout.
FERDINANDO But if they won't bring it!
FILIPPO Be patient. They must be busier than usual. We're giving a luncheon today. There are going to be eleven or twelve of us at the table. The servants can't do everything all at once.
FERDINANDO *(aside)* It looks as if we're not going to get anywhere this morning. *(to Filippo)* By your leave, Signor Filippo.
FILIPPO Where are you off to?
FERDINANDO To have my hot chocolate someplace else.

FILIPPO My dear friend, just between you and me, I wouldn't want anyone to hear us, but I must say you really are a bit greedy.

FERDINANDO I have a weak stomach. I hardly eat anything at night.

FILIPPO On the contrary, it seemed to me that last night, at that fine supper at Signor Leonardo's, you did yourself proud.

FERDINANDO Oh, last night was an exception.

FILIPPO If I'd eaten all you ate, I'd fast for three days. *(servant brings a cup of chocolate)*

FERDINANDO Ah, here's the hot chocolate.

FILIPPO Aren't you going out for yours? Don't let me stop you. I'll take this one.

FERDINANDO Have I said something to offend you?

FILIPPO No, I'm not easily offended. But please, feel free to go. I'll take this cup.

FERDINANDO You really are too kind, Signor Filippo. But, since we're good friends, I don't want to insult you. I'll take it. *(takes the cup of chocolate)*

FILIPPO Very well, sir. Your good manners do you credit. *(to the servant)* Whip me up a cup, please.

SERVANT Sir, unless Brigida gets back soon, we've run out.

FILIPPO Didn't you brew some last night, as you usually do?

SERVANT Yes, sir; but now there's none left.

FILIPPO Well, my daughter didn't drink it, my sister didn't drink it, Signor Guglielmo didn't drink it. Where on earth has all the chocolate gone?

SERVANT That's all I know, sir. All I know is that there's none left in the chocolate pot.

FILIPPO Oh, well, if there's none left, I'll just have to do without, won't I? Please don't let it trouble you, I'm accustomed to this sort of thing.

FERDINANDO This is delicious! Your chocolate is nothing short of perfection!

FILIPPO I see to it that it's made without sparing expense.

FERDINANDO With your permission, sir, I think I'll go out for a walk.

FILIPPO Come over here. Let's play a couple of hands of piquet.[4]

FERDINANDO Right this instant?

FILIPPO Yes, now, while there's no one about. If I wait till after dinner, they'll start cutting the cards and playing their own games, and I won't find anyone to give me the time of day.

FERDINANDO My dear Signor Filippo, I don't feel like playing right now.

FILIPPO A couple of hands, just to humour me.

FERDINANDO I'm sorry, but I do need a walk. Later ... later ... we'll play later on. *(aside)* Can you imagine me wanting to sit around playing penny ante with this old buzzard! *(exit Ferdinando)*

FILIPPO I was right! No one pays me the slightest attention. They all have a good time at my expense, but, if I want to have fun, I have to go down to the apothecary's and play chequers with him. Oh! Signor Fulgenzio was right. But it's too late to go back. I'm here in the country again for the season. If I get my daughter married off, I'll rent the house and the property and forget about coming to the country. But I can't bear not going to the country! If I don't have company, I might as well be dead. What can I say? I guess I've been spoiled. What's mine is not mine; it's there for them to devour; but I always end up with the short end of the stick! *(exit Filippo)*

Scene 6

A drawing room in Signora Costanza's house. Costanza and Rosina.

COSTANZA My dear niece, there's a girl! How pretty you look. Your hair is just perfect.

ROSINA This morning I put everything I could into doing my hair tastefully.

COSTANZA That's good, because today, at Signor Filippo's, all the beauties of Montenero will be there, we'll see some magnificent coiffures.

ROSINA Oh, yes! We'll see the usual caricatures: furies, lions' heads, antique medallions.

COSTANZA You're right, they do make frights of themselves.

ROSINA They can have their hairdressers. I've no time for them. All they do is copy the latest fashions, without a thought for whether the fashion suits the person's face and figure or not.

COSTANZA You are quite right. It is monstrous to see a dainty little face peering out of a massive beehive of hair which alters its whole appearance.

ROSINA I can't understand why we haven't seen Signor Tognino yet. He told me he'd come round for lunch.

COSTANZA Oh, don't worry, he'll be here. He's obviously fond of you.

ROSINA Yes, if I were willing, he'd marry me tomorrow.

COSTANZA A doctor's profession is a respectable profession, when all's said and done; and you'll be able to hold your head high in any company.

ROSINA It's a pity it'll be so long before he's ready to practise.

COSTANZA Oh, come now! How long can it take? He's been away studying in Pisa,[5] he'll soon have his degree, and he'll be practising medicine in no time at all.

ROSINA They say he doesn't know much, and that he'll have trouble passing his exams if he doesn't study a bit harder.

COSTANZA Oh, you make me laugh. It doesn't take much to become a doctor. A little memory, a few contacts, and there you have it in no time. Once he is a doctor, a practice will come easy. His friends and our friends will soon get him one.

ROSINA And how about experience?

COSTANZA The experience will come with the practice.

ROSINA I envy his first patients!

COSTANZA If he's lucky, everything will work out for the best.

ROSINA And will his father be happy then?

COSTANZA I hope so. The good doctor, if I may say so myself, has a soft spot for me.

Scene 7

Enter *Ferdinando.*

FERDINANDO *(offstage)* Anyone at home? May I come in?

COSTANZA *(into the wings)* Come in, come in. Make yourself at home. *(to Rosina)* It's Signor Ferdinando.

ROSINA What does that nuisance want?

COSTANZA Don't you know? He is one of those people who stick their noses in everywhere; you have to be nice to him, he has such a cutting tongue.

ROSINA It makes my blood boil, the way he takes advantage of that old woman.

FERDINANDO Your servant, ladies, your most humble servant.

ROSINA Your servant, sir.

COSTANZA Your humble servant, sir.

FERDINANDO My heavens! What beauties are these?

ROSINA You're teasing us, sir.

FERDINANDO Are you here all alone? Don't you have company, isn't anyone here?

COSTANZA No one's been here so far this morning.

FERDINANDO Hasn't the good doctor been round to see you yet this morning?

COSTANZA No, sir. He's gone to Maremma on a visit.

FERDINANDO And the doctor-to-be hasn't shown up?

COSTANZA Not yet.

FERDINANDO Ah, a capital specimen that lad! But what am I saying? I was forgetting that he's the idol of Signora Rosina. Forgive me, Signora, but you are a talented young lady. I don't think even your partiality for him would make you go so far as to consider him a wit.

ROSINA I never said he was witty, but I don't think it's right to make fun of him.

FERDINANDO No, no, he has his good points, he's very polite. *(aside)* I may as well humour her.

COSTANZA Signor Ferdinando, would you like me to have them make you some coffee?

FERDINANDO Thank you so much, but I never take coffee in the morning.

COSTANZA I'm sure you've had your hot chocolate.

FERDINANDO Yes, it was perfectly foul!

COSTANZA Where did you have such vile hot chocolate?

FERDINANDO Where I'm staying, at Signor Filippo's. He spends a fortune, all he can afford and more, and he gets the worst kind of service.

ROSINA He's invited us to lunch today.

FERDINANDO Oh, yes? Then you'll see for yourselves what unpalatable stuff – if there are twelve guests, there's enough for twenty-four, but without any taste, without any refinement: the worst quality meat, plates piled high with food, mountains of badly cooked, badly seasoned stuff, swimming in fat, loaded with spices, stuff that takes your appetite away just to look at it, let alone eat it.

COSTANZA I must say they served a very nice supper last night at Signor Leonardo's.

FERDINANDO Yes … nice if you like, but nothing exceptional!

COSTANZA The spitted quail were delicious.

FERDINANDO Yes, but how many were there? I'm sure there weren't eight birds each.

ROSINA I fancied the tuna.

FERDINANDO Oh, really now! The oil in the dressing was inferior. If it isn't the top quality oil from Lucca, I can't stand it.

ROSINA Oh! Do you see who's coming, aunt?

COSTANZA Yes, yes. Tognino!
FERDINANDO I am delighted that Signor Tognino is coming.
COSTANZA Please, Signor Ferdinando, don't tease the poor boy.
FERDINANDO I'm surprised at you, Signora Costanza. I could never …
ROSINA Because, if we wanted to bring up the subject of Signor Ferdinando and his old dowager, we'd have plenty to talk about.
FERDINANDO *(ironically)* Now you leave my old dowager out of it. She's my idol.
COSTANZA She's your idol all right. I know exactly what you mean.

Scene 8

Enter *Tognino.*

TOGNINO Good morning, ladies. What are you up to? Are you well this morning? I'm delighted.
ROSINA Good morning, Signor Tognino.
FERDINANDO *(with exaggerated deference)* Oh, my dear, dear Signor Tognino, I have the honour of declaring myself your most humble servant.
TOGNINO *(greeting Ferdinando)* Your servant, sir.
COSTANZA Did you sleep well last night?
TOGNINO Yes, madam.
ROSINA Did the supper upset you?
TOGNINO Upset me? Why should it upset me? It didn't upset me at all.
FERDINANDO And what's more, if it had upset him, doesn't he know all about medicine? Couldn't he take care of himself?
TOGNINO Yes, sir. I could take care of myself.
FERDINANDO For someone who'd eaten too much, someone with a case of indigestion, what would you prescribe, Signor Tognino?
ROSINA Oh, come on, he's not a doctor yet, so he can't be expected to know about these things.
TOGNINO On the contrary, ma'am. I do know.
FERDINANDO He knows, madam, he knows perfectly well, and, if you'll allow me to say so, you're doing him a disservice, you're not giving him the credit he deserves. Tell me, Signor Tognino, what would you prescribe?
TOGNINO I would prescribe cassia, manna, senna pods, cream of tartar, and Epsom salts.[6]
COSTANZA You mean, one or the other.

FERDINANDO Or all together, if need be.
TOGNINO Or all together, if need be.
FERDINANDO Bravo! Bravo for the little doctor!
ROSINA Come on, now, let's change the subject.
COSTANZA *(to Tognino)* What time did your father leave?
TOGNINO I was asleep when he left, so I don't know what time it was.
COSTANZA Didn't anyone at home tell you what time he left?
TOGNINO They told me, but I don't remember.
FERDINANDO *(aside)* Oh, what a brilliant conversationalist!
ROSINA And when do you think he'll be back?
TOGNINO I think he'll be back when he's done what he went for.
FERDINANDO No doubt about it. He's absolutely right. It really is amazing. So articulate for his age!
ROSINA *(to Ferdinando)* Come, now, sir. I've told you once and I'll tell you again: Watch out for yourself, and don't make fun of other people.
TOGNINO *(to Ferdinando)* Is Signor Ferdinando making fun of me?
COSTANZA *(to Tognino)* Tell me, have you had lunch?
TOGNINO No, that's what I'm here for.
ROSINA And I was expecting you. We'll have lunch together.
FERDINANDO Well! Signor Tognino is a lucky fellow!
TOGNINO What do you mean, lucky?
FERDINANDO Because he has all the young ladies running after him.
COSTANZA *(to Ferdinando)* Let's stay away from that topic.
ROSINA *(softly to Tognino)* Poor Tognino, don't pay any attention to him.
TOGNINO *(softly to Rosina, stamping his foot)* When we're married, I won't allow him in the house.
FERDINANDO What's the matter with Signor Tognino?
COSTANZA Leave him alone.
FERDINANDO But I'm fond of him.
TOGNINO *(scowling)* I don't care whether you like me or not.
FERDINANDO Oh, how charming, how sweet, how delightful!

Scene 9

Enter *Tita.*

TITA *(to Costanza)* Madam, you have a visitor.
COSTANZA Who is it?

TITA Signora Vittoria.
COSTANZA *(to Tita)* Show her in. What an honour!
TOGNINO What about lunch?
ROSINA Do you mind, aunt, if we go and have lunch?
COSTANZA Tita, conduct my niece and Signor Tognino to the dining room and give them something nice to eat, and stay with them, don't leave them alone.
TITA Very well, madam. *(exit Tita)*
FERDINANDO *(ironically, aside)* What tact! What surveillance! What admirable caution!
ROSINA *(to Tognino)* Come along, let's go in.
FERDINANDO A hearty appetite to Signor Tognino.
TOGNINO Thank you. Your servant, sir.
FERDINANDO Drink my health.
ROSINA *(to Ferdinando)* Oh, you make my blood boil!
FERDINANDO Long live Signor Tognino!
TOGNINO *(to Ferdinando)* Oh, you make my blood boil!
ROSINA Let's go. *(she takes Tognino by the arm and drags him clumsily offstage)*

Scene 10

Costanza and Ferdinando, followed by Vittoria.

COSTANZA Well, dear Signor Ferdinando?
FERDINANDO Well, dear Signora Costanza. If you can keep a straight face, I have to hand it to you.
VITTORIA Your servant, Signora Costanza. Forgive me if I'm tardy in paying my respects.
COSTANZA What on earth do you mean? It's an honour whenever you come. I consider it a favour. Please sit down. *(they sit down)*
FERDINANDO *(softly to Vittoria, as he sits down)* What do you say, eh? What's that outfit she's wearing?
VITTORIA *(aside to Ferdinando)* All in the worst possible taste! She doesn't even know how to dress.
COSTANZA *(aside)* Oh, blast her! She's wearing a "mariage," the very latest fashion. *(the two women study each other surreptitiously, without speaking)*
FERDINANDO *(aside)* They've been struck dumb, they're not speaking. *(addressing Vittoria and Costanza)* So, ladies, what do you think of the weather?

VITTORIA Oh, not too bad, considering the season.

COSTANZA *(aside)* Now I know why she came to see me, to show off her new dress. But I'm not going to give her the satisfaction, I'm not going to make any comment.

FERDINANDO Signora Vittoria is looking magnificent, she is dressed with such taste.

VITTORIA Oh, it's nothing, just a little dress in the latest style.

COSTANZA Does Signora Vittoria plan to stay long in the country?

VITTORIA As long as the holidays last.

FERDINANDO I just love the colours!

VITTORIA With this kind of dress, the harmony of the colours is everything.

COSTANZA *(aside)* The harmony of the colours indeed!

FERDINANDO Now, that's what I call dressing with taste!

COSTANZA I expect you've been invited by Signora Giacinta as well this morning.

VITTORIA Yes, Signora. Are you going, too?

COSTANZA Oh, how can one refuse?

VITTORIA Are you going on foot, may I ask, or by carriage?

COSTANZA Oh, I'm going on foot. I don't have a carriage, I'm not made out of money; but even if I did, it's so close, it would seem an affectation.

VITTORIA Oh, that's not the point. It's a question of noblesse oblige …

COSTANZA While we're on the topic of noblesse oblige …

FERDINANDO There will be plenty of guests, I believe, this morning.

VITTORIA As far as I am concerned, come one, come all. I'm not going to let myself be influenced. I'm going just like I am, in informal attire.

FERDINANDO But, Signora, that's a dress you can wear on any occasion.

COSTANZA *(aside)* Curse him! What a chatterbox!

FERDINANDO What do you say, Signora Costanza? Isn't it a magnificent dress, and what taste!

COSTANZA Sir, all you seem to be able to do is to interrupt people when they're talking. *(to Vittoria)* What time do you plan to go to Signora Giacinta's?

VITTORIA *(aside)* I can see this dress is driving her crazy. *(to Costanza)* Let me see, Signora, I still have a couple of people to call on, and then I'll go to Signora Giacinta's. If it's still early, we'll have a game of cards.

COSTANZA Oh, if it is cards you want, in that house they play at all hours. It would be fine if they played for low stakes, but that blessed faro will be the ruin of somebody sooner or later.

FERDINANDO I never heard of anyone being ruined by it yet.

VITTORIA This year, to tell you the truth, I've lost as much at cards as I care to: and, on top of that, I've had other expenses. I like to dress well. Every season I like to buy something new. We all have our passions. Mine's dressing well, and dressing in fashion. This year, for instance, the latest thing is the "mariage" style, and I was one of the first to have one.

COSTANZA *(aside)* She really does turn my stomach. I can't stand her.

FERDINANDO Yes, elegance certainly does make people stand out.

VITTORIA What do you say, Signora Costanza, you're a woman of taste, do you like this dress?

COSTANZA Madam, I didn't want to say anything, I'm accustomed to speaking my mind, and I can't stand flattery. On the other hand, criticizing other people's things isn't polite. But, since you insist on knowing the truth, I don't like it one bit.

VITTORIA You don't like it?

COSTANZA What can I say? I may have bad taste, but I don't like it.

FERDINANDO My goodness! This is something! What is it you don't like?

COSTANZA What does the commender find so handsome, so marvellous about it? What is it but an ordinary silk dress decorated in more than one colour, like a servant's uniform? With all due respect, I don't like it, and I don't think it deserves so much praise.

FERDINANDO Oh, well, there's no accounting for taste.

VITTORIA Signora Costanza, I didn't come here to criticize your dresses. *(they get to their feet)*

COSTANZA Neither did I, excuse me …

FERDINANDO I see Signora Vittoria has decided to leave. If she wishes, I'll accompany her.

VITTORIA I'd be delighted.

COSTANZA You may go with whomever you please.

VITTORIA Your humble servant.

COSTANZA Your devoted servant.

FERDINANDO My respects, Signora Costanza.

VITTORIA *(aside)* It's my own fault, I should never have come. Poor creature, so proud, and so ignorant. *(exit Vittoria)*

FERDINANDO *(aside)* What a subject for a musical cantata! The clash of ambition and envy. *(exit Ferdinando)*

COSTANZA A fine lady, indeed! A regular princess! Nothing but debts and vanity. No substance! *(exit Costanza)*

ACT TWO

Scene 1

A room in Filippo's house. Giacinta and Brigida.

BRIGIDA Whatever can be making you so melancholy, Mistress? You don't seem to be relishing your stay in the country this year.

GIACINTA I curse the day and the hour that I came here.

BRIGIDA Why so?

GIACINTA Oh, leave me alone, don't upset me any further.

BRIGIDA But I absolutely insist on knowing. My mistress has never had any secrets from me, I hope she is not going to cut me out now.

GIACINTA Brigida, dear, I know I've been mad, that I am mad, and that my madness will be my undoing.

BRIGIDA But why? Are you sorry you're marrying Signor Leonardo?

GIACINTA No, I don't regret that. Leonardo is a worthy person, he loves me dearly, and he is not so intractable as to make me afraid he'll mistreat me. What I do regret, what I regret most bitterly, is that I insisted in spite of everything on having Signor Guglielmo come with us, and that

I let my father put him up in our house.

BRIGIDA Did it upset Signor Leonardo?

GIACINTA Will you please leave Signor Leonardo out of this, he has nothing to do with it. He's already suffered enough as it is. I blush at the thought of what he's been through.

BRIGIDA But what harm has Signor Guglielmo done you, then? He seems to be such a sincere and well-mannered young fellow …

GIACINTA That's just it. It's his civility, his politeness, that insinuating, sweet, pathetic, sophisticated manner of his, that has charmed me, subjugated me, made me his slave, in spite of myself. Yes, Brigida, I'm in love, as much as a woman was ever in love.

BRIGIDA What, Mistress? But how in the world …? You must have told me a thousand times you never gave him a second thought.

GIACINTA It's true, I never gave him a thought, I always treated him with indifference, I used to laugh up my sleeve at the futile attentions he showered on me. But alas, Brigida mine, this living together, this seeing each other every day, at every hour of the day, his being so considerate, the right words at just the right moment, sitting next to each other at table, feeling him brush against me from time to time (whether by accident or by design), and then ask my pardon, accompanying the apology with a sigh or two – all fatal openings, horrible traps ... I don't know, I don't know where it's all going to end.

BRIGIDA But it isn't your fault. The master's to blame.

GIACINTA You're right. I keep trying to put the blame on my father, too. The first mistake was his; but it was up to me to correct it; I was the only one who could do it, and I ought to have done it; but my cursed ambition not to be dependent on anyone, and my need to be catered to, made me pretend at first to be indifferent, and indifference became gratification, and gratification, passion.

BRIGIDA Has Signor Leonardo caught on?

GIACINTA I don't think so. I'm using all my wiles to keep it from him, but I swear to you that I'm suffering the agonies of death. Having to treat Signor Leonardo with the respect a wife owes her husband, and seeing the man who has won my heart languish and suffer is such hell I couldn't explain it if I wanted.

BRIGIDA But how is it all going to end, madam?

GIACINTA That is exactly what I don't know, and why I'm living in fear.

BRIGIDA Well, when all's said and done, you're not married yet.

GIACINTA And what would you like me to do? Go back on my word? Have them tear up the contract? I signed it, my father signed it, our relatives are party to it, it's public knowledge in town. What would people say about me? But that isn't all. If they were to discover my passion for this young man, is there anyone who wouldn't argue that I was already in love with him in Leghorn, that I insisted on having him with me in a love fit, that I had the gall to sign a contract of marriage when my heart belonged to another, and with my lover standing beside me? My reputation's at stake. It makes me cringe just to think about it.

BRIGIDA Oh, my heavens! I can't tell you how unhappy it makes me. But didn't I hear that Signor Guglielmo had a soft spot for Signora Vittoria?

GIACINTA There's not a word of truth in it! He's so clever, he's only pretending. To hide his affection for me.

BRIGIDA And is Signor Guglielmo aware that madam feels this passion for him?

GIACINTA I've managed to hide my feelings as much as I could, but I'm sure he's noticed, and what's more, that old fool of an aunt of mine, the malicious old hag, has caught on as well, and, instead of preventing it and coming up with a solution, she seems to enjoy stirring up the fire. She's a lot to blame for my weakness.

BRIGIDA Speaking of the old woman, here she comes now.

GIACINTA She has gotten childish in her old age. She commits one faux pas after another, and she thinks everyone ought to humour her.

BRIGIDA Let's speak to her. Let's tell her not to encourage Signor Guglielmo.

GIACINTA No, no, for the love of heaven, let's not say anything, let things be, we'd only make matters worse.

BRIGIDA *(aside)* So that's it! My mistress is like a sick person who's afraid of taking the medicine!

Scene 2

Enter *Sabina.*

SABINA Niece, have you seen Signor Ferdinando?

GIACINTA No, madam, I haven't seen him this morning.

SABINA And you, Brigida, have you seen him?

BRIGIDA I saw him very early this morning. He went out, and he hasn't come back.

SABINA Can you believe his bad manners! He told me last night to wait for him, and he would have his chocolate in my room this morning; and he never showed up! He spends the entire day making his rounds, he has a hundred calls to make, a hundred appointments. The more you do for these men, the more they expect! They're completely ungrateful.

BRIGIDA *(aside)* The poor little thing! These men really do treat her badly.

SABINA *(to Giacinta)* Have you had your chocolate?

GIACINTA No, madam.

SABINA Why didn't you come to my room when I called you? We could have drunk it together.

GIACINTA I didn't feel like having any this morning.

SABINA *(smiling)* Signor Guglielmo was there, too.

BRIGIDA *(aside)* What a charming old lady!

SABINA Signor Guglielmo came to visit me in my room. He had the servant bring the hot chocolate, and he was so kind as to whip it himself. If you could only have seen how elegantly he whipped it! Everything that young man does, he does well.

BRIGIDA *(aside)* She could use a little whipping herself!

SABINA What's the matter? Don't you feel well?
GIACINTA I have a bit of a headache.
SABINA I don't understand the young people of today. All I hear is stomach aches, headaches, and convulsions.[7] They all have convulsions! I wouldn't change places with one of you girls for all the tea in China.
GIACINTA You're right, aunt. You have a splendid constitution.
SABINA At least I have a good time. I don't sit around mourning the dead. I don't come to the country to be bored. What a pity Signor Ferdinando isn't here! *(to Brigida)* Call me a servant. I'm going to send someone to look for him.
GIACINTA Get along with you, Aunt, don't make such a spectacle of yourself. You're making yourself look ridiculous.
SABINA What on earth are you talking about? Me, make a spectacle? Me, look ridiculous? Aren't I allowed to have a penchant, a weakness for someone? Aren't I a widow? Aren't I a free agent? Can't I do as I please?
GIACINTA Yes, that is all true enough. But at your age ...
SABINA And what age might that be, may I ask? I'm no longer a girl, but I'm still as fresh as a daisy, and I have more wit and grace than you do.
GIACINTA In your shoes, I'd be ashamed to make statements like that.
SABINA What do I have to be ashamed of? A free woman – widowed or unmarried – is permitted to have an admirer. But two beaux at once is not permitted. I believe you catch my allusion.
GIACINTA I'm surprised, madam, to hear you talking like that. But do as you please. From now on, I'll stay out of your business, and I'll thank you to stay out of mine. *(exit Giacinta)*

Scene 3

Sabina and Brigida.

SABINA The impudent hussy! As if no one knew her secrets!
BRIGIDA Pardon the liberty, ma'am, but this is no way to behave. If you know something's afoot, it's your job to prevent it, or at least to make sure that no one finds out. We're not talking about trifles; a young woman's reputation's at stake. Would you be pleased with yourself if you were to blame for your niece's disgrace? If you see something going on, it's up to you to stop it. You certainly shouldn't be the one to stir up the fire, to egg the young

people on. The devil is powerful enough as it is. What's over is over, and there's no need to keep bringing it up, and stirring up scandal and dissension in the family.

SABINA Send someone for Signor Ferdinando.

Scene 4

Enter *Ferdinando.*

FERDINANDO Here I am, here I am. I'm right here, at your service.

SABINA *(angrily)* Where have you been until now?

FERDINANDO I went to the apothecary's. I had a little tummy ache, and I went to chew some dried rhubarb.[8]

SABINA *(sweetly)* And now, do you feel better?

FERDINANDO Yes, I feel a bit better.

SABINA *(as above)* The poor thing! So that's why you didn't come to my room for your hot chocolate?

BRIGIDA *(aside)* Did you ever see a more foolish and childish old woman?

FERDINANDO I'm so sorry I couldn't come. But I know you're fond of me and will find it in your heart to forgive me.

SABINA *(to Brigida)* Out you go!

BRIGIDA Certainly, madam, don't worry, I've no intention of interrupting your billing and cooing. *(exit Brigida)*

Scene 5

Ferdinando and Sabina.

SABINA *(aside)* Let them say what they will. As long as my Ferdinando adores me.

FERDINANDO *(aside)* Now, I get to pay for all the fun I had this morning!

SABINA My dear, dear Ferdinando!

FERDINANDO My dear, dear Signora Sabina!

SABINA Bring me a chair.

FERDINANDO But of course, right away. *(he brings her a chair)*

SABINA *(sitting)* Why don't you sit down?

FERDINANDO I have been sitting till now.

SABINA Sit down, I say.

FERDINANDO Is that an order?

SABINA Yes. I have the right to command you, and I command you.

FERDINANDO And I must obey, and I obey. *(he goes to get a chair)*
SABINA *(aside)* Oh, what an adorable boy!
FERDINANDO *(aside)* Oh, what a bore! How long is it going to go on? *(he brings the chair)*
SABINA *(aside)* Oh, how he cares for me!
FERDINANDO There you are, madam. *(he sits down)*
SABINA Come a bit closer.
FERDINANDO Yes, madam. *(he brings his chair a bit closer)*
SABINA Come on, come really close.
FERDINANDO But, madam ... I have been eating rhubarb ...
SABINA Oh, you rascal! I'll come closer myself. *(she does so)*
FERDINANDO *(aside)* The plague take you!
SABINA Dear boy, you must learn to have a little moderation. Watch how you eat. Last night you overindulged. Now that's all got to stop. At lunchtime, you'll sit next to me. I'll keep an eye on you. You'll eat what I give you.
FERDINANDO Oh, there's plenty of time from now until lunchtime. I may well be better by then, and ready to eat properly.
SABINA No, my pet. I want you to be careful.
FERDINANDO What time is it now?
SABINA *(showing him her watch)* Let's see. It's eleven-thirty. Take a look. Don't you carry a watch?
FERDINANDO I did have one once ... I don't know ... It didn't keep good time. So I left it behind in Leghorn.
SABINA But why did you leave it behind? A gentleman without a watch, especially in the country, cuts a very poor figure.
FERDINANDO You're absolutely right. I don't know what to do ... I am ashamed not to have one. I'm tempted to go back and get it.
SABINA If mine had a man's watch chain, I'd be happy to lend it to you.
FERDINANDO It's not hard to get hold of a steel watch chain: they sell them in Montenero.
SABINA Yes, we could find one, but then I'd have to go without a watch, wouldn't I?
FERDINANDO What's the point? Don't you think I know you said it as a joke, just to get a rise out of me? I'll go back to Leghorn ...
SABINA No, no, my dear. I really did mean it. Here, my precious, take it. I'll lend it to you, you know.
FERDINANDO We do understand one another, don't we? *(aside)* Well, she'll never see this again.
SABINA You see how much I love you?

FERDINANDO Dear Signora Sabina, you know I feel the same about you.

SABINA And if you continue to love me, you can have anything you want of mine.

FERDINANDO I don't love you for what I can get out of it. I love you because you deserve to be loved, because I find you attractive, because you are so adorable.

SABINA *(crying)* My precious, put that watch in your pocket, it's a gift.

FERDINANDO *(aside)* If I could laugh, I'd laugh my head off.

SABINA Listen, my child. I was married with a dowry of ten thousand crowns.[9] My first husband and I didn't have children. The money's mine, it's invested, it's mine to do with as I please. If you love me forever, who knows? I'm a year or two older than you … One day, it will be yours.

FERDINANDO Don't you want to get married again?

SABINA You rascal! Why do you think I love you? Do you think I'm just a flirt? If I didn't intend to get married, would I be carrying on with you like this?

FERDINANDO My dear Signora Sabina, what a fortunate man I would be!

SABINA My precious, all you have to do is say the word. It could be arranged in no time.

FERDINANDO And you really do have a dowry of ten thousand crowns?

SABINA Yes, and in the six years since I became a widow, it has been accumulating interest.

FERDINANDO And you're free to dispose of it as you please?

SABINA It's mine to do as I please with.

FERDINANDO In other words, you'd have no trouble making me a little settlement?

SABINA Settlement? Am I being asked for a settlement? Have I reached the point where I can't get married without making a settlement?

FERDINANDO But didn't you say that one day your dowry might be mine?

SABINA Yes, when I'm dead.

FERDINANDO Before or after, what's the difference?

SABINA And if we have children?

FERDINANDO *(aside)* Oh, the old fool! She still hopes to have children.

SABINA Come, sir, is this your disinterested love?

FERDINANDO I'm not speaking out of self-interest. What I mean is, if I had the use of that money, I could invest in a little shop in Leghorn, and make it earn double. Then I'd be well off. And my better half would be well off as well.

SABINA *(crying)* No, you ungrateful wretch, you don't love me.

FERDINANDO Oh, heavens! If you don't believe I love you, I'll do something crazy, I'll give way to despair.
SABINA Oh, no, my dearest, don't despair, I believe you. God bless you.
FERDINANDO I love you so much I can't bear it.
SABINA Oh, yes, I believe you, but don't ever speak of a settlement. Isn't it enough for me to have given you my heart?
FERDINANDO *(aside)* Well, maybe she'll come round in time.

Scene 6

Enter *Filippo.*

FILIPPO So, Signor Ferdinando, do you want to play a few hands of piquet now?
SABINA Oh, stop with your piquet.
FILIPPO I was not addressing you, madam. I was speaking to Signor Ferdinando.
SABINA Signor Ferdinando doesn't want to play.
FERDINANDO *(aside)* It's hard to say which one of the two is more obnoxious.
FILIPPO *(to Ferdinando)* Well, do you want to play, or don't you?
FERDINANDO *(getting to his feet)* Please excuse me.
FILIPPO Where are you off to?
FERDINANDO *(running off)* Please excuse me.
SABINA Let him go, he's been taking rhubarb.
FILIPPO He eats like a horse, then he complains of an upset stomach.
SABINA That's not true. He has a very delicate stomach, and every little excess affects it.
FILIPPO Where did he go for the rhubarb?
SABINA To the apothecary's.
FILIPPO That's not true. As soon as he went out this morning, I went to the apothecary's myself. I've been playing chequers till now, and he never showed up, so he can't have been there.
SABINA You're blind, you must have missed him.
FILIPPO I can see better than you can.
SABINA Signor Ferdinando would never tell a lie.
FILIPPO Want to know when he's telling the truth? When he goes about telling everyone that you're an old fool. *(exit Filippo)*
SABINA Liar, cantankerous malevolent old fool! I know why he said that. I know why he persecutes him. But yes, I do love him. I'll marry him, no matter what people say. *(exit Sabina)*

Scene 7

Giacinta, followed by Guglielmo.

GIACINTA Alas! Guglielmo will be my downfall. I don't know where to hide. He follows me everywhere. He doesn't give me a minute's peace.

GUGLIELMO Why are you avoiding me, Giacinta?

GIACINTA I'm not avoiding you, I'm minding my own business, I'm going my own way.

GUGLIELMO You're right, and I am so presumptuous as to follow you. Another woman, another woman not as kind as you are, would have sent me packing by now for harassing her. But you are so good, you put up with me. You know what it is that makes me so bold, and you have pity on me.

GIACINTA *(aside)* I don't know what it is about his words. They're spellbinding, they're like witchcraft.

GUGLIELMO If I believed I was really a nuisance, if I thought I could harm your reputation, I would leave right away, no matter what it cost. But, when I consider my conduct, I don't think I'm behaving so badly as to cause any scandal, or interfere with your peace of mind.

GIACINTA *(aside)* Alas, he's done me more harm than he knows.

GUGLIELMO Madam, I beseech you, just two words on the matter I mentioned.

GIACINTA This year, we can't complain. The fine weather is making our stay in the country most pleasant.

GUGLIELMO That has nothing to do with what I was saying.

GIACINTA What did you think of supper last night?

GUGLIELMO Nothing else matters to me, except to be honoured with your favour.

GIACINTA I wonder if lunch here today will match the good taste of the way we were treated last night?

GUGLIELMO Here in the house where you live, the welcome can only be of the finest. This is where true happiness lies. If I'm the only one with cause for complaint, it's my own fault, and not anyone else's.

GIACINTA *(aside)* Could any art be more insidious than this?

GUGLIELMO Signora Giacinta, forgive me if I'm causing you any distress. May I please say something?

GIACINTA *(somewhat heatedly)* I'd say that you've said all you wanted so far!

GUGLIELMO Don't be angry. I'll be silent, if you bid me be silent.
GIACINTA *(aside)* What was it he wanted to tell me?
GUGLIELMO My luck's getting worse by the minute. I can see that my words distress you. Signora, I shall withdraw.
GIACINTA What was it you wanted to say?
GUGLIELMO Do I have your permission to speak?
GIACINTA If it's something you can say, then say it.
GUGLIELMO I know how far I can go, and I won't go beyond it, I won't take advantage of your kindness. I shall tell you quite simply that I love you, but if my love could bring the slightest harm to your interests or to your peace of mind, I'm ready to sacrifice myself in any way you choose.
GIACINTA *(aside)* Who could possibly respond to so generous a proposal?
GUGLIELMO Have I said something that doesn't deserve an answer?
GIACINTA A young woman already engaged to someone else is not allowed to respond to such a statement.
GUGLIELMO On the contrary, a young woman already engaged can answer and must answer freely.
GIACINTA I think I hear somebody coming.
GUGLIELMO Yes, you have visitors. Please give me an answer. Just two words.
GIACINTA It's Signora Costanza and her niece.
GUGLIELMO I shall continue to ask until I get an answer.
GIACINTA *(aside)* I'm so flustered, I don't know how I'm going to receive these ladies. I'll have to make an effort to hide my feelings.

Scene 8

Enter *Costanza, Rosina, and Tognino.*

GUGLIEMO *(withdraws to one side)*
COSTANZA Your servant, Signora Giacinta.
GIACINTA Your servant, Signora Costanza.
ROSINA Your devoted servant.
GIACINTA Your servant, Signora Rosina.
TOGNINO Your servant, madam.
GIACINTA My respects, Signor Tognino.
COSTANZA I hope we haven't come at a bad time …
GIACINTA On the contrary, it's a pleasure, but I am afraid I'm not going to be much of a hostess.

COSTANZA Whatever are you saying? This isn't the first time I've been here to enjoy your hospitality.

GIACINTA Hello! Is there anyone out there? Chairs, please. *(servants bring in chairs. Softly to Guglielmo)* Why don't you come forward?

GUGLIELMO *(to Giacinta, aside)* I'm embarrassed.

GIACINTA Please sit down. *(they sit down)* Please, Signor Guglielmo, there's an empty chair next to you.

GUGLIELMO *(aside)* It's not for me, madam.

GIACINTA *(aside)* Who's it for, then?

GUGLIELMO *(aside)* Someone will be along very shortly who has more right to sit in it than I do.

GIACINTA *(aside)* If you insist on making a scene, I'll give you the answer I didn't have the heart to give you before.

GUGLIELMO *(aside)* I'll sit down, as you order. *(he sits down)*

COSTANZA *(aside to Rosina)* What do you think of that? She has a "mariage à la mode," too!

ROSINA *(aside)* So I see. These two bluebloods are in hot competition.

GIACINTA And what is Signor Tognino up to? Are you well?

TOGNINO Your servant, madam.

GIACINTA What is your father up to?

TOGNINO Your servant.

GIACINTA Didn't I hear he'd gone to Maremma?

TOGNINO Your servant.

GIACINTA *(softly to Guglielmo)* God, what an idiot!

GUGLIELMO *(softly to Giacinta)* But he's lucky in love.

COSTANZA I see you have one of the latest "mariages," too, Signora Giacinta.

GIACINTA Oh, just an inexpensive little dress.

COSTANZA Yes, that's true, but it's in quite good taste. At least I'm glad you're modest about it. Signora Vittoria, who has one a hundred times uglier, pretends she has something great … What a frightful dress!

GIACINTA Would you like to play something amusing? Shall we play cards? Do you play ombre, Signora Costanza?

COSTANZA Oh yes, madam.

GIACINTA And what about Rosina?

ROSINA At your service.

GIACINTA And Signor Tognino?

TOGNINO Oh, all I can play is bezique.[10]

GIACINTA Does Signora Rosina play bezique?

ROSINA Why do you want me to play bezique?

GIACINTA I don't know. I'd like to do my duty as a hostess. I wouldn't want anyone to feel left out. If you'd like to pair up with Signor Tognino ...

ROSINA Oh, there's really no need, Signora.

COSTANZA Come along, now. Signora Giacinta is a woman of breeding. We understand each other. But whether Signor Tognino plays or not doesn't matter. He can watch us play ombre, he can learn, he can watch Rosina.

GIACINTA You know better than I do, Signora Costanza, how careful one must be seating one's guests at the card tables.

COSTANZA Oh, yes, I know from experience. I know you have to put people together who do not dislike being together. It takes all my concentration. But what drives me crazy is that they sometimes fall out, either from jealousy or because they feel they've been insulted, and they scowl at each other, and no one knows why: one has a headache, the other a stomach ache, and it's all you can do to put two tables together. Along comes someone, for example, and she says: Tonight I want to play with So-and-So. Along comes another: Now, listen, don't put me at the same table as So-and-So or Such-and-Such, I couldn't stand it. And it would be all very well, if they were straightforward about it. The trouble is that half of the time, you're supposed to guess. You have to be so careful, remembering who's friends and who's enemies. Trying to balance the tables according to skill. Choosing the game everybody likes best. Sorting out the ones who leave early and those who stay late, sometimes putting the wife in one room and the husband in another.

GIACINTA Oh, so true. I have the same problem. You're so right. I think I hear a carriage. It must be Signora Vittoria and Signor Leonardo. Would you mind, Signor Guglielmo, going to see if it's them?

GUGLIELMO *(rising)* Of course, madam; what else can I do? This chair isn't for me.

GIACINTA If you'd prefer not to go, it doesn't really matter.

GUGLIELMO Don't worry. I'm a civilized young fellow, and I do know my duty. *(exit Guglielmo)*

GIACINTA *(aside)* It looks like I'm in for a difficult day!

COSTANZA Tell me, Signora Giacinta, is it true that Signor Guglielmo has proposed to Signora Vittoria?

GIACINTA So they say.

COSTANZA If she's going to be your sister-in-law, you ought to know.

GIACINTA We haven't gotten to know each other that well as yet.

COSTANZA And do you plan to get married soon?

GIACINTA I don't know. I can't tell you. What about you, Signora Costanza, when will you be giving away Signora Rosina?

COSTANZA Who knows, it might well happen.

ROSINA Oh, no, no one will have me.

TOGNINO *(softly to Rosina, nudging her forcefully)* No one?

ROSINA *(softly to Tognino)* Shut up, you clumsy oaf!

GIACINTA *(looking in the direction of Tognino)* I believe, unless I'm mistaken …

COSTANZA *(grinning with satisfaction)* Do you think so, Signora Giacinta?

ROSINA Sometimes appearances can be deceiving.

GIACINTA Signor Tognino is not a young man to play games.

TOGNINO Oh no? *(he plays a trick on Rosina, bursts out laughing then gets up and lumbers clumsily round the room)*

GIACINTA *(aside to Costanza)* I think he's a very nice boy.

COSTANZA *(aside to Giacinta)* He's not much of a wit.

GIACINTA *(aside to Costanza)* What does that matter? As long as he's in a position to support her.

COSTANZA *(aside to Giacinta)* Oh, yes, he's an only child.

Scene 9

Enter *Leonardo, and Vittoria on Guglielmo's arm. Everyone rises.*

GIACINTA *(going to meet her)* Your servant, Signora Vittoria.

VITTORIA Your servant, my dear Signora Giacinta. *(they embrace)*

LEONARDO Please forgive me, Signora Giacinta, if I'm later than usual in coming to see you this morning. I had to make some calls, and I had some other domestic matters that kept me busy. I hope you'll forgive this omission and not accuse me of neglecting you or of not caring enough.

GIACINTA I don't believe I ever gave you reason to complain of my being indiscreet. You're welcome whenever you can get here. If you can't come, far be it from me to compel you.

LEONARDO *(aside)* I don't know whether it's discretion or indifference.

GIACINTA Please, sit down. *(Costanza, Rosina, and Tognino sit back down in their places)* Signor Guglielmo, won't you sit next to Vittoria?

GUGLIELMO As you wish. *(he sits next to Vittoria, Giacinta sits next to Guglielmo, Leonardo sits next to Giacinta)*

VITTORIA This morning, Signor Guglielmo neglected to pay me a visit.
GUGLIELMO To tell you the truth, madam, I wasn't able to do so.
VITTORIA I'm also aware that you stayed in all morning.
GUGLIELMO Very true, madam, I had some urgent letters to write.
VITTORIA There was pen and ink at our house.
GUGLIELMO I would never take such a liberty.
VITTORIA *(irritated)* Of course, my dear friend, I understand.
GIACINTA Signora Vittoria, you shouldn't be so touchy.
LEONARDO Why don't you follow Signora Giacinta's example? She's understanding personified. She never complains that she gets too few visits!
GIACINTA I don't believe any man likes to be nagged.
LEONARDO And yet, there are some men who are glad to hear themselves reproached, and they sometimes take that reproach as a sign of affection.
GIACINTA Everyone takes things differently, and I can't stand pretence.
LEONARDO Now that I know your mind, I shall put myself out much less in order to see you.
GIACINTA You're quite free to do as you please.
COSTANZA *(aside to Rosina)* Something tells me this marriage will not be a love match.
ROSINA *(aside to Costanza)* I agree: more a marriage of duty than one of affection.

Scene 10

Enter *Sabina on Ferdinando's arm.*

TOGNINO *(aside to Rosina)* Oh, oh, here comes the old dowager.
ROSINA *(aside to Costanza)* The old dowager.
COSTANZA *(aside to Rosina)* Yes, with her young Cupid.
SABINA Your most humble servant, ladies and gentlemen.
VITTORIA Your servant, Signora Sabina.
COSTANZA My respects, Signora Sabina.
ROSINA How are you, Signora Sabina?
SABINA Well, well, I'm well. What pleasant company! *(pointing to Tognino)* And who's that young man?
TOGNINO Your servant, Signora Sabina.
SABINA Greetings, my dear. Who are you?

ROSINA Don't you know him? It's the doctor's son.

SABINA What doctor?

COSTANZA The doctor, our doctor.

SABINA Good, good, I'm delighted. What a charming young fellow. *(to Rosina)* Is he married?

ROSINA No, madam.

SABINA *(to Tognino)* How old are you?

TOGNINO Sixteen.

SABINA How is it you never come to see us?

ROSINA He's too busy.

COSTANZA He has to study.

ROSINA He never goes out.

SABINA Yes, yes, I see. Good for you! Mum's the word. Don't worry, you can count on my discretion. I'm not one of those people! Ferdinando!

FERDINANDO Yes, madam?

SABINA My precious, give me my handkerchief.

FERDINANDO Would you like the white one?

SABINA Yes, the white one. I was in a draught last night, and this eye is tearing a little.

FERDINANDO There you are. *(he gives her the handkerchief, a little put out)*

SABINA *(to Ferdinando)* What is it? You seem a little upset.

FERDINANDO *(aside to Sabina)* Oh, nothing, madam.

SABINA *(aside to Ferdinando)* Are you annoyed that I spoke to that young man?

FERDINANDO Of course not, madam. *(aside)* I'm annoyed at having to make a fool of myself in public.

SABINA *(aside to Ferdinando)* There, there, my dearest, don't be jealous, I won't talk to anyone else.

FERDINANDO *(aside)* You can talk to the devil for all I care.

SABINA *(aside to Ferdinando)* Here, take my handkerchief.

FERDINANDO *(aside)* Those ten thousand crowns are eating my heart out.

SABINA *(aside)* I'm not saying he should get the whole thing, but I should give him something.

GIACINTA Come now, ladies and gentlemen, would you like to play something? Would you like to play a hand or two of cards?

VITTORIA I'll play whatever game the rest of you want to play.

COSTANZA Let Signora Giacinta decide.

SABINA *(to Giacinta)* Count me out. I've already chosen my partner.

GIACINTA And what would my aunt like to play?

SABINA Tresette with Signor Ferdinando.[11]

FERDINANDO *(aside)* Oh, heaven help me! Now I'm in for it. *(to Sabina)* Madam, it's such a boring game.

SABINA Oh, no, sir. It's a wonderful game. In any case, what's the point of complaining? You're going to have to play with me anyway.

FERDINANDO *(aside)* This is not going to be easy!

SABINA *(to Giacinta)* Do you hear? I'm already spoken for.

GIACINTA Very well. Signora Vittoria, Signora Costanza, and Signor Guglielmo can play three-handed ombre.[12]

COSTANZA *(aside)* She didn't have to put me at the same table with that "mariage" woman.

VITTORIA *(aside, to herself)* Putting me next to her! She hasn't a clue how to set up the tables.

GUGLIELMO *(aside, to Giacinta)* Am I not worthy to play with you?

GIACINTA *(aside, to Guglielmo)* I'm surprised you have the gall to address me. *(out loud)* Signor Leonardo, Signora Rosina, and I will make up another table of ombre.

ROSINA As you wish. *(aside, to herself)* I'll probably be treated to another fine scene.

GIACINTA Are you happy, Signor Leonardo?

LEONARDO Me? It makes absolutely no difference to me.

GIACINTA If you'd like to sit at another table, please help yourself.

LEONARDO You decide, if you think the players are not well distributed.

GIACINTA I can't always know exactly what's on people's minds.

LEONARDO All I want to do is please you, but you don't make it easy.

GIACINTA Oh, it's easier than you think. Hello! Is anyone there? *(enter servants)*

GUGLIELMO Set up three tables. Two for ombre, one for tresette. *(the servants set up the tables)*

VITTORIA *(to Guglielmo)* Signor Guglielmo, you seem a bit out of sorts.

GUGLIELMO Didn't you know, madam? It's my melancholy nature.

VITTORIA You're not very affectionate, Signor Guglielmo.

GUGLIELMO On the contrary, I am more enamoured than you think.

VITTORIA *(aside)* Well, he's finally said something nice.

GIACINTA *(aside, to Guglielmo)* Good for you, Signor Guglielmo, I'm glad to hear you're in love with Signora Vittoria.

GUGLIELMO *(aside, to Giacinta)* Everyone is free to interpret things as he or she chooses.

LEONARDO *(aside, to Giacinta)* Signora Giacinta, what was that you whispered to Signor Guglielmo?

GIACINTA *(aside, to Leonardo)* Am I supposed to give you an account of my every word?

LEONARDO *(aside, to Giacinta)* I get the impression that you two are a bit too familiar.

GIACINTA *(aside, to Leonardo)* These offensive suspicions are not very ingratiating.

LEONARDO *(aside, to himself)* My position's a little too painful.

GIACINTA Come along, people, everything's ready. It's getting late. If we don't hurry, they'll soon be serving lunch.

SABINA I'm ready, for one. Let's go, "Ferdinandino."

FERDINANDO Here I am, at your service. *(aside, to himself)* I can put up with her this one time. *(he goes to sit at the back table with Sabina)*

VITTORIA Would you mind taking my hand, Signor Guglielmo?

GUGLIELMO At your service.

VITTORIA Won't you sit down, Signora Costanza?

COSTANZA *(aside)* She wants to sit on the side away from the wall, so she doesn't spoil her fine dress. *(they all sit down)*

GIACINTA Won't you join us, Signora Rosina? …

ROSINA Here I am. *(aside, to Tognino)* Tognino, come over here with me.

TOGNINO Very well, madam. *(aside)* I wish it were lunchtime! *(all sit down and start playing)*

Scene 11

Enter *Filippo.*

FILIPPO Your servant, ladies and gentlemen. *(they all acknowledge him without getting up)* Isn't there anything for me to do? Everyone's playing; isn't there a place for me at one of the tables?

GIACINTA Do you want to play, Father?

FILIPPO Isn't that what it looks like!

GIACINTA Hello! Bring another table. Go play bezique with Signor Tognino.

FILIPPO Bezique?

GIACINTA There's no other choice. Bezique's the only game Signor Tognino knows how to play.

FILIPPO Can't I play with somebody else? Can't I play piquet with Signor Ferdinando?

SABINA Signor Ferdinando already has a partner.

FILIPPO A fine state of affairs!

ROSINA Dear Signor Filippo, won't you be nice and play with Tognino?

FILIPPO I suppose I've no choice. *(to Tognino)* Let's go and play bezique, then.

TOGNINO I'm telling you now: no more than a penny a hand.

FILIPPO Yes, let's go. We'll play for a penny. *(they go over to the table. Filippo calls a servant, who then exits)* Hello there! Go to the kitchen, tell the cook to hurry up and serve the food, whether it's done or not. *(aside)* Imagine me spending an hour here playing bezique with this blockhead! *(he sits at the table with Tognino and they begin to play)*

VITTORIA *(to Guglielmo)* Couldn't you at least have stopped by this morning to say hello?

GUGLIELMO But didn't I tell you, madam, that I didn't go out this morning?

VITTORIA Yes, you told me. You seem to enjoy staying indoors. I'm beginning to think that you are a bit too attached to this house.

GUGLIELMO I don't know what grounds you have for saying so.

COSTANZA All right, people, are we playing or aren't we?

GUGLIELMO Signora Costanza is right.

VITTORIA *(aside)* Any minute now, I'm throwing down my hand on the table.

GIACINTA *(aside)* Unless my ears deceive me, Vittoria is set on creating a scene.

LEONARDO Why don't you pay attention to your game, Signora Giacinta?

ROSINA Come on and play. I led spades.

GIACINTA I trump.

ROSINA What do you mean, you trump? When trumps led just now, you couldn't follow!

LEONARDO How can she follow? Her mind's not on the game.

GIACINTA I'm doing my duty as a hostess. I can hear someone complaining, and I don't know what about.

LEONARDO *(aside)* I can't wait for this cursed vacation to end.

SABINA Ha, ha, I blitzed him, a blitz, I blitzed him![13]

FERDINANDO Bully for you. You blitzed me.

VITTORIA *(to Guglielmo)* Signora Giacinta can't take her eyes off our table.

GUGLIELMO The hostess has to keep an eye on everybody.

VITTORIA That's right, you go ahead and defend her. Trumps!

COSTANZA That is not a trump, madam!

VITTORIA How am I supposed to know what the devil I'm playing?

COSTANZA *(out loud)* Exactly, this is no way to play.

GIACINTA What's the matter, Signora Costanza?

COSTANZA Is this any way …

VITTORIA *(laughing)* Mind your own game, Signora Giacinta.

GIACINTA Excuse me. I can hear them complaining …

TOGNINO Three of a kind, three of a kind!

FILIPPO *(exasperated)* All right! All right! Three of a kind!

GIACINTA *(softly to Leonardo)* Signora Vittoria doesn't seem to like me very much.

LEONARDO *(softly to Giacinta)* What can I say? In any case, she's going to be married.

GIACINTA When?

LEONARDO Maybe it won't be too long.

GIACINTA Do you hope that Signor Guglielmo will marry her?

LEONARDO If Signor Guglielmo doesn't marry my sister, he won't be visiting your house any more either.

GIACINTA Is that so?

LEONARDO Yes, that's so.

ROSINA *(to Giacinta)* Come on, play!

VITTORIA *(aside)* I think they're talking about me.

Scene 12

Enter *servant.*

SERVANT Ladies and gentlemen, luncheon is served. *(exit servant)*

COSTANZA Thank heavens! *(she gets up)*

SABINA I want to finish my game.

FILIPPO Finish it, then; we're going in to lunch. *(he gets up)*

FERDINANDO By your leave, madam, I'm hungry. *(he gets up)*

SABINA Good for you! The rhubarb has had its effect. *(she gets up)*

TOGNINO Three pennies, Signor Filippo!

FILIPPO *(aside)* The idiot! *(out loud)* Come along, please, let's go in.

GIACINTA After you, ladies and gentlemen.

VITTORIA After you.

ROSINA I'm not going in first, that's for sure.

SABINA Come along, now, no more standing on ceremony. Your hand, Signor Ferdinando.

FERDINANDO At your service. *(he gives her his arm)*

SABINA By your leave. *(she curtseys to the group)*

FERDINANDO And if anyone's jealous, he can just eat his heart out! *(exit Ferdinando with Sabina)*

GIACINTA Come, after you, Signora Vittoria.

VITTORIA *(to Guglielmo, asking if she may take his arm)* May I?

GUGLIELMO *(offering her his arm)* At your service.

VITTORIA Allow me, bear with me.

GUGLIELMO *(aside)* Yes, I'm bearing with more than she thinks. *(exit Guglielmo with Vittoria)*

GIACINTA *(to Costanza and Rosina)* After you, ladies.

COSTANZA You go first, Rosina.

ROSINA Let's go, Tognino.

TOGNINO *(aside)* I'm going to eat my head off! *(exit Tognino with Rosina)*

COSTANZA *(about to leave, to Giacinta)* By your leave.

FILIPPO *(to Costanza)* May I have the honour of accompanying you?

COSTANZA *(to Filippo)* It's my pleasure.

FILIPPO *(to Costanza)* If you will.

COSTANZA *(to Filippo)* Honoured, sir.

FILIPPO Poor me, I am entitled to some consideration, too! *(giving her his arm)*

COSTANZA Poor Signor Filippo, he's entitled to some consideration, too! *(exit Costanza with Filippo)*

GIACINTA *(to Leonardo)* Shall we go in?

LEONARDO *(to Giacinta)* Shall I offer you my arm?

GIACINTA If you don't think I deserve it, you don't have to.

LEONARDO Oh, how cruel you are!

GIACINTA Let's not make a scene, Signor Leonardo.

LEONARDO I love you too much, Giacinta.

GIACINTA Yes, too much, when you consider my merits.

LEONARDO And you love me very little …

GIACINTA I love you as much as I can, as much as I'm able.

LEONARDO Don't drive me to despair.

GIACINTA I said: Let's not make a scene. *(she takes his arm and pulls him forcibly towards the door)*

LEONARDO *(aside)* Oh, pitiless fate! *(exit Leonardo with Giacinta)*

GIACINTA *(aside)* Oh, love, oh, engagement, oh, miserable stay in the country! *(exit Giacinta with Leonardo)*

ACT THREE

Scene 1

A wood. Brigida and Paolino.

BRIGIDA Here, here, Signor Paolino. Let's stop here and enjoy the shade.

PAOLINO What if my master's looking for me and can't find me?

BRIGIDA At the moment, they're all in the dining room having coffee. After their coffee, they'll play cards. Stay here with me for a while, that is, if my company doesn't bore you.

PAOLINO Oh, my dear Signora Brigida, I'm very fond of your company.

BRIGIDA I was really looking forward to spending half an hour or so with you.

PAOLINO You have to admit, it's easier to find the right moment, free time, and suitable places to be alone together, when you're in the country.

BRIGIDA Our masters and our mistresses can find them, so why can't we?

PAOLINO You're right, things happen in the country that wouldn't happen so easily in town.

BRIGIDA Something happened to my mistress, and I'll bet it'll be a long time before she gets over it.

PAOLINO What happened?

BRIGIDA I'm afraid I can't talk about it, but if I did tell you, it would make your hair stand on end.

PAOLINO I have to admit, something certainly has happened. My master is all on edge, and Signora Giacinta seems to be living in a daze. I was behind them, you know, serving at table, and I can tell you that between the two of them they didn't eat more than a mouthful.

BRIGIDA Who was on the other side of my mistress?

PAOLINO Signor Guglielmo.

BRIGIDA Oh, curse him! Can't he leave her alone? He'll be the ruin of this household.

PAOLINO Maybe there's something going on between him and your mistress?

BRIGIDA Oh, no, not a thing. And where was Signora Vittoria?

PAOLINO She was next to Signor Guglielmo, too.

BRIGIDA Oh, what a rascal! To go and sit between the two of them.

PAOLINO Every now and then, with that pathetic expression of his, he would say a few words to Signora Giacinta, but I couldn't make anything out.

BRIGIDA Did Signor Leonardo notice?

PAOLINO I think he did, once. In fact, when he gave me his plate to change, he did it so brusquely that he caught Signora Giacinta on the shoulder and got a few stains on her dress.

BRIGIDA He stained her new dress? My mistress must have been furious.

PAOLINO Oh, no, she passed it off with complete unconcern.

BRIGIDA That's amazing! She's obviously got something more important on her mind than her dress.

PAOLINO In fact, my master wanted to wipe it off, but she wouldn't let him.

BRIGIDA And to think that tidiness is her passion. Oh, poor girl! She's really not herself.

PAOLINO I'd be willing to bet that favourable circumstances and the opportune moment have made her fall in love with Signor Guglielmo.

BRIGIDA Get on with you! What on earth are you saying? How could you? Isn't she engaged to Signor Leonardo? And isn't there an understanding between Signor Guglielmo and Signora Vittoria?

PAOLINO Oh, I think my mistress is fooling herself. All she did at table was badger Signor Guglielmo, and he didn't answer. He didn't pay her the slightest attention.

BRIGIDA Was he talking to my mistress?

PAOLINO I'll say he was talking! At times with his mouth, at times with his elbow, at times with his feet.

BRIGIDA Oh, my goodness! If I'd been there, I'm not sure I could have kept from hitting him over the head with a plate.

PAOLINO You see? If there was nothing between them, you'd have no call to get so worked up.

BRIGIDA Come on, now. Let's talk about something else. I imagine the old dowager was sitting next to that snake-in-the-grass Ferdinando.

PAOLINO Yes, of course she was. And all she did was whisper sweet nothings in his ear, while he ate, or, to put it more accurately, wolfed down his food, as if he hadn't had a bite for four days.

BRIGIDA And my poor mistress didn't eat anything?

PAOLINO How could she, trapped as she was between husband and lover?

BRIGIDA Come along, now, don't talk like that. How did Signora Costanza and Signora Rosina acquit themselves at the table?

PAOLINO Well, they didn't acquit themselves badly, but the one who really tucked in with a vengeance, almost outdoing Signor Ferdinando, was that charmer Tognino.

BRIGIDA Was he next to his Rosina?

PAOLINO That goes without saying. And what a time they had! They never stopped whispering. Enough to make you sick to your stomach.

BRIGIDA That's another wedding in the offing.

PAOLINO It certainly looks that way.

BRIGIDA And that's another friendship that began in the country. If Signora Rosina hadn't come here, she'd have had trouble finding a match in Leghorn. As for me, I've been coming for years, and

I'm still the way I always was. All I can say is, either I have no saving graces, or maybe I'm just unlucky.

PAOLINO Signora Brigida, would you like to get married?

BRIGIDA I have the same desires other girls have, at least those who don't plan to go into a convent.

PAOLINO Where there's a will, there's a way.

BRIGIDA In my case, all I know is that so far I haven't been able to find it. And yet, I'm still young. I may not be a beauty, but I don't think I'm unsightly. I'm as capable as the next girl, and maybe more than most. My dowry, including savings and personal effects, must add up to three or four hundred crowns, and still nobody is courting me, nobody wants me.

PAOLINO I'm sorry I've got to go now, otherwise I might have something to say to you on that subject.

BRIGIDA Say what you have to say, don't leave me here in suspense.

PAOLINO I'm sorry to see you wasting your time like this.

BRIGIDA Do you have something else to propose?

PAOLINO I might have … but …

BRIGIDA But what?

PAOLINO I'm not sure you'd want to hear it.

BRIGIDA If I can't have a gentleman, a proper, genteel man like yourself, I'd just as soon stay as I am.

PAOLINO Signora Brigida, we'll talk about it later.

BRIGIDA Tonight, while they're socializing.

PAOLINO Yes, we'll have all the time we need. I'll come to your house, and we'll come out here in the woods.

BRIGIDA Oh, I don't know about the woods at night …

PAOLINO Go on, I was teasing. I'm a gentleman, I respect you, I hope things work out for the best.

BRIGIDA You make me so happy …

PAOLINO Farewell then, farewell. Till tonight. *(exit Paolino)*

BRIGIDA Who knows, maybe the country has something good in store for me, too, this year? *(exit Brigida)*

Scene 2

Giacinta alone.

GIACINTA I need to breathe for a moment. I must have a moment to myself. Let them play if that's what they want. Nothing interests me, nothing amuses me; on the contrary, everything irks me, everything sets me on edge. A fine stay in the country I'm having this year! Who would ever have thought it! Me! I used to laugh at other women pining for love, and now I've fallen harder than any of them. But why? – What a fool I was! – Why did I let myself be persuaded so quickly and easily to give my word to Leonardo, and allow them to draw up the contract? Yes, that was my mistake. I was in too much of a hurry to get married, more to be free from my father's authority than out of real desire for a husband. I thought the little love I felt for Leonardo was enough for a civilized marriage, I never thought I could fall this much in love. But now, I have to find a way out. This friendship can't go on like this any longer. I'm promised to somebody else. He must be my husband, whether I like it or not. I've got to conquer my passion. This stay in the country will end. In Leghorn, I can keep out of Guglielmo's way. I'll avoid any possibility of meeting him. How could I fail to forget him, given enough time? But, in the meantime, how am I to live here in the country? Things have reached such a point I'm afraid I won't be able to hide my feelings. A hundred eyes are on me; everyone's watching. Leonardo's suspicious. Vittoria's afraid of me. The old dowager's irresponsible, and I can't keep dissembling forever. Oh, heaven, heaven help me! I beseech you, I beseech you with all my heart.

Scene 3

Enter *Guglielmo.*

GUGLIELMO So. I've found you at last.

GIACINTA What do you want from me? Can't you leave me alone even here?

GUGLIELMO I'll leave you alone, never fear. But allow me to say two words only.

GIACINTA *(looking around her)* Hurry up, then.

GUGLIELMO I beg you to give me the answer I asked for this morning.

GIACINTA I don't remember the question.

GUGLIELMO Then I'll ask it again.

GIACINTA You don't have to.

GUGLIELMO So you remember perfectly well.

GIACINTA Go away, I implore you, and leave me in peace.

GUGLIELMO Just two words, and I'll leave right away.

GIACINTA *(aside)* Oh, what art, what enchantment is this? *(to Guglielmo)* So?

GUGLIELMO Am I to live or to die?

GIACINTA Are these questions for me to answer?

GUGLIELMO I must ask the person who has the power to command me.

GIACINTA Do you expect me to break my word to Signor Leonardo, and make a spectacle of myself in front of everybody?

GUGLIELMO I do not make so bold as to expect anything, only to plead.

GIACINTA You would do better to remain silent.

GUGLIELMO Don't expect me to quit without getting a definite answer.

GIACINTA All right then. If we must talk about it, let's talk. Consider this, Signor Guglielmo, that you and I are two unhappy people, both of us unhappy for the same reason. If all there was to our unhappiness was that it made us suffer, we might even bear it, but the worst thing is that we risk losing other people's respect, our good name, our honour. I neglect my duty by listening to you, you neglect yours by laying snares for my heart. I'm neglecting my filial respect, my duty as a wife-to-be, and my obligation to act like a decent, well-bred young woman. You're neglecting the laws of friendship, hospitality, and good faith. What will people say about us? How will we look in their eyes? Think of yourself, and think of me, too. If it's true that you love me, don't ruin me. Could you have a heart so cruel that you would sacrifice to your passion a poor unfortunate woman, who has had the weakness to open her breast to love's blandishments? Could you have a heart so black that you would fool my father, betray Leonardo, and deceive his sister? And what do you get out of all this? What reward do you expect for such shameful conduct? You can count on everything else, except my going back on my original promise. Yes, to my shame I confess it, I love you. But this confession is all you'll ever get out of me. Rest assured that I'll do everything I can in the future to forget you. I won't allow myself to be consumed by my passion and die. Whatever it costs, we must separate forever. If you have the imprudence to keep after me, I'll have the courage to find a way to shame you. I'll do my duty, even though you won't do yours. You insisted that I speak, now I've spoken. You wanted to know how I felt, now you know. You asked whether you should live or die. My answer is, I don't know what's going to happen to me, but one must value one's honour more than life itself.

GUGLIELMO *(aside)* Alas! I don't know where I am! She's confused me so much, I don't know what to answer.

GIACINTA *(aside)* Oh! What an effort I've had to make! What torment, what torture it costs me!

Scene 4

Enter *Leonardo.*

LEONARDO What! You ... out here ... Signora?

GIACINTA *(aside)* Oh my God!

LEONARDO What secret business brings you out here to meet with Signor Guglielmo?

GUGLIELMO *(aside)* Oh! Now I'm ruined for sure!

GIACINTA *(aside)* My honour's at stake, I must be brave. *(to Leonardo)* The business I have with him should concern you more than me. The honour I have of being your bride-to-be makes your family's interests my own. The word is out in Montenero that there have been promises exchanged between him and Signora Vittoria. I know that she's under this impression and has shown her affection in public. These are extremely delicate matters, on which a young woman's reputation may depend. I wasn't sure where Signor Guglielmo stood. I've been trying to find out, and this is what I've discovered. He's perfectly well aware that a man of honour ought not to take advantage of an honest girl's weakness. He knows his duty, his respect for her is appropriate to your family's position, and if you'll give him her hand, he's asking her to be his wife through me.

GUGLIELMO *(aside)* Oh my God! What a fix I've got myself into!

LEONARDO *(to Giacinta)* He's asking for her hand through you?

GIACINTA Yes, sir, through me.

LEONARDO Couldn't he find someone else besides you to ask?

GIACINTA I'm the one who talked to him. Signor Guglielmo knows what I told him. My words must have made an impression on him as a man of honour, with an honest and decent heart. It's only right that I should be the one to perform an action of this kind, an action that is bound to be applauded by everyone.

LEONARDO What does Signor Guglielmo have to say for himself?

GUGLIELMO *(aside)* Passion must give way before duty. *(to Leonardo)* Yes, my friend, if you will be so good as to grant it, I ask for your sister's hand in marriage.

GIACINTA *(aside)* Oh, his conscience has gotten the better of him.

LEONARDO *(to Guglielmo)* Sir, I will give you your answer tonight.

GIACINTA What's to prevent your promising her to him right away?

LEONARDO It's only right I should speak to my sister.

GIACINTA She's bound to be agreeable.

LEONARDO *(to Giacinta)* Come, madam. They're waiting for us for the evening stroll.

GIACINTA Let's go, by all means.

LEONARDO May I offer you my arm?

GIACINTA I'm surprised you keep making these scenes. Must you be so formal? If you don't give me your arm, who will?

LEONARDO You came out here without me ...

GIACINTA And now I want to go back to the house with you. *(she takes his arm forcibly) (aside)* Pretending doesn't come cheap!

LEONARDO *(aside)* I'm still not completely satisfied. *(exit Leonardo, accompanying Giacinta)*

GUGLIELMO Whoever saw a more singular and sadder case than mine? *(exit Guglielmo)*

Scene 5

A room in Filippo's house. Filippo and Vittoria.

VITTORIA Come over here, Signor Filippo. I'd like to have a word with you in private, here where no one can hear us.

FILIPPO Certainly, madam. In the drawing room, I might as well be a statue anyway. They're playing faro, and I don't play faro.

VITTORIA Pray tell me, where is Signora Giacinta at this moment?

FILIPPO I've no idea where she is. I don't follow her around. You think it's easy to keep an eye on you girls in the country?

VITTORIA And where is Signor Guglielmo?

FILIPPO Worse still! Do you think I know where everyone who is staying in my house goes?

VITTORIA The point is, sir, that both of them are missing.

FILIPPO Both of whom?

VITTORIA Signor Guglielmo and Signora Giacinta.

FILIPPO What of it? One of them's one place, the other another.

VITTORIA And what if they were both together?

FILIPPO Oh, if that's what you're getting at, my daughter is no coquette.

VITTORIA I'm not saying that she is. All I know is that at the gaming table, they're the only topic of conversation, and seeing that both of them have disappeared …

FILIPPO Disappeared?

VITTORIA They're both missing, and nobody knows where they are.

FILIPPO My goodness, my goodness. What does Signor Leonardo have to say about this?

VITTORIA My brother has gone out looking for them.

FILIPPO If I find anything … If I discover … I'm going this instant … But here comes Signor Leonardo, let's hear what he has to say.

Scene 6

Enter *Leonardo.*

LEONARDO Signor Filippo, would you be so kind as to allow me to write a letter?

FILIPPO Make yourself at home. You'll find pen, ink, and paper over there.

VITTORIA *(aside)* He seems distressed. Something must have happened.

FILIPPO Tell me, Signor Leonardo, do you know where my daughter is?

LEONARDO *(sitting down at the writing desk)* Yes, sir.

FILIPPO Where is she?

LEONARDO *(as above)* Downstairs, in the drawing room.

FILIPPO And where has she been until now?

LEONARDO *(as above)* She went out to call on our farm manager's wife. She came down with a fever last night.

FILIPPO Whom did she go with?

LEONARDO By herself.

FILIPPO She went by herself?

LEONARDO Yes, sir.

FILIPPO Didn't Signor Guglielmo go with her?

LEONARDO Why should Signor Guglielmo go with her? Can't she go to the farm manager's on her own? If she needed company, couldn't I have gone with her?

FILIPPO Do you hear that, Signora Vittoria?

VITTORIA *(to Leonardo)* You heard what they were saying in the drawing room. I know you were upset by it, too.

LEONARDO We're quick to think evil, we're all too ready to jump to unwarranted conclusions. I went out to look for her, I found her alone at the farm manager's wife's, and I accompanied her back to the house myself. *(aside)* I have to explain it this way. Not everyone would be convinced by their explanation of why they were in the wood. I'm not entirely convinced myself. *(starting to write)*

FILIPPO Did you hear, Signora Vittoria. My daughter is not capable …

VITTORIA *(to Leonardo)* Is Signor Guglielmo back too?

LEONARDO *(writing)* He's back.

VITTORIA *(to Leonardo)* And where had he been?

LEONARDO *(as above)* I don't know.

VITTORIA *(ironically, to Leonardo)* Maybe he went to call on the farm manager!

LEONARDO *(as above)* Be prudent, Sister, be prudent!

VITTORIA *(to Leonardo)* Prudence isn't my strong point, and I wouldn't want you to have too much.

LEONARDO Let me finish this letter.

VITTORIA Are you writing to Leghorn?

LEONARDO I'm writing wherever I please. Signor Filippo, I'd like to ask you a favour. Would you be so kind as to send one of your servants to look for my valet, and to tell him to come here right away. If I'm not here when he arrives, I'll be at the coffee house this evening, and he should be sure to meet me there.

FILIPPO Yes, sir. I'll go right away. *(aside to Signora Vittoria)* Signora Vittoria, I'll thank you to have a better opinion of me, and my family, and my household. That's all. A word to the wise! *(exit Filippo)*

Scene 7

Leonardo writing, Vittoria.

LEONARDO *(aside, then writing)* This looks like the best thing to do.

VITTORIA Tell me, Brother, are you pleased with Signora Giacinta's behaviour?

LEONARDO *(writing)* Yes, madam.

VITTORIA You shouldn't be too pleased, considering the way things look.

LEONARDO *(writing)* I couldn't be more pleased.

VITTORIA And with Signor Guglielmo?

LEONARDO *(writing)* With him, too.

VITTORIA You think he's behaving well, also?

LEONARDO *(writing)* Signor Guglielmo is a gentleman and a man of honour.

VITTORIA And yet, I know that everyone else …

LEONARDO *(angrily)* Will you please let me write, you never- ending nuisance!

VITTORIA Let me tell you one thing, then I'll get out of your way.

LEONARDO *(writing)* What is it you want to say?

VITTORIA Didn't he once say he felt some attraction for me?

LEONARDO *(writing)* Yes, madam.

VITTORIA And how can you believe it?

LEONARDO *(writing)* I can believe it.

VITTORIA You can believe it?

LEONARDO *(aside, continuing to write)* Oh, you're beginning to get on my nerves!

VITTORIA Has he pursued the matter further with you?

LEONARDO *(as above)* Yes, he has.

VITTORIA He has?

LEONARDO *(as above)* Yes. Now let me finish.

VITTORIA And nobody tells me a thing about it? …

LEONARDO I'll tell you, if you let me finish this letter.

VITTORIA Go ahead, finish. *(aside)* I don't know what to believe. I may have been mistaken. Maybe my jealousy got the better of me. *(to Leonardo)* When did Signor Guglielmo speak to you?

LEONARDO Once and for all, will you be quiet? I wish your tongue would dry up. *(aside)* An effective letter takes some thought, and she keeps on tormenting me. *(he reads the letter over to himself)*

VITTORIA *(aside to herself)* I'm burning up, I'm dying of curiosity.

LEONARDO *(aside, to himself)* Yes, yes, that's good. It will seem natural. As long as it's properly handled.

Scene 8

Enter *Brigida.*

BRIGIDA They've finished playing. They want to go out for a stroll to the coffee house, and they sent me to ask if you'd like to go with them.

LEONARDO *(getting up)* Let's join the others.

VITTORIA Don't you have something to tell me?

LEONARDO I'll talk to you later this evening.

VITTORIA Give me a clue at least.

LEONARDO This is neither the time nor the place.
VITTORIA But I can't wait!
LEONARDO You've got to be the most impatient woman in the world! *(exit Leonardo)*

Scene 9

Vittoria and Brigida.

VITTORIA Tell me, Brigida, where did your mistress go today after lunch?
BRIGIDA How should I know? I haven't the faintest idea.
VITTORIA And how is the farm manager's wife?
BRIGIDA The farm manager's wife? As far as I know, she's fine.
VITTORIA Didn't she come down with a fever last night?
BRIGIDA What fever? Then how come she helped out in the kitchen for today's lunch?
VITTORIA *(aside)* What did I tell you? They're all pulling my leg, they're all making a fool of me. But that stupid brother of mine really makes me sick!
BRIGIDA Aren't you going to the coffee house with the others?
VITTORIA Did Signor Guglielmo and Signora Giacinta come back together?
BRIGIDA I know nothing about it. I'm not the person to ask. My mistress is an honest and well-bred young woman, and, if there are good-for-nothing young men, you can't blame well-behaved and decent young women. If you want to go, go. If you don't, I've done my duty. *(exit Brigida)*
VITTORIA She makes me even more suspicious. That's enough. It won't be long till it's evening. Let's hear what Leonardo has to say. My lips are sealed. But if they force me to talk, they'll hear things they never heard before. *(exit Vittoria)*

Scene 10

A country scene with a coffee house and one or two houses. Two or three benches for the patrons. Tita and Beltrame, coffee house waiters.

BELTRAME Tita, do you have a good appetite?
TITA I'll say I do! I can't wait till suppertime!

Beltrame This morning, at Signor Filippo's, we thought we'd get a good spread; and there wasn't enough to take the edge off your hunger.

Tita The plates came back from the table sparkling clean. They didn't even leave the bones.

Beltrame And what did we get, of the little left over?

Tita They took the lot – the farm manager, the farm manager's wife, the washerwoman, the other servants, they all wanted their share.

Beltrame Don't forget, they did us the favour of making a soup just for us.

Tita What a soup! It tasted like dishwater.

Beltrame The wine was atrocious!

Tita The watered-down wine they give to the wounded!

Beltrame If there'd only been bread …

Tita If you wanted bread, you had to go down on your hands and knees!

Beltrame I did get my hands on a nice piece of beef, and to tell you the truth, it was like cutting butter.

Tita And I spotted a bony piece of chicken which luckily still had a whole wing left on it, I wolfed it down in two bites.

Beltrame The macaroni wasn't bad.

Tita I liked those meatballs as well.

Beltrame If the roast had been hot, it wouldn't have been half bad.

Tita Yes, it was milk-fed veal. I wrapped a piece up for tonight.

Beltrame I got four pies and a hunk of Parmesan cheese.

Tita But if it'd been a proper lunch, we could have carried out a whole tablecloth full of food.

Beltrame And if there hadn't been so many eyes on us.

Tita I know just what you mean. If there was anything left on the plates, the house servants watched us like hawks, in case we put the stuff in our pockets.

Beltrame I'm not one of those people who line their pockets with leather![14]

Tita You won't catch me stooping that low, either. I eat what's available, if there's anything available; if not, better luck next time.

Beltrame A bit more, a bit less, the main thing is to survive.

Tita Oh, here comes company, let's make ourselves scarce.

Beltrame Here comes the old dowager, ahead of them all.

Tita My God, can she eat, the old dowager!

Beltrame What about Signor Ferdinando?

Tita And your cute little Signor Tognino?

Beltrame Hey, did you see how well he handled himself with that girl?

TITA You bet I did!
BELTRAME If it comes off, it's going to be some marriage!
TITA Appetite hitched to starvation! *(exit Tita)*
BELTRAME Want and necessity spliced! *(exit Beltrame)*

Scene 11

Enter *the following couples: Sabina and Ferdinando, Giacinta and Leonardo, Vittoria and Guglielmo, Rosina and Tognino, Costanza and Filippo. They sit down. One of the two waiters comes in and takes their orders, going from one to the next. They order.*

GIACINTA Coffee.
LEONARDO A glass of cold water.
ROSINA An iced lime drink.
TOGNINO A cup of hot chocolate.
VITTORIA Coffee with no sugar.
COSTANZA Lemonade.
FILIPPO Water with lime juice.
FERDINANDO A glass of rosolio cordial.
SABINA And bring me a fruit sherbet.
VITTORIA *(aside to Guglielmo)* You know what my brother's going to say, and you don't want to be the one to tell me?
GUGLIELMO *(aside to Vittoria)* Forgive me, madam, it's up to him, it's not my prerogative.
VITTORIA *(aside to Guglielmo)* If you really cared for me, you'd be more obliging.
GIACINTA *(aside, watching Guglielmo)* I can put up with anything, but seeing him over there with my own eyes drives me to distraction.
LEONARDO *(aside to Giacinta)* What's the matter, Signora Giacinta?
GIACINTA I can't stand this coffee house. They keep you waiting half an hour for a cup of coffee.
LEONARDO You must be patient. Didn't you hear? There are ten of us, and everybody ordered something different.
GIACINTA I'll be patient then. *(aside to herself, trembling)* I'm so sick of being patient, I can't stand it any more.
ROSINA *(aside to Tognino)* Did you hear that? Her ladyship wants to be served right away.
TOGNINO *(aside to Rosina)* Curses! I forgot to ask for a couple of cakes.

ROSINA *(aside to Tognino)* Are you hungry already?

TOGNINO *(aside to Rosina)* I'll say I am! I missed my afternoon snack.

FILIPPO *(aside to Costanza)* Don't you have anything to say for yourself, Signora Costanza?

COSTANZA *(aside to Filippo)* What do you expect me to say?

FILIPPO *(aside to Costanza)* Tell me something. Is it true your niece is in love with that idiot Tognino?

COSTANZA *(aside to Filippo)* I know nothing about it. To tell you the truth, that kind of thing goes in one ear and out the other. After all, she isn't my daughter.

SABINA *(aside to Ferdinando)* The air seems to be getting a bit humid. I wouldn't want to catch cold.

FERDINANDO *(aside to Sabina)* Poor thing! Put something on your head. Don't you have a hood?

SABINA *(aside to Ferdinando)* No, wait a minute. *(she takes a parasol out of her bag)* Hold this parasol for me.

FERDINANDO *(aside, to himself)* Oh, poor me! *(aside to Sabina)* Am I supposed to sit here for half an hour holding this damn thing?

SABINA *(aside to Ferdinando)* When you love someone, nothing's a nuisance, nothing's a bother.

FERDINANDO *(aside to Sabina)* So, you don't love me.

SABINA *(aside to Ferdinando)* Why not?

FERDINANDO *(aside to Sabina)* Because you find it a bother to make me a miserly settlement.

SABINA *(aside to Ferdinando)* Oh, you're still harping on that?

FERDINANDO *(aside to Sabina)* A settlement, madam, or it's goodbye Ferdinando!

SABINA *(aside, weeping and wiping her eyes)* Oh, how could anyone be so ungrateful? *(the waiters enter, bringing the orders and mixing them up)*

TOGNINO The chocolate was mine.

ROSINA I ordered that lime drink.

COSTANZA The lemonade goes here.

SABINA That's my sherbet.

LEONARDO A glass of water.

VITTORIA Coffee!

GIACINTA Coffee! *(they serve her the coffee)* You idiots! I didn't ask for coffee without sugar.

FERDINANDO Am I going to get my rosolio?

FILIPPO *(to the waiter)* Young man! So you've learned the lesson as well? You already know I'm always supposed to come last? Now that everyone else has been served, maybe you'll do me the favour of bringing me the water and lime juice I asked for.

Scene 12

Enter *Paolino.*

PAOLINO *(gesticulates to catch Leonardo's attention)*
LEONARDO *(getting up)* I'm coming. *(to Giacinta)* Excuse me a moment. I must have a word with my servant. *(he goes off to one side with Paolino)*
GIACINTA *(to Leonardo)* Don't mention it. *(aside, to herself)* I'd give anything to hear what Guglielmo and Vittoria are saying.
FERDINANDO *(to Sabina, as he gets to his feet)* By your leave, madam.
SABINA *(to Ferdinando)* And where do you think you're going?
FERDINANDO *(going over to take Leonardo's place)* I'll be back in a minute.
SABINA *(aside to herself)* Oh, what a rascal! He loves me dearly, but he teases me a thousand times a day.
FERDINANDO *(to Giacinta)* Oh, my God! I couldn't take any more.
GIACINTA *(to Ferdinando)* I'm surprised at you. How could you have the heart to make fun of my aunt! She's old and foolish, but she's a decent woman.
FERDINANDO *(to Giacinta)* Who? Me, Signora …?
GIACINTA You'd better not say any more.
FERDINANDO So, Signora Rosina, are you having a good time?
ROSINA Leave me alone, I don't want anything to do with you.
FERDINANDO *(aside)* Well, so much for that. I can't help anyone here! *(he goes back to sit with Sabina)* I'm back again, my precious darling.
SABINA *(to Ferdinando)* I shouldn't even look at you. But I don't have the heart to go through with it.
LEONARDO *(aside to Paolino)* Yes, find someone to copy the letter, or copy it yourself and disguise your handwriting. Seal it, put my name and address on it. Then, when we're at Signor Filippo's right after dinner, come and bring me the letter, as if it had come by post from Leghorn. Find someone you can coach to back up your story. You'll know what to do when you hear the contents of the letter. Now do your best, I assure you it's vitally important.
PAOLINO I'll do just as you say. *(exit Paolino)*
GIACINTA *(aside, to herself, getting to her feet)* This scene has gone on long enough, I can't stand it any more. I want Guglielmo to make up his mind to marry Vittoria, but I can't bear to see him with her any more.

GUGLIELMO *(aside, to himself)* Giacinta is at her wits' end. Maybe she doesn't realize what I'm going through.

LEONARDO *(to Giacinta)* I'm back again. You seem very agitated.

GIACINTA The air out here is absolutely unbearable.

LEONARDO Let's go back to the house, if you wish.

VITTORIA *(getting up)* Yes, let's go back, let's go back. *(aside)* I can't wait to find out, and there's no way this cold fish is going to tell me anything. *(Vittoria gets up, and everybody else gets up to leave)*

SABINA Let me walk on ahead. You know I've always been shortsighted. *(aside to Ferdinando)* Come on. I don't want anyone ahead of us hearing what we are saying.

FERDINANDO *(aside to Sabina)* Yes, let's go on ahead. We can discuss the settlement.

SABINA *(aside)* Damn you! *(she takes his hand angrily and they exit together)*

GIACINTA Please go on ahead, if you wish.

VITTORIA *(to Giacinta)* Oh, no, after you. Let's go back in the order we came in.

LEONARDO *(giving Giacinta his hand)* Come now, let's not make a fuss.

GIACINTA *(aside to herself)* Oh, heavens! I feel like I'm going to the scaffold. *(exit Giacinta with Leonardo)*

VITTORIA *(aside to Guglielmo)* Oh, I'm afraid you have bad news for me, Signor Guglielmo.

GUGLIELMO *(aside to Vittoria)* Why, Signora?

VITTORIA *(aside to Guglielmo)* You look too melancholy.

GUGLIELMO *(aside to Vittoria)* It's my nature. *(exit Guglielmo and Vittoria)*

COSTANZA *(aside to Rosina)* Well, Rosina, what do you make of it?

ROSINA I see storm clouds brewing. *(aside to Tognino)* Oh, my dearest Tognino, let's go. *(exit Rosina with Tognino)*

COSTANZA Shall we go, Signor Filippo?

FILIPPO Yes, here I am. Wouldn't you know it: last again! *(exit Filippo with Costanza)*

Scene 13

Evening. A drawing room in Signor Filippo's house, with candles, etc. Brigida and servants.

BRIGIDA Look sharp, now, light up the lamps. I saw them coming, through the window. *(the servants light up the lamps) (aside)* I hope Paolino is on his way, too. In the seven or eight days left till the end of our stay, I hope to bring my business to a satisfactory conclusion. Oh, wouldn't it be wonderful, with so many weddings, if mine could be the first one of all! *(to a servant)* Listen, if Paolino, Signor Leonardo's manservant, shows up, let me know. *(to another of the servants)* I have to stay here to help the ladies off with their shawls. Ah, here they come now.

Scene 14

They all enter, in the same order as before. Brigida takes the ladies' shawls. The servants take the gentlemen's hats.

SABINA Oh my! I'm quite exhausted. *(she sits down) (to Ferdinando)* Come and sit over here.

FERDINANDO *(sitting down beside her)* Here I am. *(aside)* This business is dragging on too long. Tomorrow, it's fish or cut bait!

GIACINTA If you'd like to sit down, there are chairs over here. *(everyone sits down; Filippo is left without a chair)*

FILIPPO Isn't there a chair for me?

BRIGIDA I'll get you one, I'll get you one, sir.

FILIPPO Yes, do bring me a chair, too. You are really too kind!

BRIGIDA *(bringing him a chair)* Here you are, sir.

FILIPPO *(aside, as he sits down)* Next year, I'll show them who's in charge in my own house.

VITTORIA *(getting up)* May I have a word with you, Brother?

LEONARDO *(aside, getting up)* I knew it. She's simply dying of curiosity.

VITTORIA So, what do you have to tell me?

LEONARDO *(aside to Vittoria)* I'll put it as briefly as I can. Guglielmo has asked for your hand in marriage.

VITTORIA *(aside to Leonardo)* Really? *(she looks across at Guglielmo with an ecstatic smile. Guglielmo catches her eye and looks the other way)*

LEONARDO *(aside to Vittoria)* So, it's up to you to decide.

VITTORIA *(aside to Leonardo)* Oh, if you're agreeable, I couldn't be happier!

LEONARDO *(calling Guglielmo)* May I trouble you, Signor Guglielmo?

GUGLIELMO At your service, sir. *(aside)* Like a lamb to the slaughter!

GIACINTA *(anxiously attempting to eavesdrop)*

LEONARDO My sister was pleased to hear of your kind proposal and is ready to give her consent.

GUGLIELMO Very well.

VITTORIA Very well? Is that all you can say, "Very well"?

GUGLIELMO Madam, what would you like me to say?

VITTORIA I can't figure you out. It's impossible to tell if you're pleased or disgusted.

GUGLIELMO Bear with me. That's how I am.

VITTORIA *(aside)* Once he's my husband, he may liven up.

LEONARDO Signor Filippo, Signor Ferdinando, may I have a word with you?

FILIPPO Of course! *(he gets up and comes forward)*

FERDINANDO At your service. *(he also gets up and comes forward)*

LEONARDO Will you agree to be witnesses to the exchange of promises of marriage between Signor Guglielmo and my sister, Signora Vittoria?

GIACINTA *(aside, flinging herself desperately into a chair)* It's all over!

FILIPPO Good for you, sir!

FERDINANDO I couldn't be happier!

SABINA *(aside to Ferdinando)* There, you see, that's the way it's done.

FERDINANDO *(aside to Sabina)* The settlement, and we'll do it.

SABINA Curse you and your settlement! *(she goes to sit down)*

LEONARDO In a moment, we'll put it in writing, and you gentlemen can sign as witnesses.

FILIPPO Yes, sir.

FERDINANDO If you'd like me to draw up the contract, I've done others. I'll have it ready in no time.

VITTORIA We'd be delighted.

LEONARDO Yes, please, go ahead.

FERDINANDO I'm off right away. *(aside)* I wouldn't want to be left out of the wedding. *(exit Ferdinando)*

VITTORIA *(to Guglielmo)* You have nothing to say, sir?

GUGLIELMO I fully approve. What else do you want me to say?

VITTORIA You seem to be acting more from constraint than from love.

GUGLIELMO On the contrary, I'm doing what love constrains me to do.

VITTORIA *(aside)* Well, that's something! For once he's admitted he loves me. *(to Guglielmo)* Come along, then, let's go and sit down. *(they sit)*

COSTANZA My congratulations, Signora Vittoria.

VITTORIA Thank you.

ROSINA *(to Vittoria)* Congratulations.

VITTORIA Much obliged.

ROSINA *(aside to Tognino)* You see? They went through with it.

TOGNINO *(giggling, aside to Rosina)* And we'll go through with it, too.

Scene 15

Enter *Paolino.*

PAOLINO *(to Leonardo)* Sir …

LEONARDO What is it?

PAOLINO A messenger, sent especially from Leghorn, brought this urgent letter for you.

LEONARDO Let's have a look. Give it to me. *(he gets up, takes the letter, and opens it) (to Filippo)* It's from Signor Fulgenzio.

FILIPPO Oh, yes, our old friend. And what does he say?

LEONARDO My goodness! This news is upsetting. Listen to what he says. *(reading aloud)* "My dear friend, I hasten to write to you, and I'm sending a man especially, to tell you that your Uncle Bernardino has been sick for three days with a chest ailment and is close to the end. The doctors give him only a few more hours to live. He has sent for a lawyer, so I suggest you have a thought for your interests. Your fortune is at stake. I would advise you to return to Leghorn at once."

FILIPPO Goodness gracious! My advice, too, is not to waste a moment. They say he's worth more than fifty thousand.

VITTORIA Yes, of course, go at once, go at once. I'll come with you.

LEONARDO I'm sorry to have to desert the company.

VITTORIA In any case, Signor Guglielmo will come with us.

GUGLIELMO *(aside)* It seems as if the whole world's against me.

GIACINTA *(aside)* Yes, it's better for me. It's eating my heart out, it's killing me, but a line has to be drawn somewhere.

LEONARDO Paolino, go to the post house at once and order four horses. Have the carriage ready. We'll take the carriage to Leghorn. There are four of us: Signor Guglielmo, my sister, myself, and you. There's no need to pack.

PAOLINO Right away, sir.

BRIGIDA *(aside to Paolino)* Paolino!

PAOLINO *(aside to Brigida)* Yes, my dear!

BRIGIDA *(aside to Paolino)* Are you leaving?

PAOLINO *(aside to Brigida)* Yes, but I'll be back to pick up our stuff.

BRIGIDA *(aside to Paolino)* For heaven's sake, don't forget me!

PAOLINO *(aside to Brigida)* No danger of that. I give you my word. *(exit Paolino)*

BRIGIDA *(aside)* Oh, poor me! Just when everything was going splendidly, I have to swallow this disappointment. *(exit Brigida)*

FILIPPO *(to Leonardo)* When you get to Leghorn, write to us at once. If you come back, we'll be waiting. If you don't, we'll be there soon ourselves.

VITTORIA There's no time to lose. Signora Giacinta, forgive the inconvenience. Think of me when I'm gone. I hope to see you soon in Leghorn.

GIACINTA Yes, my dear, until soon. *(they embrace)*

GUGLIELMO *(aside)* My knees are trembling. I can't breathe.

LEONARDO *(to Vittoria)* Don't you want to wait till the contract is signed?

VITTORIA Oh, yes! It has to be signed. *(shouts offstage)* Hello there, Signor Ferdinando, are you finished?

Scene 16

Enter *Ferdinando.*

FERDINANDO Coming. Coming. Now what's going on? Are you going? Are you leaving us?

VITTORIA Is the contract ready?

FERDINANDO Yes, here it is.

GUGLIELMO Excuse me. Can't we get it drawn up in Leghorn? Wouldn't it be better to have it drawn up by a lawyer?

FERDINANDO But it's already done.

GUGLIELMO We still have to read it, we still have to sign it. Signor Leonardo, my advice is not to waste time. We'd best leave at once. We'll have the contract drawn up in Leghorn. I'm ready, I'm with you. I won't leave your side.

LEONARDO You may be right. We'd better get going. We'll do it in Leghorn.

GUGLIELMO *(aside)* I breathe again. Who knows what may happen.

LEONARDO Signora Giacinta, come quickly. Keep my place in your heart. *(he takes her hand)* Signor Filippo, farewell. *(they embrace)* Your servant, everyone. *(aside)* We'll work things out in Leghorn. *(exit Leonardo)*

VITTORIA Goodbye again, Signora Giacinta. Ladies. Signor Filippo. Your servant, everyone. Let's go. *(she takes Guglielmo by the hand)*

COSTANZA Have a safe journey.

ROSINA Have a safe journey.

SABINA Have a safe journey.

GUGLIELMO *(somewhat annoyed, to Vittoria)* Leave me alone. *(to Filippo)* Signor Filippo, excuse me, and thank you.

FILIPPO Good-bye, see you in Leghorn.

GUGLIELMO *(visibly moved)* Signora Giacinta … forgive me …

GIACINTA Have a good journey. *(aside)* I can't bear it.

VITTORIA *(to Guglielmo)* What the devil's the matter? You're not crying?

GUGLIELMO *(resolutely)* Let's go.

VITTORIA That's better! Let's go. *(exit Vittoria with Guglielmo)*

FERDINANDO Signora Sabina!

SABINA Yes, what is it?

FERDINANDO Here, I have a present for you.

SABINA What is it?

FERDINANDO A marriage contract.

SABINA Is it for me?

FERDINANDO No, this one's not really for you. Because yours has to mention the settlement.

SABINA Come along, now. This is insolence, sir, and I'm sick and tired of it. You've had what's coming to you, and you should be grateful. You ingrate, you mercenary, you miser! *(exit Sabina)*

FERDINANDO The old dowager is incensed. My settlement has gone up in smoke. For me it's all over. *(exit Ferdinando)*

COSTANZA Signora Giacinta, we don't want to bother you further.

GIACINTA Are you planning to leave?

FILIPPO Don't you want to stay and play cards?

COSTANZA I really ought to go home.

GIACINTA Go ahead, as you please.

COSTANZA *(aside to Rosina)* Let's go. While we have Tognino in the right frame of mind, let's not let him off the hook.

ROSINA *(to Giacinta)* Your humble servant, madam. Excuse me. *(exit Rosina)*

TOGNINO *(to Giacinta)* Your servant. Excuse me. *(exit Tognino)*

FILIPPO *(to Costanza)* Let's be going. I'll walk you home.

COSTANZA It's very kind of you. *(aside)* At least the old gentleman's harmless. *(exit Costanza)*

FILIPPO *(aside)* If there's nothing else for it, I'll just have to play a couple of games of bezique with the pipsqueak! *(exit Filippo)*

GIACINTA Thank heavens I'm alone. I can give free vent to my passion, and own up to my weakness … Ladies and gentlemen, at this point the author, with all the power of his imagination, had prepared a long speech of despair, a regular conflict of emotions, a mixture of heroism and pathos. I thought it best to omit it, to avoid boring you further. Picture for yourselves what a woman prey to the promptings of honour and cursed by the cruellest of passions might be going through. Imagine you hear her blaming herself for not safeguarding her heart as she should have, then finding excuses for herself in accident, circumstance, and the delights of a stay in the country. The play doesn't appear to be over; yet it is over, since the plot of the Adventures is complete. If there are still some loose ends left to tie, they may well provide matter for a third comedy, which we will have the honour of presenting in due course, in the meantime, thanking you for your kind indulgence towards the two we have performed so far.

END OF THE ADVENTURES

NOTES TO ADVENTURES IN THE COUNTRY

All notes to *Adventures in the Country* are taken from the edition of the Holiday Trilogy translated by Anthony Oldcorn.

1 *Il teatro comico*, of which there exists an English translation by John W. Miller (Lincoln, NE: University of Nebraska Press, 1969), is the meta-theatrical program piece which opened the 1750–1 winter season, introducing the famous "sixteen new comedies" promised in a publicity stunt by Goldoni, and actually produced and staged by the Medebach company. *La bottega del caffè* and *I pettegolezzi delle donne* were in fact two of the sixteen new plays.

2 Maremma, or more properly "the Maremma," was a marshy, wooded coastal area to the south of Leghorn, since to some extent reclaimed, but proverbial, at least since Dante's time, for its wildness. The major town in the area is Grosseto.

3 Among the many card games mentioned here and elsewhere by Goldoni, himself an expert and enthusiastic cardplayer, faro was, as we remarked in note 12 to *Off to the Country* (p. 220), the gambling game par excellence, preferred by professional gamblers, since it offered a chance to win (or lose) considerable sums of money. Ferdinando's winnings at faro, in fact, make up more than half of his total winnings. The other games listed, known

in Italian as "giochi di società" and in French as "petits jeux" – minchiate (a variant form of "tarots," or "tarocchi," another game mentioned later), primiera ("primero" is mentioned twice by Shakespeare, in *King Henry the Eighth* and in *The Merry Wives of Windsor*), trentuno ("thirty-one," a game for any number of persons, the object being to hold three cards of the same suit whose face value adds up to thirty-one) – though more or less risky, could not touch faro.

4 The French game of piquet (in Italian picchetto, and pronounced "peekay" or "picket" in English) is, according to Professor Hoffmann, "the best game of cards for two persons that exists," "the most noble as well as the most interesting card game after whist, with which, indeed, it will, on intellectual grounds, bear fair comparison." Hoffmann continues: "It is somewhat difficult to describe clearly, but a little perseverance and attention will soon master it ... We have known intelligent children under their teens, having once learnt the game, to play it very correctly." It is Filippo's favourite game.

5 Pisa was the major university in Tuscany, drawing students from Florence, Leghorn, Lucca, etc. The Venetian equivalent was Padua. Goldoni knew the university, since he himself practised law in Pisa between 1745 and 1748. Pompous quack doctors were fair game in traditional comedy, but, in sceptically portraying the budding doctor's hopes for advancement by means other than of professional competence, Goldoni may have had his own father's medical career in mind.

6 Tognino's is a rote list of the natural laxatives commonly prescribed by traditional internal medicine. Taken all together, their effect could be devastating!

7 Fainting fits were known as "convulsions." They could be brought on by excessively tight clothes or eating disorders, though women frequently resorted to fainting to get out of a difficult situation.

8 Dried rhubarb root was a commonly prescribed purgative and stomachic. We will later learn from Filippo that Ferdinando is making it up and never went near the druggist's. In a moment, however, he will use the nonexistent rhubarb on his breath as an excuse for not wanting to get too close to Sabina.

9 The reader who is following the financial ins and outs will note that Sabina's dowry of ten thousand crowns is slightly higher that Giacinta's eight thousand (see *Off to the Country*, 3, 1, p. 199). In *Off to the Country* (2, 9, p. 187), we also learned that Filippo has a debt of one thousand crowns, or one-eighth of Giacinta's dowry, with Fulgenzio.

10 Bezique (Fr. bézique, It. bazzica), a forerunner of pinochle (still the fourth most popular game in America), was usually played by two players with

a thirty-two-card piquet deck (i.e., no twos, threes, fours, fives, or sixes). Scarne's *Encyclopedia* has a chapter on its modern variants.

11 Tresette ("three-seven," the final "e" is pronounced) derives its name from the fact that its rules allow for three- and seven-card combinations. It is still the most popular partnership game in working-class Italy, and is occasionally played one on one. It calls for considerable strategy.

12 Three-handed ombre (from the Spanish hombre, but pronounced "omber") was extremely popular in the eighteenth century, and is the mock epic game played by Belinda, the Baron, and Sir Anonym in Alexander Pope's *Rape of the Lock*. Richard Seymour, in his *Court Gamester* (1719) describes it as "the most delightful and entertaining of all Games, to those who have anything in them, of what we call the spirit of Play." Geoffrey Tillotson's edition of Pope's poem (London: Methuen, 1940) has an appendix with a detailed excursus on the game of ombre. The game pitted the two remaining players against the dealer ("the man," hombre – though in Pope's case the dealer is Belinda, a woman), who called trumps: "Let Spades be Trumps! she said, and Trumps they were."

13 The phrase Sabina uses in Italian, "gli ho dato un cappotto," could have been translated more literally in eighteenth-century English: "I capotted him." Like the modern "blitz" or "shut out," the expression signifies to win a game without conceding a single trick to one's opponent.

14 This short scene between Tita and Beltrame is one of the few concessions in the trilogy to the fossilized stereotypes of the old commedia dell'arte, in which servants were presented as constitutionally starving and obsessed with the procurement of victuals. Leather-lined pockets could be used to stow food. In point of fact, since a fair portion of a servant's compensation was paid in kind, his well-being depended on the mutual loyalty existing between him and his master. It speaks well for Leonardo's fairness that his servant Paolo, whose cash wages are six months in arrears, is prepared to put up his own savings if need be to help his master out of a jam.

Back from the Country

Prose comedy in three acts
Performed for the first time in Venice at the Teatro San Luca on 28 November 1761

Figure 17 *Back from the Country* (Il ritorno dalla villeggiatura)

Figure 18 *Back from the Country* (Il ritorno dalla villeggiatura), act 1, scene 1

Figure 19 *Back from the Country* (Il ritorno dalla villeggiatura), act 2, scene 8

Figure 20 *Back from the Country* (Il ritorno dalla villeggiatura), act 3, final scene

The Author to the Reader

Few Authors, to my knowledge, ancient or modern, ever took it upon themselves to compose more than one Comedy on the same subject. The only examples I am familiar with are Le menteur [The Liar] and La suite du menteur [The Sequel to the Liar], two comedies in part translated and in part imitated by Corneille from the Spanish author Lopez [sic] de Vega.[1] But, allow me to observe that La suite du menteur has nothing to do with the Comedy that precedes it. It is true that Damon, the Liar, and his servant, Cliton, are the same characters in both, and that in the second, mention is made of some of the adventures of the first, but the subject could not be more different, and the character of the Liar himself has changed: for, in the first play, Damon lies accidentally, and in the second he lies out of generosity, and almost from unavoidable necessity. I had no intention, then, of imitating anyone when I began to attempt a second Comedy following the first, and a third following the previous two. The first time this happened to me was after the successful outcome of the Putta onorata. Commedia veneziana [The Honest Wench. A Venetian Comedy] to which I wrote a sequel entitled La buona moglie [The Good Wife].[2] Pamela and Pamela maritata [Pamela Married] are two other comedies which display the same continuity.[3] Emboldened by the success of two consecutive comedies, I tried for three. I was so successful in this venture with the Tre persiane [Three Persian Plays] that the audience was ready and eager for a fourth, and, encouraged again by this fortunate upshot, I composed the present three comedies with the same kind of link. With this difference, however: that the others I imagined one after the other, and these three all three at once.

What is so difficult (someone may ask) about composing three Comedies on the same subject? The plays you now bring before the public make up one single Comedy, divided up into nine acts. Calisto e Melibea is a Spanish Comedy with fifteen acts, so there is nothing surprising in your composing one with nine.[4] My answer to someone objecting along these lines would be, that Calisto e Melibea could not be performed in a single evening, nor could it be divided into three separate performances, for the action of this Comedy, irregular and scandalous as it is, will not tolerate any division. Each of my three Comedies, on the other hand, begins and ends in such a way that someone seeing the second without having seen the first will be satisfied, since he will find the Comedy intelligible, with its own beginning and end, and the same can be said of the third.

It is true that, at the end of the second play, this third play is promised, and that I deliberately left certain things unresolved so as to continue the subject into the next one; still, with another ten lines the plot of the second play could have been closed perfectly. I wanted, however, to leave myself free to write a third Comedy, which would serve as conclusion to the other two, so as to prove the folly of extravagant trips to the country. All the characters of the first and the second play are once again present in this one, with the exception of Sabina, who remains in Montenero, but is not completely forgotten, since a letter arrives in time to remind us of her.

This continuity of characters, interests, and passions will not seem a matter of indifference or an easy task to anyone with experience of this sort of theatrical composition. It remains for me to say a word concerning the character of Bernardino, introduced for the first time in this Comedy. A character who appears in a single scene, unless he be a Servant, a Notary, a Messenger, or something of the sort, would normally be superfluous or introduced injudiciously. The Reader will see for himself that Bernardino is not superfluous, and he will also realize that such an odious character may be tolerated, even enjoyed in a single scene; but would become obnoxious and unbearable were he to appear a second time.

Dramatis Personae

FILIPPO	*a good-natured old city-dweller*
GIACINTA	*Filippo's daughter*
LEONARDO	*in love with Giacinta*
VITTORIA	*Leonardo's sister*
GUGLIELMO	*in love with Giacinta*
COSTANZA	*a country neighbour*
ROSINA	*her niece*
TOGNINO	*a simple-minded young man, in love with Rosina*
BERNARDINO	*Leonardo's uncle*
FULGENZIO	*an elderly friend of Filippo's*
FERDINANDO	*a freeloader*
BRIGIDA	*Giacinta's maidservant*
PAOLINO [PAOLO]	*Leonardo's manservant*[5]
CECCO	*a servant*
[PASQUALE	*Bernardino's manservant*][6]
OTHER SERVANTS	

As in the first play of the trilogy, the action takes place in Leghorn.

ACT ONE

Scene 1

A room in Leonardo's house. Enter *Leonardo, followed by Cecco.*

LEONARDO It's three days since I got back to Leghorn, and there's still no sign of Signora Giacinta and Signor Filippo. They promised they'd come right back to Leghorn themselves, if I didn't go back to Montenero; but they still haven't arrived, and I haven't heard from them, either. I wrote them a letter, but they haven't answered. They should have gotten my letter yesterday, and I should have had their answer today. It's already late, though, it should have been here by now. If they haven't written, it probably means they're on their way.
CECCO Sir.
LEONARDO What is it?
CECCO There's somebody asking for you.
LEONARDO Who is it?
CECCO A young man with a bill. I think it's the grocer's boy.
LEONARDO Why didn't you tell him I was out?
CECCO That's what I told him yesterday, and the day before yesterday, just like you told me, but, seeing he comes round three or four times a day, perhaps you'd better talk to him yourself and get rid of him somehow.
LEONARDO Go tell him I have given Paolino instructions to settle our account. Tell him Paolino is expected back from Montenero any moment now, and, as soon as he gets here, he'll settle.
CECCO Very good, sir. *(exit Cecco)*
LEONARDO Oh, dear, my affairs keep on going from bad to worse. And this year our stay in the country set me back even more than usual.
CECCO Sir, the candle man's here.
LEONARDO You idiot! Why didn't you tell him I was out?
CECCO I told him what I always tell him: I'll see if he's in; I'm not sure he's in; and he said: If he isn't, I have orders to wait till he gets back.
LEONARDO Impertinence, that's what it is! Tell him to leave the bill, I'll send someone to the shop to pay it.
CECCO Very good, sir, I'll tell him. *(exit Cecco)*
LEONARDO You'd think they had nothing better to do; you'd think they hadn't a crumb of bread to their names! They're always there with

their bows drawn back, ready to skewer the hearts of gentlemen who can't afford to pay.

Cecco He's gone away, too. He wasn't too pleased; but he's gone. Here's the bill. *(gives him the bill)*

Leonardo *(tearing it up)* Damn this and all bills!

Cecco *(aside)* Bill lacerated, debt liquidated!

Leonardo Go over to Signor Filippo's, and see if they're back, by any chance.

Cecco Right away, sir. *(exit Cecco)*

Leonardo I'm a nervous wreck. In the first place, because I'm in love with that cruel, ungrateful Giacinta, and secondly, because, in my present financial condition, my only hope for salvation is her dowry. *(re-enter Cecco)*

Cecco Sir …

Leonardo Hurry up! Why haven't you gone where I sent you?

Cecco Something else has come up, sir.

Leonardo What is it this time?

Cecco Here it is, sir. It's a summons.

Leonardo I know nothing about summonses. I don't accept summonses. They can take it to my lawyer.

Cecco Your lawyer's out of town.

Leonardo And where the devil has he gone?

Cecco He's gone to the country.

Leonardo Curse him! My lawyer in the country as well! I can't believe he would abandon his own interests and those of his clients, for the sake of a good time! I pay him, I come up with his retainer, I make everyone else wait for their money so I can pay him, I rely on him to assist and defend me; and, when I need him, where is he? He's nowhere in sight, he's off to the country! A summons for me? Where's the officer who served it?

Cecco The officer's gone. He handed it over, wrote my name in his register, and left right away.

Leonardo I don't know what to do. I'll have to wait for my lawyer. Come along, hurry. Go see if they're back.

Cecco I'll go right away. *(exit Cecco)*

Leonardo Nothing but trouble! Summonses … suits … But, by heavens, what can I do if I don't have the cash! They keep hounding me. They are bound and determined to have me do the impossible! If they'll only be patient, I'll pay them. When I'm in a position to pay them, I'll pay them.

CECCO Sir, on my way downstairs I ran into Signor Filippo's servant. He was on his way over to inform you and Signora Vittoria that they're back in Leghorn.

LEONARDO Show him in.

CECCO He's gone. He showed me a list of thirty-seven houses he had to call at before noon to announce their arrival.

LEONARDO Bring me my hat and my sword.

CECCO Yes, sir. *(exit Cecco)*

LEONARDO I can't wait to see Giacinta. Who knows what kind of a welcome she'll give me in Leghorn, after what transpired in the country? Guglielmo is still putting off signing the marriage contract with my sister. I'm tossed on a turbulent sea, drowning in debts, and besieged by creditors.

CECCO *(handing him his hat and sword)* There you are, sir.

LEONARDO See if there's anyone in the hall or on the stairs or at the bottom of the stairs.

CECCO Very good, sir. *(exit Cecco)*

LEONARDO I'm always afraid I'll meet someone who'll embarrass me. To get to Signor Filippo's I'm going to have to go the long way round, so I don't have to pass my creditors' shops. *(re-enter Cecco)*

CECCO Sir, there are two tradesmen waiting.

LEONARDO Waiting? Do they know that I'm here?

CECCO Yes, they know. That fool Berto told them you were in.

LEONARDO Who are they?

CECCO The tailor and the shoemaker.

LEONARDO Send them away. Make them go away.

CECCO What shall I tell them?

LEONARDO Tell them whatever you like.

CECCO Couldn't you give them something on account?

LEONARDO Send them away, I tell you.

CECCO But sir, they won't go. And this isn't the first time. They're quite capable of hanging around until nightfall.

LEONARDO Do you have the keys to the little secret door?

CECCO The key's in the lock, sir.

LEONARDO Good, I'll go out that way.

CECCO Be careful on the stair, sir. It's dark and steep.

LEONARDO I don't care, I'm going out that way.

CECCO There are cobwebs all over, you'll get your clothes dirty.

LEONARDO *(about to leave)* What of it? Who cares?

CECCO Do you want them to wait outside?

LEONARDO Yes, let them wait till the devil comes to take them!
(exit Leonardo)

Scene 2

Cecco, then enter Vittoria.

CECCO These are the delectable fruits of a nice little stay in the country!
VITTORIA Where is my brother?
CECCO *(softly)* He's not here, he went out.
VITTORIA What are you whispering for?
CECCO So as not to be heard by certain persons out there in the hall.
VITTORIA If they're out in the hall, they must have seen him leave.
CECCO No, madam, he went out by the secret door.
VITTORIA A silly thing to do, if you ask me! And rude besides! He has visitors in the hall, and he goes out without acknowledging their visit, without so much as taking his leave? If they're our kind of people, I'll see them myself.
CECCO Will you see them, then, madam?
VITTORIA Yes, who are they?
CECCO The tailor and the shoemaker.
VITTORIA Whose?
CECCO The master's.
VITTORIA And what do they want?
CECCO Nothing. Just to be paid the balance we owe them.
VITTORIA And why didn't my brother oblige?
CECCO I don't believe he's in a position to do so at present.
VITTORIA *(aside)* Oh, poor us! *(to Cecco)* See you don't go saying things like that in front of anyone else. In fact, do what you can to keep it a secret. Now, try and send those people away politely, so they don't kick up a fuss and give the family a bad name. My brother refuses to understand that when there are bills to be paid, you either pay up or you treat people politely.
CECCO *(aside)* My mistress talks a good line, but she doesn't practise what she preaches any more than he does.
VITTORIA Where did Signor Leonardo go?
CECCO To call on Signora Giacinta.
VITTORIA Is she back?
CECCO Yes, madam.

VITTORIA Since when?

CECCO Since this morning.

VITTORIA *(incensed)* And she didn't send me word?

CECCO Yes, madam. She sent over a servant with a message for you and the master.

VITTORIA Why wasn't I told?

CECCO Forgive me. I've been in a daze. If you knew the problems that have come up this morning …

VITTORIA I didn't see how she could have neglected her social duty to inform me.

CECCO I hear a racket out in the hall. Excuse me.

VITTORIA Send that riff-raff away.

CECCO *(aside)* Wouldn't you know it. It goes without saying. When honest workingmen ask for their livelihood, they're all riff-raff.[7] *(exit Cecco)*

VITTORIA I'll have to pay her a visit.[8] She was the last to come back, so I should be the first to go pay my respects. I'll go, but I certainly don't relish the idea. I never could stand her; but now, after all that transpired in the country, the very thought of her is enough to make my blood boil. Guglielmo has been putting off signing the contract. I hardly ever get to see him, I'm extremely upset.

CECCO Madam, Signor Fulgenzio is here. He asked to see the master, and when I told him he was out, he said he'd wait. Would you like to see him?

VITTORIA Yes, yes, show him in. Did the others go away?

CECCO They're having a word with Signor Fulgenzio. *(exit Cecco)*

VITTORIA Here comes the old sourpuss who robbed us of the pleasures of the country, just when we were starting to enjoy them! I can't wait to give him a piece of my mind!

Scene 3

Enter *Fulgenzio.*

FULGENZIO *(aside)* Alas! Wretched household! How low you've sunk!

VITTORIA Bravo, good for you, Signor Fulgenzio.

FULGENZIO Your servant, madam.

VITTORIA What on earth possessed you to write to my brother that our uncle was at death's door and make us rush headlong back to Leghorn?

FULGENZIO I haven't written one line to your brother since you left town, and your uncle is in the best of health. I haven't the faintest idea what you're talking about.

VITTORIA But I saw the letter with my own eyes.

FULGENZIO What letter?

VITTORIA The one you wrote.

FULGENZIO To whom?

VITTORIA To my brother.

FULGENZIO Madam, I'm afraid you must have dreamed it.

VITTORIA What do you mean, dreamed it? Didn't we rush back to Leghorn to get here before my uncle died?

FULGENZIO Who told you that nonsense?

VITTORIA Your letter.

FULGENZIO *(incensed)* Confound it! You're going to make me lose my temper. I told you I didn't write it. I couldn't have written it, and I didn't write it!

VITTORIA So what's the meaning of all this?

FULGENZIO What's the meaning? I'll tell you the meaning: plots, inventions, tricks.

VITTORIA Whose tricks?

FULGENZIO Your brother's.

VITTORIA What do you mean, my brother's?

FULGENZIO Your brother's. Who so far has been leading the most insane and disorderly existence imaginable. I was told his affairs were headed for disaster, but I didn't think things had gone this far! I regret that I ever got involved in this marriage business. I'm sorry if I said anything to give Signor Filippo a good opinion of a man who's not worthy of marrying his daughter.

VITTORIA Signor Fulgenzio, you are a true gentleman, and I appreciate these flattering words, to say nothing of your generous intention of ruining my brother.

FULGENZIO He's ruined himself. It's my natural instinct to do good, but only when one person's good doesn't harm or dishonour someone else.

VITTORIA If your instinct is to do good, the very least you could do is find a way to get rid of these insolent tradesmen, who think nothing of dragging our name in the mud for a handful of silver.

FULGENZIO Until now, I could and I did. Thanks to me, they all went away. Oh, I gave them no guarantees, because I'm not that crazy, but, with my reassurances, I got them to go away and not take the drastic measures they had in mind. But, my dear lady, if they're not going to be paid, then at least don't insult them! Don't call them insolent! When your brother needed them, did he abuse and insult them? Or did he try to win them over and keep them happy with flattery, sweet talk, and soft soap, so they'd keep serving him and serving him well? And now that they're back for the fifth, sixth, or seventh time to ask for what's coming to them, and wasting a working day struggling to get paid, the brother hides and the sister insults them! This is injustice, this is ingratitude, this is tyranny!

VITTORIA It is no use your spouting your sermons at me.

FULGENZIO I know that only too well. It's like preaching to the deaf.

VITTORIA Go preach to my brother. He needs it more than I do.

FULGENZIO And where is your brother?

VITTORIA He's gone to call on Signora Giacinta.

FULGENZIO Ah, are they back, too? I'm delighted …

VITTORIA Don't you dare go over there creating an unnecessary fuss.

FULGENZIO I shall do what I think must be done.

VITTORIA Don't risk breaking up a marriage contract. That kind of thing just isn't done.

FULGENZIO Oh, my dear lady … excuse me …. Do you want to know what just isn't done? Spending more than you can afford; going into debt for the sake of a good time; exhausting and insulting your creditors. *(exit Fulgenzio)*

Scene 4

Vittoria, then enter Ferdinando.

VITTORIA No one can deny that he's speaking the truth, but when he hits home, it hurts.

FERDINANDO *(from offstage)* Hello, who's there? Is anybody home?

VITTORIA Oh, it's Signor Ferdinando. He'll have news for me. Come in, come in, sir. Here I am.

FERDINANDO *(bowing)* My respects, Signora Vittoria.

VITTORIA Your servant, sir. Welcome back.

FERDINANDO Much obliged, madam. But I didn't expect to be back here so soon.

VITTORIA I expect you came back with Signor Filippo and Signora Giacinta.

FERDINANDO Yes, and we had such a pleasant journey! Another two hours, and I would have come down with a fever!

VITTORIA Why so?

FERDINANDO Because Signora Giacinta did nothing but sigh, Signor Filippo slept all the way from Montenero to Leghorn, the maid seemed to be mourning the dead, and I suffered the most excruciating boredom.

VITTORIA What did Signora Giacinta have to sigh about?

FERDINANDO She had … she had … a head full of foolish ideas – so many foolish ideas I blush for her.

VITTORIA Just what do these foolish ideas consist of?

FERDINANDO Let's change the subject. Have you heard the news?

VITTORIA What news?

FERDINANDO About little Tognino.

VITTORIA The doctor's son?

FERDINANDO Yes, his father came back and found out he wanted to marry that girl. He threw him out of the house, and Tognino had no idea where to turn for room and board. Signora Costanza, who doesn't want her niece's wedding to cost her a cent, wasn't too happy about taking him in, but in the end she had no other choice. She put him in with her servant, she feeds him, but there isn't a whole lot to chew on, and the boy does have quite an appetite. They said they'd be back in Leghorn today. They plan to bring Tognino with them, sue his father for child support, have him marry the maiden, and get him a doctor's degree from Idiot College.

VITTORIA A charming tale, but of no great interest to me. I'd rather you tell me more about Signora Giacinta's bout of melancholy.

FERDINANDO Forgive me, it's not my way to meddle in other people's affairs.

VITTORIA You've already meddled enough to arouse my suspicions, now it's up to you to dispel them.

FERDINANDO But what could you possibly suspect?

VITTORIA The same thing I suspected even before we went to Montenero.

FERDINANDO I don't know what was on your mind then, or what's on your mind now.

VITTORIA If she was sighing, something must have been bothering her.

FERDINANDO Naturally.

VITTORIA I shouldn't think she was sighing on account of my brother.

FERDINANDO It never occurred to me to think she might be sighing for him.

VITTORIA So for whom, then?

FERDINANDO *(laughing)* Who can tell? Couldn't she have been sighing for me?

VITTORIA No way! Not for you! But maybe she could be sighing for somebody else.

FERDINANDO Oh, by the way, I lost my beloved. Signora Sabina doesn't want me any more. When I spoke of a settlement, she took offence, she got highly insulted, she refused even to see me. Worse than that. Did you hear anything so ridiculous? For fear she might have to travel with me, she refused to come back to Leghorn. She stayed on in Montenero. Now I think she's so ashamed of her childish behaviour that she's afraid to come back to town to be the butt of everyone's jokes.

VITTORIA And you are the one we have to thank for this work of charity!

FERDINANDO I was only trying to keep myself amused, and to give the rest of you something to talk about.

VITTORIA *(ironically)* You should be really proud of yourself!

FERDINANDO I don't feel I did anything to deserve criticism. I should have thought it much worse if I'd courted two unmarried women, pretending to love one in order to cover up my passion for the other.

VITTORIA And just where are you aiming those words?

FERDINANDO I aim at the air. Let the air carry them wherever it will.

VITTORIA These are horrible, poisonous words, words that go right through my heart.

FERDINANDO Why, what do they have to do with you? I didn't mean you.

VITTORIA And why was Signora Giacinta sighing?

FERDINANDO You'll have to ask her.

VITTORIA And who's the one paying court to two women?

FERDINANDO You'll have to ask him?

VITTORIA And who is this "him"?

FERDINANDO Signor Him in the accusative case, Signor He in the nominative. Nominative hic, he, genitive huius, of him. Signora Vittoria, you seem to be quite out of sorts this morning. I hope to have the honour of seeing you later. I'm off to the coffee house, where everybody's waiting, anxious to hear the adventures of Montenero. I have enough material for two weeks' worth of conversation. I'll have all of Leghorn in stitches, I'll have half the world laughing. *(exit Ferdinando)*

VITTORIA Oh, what a vicious tongue! Did you ever hear anything like it? He's filled me with misgivings. I've had my suspicions, my doubts and anxieties for some time; and along he comes and gives me the coup de grâce. I have bad news on the home front, our affairs are going badly, my heart couldn't be in a worse fix. Oh, poor me! I'm certainly paying for my pleasures in the country! Better for me never to have gone! *(exit Vittoria)*

Scene 5

A room in Filippo's house. Brigida and Giacinta.

BRIGIDA Come now, mistress, don't be so pensive. Enjoy yourself, be happy. Remember, melancholy can play nasty tricks.

GIACINTA If you want my opinion, I'm not melancholy at all any more, I'm so happy in fact that I wouldn't change places with a queen. Now that I no longer see him, I feel reborn. I feel wonderful, I've never felt better.

BRIGIDA Excuse me, let's get one thing straight. Whom do you mean by "him"?

GIACINTA How can you be so slow on the uptake? Isn't it obvious that when I say "him" I mean Signor Guglielmo?

BRIGIDA *(aside)* I was afraid for a minute that "him" might be her husband-to-be!

GIACINTA *(passionately)* Am I wrong to be scornful, resentful, and nasty? Could he have done me any more harm than he did? To bring me so low? To make me fall so madly in love? What a miserable existence I led on his account! Was there a pang or an anxiety he didn't make me endure? I didn't have a moment's peace. He was out to entrap me from the very first day. Oh, how artfully he stole his way into my heart and my mind! What calculating words! What languorous, treacherous glances! What a studied performance! How clever he was finding moments to be alone with me, what sweet phrases he came up with, and how gracefully he spoke them!

BRIGIDA *(aside, ironically)* Oh, no, he's not on her mind any more, I can tell!

GIACINTA That's enough! Thank heavens I got over him. It's as if I'd had an illness, and now I'm completely cured.

BRIGIDA If you don't mind my saying so, I think you still have a little convalescing to do.

GIACINTA *(making an effort to appear unconcerned)* No, you're wrong. I'm healthy, as healthy as I ever was. Now all I can think about are the preparations for my wedding. I have already planned everything I want my father to do. As for the groom, I absolutely refuse to have Signor Leonardo get his sister involved. I don't want her put in charge of my trousseau. First of all, it's not her prerogative, because she's single, and, on top of that, she has bad taste. She dresses badly herself, and I'm sure she would do even worse by me. That's all I have on my mind at present: my head's full of dresses, accessories, jewellery, Flanders lace, Venetian lace, silk embroidery, shoes, bonnets, fans. That's all that interests me now, and that's all I can think about.

BRIGIDA And among all these thoughts don't you feel a little love now and then, a smidgin of affection for the groom?

GIACINTA I hope to love him tenderly one day. I have heard tell of lots of people who married for love, and got bored and regretted it in no time. And others who went into it out of a sense of duty or mere resignation, without much real affection, and ended up living happily till the day they died.

BRIGIDA One thing's for sure, madam, so far you're in no danger of getting bored from loving him too much. I pray to God that the bond that unites you will get stronger with time.

GIACINTA Yes, that's the way it must be, and the way it will be. I accept Signor Leonardo as the husband destined for me by heaven and given me by my father. I know I must love and respect him. As far as respect goes, I'll do my duty. As far as love goes, I'll do what I can.

BRIGIDA Excuse me, ma'am. But since you intend to respect him so well, is it true that you'll never do anything against his wishes?

GIACINTA Yes, but respect has to be mutual. If I respect him, he must respect me, too. So, he mustn't go treating me disrespectfully and considering me his slave.

BRIGIDA *(aside)* Wouldn't you know it! She's willing to respect her husband, but on her own terms!

GIACINTA It's been some time since that hothead Guglielmo tried to call on me.

BRIGIDA If he did come, I expect you'd refuse to receive him.

GIACINTA And why shouldn't I receive him? Why should I be a coward and show him I'm afraid of him? Am I not my own mistress? Don't I have the strength to see him and talk to him with indifference? I admit I've been weak in the past, but, in the three days since I last saw him, I've had time to come to my senses and fortify my head and my heart. I'm going to have to get used to seeing him, just as I see lots of other people. He's going to marry my sister-in-law. One way or another, we're going to have to spend time together. What would people say if I kept out of his sight? No, no, I'm going to start early getting accustomed to treating him as if I'd never been in love with him or never even known him. And I'm quite capable of doing it, I have the courage to do it, you'll see how clever and how good I'll be at it.

BRIGIDA What if Signor Leonardo doesn't want you to have anything to do with him?

GIACINTA Then Signor Leonardo would be insane. Why should he object to my seeing his brother-in-law?

BRIGIDA Don't you know how touchy people are when they're jealous?

GIACINTA Signor Leonardo knows I won't stand for jealousy.

BRIGIDA Strictly between ourselves, though, you must admit you've given him cause now and then.

GIACINTA What's done is done. He got the satisfaction of Guglielmo giving his word to marry his sister, and he will marry her, and that should be enough. When all's said and done, Guglielmo is an honest, decent young man, and I'm an honourable woman. It would be irresponsible to think otherwise.

BRIGIDA *(aside)* Whatever she may say, she'll never convince me that the wound is perfectly healed.

Scene 6

Enter *servant.*

SERVANT Madam, Signor Guglielmo is here and would like to pay his respects.

BRIGIDA *(aside)* Now we'll see how clever she is!

GIACINTA *(aside)* Alas! What can be the meaning of this fire that suddenly seethes up inside me?

BRIGIDA *(aside)* Oh, the poor thing! How red in the face she's become!

GIACINTA *(aside)* Oh, I must be brave. We must conquer this unworthy passion. *(to servant)* Show him in. He's welcome. *(exit servant)*

BRIGIDA Be brave, mistress.

GIACINTA What do you mean, be brave? Why are you telling me to be brave? What should I be afraid of? *(aside)* Here he comes. Oh, heavens! I'm trembling all over. My passion betrays me, my courage has fled. *(to Brigida)* Brigida, I've suddenly got stomach cramps and I have to leave the room. You receive Signor Guglielmo, and give him my excuses … *(aside)* Oh, I could kill myself with my own hands! *(exit Giacinta)*

Scene 7

Brigida, then enter Guglielmo.

BRIGIDA So much for valour! So much for courage! Poor girl! She's a woman, too – flesh and blood like the rest of us. *(enter Guglielmo)*

GUGLIELMO Where is Signora Giacinta?

BRIGIDA She asked me to make her excuses.

GUGLIELMO But the servant said she was here.

BRIGIDA She was here, in fact, but her father sent for her. *(aside)* If I say she has a stomach ache, he won't believe me, it's a feeble excuse.

GUGLIELMO I'll wait till she's free.

BRIGIDA What do you want with her, sir, if I may ask?

GUGLIELMO Am I supposed to account for my actions to you? I want to fulfil my social obligations, pay my respects, tell her I'm happy she's back. That's what I want. There, is your curiosity satisfied?

BRIGIDA Very well, sir, I'll give my mistress your compliments, and it'll be as good as if you'd given them in person.

GUGLIELMO Aren't I allowed to see her?

BRIGIDA There'll be plenty of time for that. She's still tired from the journey.

GUGLIELMO I consider this an insult. I'm a man of honour, and I don't think I deserve to be treated like this.

BRIGIDA My dear sir, you may take it however you like. I don't know what to tell you. *(aside)* I'd like to try and break up this relationship if I can.

GUGLIELMO Tell Signora Giacinta I'm engaged to Signora Vittoria.

BRIGIDA I think she already knows that without my telling her.

GUGLIELMO If it weren't for this fact, I wouldn't presume to come here and disturb her.

BRIGIDA By virtue of that fact, you'll have every opportunity to pay your respects, and to tell her whatever you like.

GUGLIELMO Are you saying you won't tell her anything?

BRIGIDA Nothing at all, if that's all right with you.

GUGLIELMO Is Signor Filippo at home?

BRIGIDA I don't know, sir.

GUGLIELMO What do you mean, you don't know? A moment ago you said he had sent for Signora Giacinta.

BRIGIDA If I said he sent for Signora Giacinta, why do you ask if he's home?

GUGLIELMO I must say, your behaviour is a little unusual.

BRIGIDA Excuse me ... I have things on my mind, too ... *(aside)* He's right, in a way. I let myself get carried away.

Scene 8

Enter *Leonardo.*

LEONARDO *(aside)* What's this? Guglielmo here? As soon as Giacinta gets back!

BRIGIDA *(aside)* Now here comes Leonardo. And this wretched Guglielmo just wouldn't go away.

LEONARDO *(to Brigida)* Where is Signora Giacinta?

BRIGIDA *(to Leonardo)* She's in there with her father.

GUGLIELMO *(greeting Leonardo)* My dear friend.

LEONARDO *(brusquely to Guglielmo)* Your servant, sir. *(to Brigida)* Ask her if I may be allowed to pay my respects.

BRIGIDA Yes, sir. Right away. Excuse me: isn't Paolino back yet?

LEONARDO No, he's not back yet.

BRIGIDA Could you tell me when he's expected?

LEONARDO Are you going to go, or aren't you?

BRIGIDA I'm going, I'm going. *(aside)* Oh, a fine thing! I'm as nervous as they are. *(exit Brigida)*

LEONARDO You're very eager to pay your respects to Signora Giacinta.

GUGLIELMO It's no more than my duty.

LEONARDO You're not so attentive or polite towards your fiancée.

GUGLIELMO Please tell me in what way I've erred.

LEONARDO Don't make me spell it out.

GUGLIELMO If you don't spell it out, I won't know what you're getting at.

LEONARDO Have you seen Signora Giacinta?

GUGLIELMO No, sir. I came here to pay my respects, but so far I've not been allowed to. But they won't keep you away from her, therefore I beg you to intercede on my behalf, so that I may perform my duty towards her.

LEONARDO Signor Guglielmo, when do you plan to marry my sister?

GUGLIELMO My dear friend, I don't believe that a marriage between civilized people should be concluded without the customary formalities.

LEONARDO In the meantime, however, why put off signing the contract?

GUGLIELMO We can sign it whenever you like.

LEONARDO Then let's sign it before the day's out.

GUGLIELMO Very well.

LEONARDO Would you be so good as to go to the notary and inform him?

GUGLIELMO Very well, I'll go and inform him.

LEONARDO You'd better go at once, if you want to catch him in.

GUGLIELMO Yes, I'll go at once. I beg you to give Signora Giacinta my regards, and tell her I came to pay my respects. *(aside)* I must pretend. I won't be happy till I've talked to her again. *(exit Guglielmo)*

Scene 9

Leonardo, then enter Brigida.

LEONARDO I still can't make this fellow out. First he arouses my suspicions, but then he can make me feel sorry I mistrusted him. His eagerness to see Giacinta seems a bit exaggerated, but, if he were guilty of some dishonourable passion, he wouldn't dare talk to me the way he does, and he wouldn't be so willing to expedite the marriage contract with my sister.

BRIGIDA Sir, my mistress sends her regards, she thanks you for your attentions, and she asks you to forgive her if she's unable to receive your respects this morning in person. She's not well, she needs rest.

LEONARDO Is Signora Giacinta in bed?

BRIGIDA She's not actually in bed, she's lying down on the sofa. She has a headache, and conversation is too much for her.

LEONARDO And I'm not allowed to see her, to pay my respects, to hear about her indisposition from her own lips?

BRIGIDA What I told you is what she told me.

LEONARDO *(incensed)* Very well, then. Tell her I'm sorry to hear about her illness, I can imagine what caused it, and for my part I'll do all I can to restore her to health.

BRIGIDA Sir, I hope you don't think …

LEONARDO *(as above)* Go tell her what I said.

BRIGIDA *(aside)* He's right, I have to admit he's right. She's totally blinded, all her virtues have gone up in smoke. *(exit Brigida)*

Scene 10

Leonardo, then enter servant.

LEONARDO Oh, yes, I deserve it. I deserve even worse. I should have realized before now that she feels neither love, respect, nor gratitude for me. My attentions are wasted on her, my hopes are in vain. Heaven help me if I should ever end up married to her! But am I to let her go? Am I to give her her freedom, so that she can shame me and dishonour my family by marrying Guglielmo? Can I let that worthless scoundrel mock me and the promise he made to my sister? No, we can't let them get away with that! I'll forget the ungrateful woman sooner or later, but I won't take this insult lying down! I'll find a way to get even. I'll get even whatever it costs. Even if it means my ruin, my downfall! I'm in dire straits, true enough, but I can still afford this satisfaction. I'll show the world I still have some fight left in me, and a sense of honour! Yes, you traitress, yes, my perfidious friend, I'll get even, you'll pay!

SERVANT Sir, one of your servants brought you this letter.

LEONARDO Where is he?

SERVANT He asked me if you were here, I said you were, he gave me the letter, and left.

LEONARDO All right, all right. That's all. *(reads the letter over to himself)*

SERVANT *(aside)* This gentleman is very upset, and my mistress is furious, too. They went to the country all smiles, and they came back with chips on their shoulders! *(exit servant)*

Scene 11

LEONARDO *(alone)* Oh, no! What's this? What dreadful news from Paolino! My country property seized? The furniture in my villa impounded? Even the linen, the place settings, and the silverware I borrowed? Paolino himself placed under arrest per order of the judicial authorities? This is the last straw, my reputation is finished. Montenero is still full of people from town. What will they say about me? Oh, how they'll drag my name in the mud! What was the point of my putting on such an elaborate front, if now my financial straits become public knowledge, and my ambition stands condemned? Oh, what a terrible, humiliating blow! Giacinta and Guglielmo will laugh at me, too. And to think I was plotting revenge! Do I have a worse enemy than myself? Oh, what a madman, what a fool, I'm my own worst enemy! *(exit Leonardo)*

ACT TWO

Scene 1

Leonardo's room.

LEONARDO *(alone)* I don't know what to do. I rack my brains and, instead of coming up with a solution, I'm driving myself to despair. I don't know how I can survive in Leghorn, and I have neither the means nor the courage to leave. What will Signora Giacinta think of me? How can I expect Signor Filippo to give me his daughter and a dowry of eight thousand crowns in the calamitous state that I'm in? Alas, poor me! And, in the midst of my other misfortunes, love continues to plague me. Oh, heavens! Here comes Signor Fulgenzio. The very sight of him makes me blush. I remember his warnings, his advice; I know I was wrong not to listen.

Scene 2

Enter *Fulgenzio.*

FULGENZIO *(aside)* Ah, there he is – the madman, the prodigal son, the fanatic!

LEONARDO My respects, my dear Signor Fulgenzio.

FULGENZIO *(stiffly)* Your servant, sir. Did you enjoy your stay in the country?

LEONARDO My dear sir, please don't ever mention the country again! I've conceived such a hatred for the country that I wouldn't go off to the country again if you paid me.

FULGENZIO Yes, an excellent decision. The trouble is you made it a little too late!

LEONARDO Better late than never.

FULGENZIO *(heatedly)* As long as there's still time, and as long as the decision is provoked by the desire to do right, not by impotence!

LEONARDO I don't believe I'm so far gone …

FULGENZIO Tell me, how could you be more ruined than you are? Do you think you can pull the wool over my eyes, too? I'm amazed at you. I'm amazed you could have the gall to embarrass a man in my position by having him ask a young woman to marry you. You knew how you stood. This is what I call an imposture, an out-and-out swindle. For my part, my options are clear: I shall tell Signor Filippo the truth; then he can do as he likes; I wash my hands of the whole business. And I'm making a solemn resolution not to get mixed up in anything like this ever again.

LEONARDO Oh, Signor Fulgenzio, for the love of heaven, don't drive me to the extremes of despair. You know my plight, have pity on me. I'm in a pitiful fix, I have nothing and no one to turn to, I shall be forced to give in to the last act of a desperate man. Without cash, without credit, without friends, without assistance, my life is nothing but shame and suffering. Help me, Signor Fulgenzio, help me. I'm on the brink of disaster, don't let my family come to a tragic end, don't let me make the ultimate spectacle of myself.

FULGENZIO If you were a son of mine, I'd be tempted to break every bone in your body. Yes, that's how your kind talk: I'm desperate, I'll hang myself, I'll drown myself! What should I care, you're no concern of mine. But I'm human, I recognize my humanity, I have a soft spot for everybody. You deserve to be left to stew in your juice, but I don't have the heart to do it.

LEONARDO Oh, God bless you! You're saving more than a man, you're saving a whole ruined family. Free me from my shame, my misery, from the throng of my creditors.

FULGENZIO Not so fast! What's the idea? Do you think I'm about to ruin myself to help you out? Do you think I'm about to pay off your debts, so you can run up some more?

LEONARDO No, Signor Fulgenzio, never again!

FULGENZIO I don't believe a word you say.

LEONARDO So what do all your previous offers boil down to?

FULGENZIO What they boil down to is this: I'm willing to use my influence with your Uncle Bernardino, with a person, in other words, who has more call to help you in your difficulties than I have and is better equipped to do so. And by spending my time, efforts, words, and counsel on your behalf, I'm already doing more than anyone could reasonably expect.

LEONARDO Sir, I'm in your hands, but, I warn you, you'll get nowhere with my Uncle Bernardino.

FULGENZIO And why won't I get anywhere?

LEONARDO Because he's a close-fisted old miser who wouldn't part with a penny to save his own life. And besides, he has such an insulting manner that nobody can stand him.

FULGENZIO Be that as it may, we must take this first step, we have to start here if we're going to get anywhere. If your own uncle won't help you, who do you think will?

LEONARDO You're right, I can't argue. It's just as you say.

FULGENZIO Come along, then.

LEONARDO *(getting ready to leave)* All right, I'll come, though I couldn't feel less like it.

Scene 3

Enter *Vittoria dressed in her best to go out.*

VITTORIA A word with you, Leonardo.

LEONARDO Get it over with quickly, I've no time to waste.

VITTORIA I wanted to ask you if you'd like to come with me to Signora Giacinta's.

LEONARDO I'd love to come, but I can't at the moment. You go, and let me know how she is, what kind of a welcome she gives you, what she says about me, and how she feels about our getting married.

VITTORIA Haven't you seen her yet?

LEONARDO No, I haven't gotten to see her so far.

FULGENZIO *(aside to Leonardo)* Hurry up, Signor Leonardo.

LEONARDO *(to Fulgenzio)* I'm coming.

VITTORIA Brother, dear, you know what she's like. If you start slackening off your attentions, I wouldn't give much for your chances.

LEONARDO Signor Fulgenzio, I don't think half an hour more or less would make that much difference.

FULGENZIO *(aside to Leonardo)* Your uncle has an early lunch, and after lunch he usually takes a nap.

LEONARDO *(aside to Fulgenzio)* Let's not waste any more time, then.

VITTORIA If she asks about you, if she complains you don't seem too eager to see her, what excuse should I give?

LEONARDO *(aside to Fulgenzio)* Couldn't we put off going to my uncle's till after lunch?

FULGENZIO *(aside to Leonardo)* Do you want your house swarming with creditors again?

LEONARDO *(aside to Fulgenzio)* Oh my God, it would be more than I could take.

FULGENZIO *(aside to Leonardo)* Let's go, then. Forget this little heartache.

VITTORIA Brother, after what happened in the country, I can't get over your apparent lack of concern for a matter that should vitally affect you.

LEONARDO *(aside)* She's right, Vittoria makes sense. Indifference is a dangerous tactic. Giacinta doesn't appear to be overenamoured of me, she could use anything as an excuse.

FULGENZIO *(aside to Leonardo)* Either you come or I'm leaving.

LEONARDO *(aside to Fulgenzio)* One more minute, for pity's sake!

VITTORIA *(aside to Leonardo)* Listen. You haven't forgotten Giacinta's visit to the farm manager's wife in Montenero?[9]

LEONARDO *(aside)* Oh, how that cruel reminder strikes home! *(to Fulgenzio)* Signor Fulgenzio, couldn't you go by yourself to Uncle Bernardino's, couldn't you talk to him yourself, and come to some kind of agreement ...

FULGENZIO *(preparing to leave)* I see how the land lies. Good day, sir.

LEONARDO No, wait! I'll come with you. *(aside)* Wherever I turn, all I see is rocks, tempests, sheer cliffs. *(to Vittoria)* You go on ahead, and tell Signora Giacinta ... I can't decide what ... Tell her whatever you like. *(to Fulgenzio)* Let's go. *(aside)* I'm at my wits' end, I don't know what I want. I get more fearful, more hopeless, more desperate by the minute. *(exit Leonardo with Fulgenzio)*

Scene 4

Vittoria, then enter Guglielmo and Ferdinando.

VITTORIA That old fool couldn't be ruder if he tried. But in our present predicament, I can only conclude that my brother must need him, so we have to put up with him. Oh, oh! Here comes Signor Guglielmo! It's about time he came round to see me! But he has that boorish Ferdinando with him. It's as if Guglielmo were doing it on purpose, as if he were trying to avoid being alone with me. That's a sign of faint love. I'm getting more and more suspicious by the minute.

FERDINANDO *(aside, to Guglielmo)* But, my dear friend, I have business to attend to, I can't stay too long.

GUGLIELMO *(aside, to Ferdinando)* Please be patient. It'll be a short visit. I need to talk to you. *(aside, to himself)* Since it's my bad luck to have to come here, I can use the company of a third party.

VITTORIA *(aside)* These two gentlemen have some deep secrets!

FERDINANDO *(bowing)* My respects to Signora Vittoria.

VITTORIA *(to Ferdinando)* To what do I owe the extreme pleasure of your most gracious visit?

FERDINANDO I'm here to accompany my friend.

VITTORIA Is Signor Guglielmo afraid of coming alone?

GUGLIELMO Forgive me, madam. Until I have the honour of becoming your husband, I feel that your good name requires this precaution.

FERDINANDO Incidentally, my friends, when is this wedding going to take place?

VITTORIA Whenever the gallant Signor Guglielmo decides.

GUGLIELMO Madam, you know better than I do that a marriage is not something you can leap into.

FERDINANDO Have you signed the contract yet?

VITTORIA No, sir. He's not found time yet to perform that overwhelming task, which can be done in a second, and which was supposed to be done as soon as we got back to Leghorn.

GUGLIELMO I haven't been able to get hold of the notary.

FERDINANDO What do you need a notary for? Contracts like that can be arranged privately. I offered you my services myself in Montenero. I can do it here, if you wish.

VITTORIA If Signor Guglielmo is willing.

GUGLIELMO To tell you the truth, Signor Leonardo instructed me to get hold of the notary. I've already seen him, and we agreed he should come here tonight. It hardly seems right to insult him, and I don't see why it's so urgent to move things up from the evening to the morning.

VITTORIA Very well, very well. If we're going to sign this evening …

FERDINANDO I thought Signora Vittoria already knew the contract was to be signed today.

VITTORIA And what made you think I knew?

FERDINANDO Because you're wearing your wedding dress.

VITTORIA No, sir, you are wrong. I dressed up a little to go visit Signora Giacinta.

GUGLIELMO Do you plan to go to Signora Giacinta's now?

VITTORIA Yes, of course. Since I have to go through with this formality, I may as well get it over with right away.

GUGLIELMO Are you going alone?

VITTORIA I wanted my brother to come with me, but his business wouldn't permit it.

GUGLIELMO I'll accompany you, if you wish.

VITTORIA *(ironically)* Oh, Signor Guglielmo, I'm so grateful for your kind consideration! This is the first time you've been so nice to me. No, no, sir, I wouldn't dream of putting you out.

FERDINANDO *(aside)* This visit's finally becoming amusing.

GUGLIELMO Forgive me, madam. I don't think we could do better than to go there together. I owe Signor Filippo and Signora Giacinta a visit myself. If I go there with you, you shouldn't take it badly.

VITTORIA I was thinking of your sensible remark earlier. As long as we're not married, we shouldn't be seen out together.

FERDINANDO She's right. There speaks the voice of prudence. You go hurry up the notary. I'll have the honour of accompanying her to Signora Giacinta's.

VITTORIA And it wouldn't be a bad idea if when I get back, in an hour or so at most, you were to be waiting here with the notary.

GUGLIELMO So, you prefer to go with Signor Ferdinando?

VITTORIA Yes, I'd rather go with him than go alone.

GUGLIELMO You're willing to go with him, but not with me.

FERDINANDO When I offered, I thought I was doing both of you a favour.

VITTORIA *(to Guglielmo)* If I go with him, no one can criticize me.

GUGLIELMO Very well, madam, I see. You find my unpleasant character annoying. Signor Ferdinando is witty and brilliant. You're wasting no time letting me know I'll be an unhappy husband. Let's speak plainly, madam: if you don't like me, you're still free to break things off.

VITTORIA If I wasn't in love with you, I wouldn't be concerned at your coldness, and I wouldn't be insisting so much on your speeding up signing the contract.

GUGLIELMO You say you love me, yet you show preference to someone else to my face!

FERDINANDO Come, friend, don't tell me you're jealous.

VITTORIA *(to Guglielmo)* I never thought you'd get an idea like that.

GUGLIELMO I don't think things without a reason, I judge by what I see.

VITTORIA Signor Guglielmo, speak to me sincerely.

GUGLIELMO I can't speak more straightforwardly than I'm speaking already. I tell you, you're doing me an injustice, and I don't believe I deserve it.

VITTORIA *(aside)* So he loves me more than I thought.

FERDINANDO Friends, if I'm in the way, I'll leave immediately.

GUGLIELMO No, no, stay and accompany Signora Vittoria.

VITTORIA No, my dear Signor Guglielmo, don't take it so badly. I apologize if I said anything to upset you. I couldn't love you more dearly. I'm to be your wife, and I'll do whatever you think best. I'll go with you to Signora Giacinta's. Or I'll forget about going altogether, if that's what you prefer.

GUGLIELMO Our social obligation requires both of us to make this gesture of politeness.

VITTORIA Let's go immediately, then. Forgive me, Signor Ferdinando, if I don't take advantage of your offer.

FERDINANDO As you prefer, madam. It's all the same to me.

GUGLIELMO Perhaps Signor Ferdinando will be so good as to accompany us.

VITTORIA But it's not necessary …

GUGLIELMO Oh, yes, madam, it is necessary, to satisfy that principle of modesty and decorum which I mentioned earlier, and which you later approved of.

FERDINANDO In other words, I must play the chaperone.

VITTORIA Oh! Signor Guglielmo, if it's true that you love me …

GUGLIELMO Come, let's go, before it gets too close to lunchtime.

VITTORIA I'm ready. Whatever you prefer.

GUGLIELMO *(to Ferdinando)* My friend, will you escort Signora Vittoria?

FERDINANDO *(to Guglielmo)* Shall I give her my arm?

GUGLIELMO Yes, do us the honour.

VITTORIA Why don't you escort me?

GUGLIELMO Madam, I know what's done and what's not done. All I ask is not to be ill-treated.

VITTORIA But I certainly …

GUGLIELMO Please make the best of it, madam, and take his arm.

VITTORIA *(giving her hand to Ferdinando)* I obey. *(aside)* I'm beginning to feel a bit better about the way things are going.

FERDINANDO *(aside)* I must say, they make me look silly at times. But enough of that! At least I have the consolation of knowing that there'll be a place set for me at the marriage feast! *(exit Ferdinando with Vittoria)*

GUGLIELMO *(aside)* How I had to struggle and playact for the chance of seeing Giacinta again! *(exit Guglielmo)*

Scene 5

A room in Bernardino's house. Bernardino, in an outmoded dressing gown, and the servant Pasquale, then enter Fulgenzio.

BERNARDINO *(to Pasquale)* Who is it? Who wants to see me?

PASQUALE Signor Fulgenzio would like to pay his respects.

BERNARDINO He's welcome, he's welcome. Show Signor Fulgenzio in. He's welcome.

FULGENZIO My respects, Signor Bernardino.

BERNARDINO Good day, my dear friend. What are you up to? Are you well? It's ages since I last saw you.

FULGENZIO Yes, thank heaven, I'm well, as well as someone who's beginning to suffer the infirmities of old age can expect.

BERNARDINO *(laughing)* Do as I do, don't give them a thought. A few ailments can't be helped, but if you don't give them a thought, you notice them less. I eat when I'm hungry, sleep when I'm sleepy, enjoy myself whenever I feel like it. And I don't give them a thought, not a thought. What should I give a thought to, I ask you? Ha, ha, ha! It makes no difference. You just don't have to give them a thought.

FULGENZIO God bless you, what a wonderful attitude! People who can take things like you do are lucky!

BERNARDINO *(laughing)* It makes no difference, no difference at all. Just don't give them a thought.

FULGENZIO I came here to disturb you with a matter of no little consequence.

BERNARDINO My dear Signor Fulgenzio, here I am, at your service.

FULGENZIO My friend, I must talk to you about your nephew Leonardo.

BERNARDINO Oh, his lordship Leonardo! And what's his lordship up to these days? How is his lordship?

FULGENZIO To tell you the truth, he hasn't been showing much judgment.

BERNARDINO Not been showing much judgment? I'd say he has a sight more judgment than we do. We work our fingers to the bone to earn a livelihood, and he enjoys, squanders, parties, and leads the gay life; and you say he doesn't have judgment?

FULGENZIO I can see you're speaking ironically, and that in your heart of hearts you condemn and detest him.

BERNARDINO *(ironically)* Oh, I would never presume to question the conduct of his illustrious lordship Leonardo. I have too much respect for him, for his talent, for his fine, fancy clothes.

FULGENZIO My dear friend, do me a favour. Let's be serious for a moment.

BERNARDINO Why, of course, let's talk seriously.

FULGENZIO Your nephew has come a cropper.

BERNARDINO You mean: had a fall? Did he fall out of his carriage? Did the team of six snatch the reins from the hands of the coachman?

FULGENZIO You can laugh, but it's nothing to laugh about. Your nephew has so many debts, he doesn't know which way to turn.

BERNARDINO Oh, if that's all it is, then it's nothing. His debts won't bother him, they'll bother his creditors.

FULGENZIO And if he's run out of cash and run out of credit, how is he going to survive?

BERNARDINO Not to worry, not to worry, I tell you. Let him go one day at a time to eat at the houses of all those who once ate at his house. He'll have plenty to keep him going.

FULGENZIO You keep up the same tone. Are you trying to make fun of me?

BERNARDINO Dear Signor Fulgenzio, you know I'm your friend and how much I respect you.

FULGENZIO If that's the case, listen to the way things are and answer more seriously. I must tell you that Signor Leonardo has an excellent opportunity to get married.

BERNARDINO I'm happy for him, I'm delighted for him.

FULGENZIO With a dowry of eight thousand crowns.

BERNARDINO I'm happy for him, I'm delighted for him.

FULGENZIO But unless he can put his house in order, he won't get the daughter, and he won't get the dowry.

BERNARDINO What? A man like him? All he has to do is stamp his foot and the money comes up out of every crack!

FULGENZIO *(aside)* Now I'm losing my patience … Leonardo warned me. *(angrily, to Bernardino)* I tell you, your nephew is ruined.

BERNARDINO *(with mock seriousness)* Oh, yes? Well, if you say so, it must be so.

FULGENZIO But he could easily recover.

BERNARDINO Oh, good! He'll recover.

FULGENZIO But he needs your help.

BERNARDINO Oh, no! That can't be!

FULGENZIO But he's relying on you.
BERNARDINO Not his lordship! Impossible!
FULGENZIO It's the truth, I tell you. He's counting on your kindness and affection. And if I weren't afraid you'd receive him unkindly, I'd have him come here in person to apologize and ask your forgiveness.
BERNARDINO Forgiveness? Why ask me for forgiveness? Come on, you're pulling my leg. I don't deserve all this deference, in my case these formalities are uncalled-for. We are friends, we are relatives. Signor Leonardo? Oh, craving Signor Leonardo's indulgence, he needn't be so formal with me.
FULGENZIO If he comes to see you, will you give him an affectionate welcome?
BERNARDINO Why shouldn't I give him an affectionate welcome?
FULGENZIO By your leave, then, I'll get him to come.
BERNARDINO He's welcome, whenever he feels like coming, he's welcome.
FULGENZIO With your permission, then, I'll have him come over.
BERNARDINO Where is Signor Leonardo?
FULGENZIO He's out there in the hall, waiting.
BERNARDINO *(taken aback)* In the hall, waiting?
FULGENZIO I'll bring him in, if it's all right with you.
BERNARDINO Yes, go ahead, bring him in.
FULGENZIO *(aside)* When he hears him in person, maybe he'll be moved. I'm getting fed up with my role in all this. *(exit Fulgenzio)*

Scene 6

Bernardino, then enter Fulgenzio and Leonardo, then Pasquale.

BERNARDINO Ha, ha, the old fox! He brought him along. He charged into the breach himself, and now he's bringing in reinforcements for a fresh assault!
FULGENZIO Here is Signor Leonardo.
LEONARDO Pray forgive me, Uncle …
BERNARDINO Oh, Milord Nephew! My humble respects. And how do you do? Well, I trust? And how is milady your sister? What is my dear little niece up to? Did you have a nice time in the country? Did you come back in good health? Are things going well? Yes? Well, get along with you then, I couldn't be happier.

LEONARDO Sir, I don't deserve to be received by you with the affection to which your kind words bear witness. I therefore have reason to fear that you wish to veil with your excessive benevolence the reprobation I merit.

BERNARDINO *(to Fulgenzio)* What do you think of that, eh? Isn't he a talented young fellow? What delivery! What a fine speech!

FULGENZIO Let's skip the superfluous speeches. You know what I told you. He's in dire need of your kindness and is making a fervent appeal …

BERNARDINO … that I might … in whatever way I can … if only I could …

LEONARDO *(hat in hand)* Oh, Uncle …

BERNARDINO Put your hat back on.

LEONARDO I regret that my misconduct …

BERNARDINO Put your hat on your head.

LEONARDO Has brought me to this pass.

BERNARDINO Allow me. *(puts Leonardo's hat on for him)*

LEONARDO And unless you help me …

BERNARDINO *(to Fulgenzio)* What's the time?

FULGENZIO *(to Bernardino)* Listen to him, if you will.

LEONARDO Oh, my beloved Uncle … *(takes off his hat)*

BERNARDINO Your most humble servant. *(takes off his nightcap)*

LEONARDO Don't turn your back on me.

BERNARDINO *(nightcap in hand)* Oh, I wouldn't dream of doing something as rude as that for the world.

LEONARDO *(hat in hand)* My only mistake was my over-extravagant stay in the country.

BERNARDINO If you'll allow me. *(puts his nightcap back on)* Did you have many guests this year? Did you have a nice time?

LEONARDO All foolishness, sir. I confess it. I see it now. I regret it with all my heart.

BERNARDINO Is it true you're getting married?

LEONARDO I'm supposed to, and a dowry of eight thousand crowns could put me back on my feet again. But unless you help me out with a few of my debts …

BERNARDINO Yes, indeed. Eight thousand crowns is a pretty sum.

FULGENZIO His fiancée is the daughter of Signor Filippo Ganganelli.

BERNARDINO Excellent, I know him. A real gentleman! A man who knows how to vacation. A good-natured, good-humoured man. An excellent match. I couldn't be happier.

LEONARDO But unless I find a remedy for part of my misfortunes at least …

BERNARDINO Please give my kindest regards to Signor Filippo.

LEONARDO Unless I find a remedy, sir, for my misfortunes …

BERNARDINO And give him my congratulations too.

LEONARDO Sir, you're not paying attention.

BERNARDINO You're right, sir. I hear you're going to be married, and I'm happy for you.

LEONARDO And you don't want to help me?

BERNARDINO What's the bride's name?

LEONARDO Can you have the heart to abandon me?

BERNARDINO Oh, how happy I am to hear that my nephew's getting married!

LEONARDO Thank you, sir, for your good wishes. You may rest assured that this is the last time I will ever darken your doorstep.

BERNARDINO Your most humble servant.

LEONARDO *(to Fulgenzio)* What did I tell you? My stomach's in knots. I can't stand him. *(exit Leonardo)*

BERNARDINO My respects to my nephew.

FULGENZIO *(indignant to Bernardino)* Your servant, sir.

BERNARDINO Good day, my dear Signor Fulgenzio.

FULGENZIO If I had known what to expect, I'd never have come to disturb you.

BERNARDINO Any time. Day or night, at any hour.

FULGENZIO You're worse than a dog.

BERNARDINO Good for you, sir, good for you! Bravo, Signor Fulgenzio!

FULGENZIO *(aside)* I could cut his throat with my own hands! *(exit Fulgenzio)*

BERNARDINO Pasquale!

PASQUALE Sir?

BERNARDINO You can serve lunch now. *(exit Bernardino)*

Scene 7

A room in Filippo's house. Giacinta and Brigida, then enter servant.

BRIGIDA No, madam, it's no use saying: I'll say this, I'll do that, this is how it's going to be, that is how I'm going to behave. There are circumstances over which we have no control.

GIACINTA But surely, if the circumstances are repeated, what happened to me this time won't happen again?

BRIGIDA I pray to heaven things turn out that way, but I have my doubts.

GIACINTA But I couldn't be more certain.

BRIGIDA What makes you so certain?

GIACINTA Listen, you have to agree that fate's on my side. As upset as I was, I picked up a book, to take my mind off my problems. I picked it up at random, but I couldn't have run across a more appropriate text. It's called *Remedies for Spiritual Ailments.*[10] Among other things, I learned this: "When a person's mind is occupied with an unpleasant idea, he or she must try to introduce an opposite idea into his or her mind." It says that our brains are full of an infinite number of "cells," in which lots of different ideas are locked up and ready to be unlocked. Our "Will" can lock and unlock these "cells" as it pleases, and "Reason" tells "Will" to lock one up and unlock another. For example, if the cell that makes me think of Guglielmo opens up in my brain, all I have to do is call in Reason, and all Reason has to do is make Will open the drawer containing the ideas of duty, virtue, and good reputation; or, if these are hard to locate, all you have to do is concentrate on the most indifferent things, such as clothes, needlework, card games, lotteries, conversation, tables, walks, and the like. If Reason's unwilling, and Will isn't ready, you just shake the machine, make violent gestures, bite your lips, laugh out loud, until the fantasy clears, and the cell containing the bad thought shuts down, and the one selected by Reason and put forward by Will opens up.

BRIGIDA I wish I knew how to read. I'd ask you to let me read a page or two of that book, too.

GIACINTA Why? Do you have thoughts that bother you, too?

BRIGIDA I have one, madam, that never leaves me, not even when I'm asleep.

GIACINTA Tell me what it is. Maybe I can tell you what cell to unlock to drive it away.

BRIGIDA To be perfectly honest, madam, I'm desperately in love with Paolino, and he has promised to marry me. Now he's in Montenero on an errand for his master, and nobody knows when he'll be back.

GIACINTA Oh, Brigida, this idea of yours is not such a wicked idea, it's not likely to cause you such trouble that you need to make an effort to drive it away. It's not a bad match for either one of you. I see no objection to your marriage. All you have to do is to open up the cell of hope, without closing the cell of love.

BRIGIDA To tell you the truth, madam, I figure both are already wide open. *(enter servant)*

SERVANT Madam, Signora Vittoria, Signor Ferdinando, and Signor Guglielmo are here to pay their respects.

GIACINTA *(aside)* Oh my heavens! *(to servant)* It's nothing, it's nothing. Show them in, they're welcome. *(exit servant)*

BRIGIDA Now, we'll see if your system works, mistress.

GIACINTA Yes, I'm glad to have the chance to try it.

BRIGIDA Remember what you're supposed to do.

GIACINTA I've already started. The minute a troublesome thought came to bother me, I drove it out at once by thinking of Signor Ferdinando, who is a merry person who will make me laugh till I cry.

BRIGIDA That's the way, madam! Laugh and shake up the machine, and enjoy yourself.

Scene 8

Enter *Vittoria, Guglielmo, and Ferdinando.*

VITTORIA Welcome back to town, my dearest Giacinta!

GIACINTA *(gaily)* I'm happy to be here. I'm so happy to see you! Gentlemen. Quickly, bring some chairs.

FERDINANDO Is Signora Giacinta well?

GIACINTA Well, very well. I never felt better.

GUGLIELMO I'm happy to see you so well.

GIACINTA Thank you, thank you. Quickly, the chairs. Here, give me a chair! *(snatching a chair)*

BRIGIDA *(aside)* She needs to shake up the machine!

GIACINTA *(gaily)* Come along, now. Sit down. Take a seat. What's new in Leghorn?

VITTORIA I haven't heard anything especially new.

GIACINTA Here, here. Signor Ferdinando knows everything, he goes everywhere. He'll tell us what's new in town.

FERDINANDO Madam, I got here this morning like you did. What can I tell you? Unless Signor Guglielmo has something to tell us …

GUGLIELMO There is news, but I can't repeat it here.

GIACINTA *(to Ferdinando, hitting him forcefully on the arm)* Come, sir, tell us something amusing.

FERDINANDO I don't know what to tell you.

VITTORIA If we can't hear the whole thing, at least let's hear part of what Signor Guglielmo has to say.

GIACINTA *(to Ferdinando, hitting him on the arm again)* No, you, you tell us something!

BRIGIDA *(aside)* Now she's shaking up Signor Ferdinando's machine!

FERDINANDO Madam, have you made up your mind to break my arm?

GIACINTA Oh, you poor thing! You poor delicate thing! Did I hurt you?

GUGLIELMO A little charity, madam, a little charity!

GIACINTA *(aside)* Oh, damn you! *(to Ferdinando)* Oh, but how amusing our Signor Ferdinando is! He makes me laugh, he makes me die laughing; when I laugh so heartily, I get quite out of breath.

VITTORIA What's gotten into you today, Signora Giacinta, that you're so cheerful?

GIACINTA I don't even know myself! I feel so gay, so light-hearted today, I never felt anything like it.

FERDINANDO There must be a reason.

GUGLIELMO It's probably because her wedding day's getting closer.

GIACINTA *(aside)* Oh, I wish his tongue would dry up! *(to Vittoria)* That's a very pretty dress, sweet Vittoria.

VITTORIA It's just an ordinary little dress.

FERDINANDO She's beginning to act like a bride-to-be as well.

GIACINTA Did you have it made this year?

VITTORIA No, to tell you the truth, it's last year's.

GIACINTA It's still very fashionable.

VITTORIA Yes, I had it altered a bit.

GIACINTA Did Monsieur de la Rejouissance make it?

VITTORIA Yes, the same tailor who made my "mariage."

FERDINANDO Speaking of "mariages," ladies, when are your weddings going to be?

GIACINTA *(giving Ferdinando a big push)* You have a very bad habit of interrupting when people are talking …

FERDINANDO You've decided you're going to persecute me this morning.

GIACINTA You're right, I've every intention of persecuting you. I'm helping my poor old aunt get her own back. You treated her so badly.

FERDINANDO What did I do to Signora Sabina?

GIACINTA What did you do to her? The very worst thing you could do! *(looking at Guglielmo as she speaks)* You spotted her weakness, and you took advantage of her. You made her fall desperately in love. A man of honour shouldn't behave that way, a gentleman shouldn't try to make an old lady – or a young one, for that matter – fall in love, when that love can never have a decent outcome. And when he knows he's compromising the interests or the good name of a woman – whether she be a single woman or a widow – he has a responsibility to give up and back off and not to continue to pursue her, to pester her with visits and importunate attentions and pretences. That is barbarous, dangerous, inhuman behaviour. *(Ferdinando turns to look at Guglielmo as well)*

GIACINTA *(to Ferdinando)* I'm talking to you, I'm talking to you. It's no use your looking the other way! It's you I'm talking to!

FERDINANDO *(aside)* The kidding has gone too far. Her digs are becoming impertinent.

VITTORIA *(aside)* Signora Giacinta is getting very worked up. In a way, she's right, but she came down on him a bit heavily.

GUGLIELMO *(aside)* Poor Ferdinando! He doesn't realize who her words are meant for. He's getting what's intended for me.

FERDINANDO *(aside)* I'm not going to sit here and wait for things to get worse. *(getting up)* By your leave … ladies … Guglielmo …

GIACINTA Where do you think you're going?

FERDINANDO I know where I'm not wanted.

GIACINTA *(with forced gaiety)* Come on, now, don't make a scene. Stay where you are.

VITTORIA Poor man! You shouldn't have told him off like that.

GIACINTA Come along, now. Sit down. I was joking. *(makes him sit down forcibly)* Poor Signor Ferdinando! Did you take it to heart?

FERDINANDO Madam, when a joke gets out of hand …

GIACINTA *(gaily)* Oh, here comes my father. Now the entertainment's complete! Old as he is, God bless him, he could still keep half the world entertained. He's a hundred times livelier than I am.

VITTORIA *(softly to Guglielmo)* Giacinta's in a fantastic mood today.

GUGLIELMO *(aside, softly to Vittoria)* Yes, you're right. *(aside, to himself)* But I think she's squirming inside. If I have to suffer, let her suffer a bit too.

Scene 9

Enter *Filippo.*

FILIPPO Your servant, ladies and gentlemen.

VITTORIA How nice to see you, Signor Filippo.

FILIPPO Are you staying to lunch?

VITTORIA Oh, no, sir. I just came to pay my respects.

GIACINTA *(aside)* She didn't have to bring him along.

FILIPPO If you'll do me the honour, you're welcome. You'd be doing me a favour. It would be just like being in the country.

VITTORIA As far as I'm concerned, thank you, but I'm expecting visitors today, and I have to be home.

FILIPPO *(to Vittoria)* What news of Signor Leonardo?

VITTORIA He's well. Haven't you seen him yet?

FILIPPO He hasn't favoured us yet, though I'm looking forward to seeing him. Is his uncle alive or dead?

VITTORIA He's alive, he's alive. He recovered, he has no intention of dying.

FILIPPO Would you believe it? And the doctors had given him up for dead! I'm delighted; poor fellow! Tell Signor Leonardo to be so good as to come and see us, I must talk to him. We have to arrange this wedding with my daughter.

GIACINTA *(aside)* There he goes! All they seem to talk about is weddings!

VITTORIA I'll tell him, sir. I think he'll be delighted.

GUGLIELMO Signor Leonardo is not very attentive. He doesn't treat Signora Giacinta as well as she deserves.

GIACINTA *(aside, wiping her brow with her handkerchief)* What is it about his odious words? They even make me perspire. *(enter servant)*

SERVANT Ladies and gentlemen, Signora Costanza sends her respects, and requests to inform you that she's back in Leghorn with her niece. *(exit servant)*

GIACINTA *(with forced gaiety)* Good for her! What wonderful news! I bet the young doctor came with them. We'll get to hear the latest about this marvellous marriage. I intend to make the most of dear little Tognino.

FERDINANDO Nothing but marriages! Nothing but weddings! First, Signora Vittoria and Signora Giacinta … and now Signora Rosina! *(getting up)*

GIACINTA *(aside)* I hope you come down with a fever! *(to Vittoria)* Oh, I want to go see them right away. I'm burning up with curiosity. Will you come too, Signora Vittoria?

VITTORIA I'll go, but not right now.

FILIPPO It's lunch time. Why do you have to go now?

GIACINTA Yes, you're right. I'll go after lunch. I have to get dressed, I have to do my hair, I have to put on my make-up …

VITTORIA Signora Giacinta, we'll get out of your way. *(getting up)*

GIACINTA Good-bye, sweet Vittoria.

Vittoria Your servant, Signor Filippo.

Filippo I hope to have the honour of seeing you again soon. Don't forget to tell Signor Leonardo.

Giacinta *(annoyed, to Filippo)* You have a bad habit of repeating everything a hundred times! Do you think everybody else's memory is as bad as yours?

Filippo *(to Giacinta)* Come, come, Signora, don't jump down my throat!

Vittoria *(leaving)* Until later, then.

Giacinta Goodbye.

Guglielmo *(greeting Filippo and Giacinta)* Your servant.

Filippo My respects, Signor Guglielmo.

Guglielmo *(bowing, leaving)* My respects to Signora Giacinta.

Giacinta *(to Guglielmo)* Your servant, your servant. *(to Ferdinando)* The young doctor will give us a good laugh.

Ferdinando *(leaving)* He certainly will. Your servant.

Filippo *(to Ferdinando)* Your servant.

Giacinta *(to Ferdinando)* Your servant, sir. *(exit Guglielmo, Ferdinando, and Vittoria)*

Filippo If you're going to get ready to go out, hurry up. I'm hungry and I'd like to go in to lunch. *(exit Filippo)*

Scene 10

Giacinta, then enter Brigida.

Giacinta I'm at my wits' end. I don't know if I'm standing on my head or on my heels.

Brigida Mistress, how goes the machine?

Giacinta Oh, leave me alone. Don't try to get a rise out of me with your wisecracks.

Brigida Madam, I have something to tell you, but I wouldn't want you to get more worked up than you already are.

Giacinta What is it you want to tell me?

Brigida Unless you calm down, I won't tell you.

Giacinta Come on, have a little compassion. I deserve it. Tell me, I promise not to get angry.

Brigida As Signora Vittoria was going downstairs, on Signor Ferdinando's arm …

Giacinta On Signor Ferdinando's arm? Wasn't Signor Guglielmo giving her his arm?

BRIGIDA No, madam, Signor Ferdinando was giving her his.
GIACINTA *(aside)* What have I always said? Guglielmo can't stand her.
BRIGIDA So, as they were going downstairs, Signor Guglielmo was a few steps behind. He called to me under his breath …
GIACINTA And what did the impertinent fellow say?
BRIGIDA If you're going to get angry, I won't say any more.
GIACINTA I'm not angry, I'm listening dispassionately. What did he say?
BRIGIDA He was holding a letter …
GIACINTA A letter for whom?
BRIGIDA For you.
GIACINTA A letter for me? And were you foolish enough to accept it?
BRIGIDA Oh, no, madam, no, I didn't take it. *(aside)* If I say I took it, she'll scratch my eyes out!
GIACINTA *(aside)* A letter for me? Whatever would he dare to write me?
BRIGIDA *(aside)* I didn't want it. He made me take it.
GIACINTA *(aside)* On the other hand, it could have been very useful for me to know how he's feeling at present.
BRIGIDA *(aside)* I'll throw it in the fire.
GIACINTA Did he say anything when he tried to give you the letter?
BRIGIDA Nothing at all, madam.
GIACINTA How did you know he wanted to give you a letter?
BRIGIDA He called me, and I saw he was holding a piece of paper.
GIACINTA And how did you know it was for me?
BRIGIDA He told me so.
GIACINTA So he did speak.
BRIGIDA It doesn't take long to say a couple of words.
GIACINTA And why did you refuse to take the letter?
BRIGIDA Because the man is a nuisance, and he won't leave you alone.
GIACINTA Just my luck! You always do the wrong thing. I couldn't be more curious. I'd give all I possess in the world to be able to see that letter you refused to accept.
BRIGIDA But madam, I …
GIACINTA You always have to play the smart-aleck, know-it-all schemer.
BRIGIDA Oh, I know you, madam. You're saying that to find out if I took it or not.
GIACINTA *(sweetly)* Brigida, did you take that letter?
BRIGIDA If I'd taken it, would you have me whipped?
GIACINTA No, my dear, I'd thank you, I'd bless you, I'd give you a nice present that would make you happy.
BRIGIDA *(aside)* I don't know whether to believe her.

GIACINTA *(sweetly)* Brigida, did you take it?
BRIGIDA Well, to tell you the truth, I was afraid he might give it to somebody else, so I thought it best to take it.
GIACINTA Oh, give it to me, or you'll kill me.
BRIGIDA Here it is. Did I do the wrong thing to take it?
GIACINTA No, bless you. Let me see it.
BRIGIDA There you are.
GIACINTA Oh, heavens! My heart is racing, my hand is shaking. Oh, this letter could destroy me!
BRIGIDA If you want my advice, madam, burn it, don't read it.
GIACINTA Go away. Leave me alone.
BRIGIDA Oh, no, let me stay. I won't leave you alone.
GIACINTA *(indignantly)* Go away, I tell you. Don't bother me.
BRIGIDA All right, madam, as you wish. *(aside)* Wouldn't you know it, my nice present turns out to be scolding and insults! *(exit Brigida)*

Scene 11

GIACINTA *(alone)* As if he weren't content with pestering me with visits, he has to insult me with letters. But nothing he has to say will make any difference. My mind is made up. I'll give him an answer that will shame him and make him give up and leave me alone. He's forgotten what I had the courage to tell him in the woods at Montenero! I'll remind him in writing. Let's see what he had the gall to write. *(opens the letter, sits down, and starts reading)* "Mademoiselle, I came to pay my respects this morning. I was not permitted. Your maid treated me rather rudely ..." Brigida can be very forward and petulant at times. Why treat people impolitely? Even if I didn't want to see Signor Guglielmo, that didn't entitle her to give him impertinent answers. "When your future husband arrived, the man who will have the happiness of possessing your hand and your heart ..." Oh! I wouldn't be so sure about my heart. "He compelled me to leave, in a manner no less harsh and insulting ..." What? In my own house? He's already playing the boss? Giving orders before he's entitled? Oh! This is something I won't stand for. But, poor Leonardo, doesn't he have cause for suspicion? Loving me as he does, aren't his outbursts understandable? If he's going to marry me, isn't he entitled to resent anyone he sees as a rival, anyone who upsets him or gets under his skin? Yes, Leonardo is right, and Guglielmo is wrong. "I don't know when I will have the good fortune to see you again." Would to God I never see him again! "Therefore, I have dared to write you this humble note for two reasons. The first is to point out to you that I have never failed in my respect ..." You can't say he's not courteous and polite. "And to assure you that you will not have to suffer any further harassment on my part, as I promise you on my honour that, even if it kills me, I will avoid any unwanted meetings in future." This virtuous self-denial is quite to his credit. Oh! If only I'd discovered the delicacy of his feelings earlier! But there's no help for it now. My reputation, my engagement to Signor Leonardo, and my hostile fates all decree it. "The second reason that leads me to trouble you with this letter springs, you may rest assured, not from malice, but from a sincere and loyal heart. It is publicly rumoured, indeed, known for certain, that Signor Leonardo is in such dire financial straits and so ruined that there is no way he can afford the expense of a marriage; nor will your father consent to see you humiliated." Oh, heavens! What a cruel blow! What a reversal of fortune! What unexpected news! "Continue to love the man who is to be your husband. But if things should ever change, if ever, through no fault of your own, you should find yourself at liberty, allow me to say that I'm still a free man, that I still have not signed the contract, nor will I be induced to do so until you are married. I dare say no more. Forgive me. With the greatest respect and the sincerest resignation, your humble servant ..." Oh, this is all I needed to throw me into the worst possible agitation! Can I believe this letter? But he wouldn't dare make up a lie that could be so easily checked. And, if Leonardo is ruined, does that mean I'm free to leave him? That choice is up to my father. And if my father were weak enough to agree to sacrifice me, would I be obliged to consent to my ruin? No, I would not. There's no reason in the world for going through with this kind of engagement. And once released from my promise to marry Leonardo, could I give my hand freely to Guglielmo? What does my heart say? What does my head say? Oh, heart and head speak two different languages. My heart urges me to hope, my head keeps reminding me of all the right and virtuous rules of behaviour. What has kept me till now from breaking off an engagement that is not irreversible, and choosing, instead of a husband I love so little, someone I feel I could love? Nothing else but my reputation, my justifiable fear of being criticized; no reversal of poor Signor Leonardo's fortune could ever excuse such weakness on my part. The fact that it was I who engineered Vittoria's and Guglielmo's engagement prevents me absolutely from being the cause of their breakup. This letter of Guglielmo's is meant to test my virtue. I must resist at all costs. I must abandon Leonardo if he doesn't deserve me, but I mustn't steal his sister's husband. I must suffer and die. But I must conquer, I must be victorious. *(exit Giacinta)*

ACT THREE

Scene 1

A room in Signor Filippo's house. Fulgenzio, Leonardo, and a servant.

FULGENZIO *(to servant)* How long is it since Signor Filippo went in to lunch?

SERVANT Quite a while, sir. The fruit has already been served, so they'll soon be done. Would you like me to tell him ...

FULGENZIO No, no. Let him finish eating. I know how much he enjoys his food. He hates being interrupted at table. Don't say anything for the moment; when they're through, you can tell him I'm here.

SERVANT Very good, sir. *(exit servant)*

LEONARDO I hope to God Signor Filippo has had no wind of my bad luck and my irregularities.

FULGENZIO He only got back to town a few hours ago, and he hasn't gone anywhere, so he probably knows nothing.

LEONARDO I'm so ashamed and embarrassed, I'm afraid to show my face anywhere. That miserable old uncle of mine made my shame and humiliation complete.

FULGENZIO May the plague take the penny-pinching old skinflint!

LEONARDO Didn't I tell you, Signor Fulgenzio? Didn't I warn you what to expect from that heartless monster?

FULGENZIO I would never have believed it! It would have been one thing if he'd said: I don't have the cash, I can't afford to foot the bill, I want nothing to do with it. What really upset me was the insulting way he treated us, the constant sarcasm, the blatant mockery.

LEONARDO I faced this humiliation for your sake, I went through with it to please you.

FULGENZIO What can I say? I'm truly sorry; on the other hand, we had to give it a shot, and I'm glad we did. If it turned out badly, it wasn't our fault. I'm not going to abandon you now. I'm even more involved in your affairs. I promised to help you, and help you I will. Get a hold of yourself, calm down, I'll help you.

LEONARDO You're right, heaven watches over everybody. Your kind heart and generosity are a godsend to me.

FULGENZIO Now, let's give Signor Filippo a second try. I'm confident we'll succeed. But even if we don't, you mustn't lose heart, I'm certainly not about to let you go under.

LEONARDO Your scheme couldn't be better thought out, and Signor Filippo's good nature is a point in our favour. Still, I think it's going to be difficult to persuade Giacinta to leave Leghorn and come with me so far from home.

FULGENZIO Unless there are more important objections to going through with the wedding, then, whether she likes it or not, she'll just have to come with you.

LEONARDO You're right, but I'd like her to come because she loves me, and I'm very much afraid she'll object.

FULGENZIO It's true Signora Giacinta can be quite capricious and headstrong at times. I realized that when she insisted on taking that young dandy along with them. By the way, how did things turn out in the country?

LEONARDO What can I say? I had my share of anxieties and setbacks. In the end, though, Signor Guglielmo gave his word he would marry my sister.

FULGENZIO Yes, yes, I know: another fine product of your stay in the country! If it works out, it'll be a miracle! *(aside)* Oh, permissiveness, permissiveness! I can't get over the way girls get married these days!

LEONARDO Here comes Signor Filippo.

FULGENZIO You can wait outside if you like. Let me broach the subject.

LEONARDO I'll be waiting with bated breath. *(exit Leonardo)*

Scene 2

Fulgenzio, then enter Filippo.

FULGENZIO *(aside)* Bah! I hate meddling, but here I am, up to my neck in it against my better judgment. Still, for better or for worse, I'm already involved, let's see if we can make it for better. *(enter Filippo)*

FILIPPO Oh, oh! Look who's here! My dear Signor Fulgenzio!

FULGENZIO Welcome back, Signor Filippo.

FILIPPO I'm pleased to see you, dear friend.

FULGENZIO Did you have a nice time in the country?

FILIPPO A wonderful time! The company was excellent. We ate well: the finest veal, superb capons, grouse, woodcock, quail, pheasant, partridge. You name it. I did myself proud, I can tell you!

FULGENZIO I'm glad you had such a good time; and now that you're back …

FILIPPO That crazy Ferdinando had us all in stitches!

FULGENZIO Yes, in the country, you always need someone around to keep people entertained.

FILIPPO He got it into his head to make a conquest of my poor fool of a sister! Just listen! What a card!

FULGENZIO There'll be plenty of time for that story. For the moment, allow me to tell you …

FILIPPO No, no, listen, if you want a good laugh …

FULGENZIO I don't feel much like laughing right now. I need to talk to you.

FILIPPO Here I am. Talk away.

FULGENZIO Signor Filippo, now that you're back in town …

FILIPPO Do you know the doctor in Montenero?

FULGENZIO Yes, I know him.

FILIPPO And do you know his son?

FULGENZIO No, I never set eyes on him.

FILIPPO Oh, what a piece of work! Oh, what a booby! Oh, what a charmer! You would have laughed your head off!

FULGENZIO There'll be time for all that. I'll be happy to listen …

FILIPPO And I had to play bezique with the idiot!

FULGENZIO My friend, if you don't intend to hear me out, please say so, and I'll leave.

FILIPPO Oh, my! What on earth are you saying? Don't intend to hear you out? My goodness! Fulgenzio, my dear friend, I'd hear you out if you showed up in the middle of the night!

FULGENZIO Then, let's get to the point. Now you're back in Leghorn, do you plan to go through with your daughter's wedding?

FILIPPO I did plan to, and I still do plan to.

FULGENZIO Have you seen Signor Leonardo yet?

FILIPPO No, I haven't seen him yet. I know he came round, but I didn't see him. But then, I'm always the last to do everything. I'll be last in this case, too.

FULGENZIO *(aside)* From what I hear, it seems he's heard nothing of Leonardo's exploits.

FILIPPO At Montenero, I was always last to do everything. Even when we went to the coffee house, the waiters served everyone else first, and me last.

FULGENZIO But in this affair we're talking about now, you're going to be first.

FILIPPO Don't worry. I know why I'm first. Because it's me who has to fork out the eight thousand crowns dowry!

FULGENZIO Tell me, in confidence, just between us: can you lay your hands on the eight thousand crowns right away?

FILIPPO To tell you the honest truth, at the moment I couldn't come up with eight thousand pennies!

FULGENZIO So, how do you plan to handle it?

FILIPPO I've no idea. I have property, I have capital investments. You don't think I could come up with the cash?

FULGENZIO Yes, you could borrow it at interest.

FILIPPO Then I'll just have to borrow it at interest.

FULGENZIO And pay four per cent per annum.[11]

FILIPPO I'll just have to pay the four per cent.

FULGENZIO Do you realize that four per cent interest on eight thousand crowns comes to three hundred and twenty crowns a year?

FILIPPO Good God! Three hundred and twenty crowns a year!

FULGENZIO Still, the wedding must go on. The contract is signed. You've already promised the dowry.

FILIPPO But I'm the kind of fellow who signs and promises because people make me sign and promise. Why didn't you mention the interest when you came to talk to me last time? Excuse me, I think I have a right to complain. If you were the good friend you say you are …

FULGENZIO But I am your good friend. If you follow my advice you'll have nothing more to worry about, and you won't lose face. I intend for you to marry your daughter without spending a penny, and without having to rely on anyone. And with the assurance that she's well taken care of, and that her dowry is safe and sound out of harm's reach.

FILIPPO If you can show me how to do that, I shall consider you the finest fellow and the shrewdest brain in the world.

FULGENZIO Tell me, don't you have property in Genoa?

FILIPPO Yes, I have something an uncle of mine left me. But I don't know exactly what it amounts to. A fellow who used to be his administrator is handling it. All he's sent me in six years has been two cases of macaroni!

FULGENZIO I was in Genoa while your uncle was alive and after he died, and I know just how things stand. The administrator's robbing you blind. Therefore, since – through your own negligence – you're making no profit whatsoever, why don't you do this? Put your property in Genoa in your daughter's name with her dowry in escrow. I'll make sure Signor Leonardo accepts the arrangement with good grace. He'll go and live in Genoa with his wife and administer the property uxorio nomine, in her name. He won't be able to dissipate or squander it, because it'll be mortgaged against her dowry. To put it bluntly, you're making nothing out of it now; with him on the spot and a little good management, it could produce double the income your eight thousand crowns could earn in Leghorn. What do you think, eh?[12]

FILIPPO Good, excellent, I'd be happy to give it to him. Let them go to Genoa, enjoy it in peace, and pay me whatever income they can, I don't care. You arrange it, then, I'm relying on you.

FULGENZIO Then, that's all there is to it. Just leave it to me.

FILIPPO Listen, couldn't we see about putting in a clause whereby Leonardo has to send me a case of macaroni now and then?

FULGENZIO Yes, of course, he'll send you all the pasta you can eat. And candied fruit from Genoa, and pomegranates from Portugal!

FILIPPO Oh, I just love pomegranates! And I just love candied fruit. It's a deal!

FULGENZIO It's a deal, then.

FILIPPO It's a deal!

FULGENZIO Will your daughter cooperate?

FILIPPO That's the problem!

FULGENZIO But can't you make her do as you wish?

FILIPPO I never got into the habit!

FULGENZIO This time, you're going to have to.

FILIPPO And I will.

FULGENZIO Everything depends on it.

FILIPPO I'll do it, I tell you, I'll do it!

FULGENZIO When do you plan to talk to her?

FILIPPO Right now, right this instant! I'll go right away. Wait here. I'll be right back with an answer. *(about to leave)* Wouldn't it be better if I brought her here, so you could talk to her?

FULGENZIO What's wrong with you talking to her?

FILIPPO I could talk to her, too.

FULGENZIO Go ahead, then, bring her here, if you like.

FILIPPO At once, right away. *(aside)* Lucky me, if it works out! If I'm left on my own, with no loss of income, I'll live like a king! *(exit Filippo)*

Scene 3

Fulgenzio, then enter Leonardo.

FULGENZIO *(alone)* Everything's going splendidly so far. As long as that flighty daughter of his doesn't throw a wrench in the works! *(enter Leonardo)*

LEONARDO Signor Fulgenzio, our troubles appear to be over.

FULGENZIO Did you hear?

LEONARDO I heard everything. I pray God Giacinta goes along with the new plan.

FULGENZIO We'll see about that in a minute. But, when all's said and done, unless her father's a complete nincompoop, his daughter will just have to make the best of it.

LEONARDO I was thinking about something else, Signor Fulgenzio. What should I do about my debts in Leghorn? Should I skip town and spoil my reputation?

FULGENZIO I thought of that, too. Once we've settled the terms of the new arrangement with Signor Filippo, you'll give me a power of attorney. You'll place your assets in my hands, and I'll vouch for you. I'll pay back your creditors, and, in due course of time, I'll restore your property, free and clear and well managed.

LEONARDO Oh, heavens! I can never find words to thank you.

FULGENZIO You can thank your Uncle Bernardino.

LEONARDO Why should I thank that old skinflint?

FULGENZIO Because I always wanted to help you, but it was thanks to him that I got involved enough to be prepared to risk my own capital if I had to.

LEONARDO But you wouldn't do it if you didn't have a kind heart.

Scene 4

Enter *Filippo.*

FILIPPO What do you think's happened? … Oh! your servant, Signor Leonardo.

LEONARDO My respects, Signor Filippo.

FULGENZIO *(to Filippo)* What is it now?

FILIPPO My daughter's gone out. They tell me she's gone to call on Signora Costanza.

LEONARDO Oh, I couldn't be more disappointed.
FILIPPO *(to Leonardo)* Did Signor Fulgenzio say anything?
LEONARDO Yes, sir, he said something.
FILIPPO *(to Leonardo)* Well, are you happy?
LEONARDO I couldn't be happier.
FILIPPO Thank heaven, we're all going to be happy!
LEONARDO How about Signora Giacinta?
FILIPPO Let's go talk to her at Signora Costanza's.
FULGENZIO We can wait till she gets back.
LEONARDO My sister's supposed to be going there, too. Maybe they're together.
FILIPPO It might be a good idea if we were to go, too.
LEONARDO You're right. We owe Signora Costanza a visit.
FILIPPO It'll give us a chance to speak to Signora Giacinta.
FULGENZIO But you can't talk freely in someone else's house.
FILIPPO If we can't talk there, we'll get her to leave with us.
LEONARDO What do you say, Signor Fulgenzio?
FULGENZIO What I say is: what's an hour here or there?
FILIPPO *(irritated)* And I say we must go at once.
LEONARDO Come on, sir. Let's not make him angry. *(exit Leonardo)*
FULGENZIO You're a stubborn man, Signor Filippo! *(exit Fulgenzio)*
FILIPPO Right! I'm a man! I know what I'm doing, I know what I'm talking about. When it comes to scheming and organizing, I take a back seat to nobody! *(exit Filippo)*

Scene 5

A room in Costanza's house. Costanza and Rosina.

COSTANZA Rosina, get yourself ready, and we'll go pay our calls.
ROSINA Where do we have to go in such a hurry? We just got back.
COSTANZA I think we should pay a call on Signora Giacinta and Signora Vittoria.
ROSINA Excuse me, Aunt, but we got back to Leghorn after them, it's up to them to call on us first.
COSTANZA That is just what I'm trying to avoid. If they come here, how do you think I'm going to receive them? Can't you see what a state this house is in? There isn't a presentable room in the place! Everything's falling apart, dilapidated, a mess.

ROSINA I must admit, there's quite a difference between this ugly old house and your pretty little place in the country.

COSTANZA The difference is that I furnished the country place myself to suit my own taste, whereas this house was furnished to suit the vulgar taste of my husband.

ROSINA Oh, my uncle isn't even aware of it. All he deals with are shopkeepers, so elegance has no meaning for him.

COSTANZA I can't stand that attitude: from now on, I'm going to spend ten months of the year in the country. There, at least, I get some respect.

ROSINA The doctor won't be coming to call any more.

COSTANZA I must say I'm sorry to have lost the doctor's friendship. I made the sacrifice for your sake. I love you, and I wanted to help you get married. You didn't have a dowry, and I couldn't provide one. If this boy hadn't come along, you might have stayed on the shelf for ages.

ROSINA I'm married, sure enough; but so far, my marriage hasn't been much of a consolation. I don't have a pretty gold ring, I don't have a pretty wedding dress, I don't have a thing to go out in. What do you think people will say?

COSTANZA You'll have all you need in due course. For the time being, you don't have to tell anyone you're married. It was done in secret, and nobody need know. Once the doctor has been pressured into giving his son an allowance, we can make the marriage public.

ROSINA As long as Tognino doesn't go telling somebody who's not supposed to know!

COSTANZA All we have to do is warn him. What happened to Tognino, anyway? He's disappeared.

ROSINA He's in there getting dressed up.

COSTANZA "Getting dressed up"? What do you mean, "getting dressed up"?

ROSINA He told me that now we're in town he intends to dress elegantly.

COSTANZA And what is he planning to wear, if all he has to his name is that old-fashioned suit he used to wear in Montenero?

ROSINA He told me he'd brought one of his father's suits.

COSTANZA His father's a foot taller than he is!

ROSINA Now, hold on! Tognino isn't that short!

COSTANZA He must go to Pisa at once and get down to studying.

ROSINA Go to Pisa at once?

COSTANZA Do you want him to waste time?

ROSINA No, but … at once?

COSTANZA How long do you expect him to wait?
ROSINA Very well. Let's make it a month at least, more or less.
COSTANZA That's enough of that! What's a day here or a day there!
ROSINA Here he comes, here he comes! He's dressed up already!

Scene 6

Enter *Tognino wearing an overlarge suit, a long three-knotted wig, and an old-fashioned hat with a feather, then enter servant.*

TOGNINO Here I am, ladies. How do I look?
COSTANZA *(to Rosina)* Oh, what an eyesore! Didn't I tell you he'd be a real sketch?
ROSINA The suit's a bit big for him, but it isn't that bad!
COSTANZA For heaven's sake, take off that suit! You look like you're wearing your dressing gown!
TOGNINO Do you expect me to go about town in my travelling clothes?
COSTANZA Don't you have the suit you usually wear?
TOGNINO No, madam.
COSTANZA What did you do with it?
TOGNINO I gave it away to the servant for helping me make off with this suit of my father's.
COSTANZA You certainly drove a good bargain!
TOGNINO It's a nice suit, it's got braid. It may be a bit long, but that doesn't matter. Well? Isn't it a good fit? What do you think, Rosina?
ROSINA You should have it taken in at the waist.
TOGNINO *(to Costanza)* Will you have it taken in for me, Aunt?
COSTANZA That's enough out of you, you lummox! And don't call me "Aunt"! For the moment nobody is supposed to know that you're married. Don't tell a soul, try to have a little common sense, don't let the cat out of the bag.
TOGNINO Count on me! I won't breathe a word!
ROSINA And it's time you began to shape up.
TOGNINO What do you mean, "shape up"?
ROSINA Learn some sense, study, learn your trade as a doctor.
TOGNINO Don't worry about my studying. I'll study as much as you like. As long as you give me enough to eat, take me out for a walk now and then, and let me play bezique.
COSTANZA Oh, the poor half-wit!
TOGNINO What's that supposed to mean: "half-wit"?
COSTANZA If you act as if you didn't have a brain!

TOGNINO I'm not going to let you insult me! *(enter servant)*

SERVANT *(to Costanza)* Madam …

TOGNINO I'm a married man, and I'm not going to stand here and let myself be insulted.

COSTANZA Hush!

ROSINA Hush!

SERVANT Oh, is Signor Tognino married?

COSTANZA *(to servant)* He doesn't know what he's saying. And you, stay out of things that are none of your business!

SERVANT Excuse me, Signora Giacinta is practically on the doorstep. She's coming to see you.

COSTANZA *(aside)* Oh, poor me! *(to Rosina)* Signora Giacinta!

ROSINA *(to Costanza)* What choice do you have? You'll have to receive her.

COSTANZA *(to servant)* Does she know I'm at home?

SERVANT She's got to know. She sent a servant on ahead, and he knows.

COSTANZA *(aside)* Then there's nothing else for it, I'll have to receive her. *(to servant)* Tell her to come in. Oh, and listen: tell her not to mind the mess. I just got back from the country, and the house is all topsy-turvy. Oh, and listen: go and order some coffee. Oh, and listen: if my husband comes home, tell him not to come in in his store clothes … either he dresses up properly or he stays in his room!

SERVANT *(aside)* Oh my God! What a snob! *(exit servant)*

COSTANZA *(to Tognino)* And you, make yourself scarce! Don't let anyone see you in that getup!

TOGNINO You think I don't know? You're sending me away so I won't drink the coffee. I want to stay!

COSTANZA Get out of here, I tell you! If you keep getting on my nerves, I'll have you thrown out like a thief.

TOGNINO Don't forget, I'm a married man!

COSTANZA Rosina, I have taken about as much as I can take.

ROSINA Come along, dearest, go in the other room. I'll bring you your coffee myself.

TOGNINO I'm a married man now, and don't you forget it! *(exit Tognino)*

Scene 7

Constanza and Rosina, then enter Giacinta.

COSTANZA *(to Rosina)* Listen, if he keeps on like this, I'm not going to be able to put up with it!

Rosina You have to make some allowance, he's only a boy.

Costanza That's right, go ahead, make excuses!

Rosina But, madam … he's my husband, what else can I do? And he was your choice, after all, I took him on your advice.

Costanza Ah, here comes Signora Giacinta! *(aside)* It's my own fault, it serves me right.

Rosina It's no use blaming him, he doesn't know any better.

Giacinta Your servant, Signora Costanza.

Costanza Your humble servant, madam.

Rosina Your devoted servant, madam.

Giacinta My respects to Signora Rosina.

Costanza Signora Giacinta, you shouldn't have put yourself out.

Giacinta No bother at all. It's no more than my duty.

Costanza I'm sorry you find me here with the house in such a mess. I'm really embarrassed.

Giacinta Please, think nothing of it. You don't have to stand on ceremony with me.

Costanza We haven't been living here long, you know, and then I went off to the country, so everything's still a mess. Please sit down. Don't mind the chair!

Giacinta Not at all, it's perfect. *(Aside to herself)* Such luxury in the country, and here she lives in a chicken coop!

Rosina *(aside to Costanza)* What do you think about that, then? She got all dolled up!

Costanza *(aside to Rosina)* Well, what do you expect? If she was coming to pay me a visit, she could hardly come in her house clothes!

Giacinta What news do you have of my aunt?

Rosina Oh, poor Signora Sabina's in the worst way. I went to see her before we left, and she gave me a letter for Signor Ferdinando.

Giacinta I'd love to hear what she wrote to him!

Rosina I'm sure Signor Ferdinando will have no problem showing it to you.

Giacinta *(aside)* I'm doing everything I can to keep my mind off it, but I have a thorn in my side that's tormenting me!

Costanza And how is Signor Leonardo, Signora Giacinta?

Giacinta He's well.

Rosina And Signora Vittoria?

Giacinta Very well.

Costanza And Signor Guglielmo?

Giacinta Is it true that Signor Tognino came back to Leghorn with you?

Costanza Yes, he came for a few days.

ROSINA He's on his way to Pisa.
COSTANZA To study.
ROSINA To become a doctor.
GIACINTA Oh, so that's it. He stopped in on his way to Pisa. And the gossips said he and Signora Rosina were married!
ROSINA Oh, is that what the gossips said?
GIACINTA Yes, but I always said you would never do anything so foolish.
ROSINA Would it really be that foolish?
COSTANZA Is your wedding going to be soon, may I ask?
GIACINTA I don't know yet. It depends what my father decides.
ROSINA And what about Signora Vittoria and Signor Guglielmo?
GIACINTA How come you came back to town earlier than usual this year, too?
COSTANZA There was nobody left in the country! Signor Leonardo and Signora Vittoria spoiled everyone's fun.
ROSINA *(to Giacinta)* And when is Signora Vittoria getting married?
GIACINTA How should I know, madam? Ask her yourself.
ROSINA *(to Giacinta)* It looks to me as if you think Signora Vittoria's getting married is foolish as well.
GIACINTA *(getting to her feet)* With your permission, ladies, I really must be going.
COSTANZA No, wait. Please stay … We'll have coffee.
GIACINTA No, thank you. Much obliged.
COSTANZA Here it comes, here it comes. Just to please me?
GIACINTA Well, I wouldn't want to slight your hospitality. *(they sit down, coffee is served) (aside)* You'd think they were doing it on purpose just to torment me.
COSTANZA *(handing Giacinta a cup of coffee)* There you are.
ROSINA *(leaving the room with a cup of coffee for Tognino)* Excuse me, ladies. *(she meets a servant coming in, confers with him, gives him the coffee and comes back)* Visitors, Aunt! We have more visitors.
COSTANZA Who's here?
ROSINA Signora Vittoria, Signor Ferdinando, and Signor Guglielmo.
GIACINTA *(aside)* Oh, poor me!
ROSINA Oh, look, you've spilled your coffee on your dress!
GIACINTA *(aside, wiping her dress)* Damn whoever it was made me stay!
ROSINA Should I bring some cold water?
GIACINTA *(irritably)* It doesn't matter, don't go to any trouble.
ROSINA Here they are, here they are.

Scene 8

Enter *Vittoria and Guglielmo.*

VITTORIA Your servant, ladies, how pleasant to see you!
COSTANZA Your servant.
ROSINA Your servant.
GUGLIELMO Your servant, ladies.
VITTORIA Oh, are you here too, Signora Giacinta?
GIACINTA I came to pay my respects.
ROSINA We are honoured.
GIACINTA *(aside)* I wish I'd broken a leg on my way over!
COSTANZA Come in. I've already apologized to Signora Giacinta. The house is only half furnished. You'll have to make yourselves comfortable as best you can.
GUGLIELMO Forgive me, Signora Costanza, if my coming here, too, is inconvenient. Signora Vittoria ran into me on the way over and persuaded me to come along.
GIACINTA *(aside)* I can see right through him … The traitor! I can see right through him!
ROSINA Not at all, it's a pleasure. I'm obliged to Signora Vittoria.
GIACINTA Tell me, Signora Vittoria, wasn't Signor Ferdinando with you?
VITTORIA Yes, Signor Ferdinando came to lunch at our house. Signor Guglielmo is not a very willing escort, so I took advantage of Signor Ferdinando's company so as not to come alone.
GIACINTA So what made him leave you alone with Signor Guglielmo?
GUGLIELMO He was with us as far as the door.
VITTORIA *(to Guglielmo)* She's talking to me and you answer? *(to Giacinta)* What concern is it of Signora Giacinta's whether Signor Ferdinando came or not?
GIACINTA It concerns me because these ladies have a letter to give him from Signora Sabina.
ROSINA Yes, that's right. Here it is. I'm supposed to deliver it into his very own hands.
COSTANZA Yes, I saw him, too, out in the hall. I wonder where he's gotten to.
ROSINA He must be somewhere in the house, he must be in another room, but I'm certainly not going to go look for him.
COSTANZA *(aside)* I wouldn't want him amusing himself getting that blockhead Tognino to talk.

GUGLIELMO So … Signora Sabina has written a letter to Signor Ferdinando?

ROSINA Yes, sir, and she gave it to me to deliver.

GUGLIELMO The correct thing for Signor Ferdinando to do would be to reply.

ROSINA He'll reply if he feels like replying.

GUGLIELMO *(eyeing Giacinta)* When someone gets a letter, it's good manners to answer.

GIACINTA First, you have to see if the letter deserves an answer.

GUGLIELMO A polite person is obliged to answer any letter: especially if it's an honest letter, written with sincerity and love.

GIACINTA Not everyone is free to love, and sometimes self-interest can be mistaken for honesty.

VITTORIA From what I'm hearing, Signor Guglielmo and Signora Giacinta are well informed about the contents of that letter!

GUGLIELMO Everybody knows about Signora Sabina's passion!

GIACINTA And everyone knows it's a passion that shouldn't be encouraged.

VITTORIA I must say I would be curious to hear this letter, too. Oh, here he comes now, here comes Signor Ferdinando!

Scene 9

Enter *Ferdinando and Tognino, followed by a servant*

FERDINANDO Come along then, my precious, my dear heart, my irresistible Signor Tognino.

VITTORIA *(aside)* Would you listen to that!

COSTANZA *(aside)* What did I say!

ROSINA *(aside)* What a nerve! That Signor Ferdinando!

TOGNINO Your servant, ladies and gentlemen!

COSTANZA *(to Tognino)* Will you please get out of here!

FERDINANDO Let him be, Signora, treat him with a little respect. He is a married man, you know.

COSTANZA Who said he's married?

FERDINANDO He told me so himself.

COSTANZA *(to Ferdinando)* There's not a word of truth in it!

FERDINANDO *(to Tognino)* Not a word of truth?

TOGNINO *(crestfallen, to Ferdinando)* Not a word of truth!

FERDINANDO Very well, then. If it's not true, I'm delighted. If you aren't married to Signora Rosina, I must inform you that I am declaring my suit. You're not going to have her, I'll marry her myself.

TOGNINO *(making fun of Ferdinando)* Cuckoo, cuckoo![13]

FERDINANDO Cuckoo? What the devil's that supposed to mean, "cuckoo"?

TOGNINO Confound it! It means that Signora Rosina …

ROSINA That's enough out of you! Tell Signor Ferdinando to go marry Signora Sabina. Here's a letter she sent him.

FERDINANDO A letter from my darling Sabina?

ROSINA Yes, sir, she gave it to me this morning.

FERDINANDO Oh, my precious little darling! I'm dying to read it.

VITTORIA We'd all like to hear it.

COSTANZA Yes, we certainly would.

GUGLIELMO *(to Ferdinando)* And remember, letters are meant to be answered.

GIACINTA *(to Ferdinando)* When they deserve an answer.

FERDINANDO Very good, we all see eye to eye on that point.

VITTORIA Read it out loud, so we can all hear.

FERDINANDO I promise I won't skip a comma. *(he opens the letter)*

SERVANT *(to Costanza)* Madam, Signor Filippo, Signor Leonardo, and Signor Fulgenzio are here to pay their respects.

COSTANZA *(to the servant)* Tell them to come in and make themselves at home; and bring us some chairs.

SERVANT *(aside)* I would if there were any more, but there aren't enough to go round. *(exit servant)*

VITTORIA This interruption's too much. I can't wait to hear that letter! *(snatching the letter from Ferdinando's hand)* Give it to me, you can't read it without us.

Scene 10

Enter *Filippo, Leonardo, and Fulgenzio.*

FILIPPO Your servant, ladies and gentlemen. *(they all rise)*

TOGNINO Oh, your servant, Signor Filippo.

FILIPPO Oh my God! What an eyesore!

TOGNINO Do you want to play bezique?

FILIPPO Don't bother me now. Giacinta, with our hostess's permission, I'd like to have a word with you.

COSTANZA Oh, please feel free.

LEONARDO *(to Filippo)* Excuse me, sir. We are here to pay our respects to Signora Costanza. You'll have plenty of time to speak to Signora Giacinta later.

FILIPPO But when I have something on my mind, I can't wait. Signora Costanza understands, I know she'll give me her permission.

COSTANZA Sir, I already said you may do as you please.

GIACINTA *(aside)* What on earth does my father want to talk to me about? I'm extremely curious.

FILIPPO *(to Costanza)* If you'll let us have the use of one of your sitting rooms, I'll have a couple of words with her. Then we'll be right back to enjoy your delightful company.

GIACINTA *(to Costanza)* If you would do us this favour …

COSTANZA I'm sorry, the sitting rooms are all cluttered. You can use the dining room, if you like.

FILIPPO Yes, yes, anywhere will do. Let's go, let's go. Excuse us. *(aside)* Oh, oh, when it comes to getting things done quickly and efficiently, there's no one to touch me! *(exit Filippo)*

GIACINTA Excuse me, I'll be back in a minute. *(aside)* Oh, my heart's all aflutter! *(exit Giacinta)*

FULGENZIO *(aside to Leonardo)* How do you think it will go?

LEONARDO *(aside to Fulgenzio)* I'm not overoptimistic! *(aside)* Oh, that Guglielmo will be the ruin of me! *(exit Leonardo)*

FULGENZIO *(aside)* If she were my daughter, she'd do as I told her, or else … *(exit Fulgenzio)*

TOGNINO *(aside)* I'll slip out into the kitchen to hear what they're saying. *(exit Tognino)*

Scene 11

Vittoria, Guglielmo, Costanza, Rosina, and Ferdinando.

GUGLIELMO *(aside)* It looks as if I'm about to hear my final sentence. Who knows if it'll be favourable or not?

FERDINANDO How long are they going to be in there talking? I'm just dying to read that letter.

VITTORIA Go on, then, if you want to read it, read it. We'll listen; there'll always be time to read it to Signora Giacinta later.

COSTANZA I can't tell a lie, I'm looking forward to hearing it, too.

ROSINA Poor woman! When she gave it to me, she was in tears!
FERDINANDO My God! Is it written in Arabic?
VITTORIA Signor Guglielmo, are you asleep?
GUGLIELMO No, madam, I'm not asleep.
VITTORIA *(aside)* I don't know how to behave with this man. He is all phlegm, and I'm all fire.
FERDINANDO I'm beginning to get the hang of it now.
VITTORIA Read it all, and don't cheat us by skipping the good parts.
FERDINANDO It'll be a pleasure. Here goes: "Heartless man," *(they all laugh moderately)* "You have wounded my heart; you are the first man to see me weep for love. If you only knew, if I could tell you all that I'm feeling, maybe I would bring tears of pity to your eyes. Alas! modesty forbids me to say any more. Since you left, I haven't eaten a bite, I haven't drunk a drop, I haven't slept a wink. Poor me! I look in the mirror and I hardly recognize myself. The roses in my cheeks are fading, and my constant crying has so weakened my eyesight that I can hardly see the paper I'm writing on. Oh, Ferdinando! My heart, my hope, my beauty …" *(everyone laughs heartily)* What's so funny? Are you laughing because she called me her beauty?
VITTORIA Poor thing, she can't see very well!
ROSINA Her eyes are all bleary!
COSTANZA All that crying!
FERDINANDO All right, all right! She recognizes true worth when she sees it, and that's all that matters.
VITTORIA Let's hear how the letter ends.
FERDINANDO It would serve you all right if I were to stop right there.
VITTORIA Oh, come on. We want to hear the rest.
FERDINANDO Where was I? Where did I leave off?
VITTORIA Are you asleep, Signor Guglielmo?
GUGLIELMO No, madam.
FERDINANDO Ah, here we are: "My hope, my beauty, for pity's sake, come to console me. Oh, yes, come! If you love me, I won't be ungrateful. If the heart I have given you is not enough, come to me, my darling, I vow and declare …" What the devil! I can't make this part out. When she wrote these two lines, her hand must have been really trembling. Now, it's getting a bit clearer. "Come to me, my darling, I vow and declare I'll make you a settlement, the settlement, a generous settlement, I promise you the settlement …" *(aside)* Again! "I promise you the settlement of all I possess. Your most faithful mistress and future wife, Sabina Borgna."

VITTORIA Bravo!
COSTANZA I'm so happy for you!
ROSINA Three cheers for Signor Ferdinando's beauty!
VITTORIA So, what will you do?
FERDINANDO A heroic decision! I shall take the next coach and go to console and succour my adored Sabina. Ladies and gentlemen, your most humble servant. *(exit Ferdinando)*
VITTORIA He is off to console himself with the settlement!
COSTANZA That poor, crazy old woman!
VITTORIA Signor Guglielmo, are you asleep?
GUGLIELMO No, madam.
VITTORIA You don't find this funny?
GUGLIELMO I don't feel like laughing.
VITTORIA *(aside)* Oh, what an ogre!
ROSINA Here they come. The confabulation is over.
GUGLIELMO *(aside, getting to his feet)* I can't wait to hear.
VITTORIA *(to Guglielmo)* You seem to be waking up, finally!
GUGLIELMO Believe me, I was never asleep. *(all rise)*

Scene 12

Enter *Filippo, Giacinta, and Leonardo.*

FILIPPO Here we are back. Excuse us, Signora Costanza.
COSTANZA It's nothing, Signor Filippo.
VITTORIA *(with exaggerated emphasis)* Well, what news do we have, my dear Brother?
LEONARDO Excellent news, Sister. First thing tomorrow morning, I'm leaving for Genoa.
VITTORIA For Genoa?
LEONARDO Yes, madam.
VITTORIA Alone, or with someone else?
LEONARDO With someone else.
VITTORIA With whom, may I ask?
LEONARDO With Signora Giacinta.
VITTORIA I imagine you'll be getting married first.
LEONARDO Without a doubt.
VITTORIA And what about us, Signor Guglielmo?
GUGLIELMO Is Signora Giacinta going to Genoa?

GIACINTA Yes, sir, I'm going to Genoa. By the grace of God, my father, and the kindness of Signor Fulgenzio. I expect you're all surprised that I'm going to Genoa. You must all be amazed that I let myself be prevailed upon to make such a radical decision at such short notice. I confess that tearing myself away from the place I was born, leaving behind the person I love more than myself … I'm talking about you, Father, my dear, dear Father. Oh! leaving behind someone I'm so deeply attached to is like tearing my heart from my breast. It's a miracle I can find the strength to go through with it. But my social position requires it, my self-respect prompts me to do it, my good name leaves me no option. Those with ears to hear will know what I mean. You, my Husband, you know what I mean; the way things stand, you could hardly have hoped for a better outcome. I shall abandon my once happy home, now a cruel reminder. I shall forget how insane I've been, how much I suffered, my moments of weakness … Yes, I shall forget, in other words, the arrogance, the vanity, the insanity of my pretentious stay in the country. If I'd stuck to the path so irresponsibly taken, who can say what pitfall I might have encountered? A change of surroundings will mean a change of outlook. This is my husband, this is the man chosen for me by the powers that be, and given to me by my father. I intend to do my duty, let others do theirs. Signor Leonardo, we must leave tomorrow: you have your business to attend to. And I'm sure I'll find plenty of chores to keep me busy. So without wasting any more time over something that can be done here and now, in the presence of my father, of our hostess, of all of these ladies and gentlemen, I offer you my hand and I ask for yours in return.

FILIPPO *(to Fulgenzio)* What do you think of that, eh? She's so touching, she brings the tears to my eyes.

LEONARDO Yes, my adored Giacinta, if your father is willing …

FILIPPO Delighted, delighted.

LEONARDO Here is my hand and with it my heart.

GIACINTA And here is mine, too … *(aside)* Oh, dear! my eyes are growing dim, I can't stand.

LEONARDO Oh, heavens! You've gone pale? You're trembling? This is a sign you don't really love me! If I thought you were marrying me against your will …

GIACINTA No, I'm not marrying you against my will. Nobody could force me, if I wasn't convinced myself. Forgive me the weakness of my sex, at least, if you see nothing commendable in my modesty. To go from being a free woman to being married is not something a woman can do without violence, without an inner commotion of ideas and emotions. To pluck one love from one's breast all of a sudden and replace it with another – to leave a father in order to follow a husband – cannot help putting a strain on a tender, sensitive, and vulnerable heart. But Reason brings me back to my senses, Virtue comes to my rescue. Here is my hand. I am your wife. *(giving her hand to Leonardo)*

LEONARDO Yes, my dearest. I am yours, you are mine. *(giving his hand to Giacinta)*

Scene 13

Enter *Tognino.*

TOGNINO *(skipping about)* A wedding! A wedding! Hurrah! They're going to get married!

COSTANZA You idiot!

ROSINA *(to Costanza)* Oh, leave him alone! You're always picking on him.

LEONARDO Signor Guglielmo, before I leave, I trust your engagement to my sister will be placed on a firmer footing.

VITTORIA I hope we can sign those papers this evening.

GIACINTA What good are papers? What good are signatures? All they're good for is to confuse us and make us uneasy. Would to God I had married Signor Leonardo the very same day I promised on paper! So many complications would have been avoided. Signora Vittoria has her dowry set aside in the bank. Let Signor Guglielmo remember his obligations, give her his hand, and marry her.

VITTORIA Are you asleep, Signor Guglielmo?

GUGLIELMO No, I'm not asleep, madam, I'm not asleep. I'm sufficiently awake to hear what people are saying and to know my duty. I'm a man of honour. If I weren't, I wouldn't have given my word. Signora Giacinta is to be commended, and so is her advice. I have always admired her virtue, and, as a final token of my respect, here I am, Signora Vittoria, ready to offer you my hand.

VITTORIA Because of the respect you feel for her, and not because of the love you feel for me?

GIACINTA Signora Vittoria is right. I'm surprised you're being so uncooperative ...

GUGLIELMO Please, don't be surprised ... I'm more reasonable than you think. Signora Vittoria, you may be sure that you have in me someone who values your qualities, a faithful husband, and a respectful consort.

VITTORIA Everything but a lover!

LEONARDO That's enough of your posturing! Either you give him your hand, or I'll put you in a convent!

VITTORIA My brother is so amusing! Signor Guglielmo, I give you my hand, not because I'm being forced to, as you seem to be, but with all my heart.

GUGLIELMO And I accept you for my wife.

VITTORIA *(tenderly to Guglielmo)* Have pity on me at least.

GUGLIELMO *(aside)* I'm more to be pitied than she is.

TOGNINO *(skipping)* A wedding! A wedding! Another wedding!

FILIPPO *(to Tognino)* All right, all right, a wedding! And when is your wedding going to be?

TOGNINO It's already been. We're married already! Yes, yes, I'm going to say it: I'm married.

COSTANZA *(to Tognino)* Oh, you fool! You thoughtless irresponsible fool!

ROSINA He's right. We can't keep it a secret. People should know, and I'm glad he said it.

GIACINTA I sympathize with Signora Costanza for wanting to conceal a marriage that some people might criticize. Let's hope that this couple will never have cause to complain of the opportunity that an overpermissive stay in the country provided. I won't say any more. I know only too well the good times I had, and how dearly I'm paying for my pleasures. Thank heavens I'm married. I'm leaving for Genoa, and I'm leaving with my mind made up to think only of duty. I wish my sister-in-law the same peace and tranquillity I wish for myself. I beg my beloved father to love me always, even when I'm far away; and, if it were not presumptuous on my part, I would urge him to take better care of his business, and to think twice about his trips to the country, and to be more careful with his money. I thank Signor Fulgenzio for the good that has come of his efforts, and, I assure you, sir, that I will never forget it as long as I live. My regards to the lady of the house; I wish every happiness to her niece and her nephew. Farewell, Signor Guglielmo. *(ruefully)* I'm leaving for Genoa with my dear husband. *(resolutely)* But before I go, I'd like to say a few words to all of you who are doing me the honour of listening. You saw us go Off to the Country; you enjoyed our Adventures in the Country; be indulgent now we're Back from the Country. If you found other people's foolish behaviour amusing, be thankful for your own common sense and restraint, and, if we haven't displeased you, give us a kind token of your appreciation.

END OF THE COMEDY

NOTES TO BACK FROM THE COUNTRY

All notes to *Back from the Country* are taken from the edition of the Holiday Trilogy translated by Anthony Oldcorn.

1 In *Le menteur* (1642), one of the models for Goldoni's *Il bugiardo* [*The Liar*], Pierre Corneille had himself imitated Mexican-born Juan Ruiz de Alarcón y Mendoza's most famous play, *La verdad sospechosa* [*Suspicious Truth*] – attributed to the prolific Lope de Vega when first published in 1630 – and in its sequel, *La suite du menteur,* Lope's own *Amar sin saber a quien* [*To Love without Knowing Whom*]. In eighteenth-century Italy, Lope was universally known as Lopez.

2 *La putta onorata* [*The Honest Wench*] was first performed in 1748, *La buona moglie* [*The Good Wife*] in 1749. *Pamela* (inspired by Richardson's novel, and Goldoni's first comedy without masks) was one of the sixteen comedies produced in 1750–1. The inferior spin-off *Pamela maritata* [*Pamela Married*] was first performed in Rome in 1760.

3 Of Goldoni's three verse plays "with an oriental theme" – *La sposa persiana* [*The Persian Bride*], *Ircana in Julfa* [*Hircana at Julfa*], and *Ircana in Ispaan* [*Hircana at Ispahan*] – the first two were performed in 1755, the third in 1756. The actress Caterina Bresciani chalked up a memorable personal success in the title role.

4 The dialogue novel *La comedia de Calisto e Melibea,* better known as *La Celestina,* probably the most celebrated Spanish work after *Don Quixote,* was published anonymously in fourteen "auctos," or acts, in Burgos in 1499. In the 1502 Seville edition, now dubbed *Tragicomedia* and attributed to Fernando de Rojas, the acts numbered twenty-one. The 1514 Valencia edition had twenty-two acts.

5 Though the servant Paolino (or Paolo) appears in the list of dramatis personae and is frequently mentioned by the other characters, especially Brigida, he does not actually appear in the third and final play.

6 Uncle Bernardino's servant Pasquale is accidentally omitted by the author from the list of dramatis personae.

7 Cecco's class-conscious remark recalls the comments of the decorator Sgualdo in the first two scenes of *La casa nova* [*The New House*] produced in the same year as our trilogy, with whose plot it has a great deal in common.

8 The rules of eighteenth-century social etiquette required that someone returning to town make this fact known. Friends already in town were then obliged to pay a call at their earliest convenience on the returnee. *Back from the Country*, not surprisingly, contains several references to this custom.

9 See *Adventures*, act 3, scene 6 (p. 269).

10 The book is, of course, Goldoni's invention, and a poke at the pseudoscientific how-to literature of the time. The vogue for books offering psychological advice, however, has not waned from his day to ours.

11 In the mid-eighteenth century, a 4 per cent interest rate was considered quite high.

12 Goldoni's legal training shows in this financial solution, as it will, in another way, in the eloquence and logic of Giacinta's speeches in the final scenes.

13 The cry of "Cuckoo!" (compare French "cocu") is not just the innocuous way of getting someone's attention it has become today. Sexist jokes about cuckoldry (the condition of a husband whose wife was unfaithful), and about the cuckold's "horns," said to be worn by the betrayed husband, abound, for example, in Shakespeare, and seem to have formed part of popular English lore for at least two more centuries. In the Mediterranean countries, the theme is just as popular today as it ever was. In the present heavy-handed allusion, presumably accompanied by the gesture representing the horns (the index and little finger of the right hand are raised, the two fingers in between and the thumb are folded into the palm which is facing the receiver – see Desmond Morris's *Gestures* [New York: Stein and Day, 1979], 120), the dim-witted Tognino, who is supposed to be denying that he is married to Rosina, implicitly admits their relationship. His cryptic utterance is to be interpreted: if you have an affair with Rosina, who is already married, you'll be a cuckold. In point of fact, the joke backfires, since, in such an eventuality, the cuckold would be Tognino!

Afterword: Goldoni Our Contemporary

CESARE DE MICHELIS
Translated by Evgenia Matt

This text would never have seen the light of day without the warm and pressing invitation of Laura Barbiani, who, as president of the Teatro Stabile del Veneto, wished to conclude the year by celebrating Goldoni with the publication of this work; I would also like to thank Luca De Fusco, who, with all his experience, kindly accompanied me on stage, as well as Eros Pagni, who recited the passages by Goldoni which appear below.

I performed this text on two occasions: on 5 November 2007 in Venice, at the Teatro Goldoni, formerly the San Luca, and on 6 November 2007 in Padua, at the Teatro Verdi.

In contradicting the traditional approach to any biographical reconstruction, let's begin with the end; it may help us to free Goldoni's story from the stereotypes built around it over the centuries and to recognize him, as the title states, as "our contemporary."

Goldoni died at a very advanced age; he was eighty-six. On 6 February 1793, a freezing and dreadful day, windy and rainy, he passed away at six o'clock in the evening at his home on Rue Pavée Saint-Saveur, number 1, on the second floor, near those beloved boulevards he often visited.

A month earlier, at the beginning of January, the National Convention had definitively cut off pensions listed on the king's roster, merely deferred before. Goldoni, reduced to poverty by this decision, counting only on the solidarity of his few remaining friends, turned to the very same Convention with a sorrowful and proud plea, referring to himself in the third person.

> Citizen Goldoni was summoned to France in 1762 so the Italian company existing in Paris at the time would adopt the Italian theatre reform that he himself had successfully carried out in Italy.
>
> Goldoni had long admired and studied the French authors and was therefore immediately intrigued by the proposal. He did not hesitate to accept it, overcoming all the difficulties that seemed to stand in the way of his departure from Italy. He left his homeland, his relatives, his friends, and his own work behind to follow his inclination, coming to live in France alongside the masters of the same art that he himself practised.
>
> Once in Paris, Goldoni felt right at home. All the men of letters knew him; all the authors kindly welcomed him.
>
> He reached the height of his fortune and glory with The Benevolent Curmudgeon, which earned him a place in the repertoire of the Comédie Française, amongst the masters of the art.
>
> His latest work, his Mémoires, was written in French and published in three volumes. It was intended to help tell the story of his life and theatre. The work did nothing but praise the talent and merit of the French nation.
>
> Goldoni enjoyed a 4,000-lira annual pension from the beginning of 1768 until 1 July of this last year; it was granted to him through the public roster.
>
> This pension was suspended by a decree of the National Assembly, and Goldoni fell into dire straits, for the pension was the only means of survival at his disposal.
>
> At a loss and uncertain, he confidently turns to the worthy representatives of the French Republic, who he hopes in all their compassion and justice will provide him with some means of support, allowing him to live out the rest of his days with his seventy-year-old wife.
>
> Old and sick at the age of eighty-six, he can no longer work or return home. He is very proud to die in France, taking the title of a French citizen to his grave. (1793, XIV, 421 SS.)

Only a few days later, despite the tumultuous atmosphere at the time, on 18 January the Committee for Public Education considered Goldoni's request and, at the suggestion of another playwright, Marie-Joseph Chénier, brother of the well-known poet André Chénier, passed it on to the National Convention with a favourable opinion.

Three days later, on 21 January, after his trial, King Louis the XVI was sentenced to death and publicly guillotined.

Around the same time, Revolutionary France, already at war with the Empire and Prussia, declared war on England and Holland. Nevertheless, on 7 February, unaware of Goldoni's death, the very same Marie-Joseph Chénier zealously took the floor of the Assembly and related the opinion of the Committee for Public Education, pleading on behalf of the Venetian playwright.

The Assembly unanimously made their decision three days later. All parties were in favor: The Plain and the Mountain, the Jacobins, Girondists, and Feuillants.

By now, the news of Goldoni's death was common knowledge. It was decided that the pension would be paid to "his" Nicoletta, left widowed and alone. The Comédie Française decided to give her all the proceeds from an extraordinary performance of *The Benevolent Curmudgeon, Le bourru bienfaisant.*

Seven days later, on 17 February, the minister of finance, Stéphan Clavière, held a particularly solemn commemoration of the deceased in the name of the French Republic.

> Citizens, Goldoni has put an end to his days of destitution. The representatives of the Nation came to his rescue after death had already taken away this consolation. He earned it: his plays are indicative of these times, times of liberty. His loathing for theatrical lasciviousness, for those farces that only amuse vile men, rendering them evermore vile, was also a sign of the fall of despotism. Goldoni reformed Italian theatre.
>
> He was such a strong supporter of the Revolution that his greatest grievance was that of being forced by illness, old age, and his companion's needs to claim a pension he enjoyed since the times of Louis XV, and whose payment had been suspended. I personally saw him passionately express the regret of not being able to throw that document into the same flame that destroyed the royalty's privileges. It won't surprise you then to know that he left some debts his widow is not in the position to pay off.
>
> Citizens, I suggest repaying Goldoni with a performance of The Benevolent Curmudgeon. Perhaps you have already come to this decision; such a tribute to Goldoni's memory is worthy of your generosity. This remarkable comedy, inspired by a great sense of justice and morals, is not far removed from our present situation. We are forced to become curmudgeons, and it is worthwhile to remember that this disposition does not exclude the will to do good.
>
> Citizens, rest assured that the public will eagerly respond to your good will. If the show ends with music that adds solemnity to this funeral oration in honor of Goldoni, the public will return home doubly satisfied. (1793, XIV, 860 SS.)

Interestingly enough, this very rapid and dramatic succession of events and decisions has drawn little attention until now. Generally, people interpret it as if it were a simple humanitarian act towards a poor old man, alone and abandoned; and yet, the fact that during those extremely critical and dramatic times for France and its newborn republic – the monarchy was abolished 21 September 1792 – the National Convention, the institutions, and the French authorities would pay Goldoni such a great deal of attention and respect deserves a more careful explanation.

This is a good starting point in order to recount Goldoni's authentic and surprising modernity; or, rather, to recognize that Goldoni, out of all of Italy's writers and men of letters, was the most important witness to the making of modernity. It's also important that the clear and explicit recognition of his role as a reformer and innovator comes from the newborn French Republic; disillusioned by his beloved Venice, he turned to France to seek out modernity and draw from its burgeoning trends.

A hundred years ago, during the bicentennial of his birth, Goldoni was regarded as the champion of a long-lost Venetian identity, and as the protagonist of that eighteenth-century era that was both magnificent and decadent.

Fifty years ago, during the 250th anniversary of his birth, both the new trends in theatre directing and the critics regarded him as an enlightened reformer, as a follower of the Enlightenment who had nobly campaigned to revive the society and culture of Venice.

Fourteen years ago, during the bicentennial of his death, the role of Goldoni and his theatre was redefined as quintessentially European. The indisputable greatness of his career was placed at the centre of a much larger backdrop, no longer simply Venetian.

Now is the time to acknowledge Goldoni as the true champion of modernity; a crucial player in the forging of modernity. It is therefore necessary to re-evaluate the long period he spent in Paris – a stay that lasted more than thirty years – often neglected by critics and remembered as a mere time of defeat in which Goldoni renounced his plans for reform and gave in to overwhelming melancholy.

The attention he received from the National Convention is an excellent starting point to reassess Goldoni outside the typical hermeneutic norms, in order to understand his greatness, so long overlooked. Hence his cursory and marginal presence in our school curricula and amid the outlines of our literary and cultural history.

Since 1789, Revolutionary France had immediately distinguished itself by recognizing the equal rights of all those who, until this time, were facing preconceived and unjustifiable discrimination: women, Jews, Protestants, and actors. France transformed Goldoni's dreams into reality; in fact, he persistently fought for the recognition of "his" actors' intellectual and artistic merits.

On the other hand, it was Marie-Joseph Chénier, the playwright who took it upon himself to protect and defend Goldoni's rights within the National Convention, who, announcing the new times of the Revolution, had written that "the stage, liberated from arbitrary obstacles, will become what it should have always been: a school of good morals." Even here, he undertook and expanded upon the dearest and most congenial of Goldoni's ideas.

Thus the parliament's intervention in favour of Goldoni should be read as ideological rather than humanitarian. Neglecting him would have been perceived as a true betrayal of the Revolution and its ideals, a stain on all of France, which the Venetian playwright chose as his second, ideal fatherland even at the cost of sacrificing his own success as an author.

In the end, Goldoni did not see Paris as a different, alternative professional opportunity – in fact, he fought his battle for more than twenty years – but rather as the real and privileged place where one can witness and partake in the atmosphere and rituals of modernity.

Only in this light do the reasons why the third part of *Mémoires* was entirely dedicated to Paris seem clear. While the first part of *Mémoires* is a typical "novel of formation" that reveals the writer's calling, the second is a true story of the comic theatre reform, a compendium of poetics, and, through description of plays, a passionate apology for a work re-evaluated *a posteriori*; a work that isn't bound by its Venetian origins but rather reintroduced as the new repertoire of the European scene.

The third part barely contributes to Goldoni's biography and bibliography. Yet it evokes the extraordinary metropolitan scene in which reformed theatre is an established instrument of moral growth and acculturation of the people, and it celebrates secular values of civil society and peaceful wisdom.

Ironically, without the third part, the other two wouldn't be as significant. Goldoni's actual presence in Paris throughout the second half of the eighteenth century confirms the essential, deep connection between the new theatre and the new world of modernity better than any abstract theorization. And while his presence in Paris didn't bring about a miracle of reform, the miracle had already taken place.

Upon arriving in Paris, Goldoni was captivated by the fervour of city life, and, above all, by its emblematic attractions.

> I was in Paris. I was happy. But I had hardly seen anything, and I was dying to see the city.
>
> I spoke about it to my friend and host. "We must begin," he said, "by paying a few visits: let's wait for the carriage." "By no means," I said, "I won't see anything in a coach. Let's set out on foot." "But it's far." "Doesn't matter!" "It is hot." "So be it!"
>
> This year, in fact, it was as hot as in Italy: for me, it was all the same. I was only fifty-three then, strong, healthy, and vigorous, and my curiosity and impatience were lending me wings.
>
> Crossing the boulevards, I had a glimpse of that vast promenade which surrounds the city and offers the passerby a cool shade in the summer and the heat of the sun in the winter.
>
> I entered the Palais-Royal. The crowds! What a gathering of every kind of people! What a charming rendezvous! What a delightful promenade!
>
> Yet the most surprising view struck my senses and mind as I approached the Tuileries! I saw that immense garden that nothing in the world compares to; I saw the whole extent of it and my eyes could not measure its length; I hastily ran through its alleys, thickets, terraces, basins, and borders; I had seen other opulent gardens, superb buildings, and precious monuments, but nothing came close to the magnificence of the Tuileries.
>
> Leaving this enchanted place, another spectacle struck me: a majestic river, wide and countless bridges, vast parades along the banks, great crowds of carriages, and a perpetual throng of people; I was stunned by the noise, fatigued by the distance, overwhelmed by the excessive heat. I was bathed in perspiration without being aware.
>
> We crossed the Pont Royal, and entered the Hôtel d'Aumont. (Memoirs, III, 2)

Goldoni often went back to describing these exemplary places that, outside any rational plan and well before the Revolution, unveiled the new world and society. They broke up traditions, customs, and hierarchies, rewarding commitment, work, and professionalism.

> The boulevards were my favourite walk. I saw them as an enjoyable and healthy resource in a very large and populous city, where the streets are not wide and the height of the buildings prevents the circulation of air.

These are bastions of great extent, surrounding the city: four rows of large trees form a vast road in the middle for carriages, with two lateral alleys for foot passengers; they allow us to see the country, and offer a multitude of pleasant views of the Parisian surroundings. At the same time, one has the opportunity to revel in the pastimes assembled there.

An immense crowd of people, an astonishing mass of carriages, of modest vendors darting through the wheels and the horses with all sorts of goods; chairs on sidewalks for those who love to watch, and those who sit to be watched themselves; splendidly decorated cafes with orchestras accompanied by Italian and French singers, pastry chefs, restaurant owners, inn-keepers, puppet shows, tumblers, barkers introducing giants, dwarfs, wild beasts, sea monsters, wax figures, automatons, ventriloquists, as well as the Cabinet of Comus – a learned physician and a mathematician who was as surprising as he was amusing.

There is still something left to say about this capital's promenades and surroundings. The Champs-Elysées, for example, is worth mentioning; this is an immense place, shaded by trees divided in quincunxes, where all the visitors seem to converge at once. And yet, there are people everywhere in the city: crowds can be found at the Bois de Boulogne, the Parc de Saint-Cloud, in Belleville, and the Pré Saint Gervais. The national decorum and joy is felt everywhere.

Paris is splendid, its surroundings are delightful, and its inhabitants are amiable; and yet, there are people who dislike it. They say, to be able to enjoy it requires a great outlay. This is untrue; no one has less money than me, yet I enjoy it, discover amusements, and find satisfaction. There are pleasures for every circumstance: limit your desires, act according to your income, and you will be comfortable here, or uncomfortable everywhere else. (Memoirs, III, 19)

Goldoni was always eager to make the reader see his definite sign of the new; the point separating the past from the present, almost as if that point were the source of his departure from Venice, where he had without a doubt proven his professional capacity, his "métier." Yet unlike Paris, that "ancient" world did not accept change; in it, his chosen direction and fulfilled path were always up for discussion.

In 1781, the year I just spoke about, the changes planned for the Palais-Royal were announced to the public, and on 15 October, the trees on the Grande Allée were given the first blow with an axe.

Oh, the number of complaints in Paris! Everyone found this walk lovely just as it was; everyone revelled in it and couldn't imagine it any more pleasant or convenient; they feared the investor's greed would prevail over the common good.

The owners of the houses surrounding the garden were the most distressed of all. They felt threatened by a new structure, which would deprive them of a view and an entrance to this delightful place; they gathered together, and made attempts to preserve their alleged rights, while jurists dissuaded them from taking action; the estate was given to the Maison d'Orléans by the king, and the duke of Chartres, now the duke of Orléans, was the rightful owner; the windows and doors looking out onto this garden were merely tolerated and, complainants notwithstanding, work had to be carried out to the public's utmost satisfaction.

But the public was distrustful; they would miss this magnificent alley that, on fine days, would gather infinite crowds, where the beauties of Paris would display all their charms, where young men would take chances, and find fortune, and where sensible men would find great amusements, at times at the expense of fools.

Every fallen tree would cause profound grief in the hearts of those present; I happened to be there when the tree of Krakow was falling down, that lovely chestnut tree that would gather the news enthusiasts; a tree that was the long-time witness to their curiosities, complaints, and lies; I made my way through the crowds and was fortunate enough to get hold of a branch that still had leaves. I immediately brought it back to the home of my acquaintances; everyone voiced their disdain for those who tore it down; deep down I was laughing: I had great faith in these projects, and I was right.

Here's the Palais-Royal: renovated, rebuilt, and completed. Say what you like, critique as you please, but I never enter it without a new delight. And the abundant crowds that visit it nowadays confirm my judgment.

The garden enclosure has been reduced, they say, but it is still vast enough to offer summer and winter alleys, and a very large space in the middle, which is never filled – there isn't enough air. Those looking only for air will prefer the Champs-Elysées, but those who care to discover company, delight, and convenience in one place will find it hard to leave the Palais-Royal behind. (Memoirs, III, 31)

Goldoni chose to live out his maturity and old age in this overwhelmingly enchanting world. It didn't bother him that the Comédie Italienne, where he should have been working, was a useless mausoleum of an irretrievable past, or that he would end up living among all those outdated relics of theatre.

The important thing is that "Paris is a world. In that city – everything carries impressive dimensions." And this is a starting point in understanding the reason behind the path he chose.

Every day in Paris, one would witness the spectacle of endless innovation, the wonder of countless technical and scientific discoveries (from magnetism and electricity to the hot-air balloon) that allowed one to experience modernity at first hand.

Therefore, the important thing is not the hardships of a completely different world nor the astonishment found therein. What counts are the emotions absorbing us, our compelling passion, and the enthusiasm that never leaves one's side. We are all too familiar with regretting the past and lamenting the present.

And just like a refrain, Goldoni would say to himself and to his close and distant friends over and over again, "I was at court, but I was never a courtier." He later explained his future intentions to a friend, Francesco Albergati.

> I have not yet attempted to be introduced at Court, but on the contrary, refused the means and opportunities to introduce myself; and if I had the misfortune of my works not seeing success in France, I would have left without a concern, for I am neither a Chevalier, nor a man of letters.
>
> The sole reason that could lead someone to welcome me with open arms would be the success of my plays. Without it, I am worth nothing; it allows me to ask but not to demand. Princes were made for granting favours, not compliments. Being able to say that I visited the king of France would mean little to me. I would much rather say: the king of France was generous to me. (1763, XIV, 302 SS.)

A few years later, he clarified his point of view in his dedication of *The Good Mother* to Stefano Guerra.

> Uniformity dominates this Country. Everyone attempts to imitate one another, and anything that would cause a caricature, is disguised in an effort to appear uniform. In spite of the study of uniformity, little character barely emerges, yet the caricature turns so light that it easily escapes the foreigner's glance. Your Excellency will remember that we made these very same observations together; but if you return here, you will see that I gathered even better ones, after moving from Paris to Versailles. The Court is the centre of the Nation. Here, the arts are used with more caution, yet truths are better developed. I have the honour to live amongst Courtiers, yet I will never learn how to be a Courtier; I cherish sincerity, which I inherited from my Country, and preserve with great pride. (1766, VII, 922)

The success of *The Benevolent Curmudgeon, Le bourru bienfaisant,* at the Comédie Française in 1771 was enough to reassure Goldoni about both the scale of his success in Europe and his far-reaching reform; enough to make him feel like a protagonist in the new world of modernity.

Everything began more than twenty years earlier, in 1750, when Goldoni felt he had reached a turning point in his artistic life; for two years, Girolamo Medebach's company had been almost exclusively performing his works on stage, at the Teatro Sant'Angelo. It was now time to take stock of the choice that drove him back to Venice, leaving his profession as a lawyer behind.

Towards the carnival's end Goldoni's latest play, *The Lucky Heiress,* failed tremendously to gain the audience's favour. Consequently, he felt the need to respond to the heckling audience with a challenge, which in turn underscores the resolve of his decision: the following season, the Medebach Company would perform sixteen of his new plays; a number equal to everything he had written until that point.

Such an endeavour is a testament to the author's courage and confidence – at this point, he was certain about both his artistic path and the means to face it fearlessly. Yet it also shows a desperate man, who was scrutinized night after night and strove to overcome his precarious standing in society.

It's not surprising that between the spring and the summer of 1750 Goldoni wrote two fundamental texts demonstrating his plan for reform, as if to underline the relevance of this challenge: *The Comic Theatre,* which, "rather than a preface to a play is a preface to all my plays," and the *Foreword,* which appeared at the front of the Bettinelli edition. By this time, his passion was almost desperately heroic.

There were early indications that Goldoni was willing to highlight his unique role and the need to write it down by sharing his own intellectual, human story; the need to separate his unusual choice from those that, to a degree, society and "the republic of letters" had already accepted.

> Virtue is equally worshipped everywhere, and Men of Letters from every country form a Republic amongst themselves. Owing this to an extraordinary, common guardian, they are fellow citizens and brothers. The distance between places, the variation in climates, the diversity of language do not render the heart and spirit of the people different, and the learned men, scattered throughout various Cities, Provinces, and Nations of the world, treat one another as inhabitants of one country, divided into

different homes. Therefore, those who look down on the Nations of others, praising only their own, are not thinking; yet those who glorify the Foreign Countries, looking down on their own Nations, are equally deceiving themselves. We can praise England's blessed, great minds, without wronging those of France; and we ourselves, can send off praise in all directions, without looking down on our good Italians. Oh, poor Italy! Your Enemies are your own Sons who, out of a certain sense of Novelty, admire all that comes from afar; and they boast about the works of foreigners, which, perhaps, received little praise in their own Country.

Your Excellency, who speaks and understands the different languages of Europe and is able to recognize and judge fine books, never believed the Italians would be surpassed in the Arts and Sciences; but that our Country, rich with the most perceptive, courageous, and sincere great minds, is merely missing its incentive, imitation, and recognition.

This is what makes the London Academy shine, as that of Paris. Yet our great minds are so scattered around Italy, that if they were united into one society, memoirs, operations, and discoveries would be born, drawing the World's applause and admiration; our volumes would be translated, as those of the Foreign Countries are now being translated into our own language.

Truth be told, what our Italy lacks is Comic Theatre, since France, England, and Spain are a great deal ahead of us in this regard. If only I had Molière's spirit, I would do for our Country what he did for his. But I am too weak to bear so much; Your Excellency may encourage me, using your eloquence to the fullest, to give me hope that my dear Nation can draw some comfort from my efforts in this matter, since, besides knowing my own self and I am not worth a lot, it is best to realize that Italy is not a Country of one Metropolis, one genius, and one people. To revel in France, it suffices to revel in Paris: to hear applause in England, it suffices to gain applause in London; this, at least, is what resonates around us, as we foresee only renowned works from those capitals.

It is the contrary for Italy: often, what one town revels in, another one does not. (1752, II, 881 S.)

Goldoni's choice was so uncommon that he doubted "whether this profession I am committed to, dishonoured for my inherent genius, were suitable for an honest man," for "the comic theatre has a reputation for being scandalous."

This choice was especially astonishing to those coming from professional bourgeois families, who seemed destined to repeat the experiences of their relatives, all committed to liberal occupations. Nonetheless, judging by the following words, his choice was inevitable: "the true, pure incentive I had for completely giving myself to this kind of study" was no more than "the invincible power of my genius for theatre."

An eighteenth-century man cannot fight his natural genius, passion, and vocation. And Goldoni didn't see any moral or cultural reasons for fighting. On the contrary, the entire culture of the century, from Locke to Rousseau, led Goldoni to support his own inclination. And it won't come as a surprise that, despite his family's advice and his early success as a lawyer, every opportunity drove young Goldoni back to the theatre.

It may appear that the playwright's professional goal was clear. It was, in fact, the result of a "choice" that Goldoni reached, rather than an "impulse." He developed "the idea of literary activity that is as much of a respectable, honourable, and productive civil commitment as any other work."

Goldoni understood that his professional choice was unusual, and as a result, wrote the Foreword of 1750 as an apology for his profession, for his "métier"; the matter of reform showed the dignity and importance of his commitment, born from a natural inclination and a careful determination.

At the beginning of the eighteenth century, the circumstances of the Italian theatre, and those of comic theatre in particular, were a disaster. Yet Goldoni's polemical fury was not adequately explained by his conformist morals alone (which were constantly contradicted by his own writing). It was explained, however, by his desire to separate his lucid, noble reform from those sordid circumstances; the more severe his judgment of the preceding theatre, the more justified his choice.

For Goldoni, analysing the crisis was useless – the essence lies in separating the noble and high tradition from the corruption of comic theatre; a tradition established by "many" who "as of late, did all in their power to regulate theatre, reuniting it with fine taste." He mentions some of the greatest names among his predecessors; from Apostolo Zeno to Metastasio, from the Abbot Conti to Scipione Maffei, without leaving out Gasparo Gozzi. Yet he also mentions the real success that changed the nature of the theatre audience.

Although Goldoni's apologetic pages reveal the reasons behind his choice, they weren't peacefully accepted; whoever worked in theatre, even in the tolerant city of Venice, bore the mark of infamy according to the current morals. And despite the city's countless theatres, the State Inquisitors went on with the ancient curse: "Remember, comic actors, you are despised by holy God, and are barely tolerated by the Prince so that you may amuse those who take pleasure in your iniquity."

It is easy to imagine the suspicion that a mercenary man of letters would arouse in a society that only pretended to accept the humanistic principles of "literary leisure": leisure would turn into a "profession" and one's colleagues would belong to that society of immoral beings which constituted the world of comic and professional theatre.

Goldoni believed in nothing but professional theatre: "it is one thing to act amongst amateurs, and another to act amongst comic actors." He stresses the enormous gap between amateur theatre performances and authentic ones: the authentic performances call for professionals in every role. They demand effort, work, and perseverance, and night after night are forced to re-examine their outcome in front of a paying public.

The real problem of reform lies in bringing the public back into theatres, starting from "noble men, learned men, men of sense, model morals, and prominent rank," who make up the best and most sought-after part of the audience, without alienating, however, the plebeian and ill-mannered public, which is necessary for the box office. Paradoxically, ticket sales are, at the same time, the limitation of professional actors "who think of nothing but money" and the measure of their success.

The steady decline of comic theatre made the public unhappy and, as a result, reduced profit and called for reform.

Comic theatre reform didn't start with the pursuit of facile success. It was built slowly, playing a role in the education of the public according to the principles of enlightenment. It began with the acknowledgment of the audience's reactions and aspirations. It grew along a pedagogical line, whose motives came from a group psychology which presented itself as the ideology of reformed comic theatre and even, in a larger sense, as the ideology of literature.

"In light of this discovery," Goldoni "immediately began to write a few plays."

This is an example of the "Galilean" revolution that separated the principles of experimental empiricism from the rules of abstract aesthetics; it united, under a carefully devised plan, the urge to devote oneself "to the desired profession of the playwright," and the plan to reform the comic theatre: reform, demonstrated through "everyone's applause."

> I certainly will not pretend that I reached this goal, whichever it may be, through a diligent and systematic study of the Works, whether educational or exemplary, in this genre of the greatest, old and new Writers and Poets, whether Greek or Latin, French, or Italian, or from other, equally cultured

Nations; yet I will be frank: though I never neglected reading the most esteemed and renowned Authors, from which only the most useful records and examples can be drawn, as from the distinguished Masters, the two books over which I pondered the most, and the worth of which I will never regret, were the World and the Theatre. The first shows me the many different types of characters that people possess; it depicts them in such a natural way that they seem to be created for the specific purpose of providing abundant themes for pleasant and educational plays; it exhibits the signs, the strength, the consequences of all human passions; it produces curious events; it informs me of the latest fashions; it instructs me on the vices and defects which are most common to our time and our nation, vices that deserve the disapproval and mockery of wise men; at the same time, it channels my attention to those few virtuous people who, through virtue, resist general corruption. No matter what I am faced with, through this book, I gather and ponder all those notions necessary to those who seek to practise, with some distinction, this profession of mine. As I leaf through the second one, the book of the theatre, it teaches me which colours one should use to represent, on the Stage, characters, passions, and events: those found in the book of the world; how they should be shaded in order to accentuate their relief; and which hues make them appear pleasurable to the delicate eyes of the spectator. I learn from the Theatre, in other words, to recognize what is best at making a strong impression on people's hearts: causing wonder, or laughter, or that delightful tickle of the human spirit, born above all from finding the faults and the ridicule in those who continue to practise, in a way that isn't too offensive, the Comic Theatre that we listen to, portrayed life-size, and in their opinion, with good manners.

I learned from the Theatre, furthermore, and I am still learning through my very own Plays, about our Nation's particular taste, for which precisely I must write, and which is quite different from the taste of other nations. At times, I observed that certain works, which I didn't think much of before, were highly praised. While others, which I held in high regard, earned me little praise and, occasionally, even some criticism. All this taught me that if I wished to render my Plays useful, I had to adjust my own tastes to those of the public, of which I am a servant, disregarding the rumours of some, either ignorant or indiscreet and difficult, who claim to create laws for the tastes of the entire People, of the entire Nation, and perhaps even of the entire World, and across the centuries, not considering that, in certain non-integral regards, tastes can change with impunity, and it is worthwhile to let the People be the masters, precisely as they are in fashion and language. (1750, I, 769 SS.)

As the themes of Goldoni's plays demonstrate, the world amounts to experience; and not merely existential experience, but culture and the experience of others. Theatre, on the contrary, amounts to work; beyond individual work, it amounts to that inexhaustible legacy of experience and knowledge; the fruit of the continuous "métier" tradition, handed down from father to son on all the boards of every stage.

Goldoni, in other words, didn't see reform outside a determined professional choice – reform can never fall from the sky. His place as the "playwright" was next to "his own" comic actors, and Goldoni was ready to share their concerns.

In the words of Brighella, "Between leisure and profession, lies the same difference found by a duellist between a small step and the sword." Goldoni knew that his professional choice held the same meaning, and at the end of 1747, he signed his first contract with Medebach, abandoning his career as a lawyer, as his destiny was united with those of comic actors. Theatre reform turned into a daily job.

In this context we can recognize the emphasis on being professional in Goldoni's writings. Far removed from the classicism of literary arts, they are entirely, radically modern. They demonstrate the extreme consequences of the duty to produce, writing according to the rules of a serial invention; invention that anticipates the twentieth century in producing a standard for successful performances.

Knowing there was no other path to reach the public, Goldoni started with comic actors and began by recognizing their human, moral dignity still rejected by contemporary society.

Once prejudices are vanquished, there must be a clear distinction between those with knowledge of their profession and those repeating the same old tricks; between those committed and willing to work and those who feign to earn an effortless living.

Goldoni's early polemic was aimed at the "conventional" roles imposed upon authors, sacrificing plot development for the sake of safeguarding the prestige of these conventions. As Benedetto Marcello pointed out in *The Fashionable Theatre,* rules and customs drastically changed opera, and were now influencing comic theatre.

The distribution of roles was not dependent on the attitude of the actors. It was dependent on their roles within the company, without paying attention to the characters they brought to the stage; at times, for example, old and frail men or women would play "young lovers" or "simple girls."

Goldoni didn't write as a man of letters who was willing to challenge history's wisdom. Instead he wished his plays to be performed and praised, while at the same time earning a living. If he was unable to suddenly get rid of these senseless rules, Goldoni was left looking for a way to avoid being overwhelmed.

By attending rehearsals and performances, and, above all, by discussing with theatre company leaders and authors, as well as partaking in their lives, Goldoni continuously redefined his plan for reform, which implied a close relationship with professional theatre; he was ready not only to recognize its strengths, but to draw as much knowledge from it as possible.

The need to fill the house every night inverted the order of things: after centuries of rigorous deductions derived from the principles of classical poetics, the "undisputable realism" of "the box office" gave new strength to inductive empiricism, which required one to begin with the end results and work his way back to the general principles with humility.

It is only natural that the work of the "playwright" couldn't be reduced to a retracing of the history of comic theatre; there were too many reasons standing in his way; first and foremost, such unpredictable comic theatre didn't need authors. Although faced with the public's vulgar laughter, Goldoni still hoped to restore dignity to his performances, giving them a more noble and compelling purpose without sacrificing that laughter.

One day Goldoni attended a *commedia dell'arte*, in which "Arlecchino worked tirelessly." The performance was packed and the crowd was thoroughly entertained, yet "a few people sitting next to me were rowdier than the rest, laughing and calling the actors scoundrels. They laughed, and called them scoundrels!"

Goldoni wasn't even thirty years old and was about to sign his first contract. The public's insults had a certain effect on him; he thought back to his initial plan and told himself, as if he were fantasizing: "Oh, if only I could make the audience laugh without them crying out 'scoundrels!'"

It seemed easy, but it was just like squaring the circle; the objective of the *commedia dell'arte* remained the same: "to make the audience laugh." Yet the bourgeois author wasn't willing to give up his pride and intellect for this one goal. Without the public's laughter neither comedy nor theatre existed, yet there had to be a way to create comic theatre without sacrificing "good taste."

Once Goldoni managed to unify the actors, who recognized his role as their leader, the playwright felt ready to face the public. Naturally, these two episodes are closely connected and therefore it is only logical that they follow one another. However, at one point, the applause forced Goldoni to acknowledge, to some extent, that improvised plays had a positive element to them as well; yet he discovered that he was not "an enemy of *commedie a soggetto*, but of those comedy actors who were unable to adequately play these roles."

Even the reformer himself is forced to stop and admire the talent of stock character actors. Goldoni's plan was not opposed to those who practised a different art form, with the intention of winning the public over: the space for Goldoni's initiative opened up where talent and success were scarce, when experience and tradition had no effect on a public that demanded something different.

The reform grew from all the weaknesses of the theatrical world – a world aware of the crisis it was in – and drew its strength from the union between the author and the actors, with the goal of winning the public back.

The comic actors were burdened by new commitments: they studied their parts, tried the characters on for size, and made them their own (or, as Goldoni would say, "supported the characters"). Not only were they now in a position to defend themselves against the stereotypes, but they also complained to the anxious public because "it is pure torture to perform while the audience is rowdy. You waste your breath to be heard and still, it is not enough." Furthermore, the actors demanded more of the audience's attention and respect for both the comic theatre and their work, for "an ignorant comic actor fails to succeed in any role at all."

It's important for Goldoni that the new comic theatre was the result not of chance but of the diligent work of a united group of honest, committed, and hard-working professionals, and that the public's approval was the fruit of this labour.

The protagonists of this reform were both the writer and the public: "If the people laugh and applaud, the comic actor will be worthy of praise."

Therefore, the public was both the patron, a judge deciding the fate of a performance, and the addressee of an educational discourse that, because it allowed that very public the right to judge, required it to be sensible and courteous, and therefore accompanied the public throughout the process of self-awareness, and moral and cultural growth.

Thus far, Goldoni accepted his position as a comic among comics, without vindicating the specificity of his profession as an original author; yet his early polemic with the Abbot Pietro Chiari gave him the uneasy sensation that the public's sudden change in mood, influenced by the slander of his enemies, was enough to push him to rethink the very project that he had been so patiently constructing for more than ten years.

The need to show his strength became apparent, as did the inevitable provocation: it was time to make it or break it; Goldoni couldn't wait to be judged by history. He was convinced that the game was played entirely on theatre stages and bookshop benches, that the public (or, as he would occasionally call it, "the people"), was the sole arbiter of his destiny. Furthermore, he was still thoroughly convinced that the people were willing to listen to him, that they would let themselves be convinced, and that they were in a position to judge.

Goldoni's theatre changed both the people's tastes and their preferences; he reshaped their culture and their sensibilities. In other words, his reform, born from the "books" of the world and the theatre, was capable of transforming the world in the same way it did the theatre.

Giorgio Strehler described this stage in Goldoni's life as "'theatrical hell'; the open acceptance of the theatrical mission, of theatre as 'something connected to the world.' 'Theatre and World' *together*, with all their good and bad, pain and struggle; *everything* would flood into the theatre, and would be lost there forever; lost in 'madness.'"

Nevertheless, the challenge ended with Goldoni's brilliant victory: on the last day of the carnival, in 1751, *Women's Gossip*, the sixteenth comedy of that *annus horribilis*, was performed, and was an absolute triumph.

The success, however, didn't alleviate any of the pressures: Goldoni had proven to the public and to himself that theatre reform could never be compared to aimless wandering. Yet the endless efforts wore him down: the playwright became critically ill, paying for his madness. He was gripped by doubt: was it all worth it?

> The tireless efforts I went through in reforming such Comic Theatre deserve at least a little compassion. It was meant only to delight the reader, and I never felt obligated to reproduce it at the Theatre. Yet if I am still unsuccessful in creating something worthy, I shall at least be excused for my circumstances. What a disastrous year! In a few days, two Characters went missing from the Company for which I write: the famous Pantaloon, Francesco Rubini, and the exceptional Brighella, Giuseppe Angeleri, who, apart from his usual mask, has played other essential roles. There go all my plans for this year. My health has never been worse. Yet it is best if I go on writing, even with a broken heart. I am certain that merely a few will pity me if my Works won't find fortune. Yet I am not deluding myself. I am accustomed to the good and the bad; as I never pretended to be praised, misfortune could never bring me down. Who can tell... perhaps a glimmer of light will shine through the dark? May God bless the Works of others, without leaving my

own behind; and only take away the public's love when envy fills my heart. (1755, IV, 7 SS.)

According to Strehler, the following stage in Goldoni's life coincided with "discovering that 'nothing' could change *because of* theatre" and, exhausted by work, Goldoni was soon overcome with discouragement.

Above all, Goldoni felt the compensation for his endless efforts was neither sufficient nor fair; meanwhile, Medebach – who brought sixteen of his plays to the stage rather than the eight established in his contract – was generous with praise and stingy with money.

It was of course Goldoni who made the protagonist of *The Venetian Lawyer* say, "We do not gain with gold, but ideas" and "I do not demand compensation for my efforts … Money is irrelevant to me … I value only my integrity, my reputation, and my respect." Yet he also added, "Men, in any profession, must not be ashamed to be rewarded for their tireless efforts." And faced with his manager's scarce generosity, he scornfully cried out: "One cannot live off fame alone!"

After a year of working relentlessly amidst the fumes of hypochondria and the stress of his neurosis, Goldoni would experience anxiety, disillusionment, and discouragement more intensely than ever.

In 1753, only two years after the sixteen new plays, as *The Innkeeper Woman* was about to be performed, and after breaking his contract with Medebach – signing a more profitable one with Teatro di San Luca – Goldoni blew off a little steam: "Having held this craft so close to my heart, having sweated so much for its sake, having suffered all the pain, what will I ever have to show for it? Insults, ingratitude, and grief."

Certainly, at this stage, the disputes with Medebach weighed heavily on the author; yet, from this point on, Goldoni's disillusion would play a more frequent part in his complaints, as when, in a conversation with his dear friend Pietro Verri, he sadly complained that "the public's approval and the theatrical cheers end when the voices go quiet."

The triumph on the last night of the carnival in 1751 was the last episode in Goldoni's peaceful, optimistic theatre reform. From here on out, he could barely tolerate his work, carried out with both the pride of a man aware of his own worth and the desperation of a man bound by the chains of need.

His profession turned into a torturous duty that provoked metaphors of violence and agony; Goldoni was "chained," "condemned," or "forced." His enthusiasm faded away and he felt "his veins drying up."

In San Luca, Goldoni will never find that kind of harmony with actors that is "essential to a good denouement of comedies." He will constantly fight for the distribution of roles, re-opening the war against the "conventions" he thought had ended years before; Goldoni will now need to defend his own professional worth to those who held the author responsible for all of the public's resentment.

This was the very moment in which Goldoni acquired a more acute critical awareness of his own existential and cultural experience. On the one hand, he carried on his commitments with tenacity – which Strehler defined as an act of "heroism." On the other, he was planning his escape to a different reality.

Certainly, at the heart of Goldoni's crisis lies, as Strehler wrote, the awareness that "the theatre *doesn't actually change* the world itself, it doesn't even change *theatre* significantly, and whatever changes are made aren't worth the struggle they cost"; moreover, "another illusion, even more disappointing, is found in the belief that human beings 'improve' because of theatre." Nevertheless, Goldoni was still convinced that nothing could interrupt or delay his appointment with modernity, with the aggressiveness of modernity, even if it meant leaving his profession as a playwright behind. Hence his final decision to go to Paris.

The years between 1751 and 1762 were the hardest for Goldoni. The anxiety and the fear of not being able to accomplish more than what he had already done clashed inside him, aggravated by his exhaustion and sickness. As he faced the uncertainty of old age in poverty, his "'indestructible faith' in theatre and in the justice of history – for what he has done, is doing and will do," his will never to give up – were tested.

Yet these years were also his most prolific: in 1756 *The Little Square* was performed. In this play it became clear how, by making himself the main protagonist of his own theatre – the way he had done countless times before – and by bringing his own life experience to the stage, Goldoni perfected the transformation of his concept of literature; 1760 was the year of *The Rude Men* and of *The New House*; 1761, of *The Holiday Trilogy;* and in 1762, as a grand finale, *The Grumpy Mr Todero, The Chioggia Scuffles,* and *One of the Last Carnival Evenings* were performed back to back.

The end of this long period of tension coincided with Goldoni's departure for Paris: on the evening of Mardi Gras, 16 February 1762, the actors at the Teatro San Luca performed the last new comedy of the season, *One of the Last Carnival Evenings.* With this play, the author left his public, announcing his departure for Paris. Goldoni confessed that "this play is an allegory." And this allegory served to barely conceal its autobiographical theme; although, at times, it actually revealed the writer's intentions.

"I turned comic actors into a society of weavers: that is, fabric manufacturers. And I granted myself the title of draftsman," Goldoni revealed, as if to highlight the "craftsman" nature of his work. This choice showed the playwright's unconventional humility; the humility, however, of one who must abide by the rules of conventional society, face the public, and accept the status quo. Yet it also revealed the pride of a bourgeois man who felt he was part of a productive activity, valuable to the fortunes of his country, and beneficial in both an economic and practical sense. Furthermore, it showed that he was aware of the difficult and complex choice that lay before him; a choice in which the various aspects of his personality would find both comfort and conflict. On the one hand, there was the optimist, convinced that he has made it; he was, after all, invited to Paris. On the other, there was also the cautious man, aware of the hardships that go along with working in a different place. In the end, there was the melancholic man, who realized that his reform didn't make it, that, after all, modernity had defeated him.

It was the Goldoni who, replacing Moscovia with Paris, would entrust Anzoletto to deliver his farewell to the public and his motherland.

> For quite a while everyone has been fond of this country's popular designs. Whether it is the skill of the designers, or that of the weavers, our tapestries captivate the mind's eye. Our workers were welcomed everywhere they travelled. When the designs were shipped away, they were appreciated; yet even this will not suffice. It is easy to see that an Italian hand, designing on site for the tastes of the Muscovites, is capable of creating a blend that will please both nations. This isn't easy, yet not impossible. The great fault, however, lies in the failure of their choice, for I am the lowest designer, and have put the most magnificent project at risk. Nevertheless, I have resolved to go. Who can tell ... My own Country accepted me without my being worthy; perhaps I will find this same fortune elsewhere. I will do my duty; on this, I stake my honour. I always have and will keep doing so; and if my inabilities prohibit the praise of my works in Moscovia, I will still strive to learn, I will return with new knowledge, new light, I will provide for my weavers, and I will serve my Motherland, which never ceased to show great mercy for me and has always been so kind.
>
> Brilliant talent has never been scarce in Venice, a city blessed in all arts, in all the sciences; and now more than ever, our surroundings are flourishing

with great minds, fine taste, and originality. Yet I have endured too much, and suffered more than I deserve.

Will I ever forget my Country? My most beloved Motherland? My Masters? My dear friends? It is not the first time I leave; yet anywhere I travel, the name of Venice remains stamped upon my heart; I could never forget the grace, and the blessings I have been granted; I have always hoped to return, and upon returning have felt consoled. Any comparison I had the opportunity to make always made my Country appear lovelier, more magnificent, and more respectable; upon returning, I always discovered even greater beauties; this time will not be any different, if Heaven will grant my return. I confess and swear on my honour: I am leaving with a broken heart. None of the temptations or fortunes, if they were bestowed upon me, could ever make up for the agony of being away from my loved ones. My dear friends, preserve your love for me. May Heaven bless you, and I mean it from my heart. (1762, VIII, 241 SS.)

***

Carlo Goldoni's *Complete Works* were edited by G. Ortolani in fourteen volumes and published by Mondadori (1935–56). Apart from the quotations taken from *Memoirs* (Paris: "Meridiani" Mondadori, 1993, edited by Paolo Bosisio), the indications in parentheses below the citations refer back to this edition.

In 1993, the publishing house Marsilio began to publish the national edition of the works of Carlo Goldoni. This series was initially directed by Sergio Romagnoli and is currently directed by me. Over forty volumes have appeared thus far.

Although Goldoni's bibliography is very rich, we should keep a few particular works in mind as an initial point of reference: the monographs of Siro Ferrone, *Carlo Goldoni* (Florence: Sansoni, 1975, 2001), and Carmelo Alberti, *Goldoni* (Rome: Salerno, 2004), as well as the biographies of Franca Angelini, *Vita di Goldoni* [*The Life of Goldoni*] (Rome, Bari: Laterza, 1993), and Ginette Herry, *Carlo Goldoni. Biografia ragionata* [*Carlo Goldoni. Annotated Biography*], Vol. 1 (Venice: Marsilio, 2007), all of which are filled with additional bibliographical references.

A chapter on Goldoni appears in my *Letterati e lettori nel Settecento veneziano* [*Men of Letters and Readers of Eighteenth-Century Venice*] (Florence: Olschki, 1979).

THE LORENZO DA PONTE ITALIAN LIBRARY

General Editors: Luigi Ballerini and Massimo Ciavolella

Pellegrino Artusi, *Science in the Kitchen and the Art of Eating Well* (2003). Edited and translated by Luigi Ballerini and Murtha Baca

Lauro Martines, *An Italian Renaissance Sextet: Six Tales in Historical Context* (2004). Translated by Murtha Baca

Aretino's Dialogues (2005). Translated by Margaret Rosenthal and Raymond Rosenthal

Aldo Palazzeschi, *A Tournament of Misfits: Tall Tales and Short* (2005). Translated by Nicolas J. Perella

Carlo Cattaneo, *Civilization and Democracy: The Salvemini Anthology of Cattaneo's Writings* (2006). Edited and introduced by Carlo G. Lacaita and Filippo Sabetti. Translated by David Gibbons

Benedetto Croce, *Breviary of Aesthetics: Four Lectures* (2007). Translated by Hiroko Fudemoto, Introduction by Remo Bodei

Antonio Pigafetta, *First Voyage around the World (1519-1522): An Account of Magellan's Expedition* (2007). Edited and translated by Theodore J. Cachey Jr.

Raffaello Borghini, *Il Riposo* (2008). Translated by Lloyd H. Ellis Jr.

Paolo Mantegazza, *Physiology of Love and Other Writings* (2008). Edited and translated by Nicoletta Pireddu

Renaissance Comedy: The Italian Masters (2008). Edited and translated by Donald Beecher

Cesare Beccaria, *On Crimes and Punishments and Other Writings* (2008). Edited by Aaron Thomas; Translated by Aaron Thomas and Jeremy Parzen; Foreword by Bryan Stevenson; Introduction by Alberto Burgio

Leone Ebreo, *Dialogues of Love* (2009). Edited and translated by Cosmos Damian Bacich and Rossella Pescatori

Boccaccio's Expositions on Dante's Comedy (2009). Translated by Michael Papio

My Muse Will Have a Story to Paint: Selected Prose of Ludovico Ariosto (2010). Translated with an Introduction by Dennis Looney

The Opera of Bartolomeo Scappi (1570): L'arte et prudenza d'un maestro Cuoco (The Art and Craft of a Master Cook) (2011). Translated with commentary by Terence Scully

Pirandello's Theatre of Living Masks: New Translations of Six Major Plays (2011). Translated by Umberto Mariani and Alice Gladstone Mariani

From Kant to Croce: Modern Philosophy in Italy, 1800-1950 (2012). Edited and translated with an introduction by Brian P. Copenhaver and Rebecca Copenhaver

Giovan Francesco Straparola, *The Pleasant Nights*, Volume 2 (2012). Edited with an Introduction by Donald Beecher

Giovan Francesco Straparola, *The Pleasant Nights*, Volume 1 (2012). Edited with an Introduction by Donald Beecher

Giovanni Botero, *On the Causes of the Greatness and Magnificence of Cities* (2012). Translated and with an introduction by Geoffrey W. Symcox

John Florio, *A Worlde of Wordes* (2013). A Critical Edition with an Introduction by Hermann W. Haller

Giordano Bruno, *On the Heroic Frenzies* (2013). A Translation of *De gli eroici furori* by Ingrid D. Rowland; text edited by Eugenio Canone

Alvise Cornaro, *Writings on the Sober Life: The Art and Grace of Living Long* (2014). Translated by Hiroko Fudemoto; Introduction by Marisa Milani; Foreword by Greg Critser

Dante Aligheri, *Dante's Lyric Poetry: Poems of Youth and of the Vita Nuova* (1283–1292) (2014). Edited, with a general introduction and introductory essays by Teodolinda Barolini. With new verse translations by Richard Lansing. Commentary translated into English by Andrew Frisardi

Vincenzo Cuoco, *Historical Essay on the Neapolitan Revolution of 1799* (2014). Edited and Introduced by Bruce Haddock and Filippo Sabetti. Translated by David Gibbons

Vittore Branca, *Merchant Writers: Florentine Memoirs from the Middle Ages and Renaissance* (2015). Translated by Murtha Baca.

Carlo Goldoni, *Five Comedies* (2016). Edited by Gianluca Rizzo and Michael Hackett, with Brittany Asaro. Introduction by Michael Hackett with an essay by Cesare De Michelis.

www.ingramcontent.com/pod-product-compliance
Lightning Source LLC
LaVergne TN
LVHW090145080826
844660LV00013B/682/J